Improving English Instruction

SECOND EDITION

ROYAL J. MORSEY

PROFESSOR OF ENGLISH
AND SECONDARY EDUCATION
BALL STATE UNIVERSITY

ALLYN AND BACON, INC.
BOSTON

Library of Congress Catalog Card Number: 69-17548

Printed in the United States of America.

To Mary and Paul

PREFACE

Authors, in books and magazine articles, and speakers, at local, state, and national meetings, have bombarded the English teacher with proposals designed to help him help students make maximum progress towards these goals: clear, thoughtful, and correct speech and writing; intelligent listening; and a lifelong devotion to worthwhile literature. But the proposals, many based on sound research, appear to have had limited influence.

Broadcasting admonitions in a classroom, from a pulpit, or in books and magazines is, psychologists say, less likely to change behavior than promoting deep personal involvement, i.e., cooperation between teacher and student, minister and parishioner, or author and reader in solving relevant problems. Hence, the wide range of ideas in this book on teaching literature, grammar, usage, listening, semantics, the nature of language, written composition, and oral composition (speech) are offered as hypotheses designed to help solve two problems confronting all English teachers: What should I teach? How should I teach what I consider worth teaching? Furthermore, even though ideas survive testing, evaluation has to continue because conditions change.

This book is predicated on the idea that progress in improving English instruction is possible when English teachers become researchers, testing promising ideas on teaching reading, writing, speaking, and listening. Action research, which calls for imagination rather than imitation, has recently received increasing attention and support. In the next decade, many English teachers will (1) identify and define significant teaching problems, (2) gather data related to them, (3) develop hypotheses that promise to solve them, and (4) test hypotheses to see whether they live up to their promise. The purpose of this book is to help such teachers get underway with the formal and informal testing of ideas on teaching English, a process which may lead to results as impressive as some achieved by researchers in medicine, agriculture, and industry.

A student teacher may need to postpone experimentation until he has had some experience as a regular teacher. But he should develop the attitude of wanting eventually to test some of the most promising of the many conflicting ideas on teaching English. Once he feels secure in the classroom, he should also develop and test his own hypotheses. If he does so consistently, he will find teaching English a satisfying rather than a frustrating profession.

The English methods student or student teacher will discover that many of the items in the "Assumptions About . . ." section which follows each chapter of *Improving English Instruction* can be used as a check on his ability to defend his beliefs about teaching English and, when he is ready, as a source of hypotheses to test through research. Just as a doctor can produce evidence to support his belief that inoculation is superior to incantation in preventing smallpox, so should the student be able to support what he considers to be the best policies and practices in his profession.

The "Ideas to Test" section that follows each of the first eleven chapters may be of little immediate help to the student teacher who may not stray from a departmental syllabus or who feels insecure when he departs from the pattern provided by a permissive critic teacher. However, student teachers unrestricted by rigid syllabi and critics have introduced paperback book clubs, have based instruction in grammar and usage on students' writing, have presented units on the nature of language, and have used supplementary materials in composition and literature units.

The English methods student and student teacher can increasingly comprehend the value of their chosen profession by pondering the role of English teachers in today's high school. The high school student's success— academic, vocational, and as a citizen—hinges heavily on how well his English teachers help him develop the ability to think clearly; to express thoughts clearly, orally and in writing; to evaluate the thoughts of others; and to use literature as an "arch wherethrough" he can acquire knowledge of "cities of men, and manners, councils, governments, himself not least." The role of English teachers is heavy with responsibility, but those who accept it will enjoy the satisfactions that come from helping others participate effectively in a democracy.

For their helpful written reactions to the rough draft of the 1965 edition of *Improving English Instruction,* I wish to thank Professors Margaret Early, Syracuse University; Wilfred Eberhart, The Ohio State University; Oscar M. Haugh, University of Kansas; Graham Pogue, Ball State University; Robert Shafer, Arizona State University; and Ingrid Strom, Indiana University. For their helpful written reactions to the 1965 edition, I wish to thank Professors Edward R. Fagan, Pennsylvania State University, and A. K. Stevens, University of Michigan.

Royal J. Morsey

CONTENTS

1

Developing Goals

Before reading this chapter, formulate clear, defensible answers to the following questions. After reading it, prepare to explain why you changed or retained your answers.

1. What is your definition of *philosophy*?

2. What is your philosophy of life? What do you want to be and do—and why?

3. What is your philosophy of education? What should the schools be and do—and why?

4. What is your philosophy of teaching English? What should the English curriculum be and do—and why?

5. Why and how is an English curriculum changed?

6. Why do the methods of an English teacher who promotes rote learning (recall) differ from those of a colleague who promotes thinking (problem solving)?

DEFINING PHILOSOPHY

Some semanticists claim it is impossible to define single words clearly and accurately. How helpful would the dictionary definition of *apple* (edible pome fruit) be if you had never seen an apple? The word *apple* points to specific objects which resemble each other fairly closely but which do vary in size, shape, color, flavor, scent, and texture. To define *apple* for a student who has never seen one, you could (1) ask him to examine the outside and inside of an apple and then eat it and (2) have him sample apple pie, sauce, strudel, dumplings, and butter. If an apple were not available, you could show him a picture; but you will agree that the flavor, scent, and texture of the object called *apple* would be absent.

You may now understand why it is difficult to define *philosophy*, a word which points to no specific object. Ask a friend to define the term and you may be subjected to a barrage of abstract words. Perhaps the best way to give meaning to *philosophy* is to ask questions about it: Why is it often defined as "the love of wisdom"? Why have philosophers seeking wisdom sought answers to these questions: Why am I on earth? What should be my role on earth? What should I value most? least? What is death? What happens after death? Why do some men insist man has free will, others that he is a puppet manipulated by his environment?[1] What are *knowledge, education, truth, beauty, liberty, justice, good,* and *evil?*

You can see that man's pursuit of wisdom produces questions unanswerable with a "yes" or "no." Although most educated men have agreed amicably that the questions have no final answers, the varying answers have sometimes led to violent verbal and physical clashes. In international affairs, conflicts arise when leaders change their concepts of right and wrong from day to day, basing decisions on a Machiavellian principle: the ends justify the means.

Many men have devoted their lives to philosophy, the search for wisdom, but not one has been able to label himself wise and make it stick. One who says he is wise is presumed to be ignorant. But men who seek knowledge and understanding challenge current clichés; they make greater contributions to man's welfare than those who accept unquestioningly the beliefs of their fathers. Americans owe much to the philosophers John Locke (1632–1704) and Jean Jacques Rousseau (1712–1778); they defined and defended ideas about the rights of man that became part of our Constitution. We are still defining, defending, and amending our Bill of Rights, tasks which may never be completed.

A PHILOSOPHY OF LIFE

Should you list your convictions about politics, economics, religion, ethics, government, education, and art, one might understand somewhat your philosophy of life. But if your behavior does not reflect the listed beliefs, are they of value to anyone? In the United States some pressure groups

---

[1] A current related question: "Will the English student soon become a puppet manipulated by the incestuous issue of the handbook and workbook—the computer teaching machine?"

give staunch oral and written support to the Constitution as they themselves work to deny individuals and groups rights guaranteed in the Bill of Rights. Many students in social studies and English classes voice acceptance of minority groups, but spurn them when they seek membership in fraternities, sororities, and some school-sponsored clubs and organizations. How many politicians' actions demonstrate that they take seriously their oath to uphold the Constitution?

To understand an individual's philosophy of life, one must scan his deeds. As you record statements reflecting your convictions about "the good life," ask yourself how often you have succeeded in translating them into behavior. Perhaps we should write essays on "This I Did" instead of "This I Believe." We all realize we sometimes fail to practice what we preach, to translate ideals into behavior. Moreover, a philosophy of life is personal—we hesitate to air our successes and failures or our convictions in an essay. And honest statements about beliefs often lead to controversy, a disturber of the even tenor of our lives. Nevertheless, an educated person has convictions he can support with evidence;[2] and, if courageous, he will, when necessary, express them and act upon them.

A PHILOSOPHY OF EDUCATION

Since one's philosophy of education is a segment of one's philosophy of life, it should be easier to pinpoint. Educational philosophers claim that an individual with a well-organized philosophy of education can provide rational answers to (1) What is education? (2) What should be the aims of education? (3) How can the aims of education be realized? An English teacher can state Questions 2 and 3 in a personal fashion: What are my goals, and why? What teaching materials and methods will help me achieve my goals, and why?

The word *education* has as many definitions as there are people. The dictionary definition ("the process of educating or being educated") is the least useful. Most high school students equate education with the ability to read, write, and solve simple mathematical problems, or with high school or college diplomas. College students identify education with learning. Asked to define *learning*, they say, "Learning is gaining knowledge about something. You learn how to drive a car, read a book, become a good citizen, teach school, or practice law." Asked about the aims of education, they mention teaching the three R's, good citizenship, and clear thinking, and passing-on, as well as improving, our social heritage. When asked who should be educated, they usually respond, "Everyone should receive as

---

[2]Can you support with evidence your stand on the statements in the "Assumptions About . . ." section at the end of each chapter?

much education as his ability warrants; a democracy's survival depends upon a well-educated citizenry."

A primitive child learned skills which had enabled his elders to survive: hunting, fishing, fighting, foraging, warding off evil spirits, preparing food, making clothing, and building shelter. He learned through listening, observing, and doing. In early America, a farm boy learned farming, and his sister housekeeping, the same informal listening-observing-doing way, but they had some formal schooling—a few days or months a year—to learn reading, writing, arithmetic, and religion.[3]

The first elementary schools in the United States, in New England, emphasized reading because it was assumed that one who learned to read the Bible could take Brobdingnagian strides towards living a good life, parrying successfully the machinations of "the old deluder Satan" and his sidekick Beelzebub. Beginners were supplied with a hornbook, a one-page pre-primer resembling a mini fraternity paddle. Pasted on the oaken paddle was a printed sheet, covered with transparent horn, providing the alphabet, numbers (0 through 9), and the Lord's Prayer. Had the paddle featured raised letters, some Puritan pupils would have carried parts of their curriculum imprinted on their heads, palms, knuckles, and posteriors. The following addition to *The New England Primer* would have won a warm welcome from Puritan parents and teachers:

> With paddle stout
> The Devil rout.

By stringing a cord through the hole in the handle, the paddle could be worn like a lavaliere. Minds sharpened by a hassle with the hornbook were primer-ready: *The New England Primer*, alias *The Little Bible*, opened with fundamental principles of the Puritan creed:

> In Adam's fall
> We sinnèd all.

> Heaven to find,
> The *Bible* mind.

Many Puritan children memorized not only *The Little Bible* but the two hundred and twenty-four stanzas of Michael Wigglesworth (1631–1705)'s

---

[3]Religious instruction was also provided by their parents.

IMPROVING ENGLISH INSTRUCTION

The Day of Doom, a best-selling summation of the Puritan faith. Think of the pride of Puritan fathers and mothers whose Patience or Prudence recited, in the presence of compatriots, Michael Wigglesworth's weighty 896-line (6072 verse feet) iambic pentameter peroration. Compatriots' praise at the end of the performance sometimes brought on a popular epilogue: selections from John Cotton's *Spiritual Milk for Babes*, a potent posset.

In the Middle Colonies, Quakers, Presbyterians, Baptists, and Catholics ran private schools with emphasis on their separate routes to religious salvation. Wealthy Southerners (mostly Anglicans) hired tutors to ground their children in the three R's and prepare their sons for entrance into English universities or American colleges. Children of poor Southerners were often given some elementary schooling by The Anglican Society for the Propagation of the Gospel in Foreign Parts, an England-based agency whose aim was mirrored in its name.

Thomas Jefferson (1743–1826) recommended elementary education for everyone and secondary education for the academically able. Benjamin Franklin (1706–1790) urged a broad program of vocational education in an academy which he helped plan. American academies, which originated in the second half of the eighteenth century, provided a more functional type of secondary education than the Latin Grammar School which had been imported from England. The Latin Grammar School prepared a few boys to meet the entrance requirements—considerable proficiency in Latin and knowledge of the rudiments of Greek—of America's Harvard (founded in 1636), William and Mary (1693), and Yale (1701), or England's Oxford (twelfth century) and Cambridge (fourteenth century).

In the 1820's, the first high school was established in Boston. When, shortly after the Civil War, the collection of taxes by states for the support of high schools was declared legal by state supreme courts, high schools rapidly supplanted academies. The college-preparatory curriculum in early high schools was gradually expanded to include history (citizenship education), science, physical education, and finally vocational subjects. Today comprehensive high schools provide preparation for citizenship, college or university entrance, and vocations.

What methods have schools used to help students attain educational goals? Before the invention of the printing press in the fifteenth century, teachers dictated from manuscripts and notes materials for students to record and memorize. When the printing press automated into limbo the monks (scribes) who copied manuscripts by hand, books gradually replaced dictation, making easier and faster the mastery of the seven liberal arts[4] (grammar,[5] rhetoric, logic, arithmetic, geometry,[6] astronomy, and music) and other subjects as they appeared in the curriculum. Recitations and written examinations measured students' grasp of subjects. Rote learning was highly prized, except in a few universities where disputations (debates) were part of the curriculum; but frequently even disputations followed fixed patterns of ideas. The principle that students should learn how to think was promoted by Socrates, but it has seldom been applied in elementary and secondary schools.

"Who should be educated?" produces conflicting answers around the world. In ancient Greece only citizens' sons, a minority group, were educated. Before Martin Luther (1483–1546) broke with the Church, few children received formal instruction in reading. Luther translated the Bible into High German, then established schools so every Lutheran child could learn to read it. For Americans, schooling was catch as catch can (Abraham Lincoln had little formal education) until well after the Civil War.

Today only a few highly industrialized countries offer more than a minimum of elementary schooling, and secondary education is accessible to only a small portion of the children in some western European countries. Rigorous academic examinations place a minority of their eleven-year-olds on the high road to secondary schools and universities, and a majority on the low road to advanced elementary and vocational schools. Switching from the low to the high road is almost as difficult as winning the Indianapolis 500 on a unicycle. Many European parents envy the educational opportunities of American children, while some of our leading citizens favor the European system, deploring the ease with which our high school graduates who have specialized in vocational courses enter colleges and universities. Vocational education has been viewed with suspicion, and its legitimacy questioned, by academicians ever since the citizens of ancient Athens equated vocational work with the labor of slaves.[7]

Except for America's emphasis on vocational training, compulsory education, universal secondary education, and a tax-supported school system (kindergarten through university), educational aims and methods have changed less than one might suppose. One who visits a secondary

[4]Originating in ancient Greece, the seven liberal arts, their content always adjusting to changing educational aims, dominated education for over two thousand years, and, of course, persist in today's curricula.

[5]Grammar emphasized literature. Grammar as we know it came into its own in the eighteenth and nineteenth centuries (see Chapter 9).

[6]One of the world's first textbooks, Euclid's *Elements of Geometry*, is still in use.

[7]See James Bryant Conant, *The Education of American Teachers* (New York: McGraw-Hill Book Company, Inc., 1963), pp. 1–14.

school class in English or social studies discovers that the passing of the recitation is a myth. The almost exclusive use of objective tests and objective "discussions" promotes the parroting of textbook information.

The principles of progressive education provoked controversy during the first half of the twentieth century but were seldom tested in classrooms. Advocates of progressive education questioned the value of memorizing facts, insisting that in a rapidly changing world students must learn to *use* knowledge to solve their problems. They believed that by using the scientific method to solve problems students acquire a tool immune to obsolescence and useful as long as they live. They pressed for the inclusion of a fourth R in the curricula of public elementary and high schools: research. When we note the phenomenal progress in transportation, communication, and agriculture stimulated by man's using the scientific method, is it not reasonable to recommend its emphasis in school curricula?

DEMOCRACY IN THE CLASSROOM

Should our schools define, defend, and exemplify the principles of democracy?

The Declaration of Independence, 1776, and the Bill of Rights, Articles I–X, in force from 1791, matched the utopian tone of Christianity's "Do unto others . . ." and "Love thy neighbor. . . ." When couched in everyday language, both documents are considered subversive by some Americans. Two statements in the Declaration of Independence are anathema to despots:

> . . . We hold these truths to be self-evident: That all men are created equal; that they are endowed by their Creator with certain unalienable rights; that among these are life, liberty, and the pursuit of happiness. That, to secure these rights, governments are instituted among men, deriving their just powers from the consent of the governed; that, whenever any form of government becomes destructive to these ends, it is the right of the people to alter or abolish it, and to institute a new government, laying its foundations on such principles, and organizing its powers in such form, as to them shall seem most likely to effect their safety and happiness. . . .

The first amendment to the Constitution, Article I, is similarly direct in defending liberty and civil rights:

> Congress shall make no law respecting the establishment of religion, or prohibiting the free exercise thereof, or abridging the freedom of speech or of the press; or the right of people peaceably to assemble, and to petition the government for a redress of grievances.

The aim of education in the Colonial period was to elude "the old deluder Satan"; but it was self-evident to the founding fathers that a government which derives its "powers from the consent of the governed" must broaden its educational aims or perish: "Promote, then, as an object of primary importance, the general diffusion of knowledge. . . . it is essential that public opinion be enlightened" (George Washington). "If a nation expects to be ignorant and free . . . it expects what never was and never will be" (Thomas Jefferson). ". . . a people who mean to be their own governors must arm themselves with the power which knowledge gives" (James Madison).

The founding fathers' philosophy of government has been an inspiration to peoples seeking relief from tyranny; but the founding fathers were in no position to translate philosophy into actuality. To obtain ratification of the Constitution they had to leave decisions about suffrage and education to the states. Even though the "consent of the governed" clause excludes no one, only a minority (6 percent during the Revolutionary period) of Americans could qualify for voting privileges until women were enfranchised in 1920. (Prior to World War I, eleven states permitted women to vote in some elections.)

The founding fathers' successors also avoided recommending educational goals and methods calculated to achieve the rights guaranteed in the Declaration of Independence and the Constitution. They insisted that a democracy's survival depends on education but shied away from suggesting specific educational aims and methods because community mores and attitudes of influential citizens often challenged the rights Jefferson and his associates deemed fundamental. Furthermore, H. K. Beale, *A History of Freedom of Teaching in the American Schools* (New York: Charles Scribner's Sons, 1941); H. H. Remmers, *Anti-Democratic Attitudes in American Schools* (Evanston: Northwestern University Press, 1963); and John C. Weiser and James E. Hayes, "Democratic Attitudes of Teachers and Prospective Teachers" (*Phi Delta Kappan*, May, 1966, pp. 476–481) illustrate that substantial numbers of high school students and elementary and secondary school teachers reject the founding fathers' precepts.

When I ask university students to define *democracy*, their responses cluster around (1) voting; (2) Lincoln's "government of the people, by the people, for the people"; and (3) the Bill of Rights. When I postpone the question until after they react to a dozen items from H. H. Remmers' polls on the Bill of Rights, I find that from one-fourth to one-half believe that freedom of the press, freedom of speech, the right to petition, and freedom from loyalty oaths should be abridged. The most startling revelation is that one-fourth or more concur that "A large mass of the people are not capable of determining what is and what is not good for them." In our classroom-attempts to define democracy three assumptions often

8

arise and are debated: (1) The degree to which a local, state, or national government or a home, church, school, lodge, or teachers' organization is democratic can be ascertained by noting to what extent its members participate in developing and carrying out its policies. (2) The members of an organization that hews to democratic principles must have faith that the majority will make the right decisions most of the time. (3) A democratic organization insists the Bill of Rights applies to all members and nonmembers.

When I ask students whether administrators and teachers are obligated to defend the principles of democracy, they reply that citizens sometimes exact harsh penalties from those who seek for themselves and others certain Constitutional rights. They say that individuals and groups are sometimes stoned, clubbed, gassed, or shot while trying to achieve rights supported by laws; and not infrequently juries free the lawbreakers when evidence of their guilt is overwhelming. They also bring up current cases of teachers fired for (1) revealing, in or out of the classroom, the discrepancies between citizens' verbalizations about democracy and their actual behavior and (2) participating in organizations that seek equal rights for all.

Students know that in some classrooms, North and South, free discussions of civil rights, foreign affairs, consumer education, or sex education can lead to dismissal. Some insist a teacher should pass-on the social heritage of the community, including its prejudices and injustices, or seek a job elsewhere; and usually several seem unaware of any restrictions on what teachers and students may discuss and investigate. They apparently agree with Leibnitz and Pope that this is the best of all possible worlds— whatever is, is right.

The courageous English teacher concerned about significant current issues will discuss them when they arise naturally from reading, writing, speaking, and listening assignments. He gives every idea a fair hearing. He questions the tyranny of students and others who strive to silence speakers with unpopular ideas. He is committed to John Stuart Mill's assertion:

> Sometimes we come, on further reflection, to find merit in the new idea; and if we do not, we understand our own views better by testing them against differing views.

Furthermore, he is not interested in selling a bill of goods. He promotes an exchange of views on controversial issues because he believes that students who are given free access to information and stimulated to use it will increasingly resort to reason rather than emotion when their assumptions are challenged by classmates, teachers, and others. Such a teacher will not hesitate to reveal his ideas, if asked, but he does not use his verbal skill to embarrass students or to win an argument. He knows that trying to impose his views on students is propaganda, not teaching.

Should the school exemplify in its aims and methods the principles of democracy, try to approximate a democracy in action? Students say that as elementary, high school, and university students, they were seldom asked to participate in developing and carrying out policies related to the subject matter they were asked to read and recite and later recall on tests. They often label student courts and student councils phony, the trappings of democracy. They accuse administrators and teachers of plotting and enforcing behavior patterns without recourse to students' ideas. They insist the conscientious student is kept docile with a club as potent as Circe's wand: the grade. The student not easily intimidated by grades may be subjected to less subtle pressures.

After the initial antagonisms towards teachers' and administrators' methods of stimulating conformity to rules are expressed, some students recall a teacher who encouraged student participation in formulating course aims, content, and methods. He is not always lauded. Apparently such a teacher may discover that (1) it is more difficult to maintain order when students are involved in planning the curriculum; (2) it takes so much time to agree on a curricular destination and route that the semester is almost over before course content can be covered; and (3) the outcomes of a teacher-pupil planned program are not easily converted into grades.

Perhaps unpopularity of democratic procedures in the classroom arises from its strangeness; most students are accustomed to following, not determining, directions. An adult's quest for certainty is shared by students; they feel safe and secure in a situation where the curricular map features a clear, unmistakable destination and a detour-free route. A teacher-arranged educational tour eliminates entirely or reduces to a minimum the frustrations and uncertainties accompanying decision making.

What are some arguments favoring experimenting with democratic processes in schools? Students, especially those with social studies majors or minors, often point out that the most serious problem confronting huge modern democracies is promoting intelligent individual and group participation in local, state, and national governments. They recall accounts of the "pure" democracies in ancient Athens and early New England (the town meeting), not always recalling that in both situations qualifications for direct participation excluded most of the governed. They admit that today suffrage is extended to most Americans who meet certain age, residence, citizenship, and education requirements. However, they indicate that direct participation in determining and carrying out crucial governmental policies is largely denied to all but well-organized pressure groups.

Voters often elect the candidate who makes the most-appealing promises. Once in office he may dismiss his promises as campaign propaganda. Decisions affecting the lives of all citizens may be made without the direct consent of the governed. Of course, politicians making "wrong" decisions can be defeated at the next election, but their control of mass media and patronage may make their mistakes palatable.

A critic is often silenced by politicians who equate democracy and patriotism with *their* decisions. When debate is needed most, it is sometimes postponed for the duration of a created emergency. A citizen concerned about crucial issues may discover he is only a spectator watching the performance of politicians over whom he has little or no control and whose opponents are often so much like them that he says, "A plague on both your houses" and stays away from the polls. He is also irked by the newspaper editor who identifies democracy with the periodic pulling of a lever in a voting booth and who appeals to reluctant voters' consciences and patriotism instead of providing pertinent information about issues and candidates.

Some educators claim that if our schools provide practice in democratic processes, citizens who reach voting age will choose political leaders who will involve the electorate in decision making. Furthermore, they feel if the method of intelligence is applied to selecting government leaders, perhaps more men of wisdom rather than merely action will be selected and elected. When winning elections depends upon campaign propaganda and image building, appeals to emotion rather than reason, many capable people avoid becoming candidates.

Local, state, and national governments are faced with what seem insurmountable problems and perpetual crises; but the people who presumably select and control the leaders who have to solve the problems usually spend from eight to sixteen years in schools that prize slavish adherence to patterns prescribed by administrators and teachers who epitomize the traditional read, recall, and recite syndrome. We laud scientists and inventors who spend a lifetime advancing one step toward the solution of a problem in agriculture, medicine, communication, or transportation by identifying and defining the problem, gathering data, developing hypotheses, and testing hypotheses. In solving problems related to civil rights, foreign affairs, poverty, and consumption of goods and services, politicians often become enamoured of a single hypothesis that is pursued indefinitely even though tests demonstrate its ineffectiveness. Furthermore, mistakes are rarely admitted and sometimes compounded because face-saving and the next election are considered more important than the national welfare. Such politicians prosper because of indifferent, uninformed, or unthinking electorates.

Schools shy away from experimentation for many reasons. A common one is the insistence by influential patrons that new goals and methods will scar the student and society. Any attempt to approximate in the high school the democratic principles presented in the Declaration of Independence and the Bill of Rights is scored by individuals and groups who believe tried-and-true traditional goals and methods are indispensable in preparing youth for college or business and industry. But Wilford Aiken's account of an exciting research project—*The Story of the Eight-Year Study* (New York: McGraw-Hill Book Company, Inc., 1942)—indicates that 1475 students graduating from experimental schools (who had been carefully matched with 1475 students from traditional schools) were in no way handicapped as college or university students.

Since the zest for experimentation on a grand scale appears to have vanished—see Chapters 8 and 9 of Lawrence A. Cremin's *The Transformation of the School: Progressivism in American Education* (New York: Alfred A. Knopf, 1961)—it might be useful for experienced teachers to test the following hypotheses on a small scale: Students in an English class that exemplifies the principles of democracy will exceed the progress made by students in a traditional class. Since the fear of handicapping college-bound students through experimentation is overwhelming in most schools, perhaps the experiment should be tried in classes that are considered academically hopeless. A teacher might teach one group of slow seventh graders the traditional way, another similar group the democratic way. Achievement, performance, and attitude tests would be given at the beginning and end of the experiment which might last for a single semester, a year, two years, or three years.

In the experimental class students would be directly involved in determining goals, content, and methods they believe would lead to improved performance in reading, writing, speaking, and listening. They would even decide how their work would be evaluated. Codes for criticism and conduct would be developed and applied by students. The teacher's traditional club, a grade, would be absent. He would be there to (1) answer questions; (2) provide requested materials; (3) give encouragement; (4) keep a daily journal on how the problems relating to goals, content, methods were attacked and resolved; (5) make the contents of the journal available to students once a week or oftener; and (6) step in, when necessary, to preserve life or limb. In the control class the teacher would provide the destination and itinerary for the curricular journey.

An experienced English teacher who is interested in testing the idea of having students make decisions rather than follow orders could limit the experiment to a three-week oral composition unit. He might even limit the planning period to two or three days; but all the students would be encouraged to participate in developing the aims, content, methods, and evaluative procedures. The first time such an idea is tested, the teacher might be the discussion leader during the planning sessions; the next time a student selected by the group could take his place. There is no reason why the teacher should not (1) discuss with students the reasons for the experiment and (2) conduct a post-mortem upon its completion. After several such small-scale experiments a teacher might be ready to develop a more formal research proposal that includes a defensible experimental design and controls.

Having students participate directly in determining the goals and methods for a unit of work is not unusual on the elementary and university (graduate) levels, uncommon on the secondary level. Shouldn't secondary students also have frequent opportunities to make curricular decisions, i.e., set worthwhile group and individual goals, develop ways of achieving them, and determine to what extent the goals and methods were successful? Even if tried on a limited scale, such a procedure should help students gain valuable experience in decision making. Most teachers claim their primary aim is to develop a thinking student and citizen, but quite often they make all the decisions in the classroom. A student who is completely dependent upon teachers for academic action is likely to cease such action when he drops out or graduates. But a student experienced in setting worthwhile academic goals and developing ways of achieving them is likely to know how to continue his education when a teacher's guidance is no longer available; and he may increasingly draw on reason rather than emotion as he participates in school, city, state, and national governments.

A PHILOSOPHY OF TEACHING ENGLISH

When high school English teachers parley, they usually agree that the following goals (recorded, with minor variations, in most English methods books) should be central in all English programs: helping students learn (1) to speak and write clearly, thoughtfully, and correctly; (2) to listen intelligently; and (3) to appreciate good literature and worthwhile current publications. Linguists have introduced a fourth objective: to help students understand the nature (evolution, structure, and function) of the English language.[8]

When the discussion turns to ways of achieving these objectives, differences of opinion arise. "There are many ways of skinning a cat,"

[8]See George Winchester Stone, Jr., ed., *Issues, Problems, and Approaches in the Teaching of English* (New York: Holt, Rinehart and Winston, Inc., 1961), pp. 1–40 and 233–46.

is resurrected and translated into "There are many effective approaches to teaching reading, writing, speaking, and listening." Recently, sixty high school English teachers were asked to respond to the following "common-sense" methods recommended in most books and articles on teaching English:

> Students should be given frequent opportunities to write, speak, and listen under the guidance of a teacher.

> Instruction in grammar and usage should be based largely on the strengths and weaknesses revealed in students' speech and writing, rather than on handbook and workbook exercises.

> English teachers should help students develop a lifelong appreciation of literature by encouraging them in every way possible to read widely from the works of reputable authors.

Almost all the teachers claimed that the typical English teacher, with five classes of thirty students each, cannot do the grading involved in giving students frequent opportunities to write. They asked, "How can anyone find time to grade one hundred and fifty papers once a week?" One teacher commented, "Even if schools followed Conant's suggestion[9] that no English teacher be assigned more than a total of one hundred students in four classes, a theme a week would still be unreasonable." But some teachers (see Chapter 6) with 150 students do provide frequent guided writing experiences for their students.

The following quotations indicate how the teachers responded to the suggestion that instruction in grammar and usage be based on the strengths and weaknesses revealed in their students' speech and writing:

(1) "Students' writing and speaking skills vary so much that instruction would have to be given on an individual basis, which takes too much time when classes number thirty or more students." (2) "Students show so many deficiencies in spelling, punctuation, capitalization, and sentence structure that each area demands a week or more of attention every semester." (3) "Handbook and workbook exercises are indispensable. They permit a well-organized approach—a series of exercises on each part of speech and each common departure from standard usage. Furthermore, the exercises can be completed in class or assigned as homework and can be graded in class by the students." (4) "Students must know the rules of good grammar before they write themes." (5) "I once tried the suggested approach, but my students showed no improvement in their next theme." (6) "I don't like the workbook-handbook routine, but my school requires

[9]James B. Conant, *The American High School Today* (New York: McGraw-Hill Book Company, Inc., 1959), p. 51.

IMPROVING ENGLISH INSTRUCTION

all students to buy workbooks. If I don't use them, parents complain to my principal."

But some English teachers (see Chapters 6 and 7) do relate instruction in grammar and usage directly to strengths and weaknesses revealed in students' speech and writing. The logic of the method appeals to students. They are interested in eliminating serious usage errors from their speech and writing, bored with detecting and correcting errors contrived by handbook and workbook makers.

All of the secondary school teachers supported the idea that students be encouraged in every way possible to read widely from works of reputable authors. But when asked how they achieved the goal, they concluded their departmental syllabi require such a thorough treatment of traditional literary selections that they and their students have little time for supplementary material. Most of them were free to develop book lists for students' "outside readings," but only a few used paperbacks. Several had organized paperback book clubs.

Recall your experiences in high school English classes you attended. What were the goals of your best and worst teachers? How did they go about trying to achieve them? If they used workbook and handbook exercises, what were the outcomes? If you wrote themes fairly frequently, how were your writing strengths and weaknesses pointed out to you? If your teachers helped you improve your oral English, how did they do it? If they helped you improve your listening skills, how did they do it? How did they help you understand the nature (evolution, structure, and function) of the English language? Which of their goals and methods do you plan to adopt? reject? Why?

One goal of the English teacher surpassing all others in importance has not been mentioned. He hopes that many of his students will develop an enthusiasm for learning which will persist all their lives. Only the individual who remains a student until he dies profits fully from the schooling he received. Too seldom does even the college student become a learner. More likely than not, he remains a pupil—one who undertakes only compulsory intellectual assignments.[10] Why is zest for learning in the very young often dulled by the time they reach high school? Is it because learning becomes increasingly verbal and memoriter as students climb the educational ladder?

REVISING THE CURRICULUM

Since almost any high school in which an English teacher might accept a position already has an English curriculum, both experienced and inex-

[10]Jacques Barzun, "Pupils into Students," *Teacher in America* (New York: Doubleday Anchor Books, Doubleday and Company, Inc., 1944), pp. 17–31.

perienced teachers are likely to help revise this curriculum rather than to develop a new one. The revisions made are commonly limited to selecting new literature anthologies, handbooks, and workbooks. However, in a few schools the objectives of the English department and the specific objectives, content, and methods for individual courses are reviewed periodically.

An English department head who believes curricular revisions should not be limited to choosing new anthologies and handbooks will, every three to five years, ask his teachers to determine whether the goals for the department and individual courses are compatible with the size and quality of the student body and faculty, the current demands of society (local, state, national, and international), and the financial support received from the community and state. If the goals are changed, revisions promising their achievement are made in the courses of study. For example, in recent years a few schools have based curricular changes on the assumption that students are more likely to develop an appreciation of American literature when the course begins with living authors and ends with Sarah Kemble Knight, Jonathan Edwards, Michael Wigglesworth, and Anne Bradstreet. And an increasing number of high schools are accepting Conant's assumption that time devoted to English should be divided equally between composition and literature.[11]

When an English department has reached a consensus on desirable curricular changes, they are usually recorded in organized fashion in syllabi. Syllabi must then be translated into specific classroom procedures. An English curriculum developed by a department or committee is only a map; it takes a conscientious, enthusiastic, imaginative, and well-prepared teacher to use the map in planning and directing a worthwhile academic journey for students. Curricular revisions are made, then, to develop better goals for students and teachers and more effective courses of study for reaching the destinations. Since curricular changes should be supported with data that prove their worth, they must, whenever possible, be preceded and followed by research.

Committees may undertake curriculum studies solely because the members are prodded by an administrator. They are not always given time to find answers to two questions: "What should be the objectives of the English department? How can they best be achieved?" To examine research in English which might help committees make defensible decisions is a burden few overworked members will assume. Research to produce evidence to justify curriculum changes or maintenance of the status quo takes time, money, and energy. But the outlook for research-based curriculum reconstruction in English is better today than ever before. The U. S. Office of Education's Division of Elementary-Secondary Research,

[11]Conant, *The American High School Today*, p. 50.

the National Council of Teachers of English's Research Foundation, and private foundations have initiated a trend that promises eventually to force curriculum committees to forsake guesswork for research. Once the values of research are proved, more time, money, and energy will probably be available.

In the chapters that follow, you will find illustrated and discussed many ideas on teaching English. May they win you to the idea that improvement in English instruction is most likely to occur when teachers, singly and in groups, evaluate continuously through research the goals, content, and methods of courses forming the English curriculum.

AN EDUCATIONAL FILM SERIES

A pictorial presentation of the aims and methods of American education is provided by *Education in America*, a series of three films: "The Seventeenth and Eighteenth Centuries," "The Nineteenth Century," and "Twentieth Century Developments." Each film runs sixteen minutes. For the nearest rental source, write to Coronet Instructional Films, Coronet Building, Chicago, Illinois 60601.

Note: Most colleges and universities preparing English teachers have rental films useful in teaching literature, grammar, linguistics, usage, composition, speech, and semantics. For an illustrative listing of such films, see *Language Arts Films* (Champaign, Illinois: Visual Aids Service, Division of University Extension, University of Illinois 61801).

ASSUMPTIONS ABOUT DEVELOPING GOALS

Prepare to explain why you accept or reject, wholly or in part, the following assumptions about developing goals:

1. The best definition of *philosophy* is "love of wisdom."
2. The questions (see page 2) raised by philosophers can be answered only with assumptions.
3. The philosophies of life and government of American and Soviet leaders cannot be reconciled.
4. W. H. Auden's "The Unknown Citizen" is a just satire on modern man's values.
5. You can discover an individual's philosophy of life from a list of his statements of belief.
6. The unexamined life is not worth living (Socrates).
7. Socrates' "Know thyself" is easily defined and illustrated.
8. Education is learning.
9. The purpose of education is to pass-on one's social heritage.

10. The purpose of education is to improve one's social heritage.

11. The purpose of education is to teach students how to think, not what to think.

12. The purpose of American schools is to define, defend, and exemplify the values of a democratic society.

13. Development of moral and spiritual values is a responsibility of our schools.

14. Much of American education is indoctrination.

15. A college or university education should be reserved for high school graduates who rank in the upper 50 percent of their class.

16. One can easily refute the objections (see pp. 14–15) to basing instruction in grammar and usage on the strengths and weaknesses revealed in students' speech and writing.

17. The suggestion that schools should develop in students the ability to use the scientific method in solving their problems is applicable only in the science laboratory.

18. A licensed physician should be permitted to identify his patient's health needs and to take measures to meet them.

19. A licensed teacher should be permitted to decide what to teach and how to teach it.

20. The assumption that most students can learn to appreciate literature and to express ideas clearly, thoughtfully, and correctly is unrealistic.

21. Content and method are inseparable.

22. The road to peace is paved with education.

23. The aims and methods of education have varied considerably in the last twenty-five hundred years.

24. An excellent overview of educational aims, content, and methods from primitive to recent times is given in the "Assimilation Charts" at the ends of chapters in Elmer Harrison Wilds' *The Foundations of Modern Education*, 1936 edition.

25. The aims and methods of American secondary education have varied considerably in the last fifty years. (See H. G. Good, "Late Pattern High Schools," *A History of American Education*, Second Edition, New York: Macmillan, 1962, pp. 438–468.)

26. One cannot successfully contest Jacques Barzun's thesis—pupils must develop into students—in Chapter 2 of his *Teacher in America*.

27. The section on "Goals, Content, and Teaching Problems" in George Winchester Stone, Jr., ed., *Issues, Problems and Approaches in the Teaching of English* (New York: Holt, Rinehart and Winston, Inc., 1961), pp. 7–15, raises crucial issues about teaching English.

28. William J. Dusel points up effectively the need for revising teaching loads in "Determining an Efficient Teaching Load in English," *Illinois English Bulletin*, Vol. 43, October, 1955.

29. Books on teaching English by J. N. Hook; Walter Loban, Margaret Ryan, and James Squire; Hans P. Guth; Abraham Bernstein; and Edwin Sauer (see Bibliography) agree on goals for teaching English.

30. The three goals for teaching English on page 13 are oversimplified.

31. The three methods of teaching reading, writing, speaking, and listening on page 14 are impractical.

32. High school English teachers should divide their time equally between teaching composition and literature.

33. One can profit from recalling and analyzing the goals and methods of one's former English teachers.

34. Teachers should be blamed for the high percentage of high school students who apparently reject large portions of our Bill of Rights. See H. H. Remmers and D. H. Radler, "The Citizen He Will Become," *The American Teen-Ager*, pp. 178–221.

35. The dropout rate in some schools could be reduced by relating instruction to the concerns of students rather than restricting it largely to rote learning of irrelevant facts labeled *English, social studies, and science.*

36. The English teacher should apply to his teaching Thoreau's admonition, "Our life is frittered away by detail. . . . Simplify, simplify."

37. Although born into a scientific age, most college and university students (undergraduate and graduate) cannot explain satisfactorily how a scientist solves problems.

38. The scientific method perpetually challenges not only theories hallowed by tradition but also theories approved yesterday by the method.

39. Our unique single-track educational system, which permits a child to enter a public kindergarten and progress through a public elementary school, secondary school, and college or university, is superior to the typical European double-track educational system, which directs most upper-class children towards the gymnasium, lycée, grammar school, and university and most lower-class children towards advanced elementary schools and vocational schools.

40. Educational aims and methods are the subject of current controversies. See Henry Ehlers and Gordon C. Lee, *Crucial Issues in Education* (New York: Holt, Rinehart and Winston, Inc., 1964) and/or Harold Full, ed., *Controversy in American Education, An Anthology of Crucial Issues* (New York: The Macmillan Company, 1967).

41. Yesterday's and today's books on English methods vary little in practices recommended. See Percival Chubb, *The Teaching of English* (New York: The Macmillan Company, 1929) and/or Thomas C. Blaisdell, *Ways to Teach English* (New York: Doubleday, Doran, and Company, Inc., 1930).

42. The complaint of Quintilian (A.D. 1st century), "Education is for the schoolroom, not for life," is applicable today. (See Royal J. Morsey,

"Piddling While Rome Burns," *Phi Delta Kappan,* Vol. 48, No. 10, June, 1967, p. 522.)

43. Cities with populations under 100,000 should have a single comprehensive high school where the children of all the people can associate with each other in curricular and extracurricular activities.

44. ". . . if we once start thinking, no one can guarantee where we shall come out, except that many objects, ends, and institutions are doomed. Every thinker puts some portion of an apparently stable world in peril, and no one can wholly predict what will emerge in its place" (John Dewey).

IDEAS TO TEST

You have probably been urged to know your students. See what you can find out by asking them to respond orally or in writing to one or more of the following questions.

1. Explain briefly what you like and dislike about English as a school subject, and why.

2. What have you read the last two weeks that was not required reading in any of your classes?

3. If you have a favorite school subject, explain why it is a favorite.

4. Without giving names, what are some of the qualities of your best teachers?

5. What occupation would you like to follow? Why?

6. What are your strongest prejudices? How did you acquire them?

7. What is literature? What can you learn from literature?

8. What are the goals English teachers try to help you achieve?

9. Why do you or why don't you like to compete with fellow students in winning good grades in English?

10. Do you think English teachers' examinations test the progress you have made in reading, writing, speaking, and listening? Defend your answer.

11. What is the meaning of *philosophy of life*? Why can't you avoid having one?

12. How does one learn and improve the following skills: swimming, reading, bicycling, writing, driving an automobile, speaking, dancing, and listening?

13. Why do you accept or reject, wholly or in part, the following statement: An American citizen should be skillful in using words.

14. How could English classes be made more interesting and worthwhile?

15. What should schools do that they do not do?

16. If at the beginning of the semester your English teacher asked you, "What should we do in this class?" what would you say? Why?

17. Ask students to identify the pressing problems confronting (1) them, (2) their parents, (3) their town or city, (4) their state, (5) their nation, and (6) mankind. Then ask them how their school is helping to solve the problems.

2

Learning: Principles and Problems

Before reading this chapter, formulate clear, defensible answers to the following questions. After reading it, prepare to explain why you changed or retained your answers.

1. How do you define *learning*?

2. If someone asked you, "What did you learn today?" what would your answer be?

3. Your comments about completed high school and college English courses have probably included, "I learned a lot in Mr. Viel's course" and "I learned very little in Mr. Wenig's course." Why did you learn a lot in Mr. Viel's course, very little in Mr. Wenig's course?

4. What conditions prevailed when you learned skills (driving a car, swimming, dancing, sewing, carpentry, cooking, sports) quickly? slowly?

5. Please complete "Students learn best when . . ." in twenty-five words or less. How can your statement be applied to English instruction?

6. Why can or can't you say your high school English teachers made effective classroom use of mass media—newspapers, magazines, radio, and television?

7. Why can or can't you say your high school English teachers made effective use of technological aids—films, filmstrips, slides, recordings, tape recorders, programed teaching machines, radio, and television?

8. Why do most high school curricula accent the separateness rather than the interrelatedness of English, science, social studies, mathematics, foreign languages, etc?

9. Why should or shouldn't slow students be taught in separate classes? Why would or wouldn't you like to teach slow classes?

DEFINING LEARNING

When a parent puts Johnny, a third grader, on the spot with, "What did you learn today?" he may say, "Aw, nuthin'!" When he is a high school senior he may say, "Nothing!" or "Not much," which indicates he has improved his usage or enhanced his knowledge in the intervening nine years. Should a visiting grandparent ask Johnny, a third grader, "What have you learned since you started to school?" he may say, "To finger-paint, read, write, and all about Indians, Christopher Columbus, the Boston Tea Party, and George Washington." Such an answer reflects the most common dictionary definition of learning: "to gain knowledge or skill."

Should one ask psychologists to define learning, they would probably say, "It is a process within an individual that brings about a change in his behavior."[1] Perhaps research will eventually give the words *process* and *change* in the psychologists' definition more exact meanings. The *change* an English teacher seeks to stimulate in his students' behavior is improvement in language skills.

SIX LEARNING PRINCIPLES

Six commonsense learning principles abstracted from the findings of researchers concerned with human and animal behavior can be applied to the classroom: Students learn best when (1) their goals are clear and vital; (2) subject matter contributes directly to achievement of their goals; (3) transfer of learning is provided for; (4) guided practice is in the skill to be learned; (5) worthwhile achievement is possible, promptly measured, and rewarded; and (6) the problem-solving approach is emphasized. These generalizations can serve as guidelines in planning an English program, course, unit, or lesson. Check the following detailed recommendations relating to goals, subject matter, transfer, practice, success, and problem solving against your experiences as a student and/or teacher. Try to determine how all or some of them might be tested in the classroom. Such an application, as you read, of past experience to present learning will incite ideas of your own. The purpose of English methods books is to stimulate creative teaching, not addiction to established or recommended patterns. If a recommended pattern does not prove its worth in the classroom, modify it or replace it.

[1]For thirteen definitions of learning by authorities in the field, see John F. Travers, *Learning: Analysis and Application* (New York: David McKay Company, Inc., 1965), pp. 2–3.

Goals

Students learn best when their goals are clear and vital. How many of your high school teachers explained their course goals? How many invited student participation in developing course goals? Most English teachers are as anxious and happy to sell learning as Carl Sandburg's fish crier (see page 61) was to sell fish; but those who keep their goals a secret presume students to be mind readers or to share their enthusiasm for language and literature. Such teachers may be right in claiming that goals will become clear as the course progresses, but most students are helped by knowing their destination and itinerary early in the semester.

An English teacher who spends a period or more at the beginning of the semester explaining his (1) goals and (2) methods (discussions, written and oral reports, supplementary readings, and tests) gives students a much-needed sense of direction and allays their fears of burdensome surprises. Because students usually schedule four or five courses, they appreciate advance notice of their responsibilities. In addition to an overview of the entire course, some teachers later present detailed aims and methods for each unit. Teachers usually state their goals and methods orally; but students welcome a written statement and an opportunity to discuss it with their teacher.

An approach to goals that reflects more accurately the learning principle "Students learn best when their goals are clear and vital" is considered too time-consuming by many teachers. However, most students value participation in setting the goals for a course; letting students assume at least part of the responsibility can ease instructional frustrations—highly motivated students are easier and more pleasant to work with than those who need hourly prodding. Involvement in decision making is currently sought by many segments of society; it should be fostered in a democracy.

A class discussion of the following questions may give the teacher insights useful in originating or revising course plans: Why in all nations are language and literature a required part of secondary curricula? Why do you accept or reject, wholly or in part, the assumption that increased skill in reading, writing, speaking, and listening provides immediate and long-term benefits? Why do some English courses lack vitality? Without mentioning teachers' names, why have you worked hard in some English classes and done much less in others? If you were an English teacher, how would you (1) defend English as a required course and (2) stimulate enthusiasm for English? To what extent have you achieved the goals set by your English teachers? If you could set your own goals for this semester's work, what would they be, and why? If a teacher

24

decides against devoting a period or more to a class discussion of students' goals, he could ask them to write an answer to, If you could set your own goals for this semester's work, what would they be, and why? The answers would give him helpful information and a sampling of students' composition abilities.

Before or soon after individual and group goals are determined, the teacher must seek an answer to, What is the present status of each student's skill in reading, writing, speaking, and listening? He can find a partial answer by administering performance, not standardized, tests. Some teachers believe that giving tests during the first week of the semester ends interest in a course. Others claim it motivates students, especially if they understand that a functional course will be derived from test results. A possible compromise is to administer a performance test prior to each unit of work. If the course begins with a literature unit, students' written interpretations of several short literary selections of varying difficulty will reveal their ability to read literature. If a composition unit is scheduled first, students could write a short composition in class, an assignment which will provide useful information about students' grasp of grammar and usage, punctuation, capitalization, sentence clearness and effectiveness, vocabulary, spelling, organization, paragraphing, and content. To be *most* helpful individual goals should (1) be determined by student-teacher analysis of performance tests and (2) undergo necessary modifications as students' performance in language skills improves, remains static, or deteriorates. At the end of the semester, the teacher can acquire information valuable for future planning by asking students to respond orally or in writing to, Why did or didn't you accomplish what you set out to accomplish at the beginning of the term?

Clear, vital goals are highly motivational. They are likely to be clear and vital when the evidence supporting them is drawn from performance tests which reveal students' reading, writing, speaking, and listening strengths and weaknesses.

Subject Matter

Students learn best when subject matter contributes directly to achievement of their goals. English teachers sometimes meet with department heads, curriculum directors, English supervisors, and college or university faculty to select and organize subject matter likely to help students improve language skills more quickly and thoroughly. They may view English instruction as a program extending from the kindergarten through the graduate school.[2] However, most senior high school staffs are concerned only with

---

[2]See Mary Columbro Rodgers, *New Designs in the Teaching of English* (Scranton, Pennsylvania: International Textbook Company, 1968), pp. 1–32.

their own program; and with or without the help of consultants, they periodically select and organize subject matter for grades 10–12 that makes for an orderly, nonrepetitive progression towards clear, vital goals. English curricula not revised periodically tend to drift towards sameness on the various grade levels, especially when handbook and workbook exercises are in the saddle and riding hard.

After a staff has developed junior or senior high school courses of study which are sequential and cumulative, each teacher must make necessary adjustments when he uses the resultant syllabi. Even if students are grouped homogeneously, he dare not assume two slow, average, or academic classes are alike. Syllabi modifications are inevitable if he pays attention to evidence provided by performance tests. Teachers and consultants may evolve "utopian" courses of study for various grade levels, but to impose their tenth-grade course of study on all tenth graders will prove as futile as trying to entice students into memorizing the *Encyclopaedia Britannica.*

Students are bored when asked to spend much of each semester completing handbook and workbook exercises or memorizing rules on the parts of speech, sentence types, punctuation marks, clauses, participles, and gerunds. They also fail to see any concrete benefits accruing from time spent on uniform spelling and vocabulary lists.[3] When subject matter contributes directly to achievement of student goals, it becomes a means to a worthwhile end. A student whose reading, writing, speaking, and listening strengths and weaknesses are revealed by performance tests is motivated by carefully selected and logically organized reading, writing, speaking, and listening experiences designed to alleviate his weaknesses and increase his strengths.

Transfer

Students learn best when transfer of learning is provided for. Our educational institutions are based on the idea of transfer. Business education teachers used to assume that students who passed shorthand, typing, and bookkeeping courses could soon become skilled stenographers, typists, bookkeepers, or secretaries. Complaints from businessmen caused business education teachers to introduce courses that simulated business-office routines. Teachers learned that students who type sixty words per minute on a speed test also need experience typing letters and completing business forms. Practice in transferring typing and shorthand skills and bookkeeping knowledge to a wide variety of business situations is now provided by most high school business education departments.

[3]See Appendix 12, Two Main Roads Diverge in the Classroom.

One who applies the cliché "ivory tower" to colleges and universities implies that what is learned there has little relevance to problems faced by most societies. He enjoys pointing out that some teachers and students of social studies do not practice good citizenship and that some mathematicians and economists are easy prey for usurers. If he chose to cap the cliché "ivory tower" with a chestnut, he could say, "Those who can do; those who can't, teach; and those who can't teach, teach teachers." However, there is evidence that our colleges and universities enjoy considerable success in developing vocational skills and modest success in passing-on the social heritage and unshackling minds. Some even stimulate thinking about ways of improving upon our social heritage.

Today there are few teachers who support the once widely accepted idea that reasoning, observing, remembering, and imagining can be developed by exercising mental muscles on difficult subjects: Greek, Latin, geometry, and science. But there are many teachers who still believe that what they teach will be automatically applied by students to new situations as they arise. They say, "Nothing we learn is ever lost; minds are storehouses from which we requisition what has been learned whenever we need it." They imply that one who memorizes an English handbook will use his knowledge about organizing a theme, paragraphing, diagraming sentences, précis writing, capitalization, a. d punctuation whenever he is asked to compose a composition. Research has produced evidence that such transfer is likely to occur only if teachers help students relate handbook material to their composition activities. A handbook proves an excellent resource when students use it to answer questions which arise as they write a composition or prepare a talk.

The English teacher cannot insure complete transfer of what his students learned yesterday, last week, or last year to what they are learning today; but he can increase transfer by helping individual students derive goals from evidence provided by performance tests. Once a student knows where he stands regarding language and where he would like to go, he and his teacher can select and organize materials that will get him to his destination with minimum dependence on transfer. Mastery of writing principles illustrated in handbooks is likely only when they are learned as part of the composition process, unlikely when they are learned in isolation. Skills are mastered through guided practice, not by storing the mind with knowledge about them. Transfer is most apt to occur when we are strongly stimulated to draw on old learning (to rack our brains), a not uncommon situation when we have clear, vital goals. Outstanding writers, speakers, sculptors, painters, teachers, and athletes improve their skills by exploiting fully what they have learned in the past.

The teacher as well as the student must bring past learning to bear on current learning. An experienced teacher may be someone who has repeated the same routine every year for forty years. A creative teacher is always revising his goals and methods. What he has learned about teaching this semester affects next semester's goals and methods. He analyzes his successes and failures to determine how he can reduce his failures and increase his successes—a procedure that insures maximum transfer.[4]

Practice

A student learns best when guided practice is in the skill to be learned. How much time in your high school English classes was devoted to practicing reading, writing, speaking, and listening? How much time was spent on segmented activities assumed to have an impact on language skills at a later date, i.e., spelling and vocabulary lists, handbook and workbook exercises, and memorization of definitions and rules?

Most teachers believe "practice makes perfect," which may be true if one foregoes a too-rigid definition of *perfect*. Some students practice "I seen" so long that "I saw" becomes almost an impossibility. However, students do often make perfect scores on objective tests that measure success in recalling facts. Many are so highly motivated they can approximate a verbatim rendition of assignments in handbooks, workbooks, and literature anthologies. "A" grades are accompanied by significant rewards: membership in honor societies; approbation from peers, parents, and teachers; scholarships; and admission to colleges and universities. Why do such students often do well in college even though through lack of guided practice their language skills are mediocre? They have acquired good study habits, possess considerable innate ability, and adjust quickly to the demands of teachers. Unfortunately their success encourages high school teachers to continue developing skilled memorizers of inert material.

Some academic, average, and slow high school students criticize among themselves the demands for rote learning still prevalent in many schools; but they know that in-class questioning of goals and methods is seldom a student's prerogative. If one asked a high-school dropout how he would teach a skill to fellow dropouts, he would probably answer, "I'd have them practice it and help them when they need help," an approach he observed coaches use on the baseball field, gridiron, and basketball court.

If memorizing is the skill you practiced most in high school and college English classes, you may resent having its value questioned. When you teach, follow a similar pattern in one of your classes, a control class.

[4]See John F. Travers, Chapter VIII, "The Transfer of Learning," *Learning: Analysis and Application* (New York: David McKay Company, Inc., 1965), pp. 136–155.

In an experimental class resembling the control class in ability, emphasize guided practice in reading, writing, speaking, and listening. In literature have students read what they can appreciate, give them a wide choice of suitable supplementary reading, provide time for in-class silent reading, and minimize attention to authors' lives and times and literary criticism. In written composition help students as they write and rewrite paragraphs, essays, and letters. Base instruction in grammar and usage on what you discover from reading their writings (including essay tests) and listening to their discussions, oral reports, and extracurricular chatter. In speech units use your time helping students prepare, present, and evaluate talks, panel discussions, readings, and plays. In a listening unit replace lectures and discussions about listening with guided listening experiences.

In order that you may compare the outcomes of the experimental and control classes, administer simple performance tests at the beginning of the experiment and the same tests at the end of the experiment. Also, have students complete a brief attitude-towards-English questionnaire at the beginning and end of the experiment. When you compare the test results of the control and experimental classes, you may not have irrefutable evidence favoring the segmented-activities approach or the guided-practice-in-the-skill-to-be-learned approach; but the evidence will probably stimulate further experimentation. A teacher who persistently and systematically provides students with opportunities for guided practice in language skills —reading, writing, speaking, and listening—will enjoy teaching and bring joy to his students. Students are quick to subscribe to Sophocles' suggestion, "One must learn by doing the thing."

Success

Students learn best when worthwhile achievement is possible, measured promptly, and rewarded. Miss Freundlich, one of my student teachers, a journalism major and English minor, and Mrs. Gutig, her high school supervisor, exemplified this principle in teaching eighteen disadvantaged tenth graders who had received "F's" in slow English classes during their first semester in a senior high school. Mrs. Gutig and Miss Freundlich's goal was to provide their students with interesting, worthwhile, and successful experiences in reading, writing, and speaking. During the last ten weeks of the semester, I spent ten hours observing them.

The two teachers selected and organized materials aimed directly at developing language skills. Reading materials included newspapers (twenty copies of Monday's edition were donated by a local paper); current popular magazines; writings of the eighteen students; and books chosen by students, teachers, and librarians. The students wrote and evaluated paragraphs and letters. They also discussed feature articles Miss Freundlich wrote for her university newspaper. Much of their writing was read aloud in small groups or to the whole class, subjected to student comment, and rewritten. Dittoed anthologies of students' best paragraphs or letters were distributed monthly and discussed. Instruction in grammar and usage was based exclusively on their writing and speaking. Speech activities—reports, panels, and readings (including simple, short, one-act plays)—centered mostly on current events of concern to students. Miss Freundlich told me that not once did students request their first-semester diet: handbook and workbook exercises and vocabulary and spelling lists.

The response of the students to the curriculum was enthusiastic. They were doing successfully what they considered worthwhile. Throughout the term comments from fellow students and teachers substituted for grades. Much of the success of the experiment must be attributed to the attitude of the two teachers. They were friendly counselors and helpers providing a new and exhilarating experience for their students: success in an academic subject. The informality they fostered never interefered with learning. From my first visit on, students came to me for help when Mrs. Gutig and Miss Freundlich were busy. One curious student who knew my role asked me, "Is Miss Freundlich doin' all right?" He beamed when I answered, "She's doin' much better than I could."

A few days before the end of the term, Mrs. Gutig told me in the presence of Miss Freundlich, "We have a problem. The principal visited our class frequently and supported us with encouragement and materials. Yesterday, when he said how pleased he was with our students' attitude and progress, I asked him about grading them. He felt giving them grades above "D" would be unfair to students in academic, average, and regular slow classes who are expected to meet higher standards and might be misinterpreted by prospective employers. He said he wasn't telling me what to do but just giving his opinion. What do you think?"

I told her if I were grading the students, most of them would receive "A's," "B's," and "C's." I said the principal's objection could be countered by indicating on the students' permanent record cards that the grades were made in a special slow class. How would you have answered Mrs. Gutig? Should one deny successful scholastic experiences to conscientious students handicapped by low I.Q.'s and economic and social deprivation? At the end of the term, I asked Miss Freundlich how Mrs. Gutig resolved the grading problem. She said every student received a "C" and all seemed pleased. Apparently the "C" was the highest grade most of them had ever earned in an academic subject. In your opinion, why did or didn't Mrs. Gutig make the right decision?

High school students usually measure success by the grades they receive. Their teachers face baffling questions: What must students do to achieve success in my classes? Can I defend my grading standards? Do I demand too much or too little from my students? Is a colleague justified in following a rigid formula: 10 percent "A's," 20 percent "B's," 40 percent "C's" 20 percent "D's" and 10 percent "F's"? How can I convince my students that grades are not the only rewards for achievement in school? These questions have no easy answers. Most teachers evolve a grading system that falls between *hard* and *easy*. Teachers who equate *hard* grading with high standards and *easy* grading with low standards rarely feel compelled to define *standards*. Is it possible a hard course may be hard because of ineffective instruction and an easy course easy because of effective instruction?

The competent English teacher emphasizes intrinsic rather than extrinsic rewards. He and his students agree on goals which seem worth achieving and then select and organize subject matter which makes achieving them highly likely. The primary rewards come from perceptible and continuous improvement in language skills. My student teacher, her high school supervisor, and their students were highly motivated because their joint venture—improving students' reading, writing, and speaking skills—produced results they valued. Academic progress of individual students ranged from little to considerable, but participation was 100 percent and enthusiastic. An outcome difficult to measure but obvious to an observer was the students' increased respect for themselves and others, brought about by two superior teachers who considered "slow-minus" students worthy of their best efforts.

Problem Solving

Students learn best when the problem-solving approach is emphasized. The success of the problem-solving approach in the classroom hinges on the kinds of problems students are asked to tackle. In early manual training classes, students learned carpentry by devoting days to each of the following skills involving boards: sawing, planing, nailing, sanding, and measuring. When they were bored to desperation doing things to boards, they turned out a broom holder, umbrella holder, or hat holder. Today high school students—future carpenters, plumbers, electricians, painters, and bricklayers—sometimes plan and build a home under the guidance of an industrial arts teacher with experience in building trades. They are highly motivated because they learn skills while solving a problem—constructing an attractive, durable, and salable home.

Some teachers judge the problem-solving approach to learning too complicated. They believe that a concern with thinking should be postponed until students' minds are knowledge laden. But even preschool children solve problems daily. They are quick to develop and test hypotheses which get them what they want, and their wants are legion. Honor-roll students use the problem-solving approach throughout their school careers: they (1) define their problem, getting "A's"; (2) collect data, from other students and by analyzing their teachers; (3) develop hypotheses, what the teacher wants; and (4) test hypotheses—apples, papers, reports, apples, extra work, compliments, conferences, and apples. If their hypotheses do not test out satisfactorily, they develop new ones.

Today some cultures have unprecedented know-how and resources; but man's perpetual problems—poverty, war, racism, disease, and crime—seem to defy solution. Primitive medicine, agriculture, communication, and transportation gradually succumbed in some cultures when men began consciously to apply critical thinking, the scientific method, to problems in these areas. Early researchers in the physical sciences were often considered heretics because they challenged traditional rituals deemed efficacious in influencing evil spirits (problem makers) and good spirits (problem solvers). Today researchers in the physical sciences are comparatively free to exercise their ingenuity. Research in the area of the social sciences is another matter; hypotheses that challenge tradition may meet with verbal or physical violence.

Even in advanced countries educational institutions continue to emphasize indoctrination. Passing-on the social heritage, not questioning it, is a common goal. Men feel threatened by new ways of solving social problems. Even researchers who consistently and persistently use the scientific method in the laboratory often reject its application to social problems, some because they believe the method is not applicable and others because they are wedded to sacrosanct absolutes. Some educators believe if students learn to use the scientific method in school, they will possess a tool that will prove useful all their lives.

How can the problem-solving approach be applied to improving students' language skills? Could not a teacher ask students to consider as problems the development of goals and methods for mastering language skills? He could then ask them to suggest ways of solving the problems. If they are weak in written composition, they could gather data by analyzing papers they have written in the past, questioning their teachers, reading the writings of fellow students, and abstracting ideas from textbooks and library books. They could then develop hypotheses on improving composition skills that relate to the whole class and to individuals. Their hypotheses about selecting a topic, narrowing it, organizing it, paragraphing, sentence structure, punctuation, capitalization, spelling, proofreading, and rewriting could be tested by writing one or more compositions. Perhaps gathering data, developing hypotheses, and testing hypotheses should be postponed until after students have written a composition and had it evaluated by classmates and the teacher. (If students feel that the compositions should remain anonoymous, names could be replaced with letters of the alphabet.)

Some teachers have posed broad problems for students. A high school English teacher and his student teacher developed a unit on "Understanding Politics." They and their students read (1) quality political novels, plays, essays, and poems and (2) political articles in current newspapers and magazines. The teachers assigned televised political speeches. In their talks, panels, debates, and written compositions, students related what they had read, heard, and thought about politics to the 1968 presidential campaign. Similarly organized units could be developed on minority groups, war, poverty, crime, religion, and economics. World literature reflects many of the problems faced by man over the last three thousand years. It and the mass media provide good sources of materials for teachers interested in experimenting with the problem-solving approach to learning.

The teacher himself is forced into using the problem-solving approach. From his first day of teaching to his last an ever-present problem is improving instruction, one that generates many smaller though no less difficult ones. He gathers data from his past experience, other teachers, books, magazines, newspapers, motion pictures, and television. He develops over the years hundred of hypotheses and tests them. The approach seems routine, but its application to instructional problems is an antidote for routine teaching. When students are helped by their teachers to use a similar approach in solving specific problems involving their language skills, they are likely to discover that learning can be exciting and rewarding.

The six teaching principles illustrated above are interrelated assumptions about stimulating learning in students that many teachers have tested. Introduce them into your course, unit, and daily-lesson plans to see how they affect your teaching and your students' learning.

FOUR LEARNING PROBLEMS

When English teachers attend meetings devoted to free discussion of learning problems, they often focus on one or more of the following: mass media, technological aids, interdisciplinary philosophy, and disadvantaged students.

Mass Media

Owners of newspapers, magazines, radio and television networks, and motion-picture studios are often economically powerful individuals or corporations whose business acumen is measured on balance sheets and profit-and-loss statements. Profits come largely from advertising; and advertisers are influenced by circulation, listening, and viewing figures. Most owners or managers of mass media predict that such figures would decline should they upgrade their current fare. Forty years ago many cities had two or more newspapers reflecting divergent views on current issues. Today in many cities, even states, leading newspapers are controlled by a single individual or corporation. Canned editorials reflecting ultraconservative political and economic philosophies are disseminated from a central office. To keep their readers and advertisers contented, such newspaper chains often slant or play down coverage of controversial local, state, national, and international problems. However, when English teachers meet they seldom choose to discuss the influence of ownership, advertising, and profit motive on mass media. They raise two questions: "How can we use mass media to improve students' language skills?" "How can we help students become discriminating users of mass media?"

A few English teachers say that mass media offer no help in developing students' language skills; they write off newspapers and magazines as purveyors of sensationalism and prejudice and television, radio, and motion pictures as distributors of trash. Teachers more discriminating in their evaluations avoid blanket indictments. They review weekly listings of television and radio guides and recommend or assign commendable offerings: political speeches and debates; reputable news reporters; interviews with authors, officeholders, representatives of minority groups, and prominent foreigners; discussions of current issues; quality-music programs; travelogues; and drama derived from literature or significant current social problems. Between September and June, I call my students' attention to motion pictures and television programs that relate to literature; but only a few students view them. One cannot impose quality viewing on students because television networks and motion-picture studios rarely release recent films for showings in schools. High school teachers say that their movie and television recommendations are seldom heeded unless they require oral or written reactions to them.

Television and movie fare stimulates much adverse and some complimentary comment from teachers in high school classrooms. Newspapers and magazines receive little classroom attention even though 98 percent of 589 students I queried three times during a nine-month period read local newspapers and 85 percent read *Life, Look, Reader's Digest,* and other popular magazines. (Sixty-three percent read unassigned books.[5]) It is a mistake to assume that students spend most of their free time peer-

[5]Royal J. Morsey, *A College Seminar to Develop and Evaluate an Improved High School English Program* (Muncie, Ind.: Ball State University, 1961), pp. 59–85.

IMPROVING ENGLISH INSTRUCTION

ing at what some teachers relish calling the boob tube, idiot box, trivia tube, or drivel dispenser. Collect information about students' mass-media habits by asking them at the beginning, middle, and end of each semester to complete a short-answer questionnaire on reading materials in the home, sections read in newspapers, favorite television programs, and movie preferences, with an estimate of time spent on each the preceding week. The questionnaires can be kept anonymous and the results summarized by student volunteers. The summary can be dittoed or placed on the blackboard and discussed. Some teachers use such summaries in planning reading, writing, speaking, and listening experiences which help students develop skill in appraising mass media.

Once a teacher discovers his students' extracurricular reading, viewing, and listening habits, he is likely to conclude that they should be helped to become more discriminating users of mass media. In achieving such a goal, he and his students need first to admit that mass media exert tremendous influence on almost everyone's ideas and behavior.[6] What people choose to (1) see and hear on television, (2) listen to on the radio, and (3) read in newspapers and magazines affects what they believe and do about issues involving poverty, crime, race, war, government, religion, education, and health. Should anyone ignore mass media completely, he would still be influenced by those who depend upon them for information and entertainment.

I have listened to many rambling classroom discussions lauding and decrying the purposes, policies, and practices of newspaper, magazine, motion picture, radio, and television owners or managers. The unsubstantiated generalizations of students are a poor substitute for defensible statements derived from specific examinations of mass media's products. For example, to point up the differences between *The Podunk Advertiser* and *The Christian Science Monitor* students must analyze both. Since probably only one copy of each paper is available, perhaps two or more students can (1) examine the papers thoroughly and illustrate in class what they discovered and (2) invite the teacher and other students to comment. Assignments can also be made requiring students to evaluate orally or in writing newspapers' (1) coverage of local, state, national, and international news; (2) editorials; (3) columnists; (4) financial news; (5) advertising; (6) sports pages; (7) cartoons; (8) comics; (9) women's pages; (10) book reviews; and (11) theater news. A somewhat similar approach can be used for magazines.

School subscriptions to quality newspapers and magazines provide an

[6]Charles S. Steinberg, "Mass Media and the Educator," Harold Full, ed., *Controversy in American Education: An Anthology of Crucial Issues* (New York: The Macmillan Company, 1967), pp. 166–171.

excellent source of materials for students assigned research on current problems and events. Schools that subscribe to *The Christian Science Monitor, The New York Times*, and *The St. Louis Post-Dispatch* are often so large that easy accessibility to the papers is lost. If asked, some students will make available to classmates their parents' newspapers and magazines. I place my copies of newspapers and magazines on a chair near the door of my classroom. The magazines have many takers, the newspapers few. To most university students a day-old newspaper seems as superfluous as a mustache cup at a girl-scout jamboree. Some English teachers ask eleventh- or twelfth-grade classes to subscribe to *The Atlantic* or *Harper's* at student rates, and a period or more each month is spent reading and reacting orally and in writing to its articles and stories. Do you wonder whether students having such an experience are more likely to subscribe to such magazines after they graduate than those who do not?

Since few students will turn from local newspapers and popular magazines to quality newspapers and magazines, the English teacher should help them evaluate their favorite reading material. A teacher's lecture on "trash" may cause resentment, but student criticism may be welcomed. A biased or unbiased editorial or column in a newspaper can be duplicated and subjected to class analysis—assumptions and facts can be isolated, weighed, and compared with writings reflecting opposite views. Instead of the teacher's declaring, "This is propaganda!" he might ask, "Why is or isn't it fair to label this editorial *propaganda?*" or "Why do you accept or reject, wholly or in part, the editorial writer's conclusions?" A teacher who issues final verdicts on what is or is not propaganda is a practicing propagandist. Students learn best through discovery and by supporting their ensuing assumptions with evidence that will survive free discussion.

Some teachers believe that separate units on mass media prove less effective than including in daily lesson plans incidental mass-media experiences which contribute directly to improving reading, writing, speaking, and listening. Other teachers believe that if students are to learn how to use—rather than be used by—newspapers, magazines, motion pictures, radio, and television, periodic mass-media units are essential. Since both approaches have much to commend them, they could be explored by the teacher and his students before a decision is made. Probably no one would recommend restricting all instruction to separate units—too many opportunities to recommend and evaluate the day-to-day offerings of mass media would be missed.

Technological Aids

Technology (applied science) has produced microscopes, telescopes, phonographs, motion pictures, filmstrips, slides, radio, television, tape recorders, and computers. These technological aids have a history highlighted by improvements and broader applications. Their classroom use came after they had filled other roles successfully. They originated when one or more individuals buttressed with knowledge and methods of acquiring knowledge developed by predecessors and contemporaries hit upon a happy hypothesis or hypotheses. Zacharias Janssen, microscope, 1590; Hans Lippershey, telescope, c. 1608; Alexander Graham Bell, telephone, 1876; Thomas A. Edison, phonograph, 1877, motion pictures, 1893; Guglielmo Marconi, wireless telegraphy, 1895; and many others would probably be astonished if they could see the products and processes their ideas have wrought in medicine, astronomy, space science, and mass media.

In 1927 the four-year high school I attended had 150 students and one of the technological aids listed above—a microscope. It and two athletic trophies reposed behind the locked glass doors of a one-shelf cabinet in the superintendent's office. Perhaps the superintendent—a coin collector and relentless disciplinarian—used the microscope to (1) detect vestiges of dates on badly worn coins and (2) identify malefactors he had cut down to size—his tongue was sharper than a scalpel. Today the school has technological aids galore; only a computer is missing.

The assumption that movie projectors, tape recorders, record players, filmstrips, slides, radio, and television are desirable adjuncts to traditional teaching resources seems unadulterated common sense. But common sense should be verified. We have no evidence that technological aids are indispensable. On the other hand, no one knows whether the classroom teacher is indispensable. Some distraught taxpayers have envisioned technological aids programed to produce elementary, secondary, and college graduates sans teachers, supplies, equipment, and school buildings.

School consolidation has increased the use of technological aids. In large schools their cost per pupil becomes negligible. Today some consolidated and city schools are investing five thousand dollars or more in video-tape machines formerly used only by television stations and networks to record programs for later broadcasting. Their portability increases their versatility in and out of the classroom. Speech and dramatics teachers claim that individual and class study of video tapes of students' speeches and plays is much more effective in stimulating improved performance than is the traditional verbal criticism. Some college, university, and high school supervisors video-tape class sessions of student teachers. The video tapes are later viewed and discussed by student teachers and supervisors. Common sense suggests the video-tape machine can help improve instruction, but only research can confirm or disprove it.

There are effective and ineffective ways of using technological aids. Many teachers apparently use them, especially films, because students welcome departures from the reading-writing-reciting routine. In some large schools English students spend one period a week in the auditorium viewing films on authors' lives, literary history, literary masterpieces, planning a composition or speech, linguistics or formal grammar, semantics, and Mortimer J. Adler's analyses of great ideas. Among films shown, students seem to prefer condensed versions of time-worn Hollywood movies derived from *Romeo and Juliet, Treasure Island, David Copperfield,* and *Great Expectations.* Introductions to the films are rare; and follow-ups, if time permits, are usually limited to students' responses to teachers' "Did you like the film?" In some schools a teacher's class session is occasionally interrupted by a note or call from the principal's office informing him a film has just arrived in the mail and asking him whether it can be shown immediately. The teacher usually acquiesces; he knows a dozen colleagues will want to show the film before it must be returned. When the student movie-projector operator appears, the teacher announces to his class, "A film has just arrived. It has been assigned to us this period." At the end of the film he says, "Did you like the film?" or "Open your books to page _____."

If technological aids are used as interludes only, they are less effective than when they contribute directly to achieving current objectives. If there is no alternative time, a teacher is justified in interrupting a composition unit to show an outstanding film version of a Shakespearean play. But if he could plan to present it during a unit on Shakespeare, his introduction to the play and the class discussion afterwards could relate effectively to unit goals. Worthwhile films unrelated to goals developed for a course or unit could perhaps be shown during free periods, at noon, after school, or in the evening. In some communities high school teachers and students arrange to see superior domestic and foreign films scheduled by a local college or university.

Programed instruction in English, with or without benefit of machines, provides for the learning of facts[7]—the content of workbooks, handbooks, wordbooks, and literature anthologies. If the student does not transfer the facts learned to written and oral composition or literature, they remain inert. The question the English teacher should keep in mind is, "What are the most effective ways of improving reading, writing, speaking, and listening?" Teaching machines and programed textbooks[8] are assumed to appeal to students because they demand activity rather than passivity,

[7]Ernest R. Hilgard, ed., *Theories of Learning and Instruction: The Sixty-third Yearbook of the National Society for the Study of Education* (Chicago: The National Society for the Study of Education, 1964), Chapters XV–XVI, pp. 354–401.

[8]If you haven't examined a programed textbook for high school students, see Joseph C. Blumenthal, *English 2600: A Programed Course in Grammar and Usage.* Revised Edition. (New York: Harcourt, Brace, and World, 1962.)

learning rates are determined by students, new learning evolves from old learning, and right answers are rewarded immediately. But there is no evidence they help students appreciate literature; speak and write clearly, thoughtfully, and correctly; and listen intelligently.

The conditioned responses programed into and rewarded by computer-type teaching machines are admirably suited for training students in societies whose leaders command all the right and wrong answers. Students having a daily rendezvous with teaching machines are unlikely to understand that most of what man calls knowledge is assumption. Progress is usually won by those who challenge revered "right" and "wrong" answers. Such individuals do not memorize knowledge and hoard it; they *use* it to gain new insights and understandings. History books laud hundreds of them who were once ridiculed, banished, jailed, or killed by institutions, leaders, mobs, or individuals wedded to superstitions deemed facts.[9]

A recent development still in the experimental stage is ETV, educational television. In the spring of 1968 there were 146 ETV stations on the air. An initial grant in 1962 accompanied the passage of the Educational Television Facilities Act allotting thirty-two million dollars in federal funds to colleges, universities, public schools, state ETV commissions, and other nonprofit groups. The purpose of ETV is to educate, a worthy objective as difficult to achieve on the air as in the classroom.[10] A distinct advantage of ETV's programs over commercial television's educational programs is they can be planned to contribute directly to educational goals of students and teachers and be shown at most-appropriate times. However, ETV has been handicapped by inability to approximate the money spent by commercial television on public relations, promotion, and personnel.

Technological aids are recognized by progressive schools as adjuncts to instruction. English teachers in such schools include them in their plans whenever they promise to equal or surpass other ways of achieving the goals of a language program. Students should learn what use will be made of technological aids when they are given an overview of course goals and methods at the beginning of the semester. If students are directly involved in making decisions about course goals and methods, they can also help determine the role technological aids will play. Teachers and students planning course objectives and methods should consult film, slide, and filmstrip catalogs of colleges, universities, state departments of education, and com-

[9]Philip W. Jackson, *The Teacher and the Machine* (Pittsburgh: University of Pittsburgh Press, 1968).

[10]*Educational Technology*, Vol. VIII, No. 13, July 15, 1968, pp. 11–16. (This twice-monthly magazine is published by Educational News Service, P. O. Box 508, Saddle Brook, New Jersey 07662. It is available only by subscription, $10.00.)

mercial firms. Listings of recordings suitable for classroom use are obtainable from the National Council of Teachers of English and from Listening Library, 1 Park Avenue, Old Greenwich, Connecticut 06870.

Whenever possible, films, filmstrips, slides, and recordings should be given an introduction by the teacher or students. The introduction should be based on a preview or prior hearing and focus the material on the goal it is supposed to help achieve. The post-mortem should provide an opportunity for students to discuss why the technological aid was more or less effective than other approaches might have been. Omitting the introduction and follow-up encourages intellectual passivity. The follow-up can also help the teacher decide whether or not a film or recording should be retained in his teaching plans.[11] Course plans should not be so rigid that teachers and students cannot take advantage of opportunities to use technological aids not foreseen when the plans were made. Excellent ideas often arise as plans are applied in the classroom, and schedules of television stations and motion-picture theaters are usually available only a week in advance.

There are numerous opportunities for simple survey research (see Chapter 12) designed to evaluate technological aids. The results of a questionnaire asking students to evaluate a film, filmstrip, a series of slides, or a recording in light of course objectives can stimulate a discussion of the strengths and weaknesses of a specific technological aid. A single question can provide a valuable writing experience for students and useful information for the teacher: If you were a teacher, why would or wouldn't you show your students the three filmed lessons you saw on *The Odyssey* (written and narrated by Gilbert Highet)?[12] Such simple survey research revealing students' thoughts and feelings can help teachers choose effective technological aids.

Interdisciplinary Philosophy[13]

Teachers who favor the interdisciplinary philosophy deplore the segregation of knowledge into compartments—English, history, mathematics, and science—and each compartment's division into one or more additional segments. In many universities the English department has fathered

---

[11]For help in using technological aids, see Edgar Dale, *Audio-Visual Methods in Teaching.* Revised Edition. (New York: The Dryden Press, 1954.)

[12]Encyclopaedia Britannica Film Corporation, 425 North Michigan Avenue, Chicago, Illinois 60611.

[13]See Edward R. Fagan, *Field: A Process for Teaching Literature* (University Park: Penn State Press, 1964), pp. 6–8, and Robert M. Gorrell, ed., *Rhetoric: Theory for Application* (Champaign, Illinois: National Council of Teachers of English, 1967), pp. 45–74.

speech, dramatics, journalism, and English-for-foreigners departments. The domain it retains is divided on the undergraduate and graduate levels into long lists of courses grouped under century, country, individuals, movements, and purpose. Consult a university catalog or city high school class schedule, and you will be struck by the separateness, not the relatedness, of the various disciplines.

The knowledge explosion originating in the Renaissance eventually led to a proliferation of subjects in elementary, secondary, college, and university curricula. During and after the Renaissance, printing presses reproduced not only Latin and Greek classics but thousands of titles in vernacular languages as well. When leaders learned that potent political and religious indoctrination depends on literacy, vernacular schools burgeoned. The industrial revolution, spurred by the systematic application of the scientific method to the production of machinery and consumer goods, eventually produced the wealth which enabled young people to remain in school for years rather than months. The ensuing rapid increase in university enrollments made possible the research which multiplied knowledge so rapidly that specialization became inevitable. Specialization created a multiplicity of disciplines with subsequent knowledge explosions in each.

Today high school, college, and university students can select from a veritable smorgasbord of subjects. Educators have long recognized that such variety presents problems. When most of what has been perceived or grasped by man's mind is available to a student, what should he select? A high school senior interested in higher education narrows his problem when he chooses a profession; but he must still choose (1) an area of specialization within the profession and (2) electives. His scores on college or university entrance examinations may shock him. After accumulating sixteen or more credits in segregated subjects—English, social studies, science, mathematics, and foreign languages—he may discover he has only a smattering of knowledge in each. Should he survive as an undergraduate and decide to enter graduate school, entrance-examination data may indicate inability to use and apply knowledge presumably acquired by pursuing several disciplines for four or more years.

Diversification has desirable aspects. What could be worse than compelling all secondary students to follow the curriculum of our eighteenth-century Latin grammar school? The problem is not to eliminate but to correlate courses in the high school curriculum. In grades 7–12 knowledge appearing under various labels—English, biology, and social studies—is further segmented into dozens of courses. Each English course is divided into units—literature, listening, grammar and usage, speech, and composition—whose relationships are seldom clear to students. How can the rigid compartmentalization of subject matter within a discipline and among disciplines be breached?

Some educators suggest, "Since verbal skills are essential to one who seeks success in any one of the disciplines, every teacher should teach reading, writing, speaking, and listening." The suggestion has been followed successfully in a few outstanding private schools. Public-school teachers say they are specialists qualified to teach only their own disciplines or they do not have the time to assume the duties of the English teacher.

Core-curriculum enthusiasts promote the interdisciplinary philosophy by having students use language skills, history, art, and music in investigating or solving problems they and their students consider vital. When sputnik appeared, the subject-matter curriculum received a boost that all but eliminated the core curriculum in the junior high school. It had never caught on in the senior high school because teachers with enough academic breadth to teach core subjects were scarce and administrators and teachers were unable to solve the course-credit problem, i.e., if Sally pursues social studies, English, art, and music in a single course, how does one divide among the subjects the course credit she earned? Furthermore, fear was expressed that in attempting to learn several subjects simultaneously, Sally might not master even one thoroughly, and her teacher might overemphasize the subject in which he felt most competent.

Core-curriculum sponsors believe the organized knowledge of various disciplines should often be brought together and applied to problems students suggest or accept as significant. For example, they say mass media have made millions of Americans sensitive to the problems arising from unjust treatment of minority groups. Why not have students and teachers identify and define the problems, gather data, develop hypotheses, and test some of the hypotheses in the home, school, church, and community? If the problem chosen is "Understanding Racial Minorities," gathering data would involve drawing on the resources of music, art, social science, and literature. Ideally teachers from these disciplines would work together, use a team approach; but since that is practical in only a few school systems, the English teacher could have his students gather materials illustrating (1) racial minorities' contributions to music, art, literature, and science and (2) the history of racial minorities in our society. In some communities students could also invite informed adults to the classroom and conduct opinion surveys among student and adult groups. In such a problem-solving situation subject-matter lines would be crossed frequently and reading, writing, speaking, and listening would serve investigative and evaluative functions. There are many alternatives to "Understanding Racial Minorities" because man is perpetually confronted with problems involving crime, poverty, religion, juvenile delinquency, international relations, consumption of goods and services, war, politics, government, pollution, health, and conservation. Drawing on several disciplines in investigating a problem demonstrates their usefulness and interrelatedness.

A single discipline's limitations in helping investigate broad problems is easily illustrated. We do not, for example, consider historians particularly adept at solving racial problems even though they may be able to give a listener or reader a much-needed detailed history of them. (An English teacher and his students consulting current history textbooks would unfortunately find little to help them understand racial minorities.) The interdisciplinary philosophy is much more in evidence in the works of the world's great and not-so-great writers and thinkers than in history books. Writers whose works are labeled *literature* do not merely gather and record facts; they interpret man's ideas and behavior and are often his severest critics. From the days of the ancient Greeks to the present, they have endured vilification and have risked their lives to define justice and expose injustice. Socrates believed in the interdisciplinary philosophy; he was not interested in knowledge for its own sake. Knowledge to him was worthwhile when it produced temperance, justice, happiness, production of goods, good government, and skill in private affairs. His pragmatic approach to learning has always appealed to students. Some scholars involved in pure research say they are interested in knowledge for its own sake; but is it not likely they are motivated at least in part by the fact that pure research often yields useful knowledge readily converted into fame and fortune?

In his *Teachers' Guide to World Literature for the High School* (Champaign, Illinois: National Council of Teachers of English, 1966), Robert O'Neal illustrates how several carefully selected literary works can focus on broad problems many students find appealing. Under "Some Thematic Suggestions," pp. xii–xiv, he presents fourteen themes. Under one, "A Search for a Better Society," he lists Hilton's *Lost Horizon*, More's *Utopia*, Orwell's *Animal Farm* and *Nineteen Eighty-Four*, Swift's *Gulliver's Travels*, and Voltaire's *Candide* and *Zadig*. In slow classes, one could use a similar theme and substitute simpler books.

Many English teachers who reject the problem curriculum do draw on music, art, history, and science to help students appreciate literature; and they use mass media in teaching literature and developing students' writing, speaking, and listening skills. This approach helps break down strict compartmentalization of disciplines and convinces students what is learned in the classroom can relate to life outside the classroom. The interdisciplinary philosophy is very much in evidence when individuals and organizations try to solve their own and society's problems. Should it eventually prevail in the classroom, school curricula may reflect a vitality that will change laggard learners into avid learners.

Disadvantaged Students[14]

Not all slow learners have poor and uneducated parents;[15] but in inner-city high schools slow classes are made up predominantly of students whose parents' income and educational levels are so low that teachers and administrators label these children *disadvantaged*. To most such students the school curriculum is a meaningless routine leading to "D's" and "F's." High schools in slum ghettos have heavy concentrations of students even less enthusiastic about the educational fare provided by their schools.[16] These two groups of disadvantaged students contribute immensely to our 40 percent high school dropout rate.

A beginning English teacher assigned a class of slow learners soon discovers an alphabetical or numerical symbol (grade) is an ineffective motivational device. Their academic ineptitude has been limelighted so often they have given up trying, and most of them have decided to quit school the moment the law permits. If the teacher examines their permanent record cards, he sees long histories of failure in academic subjects and deterioration in I.Q. scores. Should he ask them why they reject school, he may learn that for them success in school is like reaching for the moon. Many of the boys dream about earning money to buy cars and to enjoy social activities. The girls' dreams often center on marriage. Whenever a teacher has mostly slow students from one or more minority groups, his motivation problem is even thornier. They are often convinced that even if they meet school standards, their opportunities for jobs and further education are hopelessly limited or nonexistent.

The majority of students in slow classes usually come from homes with few, if any, books, magazines, and newspapers. Their parents are likely to be school dropouts preoccupied with providing a minimum of food, clothing, and shelter. Many such students live with one parent or grandparents. Disadvantaged students rarely associate with educated people and seldom know anyone who pressures them to work hard in school. Their English usage, formed in the home and neighborhood, provokes

[14]See Edward R. Fagan, ed., *English and the Disadvantaged* (Scranton, Pennsylvania: International Textbook Company, 1967), pp. 1–5.

[15]See John Holt, *How Children Fail* (New York: Pitman Publishing Company, 1964), pp. xiii–xv and 165–181.

[16]John P. De Cecco, ed., *The Psychology of Language, Thought and Instruction* (New York: Holt, Rinehart, and Winston, 1967), pp. 85–135.

severe penalties in school, the heaviest in English classes. Students whose families surround them with books, newspapers, and magazines; take them to plays and concerts; provide travel opportunities; and plan college careers even before they are out of grade school receive an extracurricular education that gives them enormous competitive advantages over disadvantaged students. Still, some teachers seem to assume that all students in their classes have had equal opportunities to learn. Students who did not work hard in the past must catch up quickly or pay for their sloth by reaping "D's" or "F's." Such teachers seem not to understand that students conditioned from birth to economic, social, and intellectual deprivation may have emotional and physical problems which a competitive school situation aggravates rather than alleviates.

For twenty years I have observed Mr. Lernen, a junior high school English teacher, work successfully with academic, average, and slow students. He believes that all his students are worthy of his best efforts. His friendliness and kindliness are not confined to the class hour or to his capable students. He greets students as they enter the room and is available after class and after school. He does not assume they have met prescribed standards because they are seventh, eighth, or ninth graders. When I observe him teach early in a semester, I recall the old saw, "Blessed are they who expect nothing, for they shall not be disappointed."

Mr. Lernen applies in his classroom the learning principles discussed in this chapter. Before he involves students in planning the semester's work, he asks them to review their past experiences in English classes. He is not shocked by his slow students' frank appraisals of the school system.[17] Early in one term they wrote compositions on "Why and How Teachers Punish Students." (I learned junior high school students are still paddled with varying vigor and strokes by male and female teachers for chewing gum, passing notes, unnecessary talking, not having assignments, and coming late to class.) When he and his slow students discuss goals and methods for the course, a jokester will occasionally suggest fun and games; but most of them are interested in improving their poorly developed language skills, especially after they learn Mr. Lernen wants first to determine where they are academically so they can progress individually as far beyond that point as possible.

Performance tests in reading, writing, and speaking are given early in the semester in all his classes. Group and individual goals evolve from what the tests reveal. In his slow classes, reading, writing, and speaking experiences focus mostly on an exchange and evaluation of their ideas on school, jobs, juvenile delinquency, racism, war, crime, poverty, and laws.

[17]Herbert Kohl, *36 Children* (New York: New American Library, 1967), pp. 177–180.

Few selections in available anthologies relate to these topics; so he provides newspapers, popular magazines, and appropriate paperbacks. He allots much time to free discussions. He begins answers to controversial questions students direct at him with "In my opinion" and ends them with, "Joe, what do you think?" He admits to his students he has few final answers to the controversial questions they often raise.

One of Mr. Lernen's student teachers, a physician's daughter, was shocked to learn from Mr. Lernen and a guidance counselor that in one of her slow classes one student often slept under bridges and in vacant buildings, another practiced prostitution at age thirteen, three used alcohol to excess, and five lived in homes some farmers would consider unfit for animals. She also discovered that several students in each of her two slow classes were being supervised by probation officers. Vandalism and stealing cars were their most common offenses.[18]

Mr. Lernen's end-of-the semester questionnaires disclose that few of his slow students change their minds about dropping out of school; but most of them appreciate a new experience, the opportunity to begin where they are academically rather than where they should be. And they always laud the curricular emphasis on their concerns rather than the teacher's.[19] If there were many, rather than few, Mr. Lernens in grades 1–12, a rapid reduction in the 40 percent high school dropout rate would be inevitable.

Some English teachers believe that students placed in slow classes feel excommunicated. They argue that heterogeneous classes can be taught effectively if students participate in setting individual goals based on the outcomes of performance tests in reading, writing, speaking, and listening. Success, they feel, should be measured by how far a student advances beyond the point where he happens to be at the beginning of the semester. Learning, they claim, is unlikely to occur when students are publicly labeled incompetent by being sentenced to slow classes; and support for learning is unlikely to come from the home when parents discover that the school is quick to classify their children failures. However, the majority of teachers believe that competition motivates learning and that homogeneous grouping provides fair competition. They seem not to realize that even in homogeneously grouped classes, no two students have identical physical and mental characteristics and academic and social backgrounds.

The failure syndrome the school often imposes on students with gene-and-environment-induced handicaps is not easy to reverse. But it can be reversed if most teachers, rather than a few, admit that long-established

[18]For grade-school backgrounds of disadvantaged students, see Jonathan Kozol, *Death at an Early Age* (Boston: Houghton Mifflin Company, 1967), pp. 1–7.

[19]For suggestions on vitalizing the English curriculum, see Herbert R. Kohl, *Teaching the "Unteachable"* (New York: The New York Review, 1967), pp. 61–64.

instructional routines, not the recalcitrance of students, are largely responsible for the 40 percent high school dropout rate and an additional 40 percent who are never really successful in school. Students from homes where education is considered the key to the professions may be bored with a trivia-filled curriculum, but they will master it because good grades spell admission to college. Disadvantaged, average, and academic students deserve a curriculum designed to open doors to a life of learning. The English teacher can open such doors if he helps advantaged and disadvantaged students set vital goals geared to where they are in mastery of language skills when they come to him and then provides guided practice in the skills.[20]

Many of the assumptions in this chapter about principles of learning, mass media, technological teaching aids, interdisciplinary philosophy, and disadvantaged students receive direct application in subsequent chapters devoted to detailed discussions of goals and methods which promise to improve instruction in specific areas: reading (literature), writing, speaking, listening, grammar and usage, and semantics.

ASSUMPTIONS ABOUT LEARNING

Prepare to explain why you accept or reject, wholly or in part, the following assumptions about learning:

1. One can explain why and how we learn.

2. Mental, physical, and environmental factors affect an individual's ability to learn.

3. We know very little about how people learn (Noam Chomsky, *Newsweek*, Vol. LXII, No. 9, August 26, 1968, p. 56).

4. A teacher and his students could profit from discussing at the beginning of a semester the six common sense generalizations about learning presented in this chapter.

5. The six common sense generalizations about learning presented in this chapter are interrelated.

6. There are specific reasons why some English courses you took lacked vitality.

7. Students are coddled too much by administrators and teachers.

8. Worthwhile learning is always difficult.

9. The current status of students' skills in reading, writing, speaking, and listening can be determined only by administering performance tests.

[20]The *Bulletin* of the NDEA Institute for Advanced Study in Teaching Disadvantaged Youth, 1126 Sixteenth Street, N.W., Washington D.C. 20036, is "available to anyone actively engaged in preparation of education personnel. Institute publications are announced in the *Bulletin*."

10. A student needs verbal skill to succeed in science, mathematics, social studies, and business subjects.

11. A teacher can help students transfer what they learned in the past to what they are learning today.

12. "Practice makes perfect" is an indefensible absolute.

13. Teachers should use fear of failure to motivate students.

14. There are reasons why debating, drama, and writing clubs (predecessors of speech, dramatics, and journalism courses) owe their origin to students rather than teachers.

15. The problem-solving approach to learning is more commendable than the fill-the-mind (storehouse) approach, but it has serious drawbacks.

16. English teachers should and can use mass media to improve students' language skills.

17. English teachers should and can help students upgrade their mass-media tastes.

18. This is the first generation who have been brought up by the mass media instead of parents (Margaret Mead, *Life*, Vol. 65, No. 8, August 23, 1968, p. 31).

19. There are effective and ineffective ways of using technological teaching aids in the classroom.

20. The portable video-tape machine promises to become the most versatile technological teaching aid ever devised.

21. The arguments for using programed teaching machines are more convincing than the arguments against. (See John F. Travers, *Learning: Analysis and Application*, pp. 178–79.)

22. The rapid multiplication of subjects (disciplines) presents serious problems for students and teachers.

23. The core-curriculum idea reflects strengths and weaknesses.

24. Most disadvantaged students entering kindergarten or the first grade already have two strikes against them.

25. Poverty is the parent of revolution and crime (Aristotle).

26. Teachers should support middle-class values in the classroom.

27. The advantages of segregating slow students outweigh the disadvantages.

28. The six principles of learning illustrated in this chapter apply equally well to slow, average, and academic students.

29. There are reasons why Jonathan Kozol's *Death at an Early Age* and Herbert K. Kohl's *Teaching the "Unteachable"* are usually greeted with vigorous approval or vigorous disapproval by teachers, administrators, and laymen.

30. Alexander Pope's assumptions about education and learning suggest that a teacher's preceptorial proficiencies must include twig-bending and aggressive bartending:

'Tis education forms the common mind:
Just as the twig is bent the tree's inclined.

A little learning is a dangerous thing;
Drink deep, or taste not the Pierian spring:
There shallow draughts intoxicate the brain,
And drinking largely sobers us again.

31. . . . a faithful study of the liberal arts humanizes character and permits it not to be cruel (Ovid).

32. To label high school curricula *trivia-filled* is unjust.

IDEAS TO TEST

1. Ask students to give oral or written answers, without mentioning teachers' names, to the following questions: In recalling former English classes, in which one did you learn the most, and why? in which one the least, and why?

2. Early in the semester ask students to identify and explain in writing what they consider to be their strengths and weaknesses in reading, writing, speaking, and listening.

3. Distribute to students a written statement of your course aims and methods at the beginning of the semester. Ask them to defend their suggested additions and deletions.

4. Give performance tests in reading, writing, speaking, and listening. Reveal the general results of the tests. Then ask each student to analyze his test results and state briefly in writing what he thinks his goals for the semester should be. At the end of each unit, ask students to explain briefly why they have or have not made progress toward achieving their goals.

5. Have students complete periodically a one-page questionnaire that reveals their use of mass media: newspapers, magazines, unassigned paperbacks, radio, and television. Tabulate the answers to the questionnaire and discuss them with students.

6. Help students plan individual reports, debates, and panel discussions evaluating specific television programs.

7. Ask individual students or panels to compare the content of two or more newspapers or two or more magazines.

8. Encourage students to share with classmates newspapers and magazines to which their parents subscribe.

9. Ask students to examine quality newspapers and magazines and explain why they do or do not appeal to them.

10. Discuss with students the classroom use they believe should be made of technological aids: films, filmstrips, slides, radio, recordings, tape recorders, and television.

11. Discuss with students the relationships between English and other subjects in the curriculum.

12. Have students present arguments for and against homogeneous grouping.

13. Ask students to identify and discuss fears that interfere with learning.

14. At the end of the term, ask students to write an unsigned answer to one of the following questions: If you had been the teacher of this class, what would you have done that I did not do? If you had been the teacher of this class, what would you not have done that I did?

3

Planning a Lesson

Before reading this chapter, formulate clear, defensible answers to the following questions. After reading it, prepare to explain why you changed or retained your answers.

1. What should a lesson plan include?
2. Are daily lesson plans essential? Defend your answer.
3. Are unit plans desirable? Defend your answer.
4. Why do you suppose teacher-pupil planning is advocated by some educators?
5. Assume you have been asked to teach William Wordsworth's 'I Wandered Lonely as a Cloud" to high school students. What will you include in your lesson plan?

"What shall I teach?" is a question confronting the student teacher asked to teach his first class. It is usually answered by the critic teacher, who tells him what to teach and gives him an overview of the semester's work in reading, writing, speaking, and listening. A regular beginning teacher about to face his first class may be helped to answer this question by departmental syllabi, the department head, or colleagues. In some schools, he is merely told which textbooks are used in the various courses.

Assume your critic teacher asks you on Friday, "How about teaching next Monday?" You answer, "I'd like to, but what shall I teach?" The critic, having heard you praise Wordsworth, replies, "Why don't you teach 'I Wandered Lonely as a Cloud'?"[1] He then tells his students, "For

[1] Whenever the author uses, presents, or refers to traditional literary selections in

Monday, read in your anthology the material on Wordsworth's life and his poem, 'I Wandered Lonely as a Cloud.' " Now that you know what you are going to teach, you need to develop a lesson plan which will help students appreciate the poem. Your plan will derive from the answers to two questions: "What results should I achieve through presenting the material?" and "How shall I go about achieving them?" The headings of a typical lesson plan are (1) *Aims* and (2) *Methods*.

Let us consider *Aims* for teaching "I Wandered Lonely as a Cloud." Whether an English teacher teaches a single poem or a poetry unit, his primary objective is appreciation. If you get your class to appreciate literature, you should be enshrined in an English teachers' hall of fame. Students who learn to do so will read after they leave your classroom, the true measure of your success. "Well," you say, "since appreciation is so important an aim, I should try to get my students to appreciate 'I Wandered Lonely as a Cloud'; but define the term a bit further."

The word *appreciation*, like *philosophy*, does not point to a specific object. However, one can make statements about this word which give it meaning. A student cannot appreciate a poem unless he understands what the author said. But his ability to paraphrase a poem does not prove he appreciates it. Appreciation also involves an emotional response, a point made by Goethe:

> A teacher who can arouse a feeling for one single good action, for one single good poem, accomplishes more than he who fills our memory with rows on rows of natural objects, classified with name and form.[2]

If a student reacts to a poem with "That's an idea I've had!" or "That's how I feel!", relating the poem to his experiential background, he probably appreciates it. Such a feeling is also indicated when he requests other poems by the same author or writes poems influenced by that author. There are, of course, degrees of appreciation. An individual usually appreciates good poems more every time he returns to them because of experiences he has had between readings.

The lament of students who dislike poetry—"I don't understand it!" —springs from their inability to relate a poet's theme to their own experiences. Teachers can, of course, try to select poetry which ties in directly

---

the text and appendix, he is not urging a bias toward such selections. They are as useful as current materials in illustrating lesson-planning principles, and student teachers are likely to teach them. Furthermore, college libraries have multiple copies of standard selections, and bookstores often carry them in several inexpensive editions.

[2]Johann Goethe, "Elective Affinities," Part II, *Novels and Tales by Goethe*, trans. James Anthony Froude and R. Dillon Boylan (London: G. Bell and Sons Limited, 1913), p. 172.

with their students' experiences. But some teachers can help students appreciate a poem that normally is Greek to them, as was demonstrated by a student teacher who was successful in helping average junior high school students appreciate Shelley's "To a Skylark."[3] The critic teacher predicted it could not be done; but the student teacher did it by reading the poem with thought and feeling and relating, through explanations and discussion questions, the many descriptive and few philosophic stanzas to his students' past and current experiences. His key discussion questions were:

1. Why does Shelley envy the skylark? Why do you or don't you share his envy?

2. In the fourth from the last stanza, Shelley says man's unhappiness is caused by living in the past and future and yearning for things he cannot have. Why do you agree or disagree with him?

3. In the third from the last stanza, Shelley blames much of man's unhappiness on "Hate and pride and fear." Why do you agree or disagree with him?

4. Shelley seems to conclude that listening to the skylark provides a kind of definition of happiness. Is he justified in drawing this conclusion? Defend your answer.

5. If the skylark could tell its story, why might it differ from Shelley's?

6. Which lines appeal to you most? Why?

7. How might one state the theme in a single sentence?

After a fifty-minute class discussion of "To a Skylark," the student teacher read it aloud again without comments and made the assignment for the next day. His success in presenting the poem derived from two masterful readings, which reflected his own deep appreciation, and discussion questions that encouraged personal responses to the poet's theme. Most student teachers read poetry effectively, but too often their discussion questions merely exacting paraphrasings of the poet's stanzas.

Once the student teacher knows what he hopes to achieve by teaching "I Wandered Lonely as a Cloud," he must decide what to do with the poem in the classroom. Recalling how his high school and college English teachers taught poetry, he resolves to discuss Wordsworth's life and the poem. He devises discussion questions that require recall of "facts" in the poem. Finally, one of Mrs. Smith's student teachers produces the following lesson plan:

[3]This poem appears on pp. 325–27.

LESSON PLAN I

William Wordsworth's
"I Wandered Lonely as a Cloud"

I. *Aims*

To help students appreciate the poem.

II. *Methods*

  A. Discussion of life and works

    1. When was Wordsworth born?

    2. Where was he born?

    3. When did he die?

    4. Where was he buried?

    5. Tell about his education.

    6. Who collaborated with him in writing two volumes of *Lyrical Ballads*?

    7. What role did his sister Dorothy play in his life?

    8. What are the names of his most famous long poems? short poems?

    9. Which volume of his poetry set off the Romantic Movement?

    10. What did he say in his preface to the 1800 edition of *Lyrical Ballads*?

    11. What can you say about his style?

  B. Discussion of the poem

    1. What is the setting of the poem?

    2. Where did the author wander?

    3. How did he feel?

    4. What did he see?

    5. What caused the flowers to seem alive?

    6. What danced beside the flowers?

    7. What effect did the scene have on the author?

  C. Assignment

Read "The Solitary Reaper" for tomorrow.

(Note: The student teacher ran out of material fifteen minutes after the session began, so he changed the assignment as follows: "You weren't very well prepared today. Spend the remainder of the period reading 'Why Art Thou Silent?' and 'The Idiot Boy.' For tomorrow, read 'The Solitary Reaper.' At the beginning of the period tomorrow you will take a twenty-five item true-false test on the four poems and Wordsworth's life. Also, memorize the fourth stanza of 'I Wandered Lonely as a Cloud.' No, Joe, you may not take the fifth; there are only four stanzas in the poem.")

Mrs. Smith's other student teacher, in another class, made his début the same day. He handed his college supervisor the following lesson plan:

LESSON PLAN II

William Wordsworth's

"I Wandered Lonely as a Cloud"

I wandered lonely as a cloud
That floats on high o'er vales and hills,
When all at once I saw a crowd,
A host, of golden daffodils;
Beside the lake, beneath the trees,
Fluttering and dancing in the breeze.

Continuous as the stars that shine
And twinkle on the milky way,
They stretched in never-ending line
Along the margin of a bay:
Ten thousand saw I at a glance,
Tossing their heads in sprightly dance.

The waves beside them danced; but they
Out-did the sparkling waves in glee:
A poet could not but be gay,
In such a jocund company:
I gazed—and gazed—but little thought
What wealth the show to me had brought:

For oft, when on my couch I lie
In vacant or in pensive mood,
They flash upon that inward eye
Which is the bliss of solitude;
And then my heart with pleasure fills,
And dances with the daffodils.

I. *Aims*
   A. To help students share Wordsworth's feelings and thoughts.
   B. To break down students' prejudices against nature poetry.
   C. To develop in students a sensitivity to their immediate environment.
   D. To point up Wordsworth's skill as a poet.
   E. To encourage the reading of poems by Wordsworth and other authors that relate to "I Wandered Lonely as a Cloud."

II. *Methods*
   A. Read the poem aloud.
   B. Discussion questions

1. Does the author do more than paint a word-picture of a beautiful scene? Defend your answer.
2. Wordsworth's sister, Dorothy, described in her journal the scene which inspired the poem: The daffodils

   . . . tossed, and reeled, and danced, and seemed as if they verily laughed with the wind that blew upon them over the lake. They looked so gay, ever glancing, ever changing.

   Why is or isn't William Wordsworth's description of the daffodils' motion more effective than his sister's?
3. Wordsworth believed nature touches both the senses and the mind. How does the poem illustrate the idea?
4. Have you had the experience Wordsworth describes in the last stanza? Explain.
5. In his preface to *Lyrical Ballads*, Wordsworth wrote: ". . . poetry is the spontaneous overflow of powerful feelings: it takes its origin from emotion recollected in tranquillity." Why does the poem exemplify Wordsworth's definition of poetry?
6. Could a competent painter do more with the scene than Wordsworth did? Defend your answer.
7. Why would few of us stop whatever we are doing to watch a host of daffodils "fluttering and dancing in the breeze"? Why do most of us develop immunities to the natural beauty in our immediate environment?
8. When you came to school today, did you see anything that deserved to be painted, photographed, or described orally or in writing? Explain.
9. Why do you like to tell others about experiences that make a deep impression on you?
10. What qualities and abilities did Wordsworth have that most people do not have? Why do you suppose he was interested in having his poem published?
11. Is Wordsworth's language simple and direct or difficult and complex? Draw on the poem to defend your answer.
12. How are the first three stanzas of "I Wandered Lonely as a Cloud" and Robert Frost's "Stopping by Woods on a Snowy Evening" similar? How do the final stanzas differ? Which of the two poems do you like better? Why?

C. Supplementary materials
   1. If time permits, compare the poem with one or more of the

following: William Wordsworth's "The World Is Too Much with Us" and "It Is a Beauteous Evening, Calm and Free"; John Greenleaf Whittier's "Snow-Bound"; Walt Whitman's "Miracles"; Emily Dickinson's "Some Keep the Sabbath"; Robert Bridges' "London Snow"; Thomas Hardy's "Afterwards"; A. E. Housman's "Loveliest of Trees"; Sara Teasdale's "Barter"; Robert Frost's "The Pasture"; and Mark Van Doren's "Morning Worship."

    2. Recommend Louis Untermeyer's *A Concise Treasury of Great Poems*, a paperback, which includes ten of Wordsworth's poems, biographical material, and interpretive comments, and William Wordsworth's *The Prelude, Selected Poems and Sonnets*, a paperback with an introduction by Carlos Baker.

D. Read "I Wandered Lonely as a Cloud" aloud once more before making tomorrow's assignment.

E. Assignment

    1. Read Wordsworth's "The Solitary Reaper" for tomorrow. Swinburne, a British poet, says of two lines[4] in "The Solitary Reaper": "In the whole expanse of poetry there can hardly be two verses [lines] of more perfect and profound and exalted beauty." We'll check tomorrow to see who was able to spot the lines Swinburne had in mind.

    2. Tomorrow's discussion of "The Solitary Reaper" will center on questions you raise and mimeographed questions I shall distribute.

Discussion Questions on "The Solitary Reaper"

William Wordsworth's "The Solitary Reaper"

> Behold her, single in the field,
> Yon solitary Highland Lass!
> Reaping and singing by herself;
> Stop here, or gently pass!
> Alone she cuts and binds the grain,
> And sings a melancholy strain;
> O listen! for the Vale profound
> Is overflowing with the sound.
>
> No Nightingale did ever chaunt
> More welcome notes to weary bands

[4]Lines 19–20.

Of travellers in some shady haunt,
Among Arabian sands:
A voice so thrilling ne'er was heard
In spring-time from the Cuckoo-bird,
Breaking the silence of the seas
Among the farthest Hebrides.

Will no one tell me what she sings?—
Perhaps the plaintive numbers flow
For old, unhappy, far-off things,
And battles long ago:
Or is it some more humble lay,
Familiar matter of to-day?
Some natural sorrow, loss, or pain,
That has been, and may be again?

Whate'er the theme, the Maiden sang
As if her song could have no ending;
I saw her singing at her work,
And o'er the sickle bending;—
I listened, motionless and still;
And, as I mounted up the hill
The music in my heart I bore,
Long after it was heard no more.

1. Dorothy Wordsworth wrote in her journal that her brother found the idea for "The Solitary Reaper" in the following passage from Thomas Wilkinson's *Tour in Scotland:*

> Passed a female who was reaping alone; she sung in Erse [Scottish Gaelic] as she bended over her sickle;—the sweetest human voice I ever heard; her strains were tenderly melancholy, and felt delicious, long after they were heard no more.[5]

a. Is Wilkinson's one-sentence prose statement of what he saw an accurate summary of "The Solitary Reaper"? Did Wordsworth borrow directly from Wilkinson? Defend your answers.
b. Why do you suppose both Wordsworth and Wilkinson emphasized the girl's song rather than her surroundings? Why is the poetic presentation of the experience superior to the prose?
2. If you were to sketch the scene, what would you play up? Why?
3. How are the last stanzas of "The Solitary Reaper" and "I Wan-

[5] Wordsworth and his sister had seen such a scene many times when traveling in Scotland.

dered Lonely as a Cloud" similar? dissimilar? Do the final two lines of "The Solitary Reaper" reflect your response to unforgettable experiences? Explain.

4. The brief passage from Wilkinson quoted above illustrates that significant changes in the English language have taken place since Wordsworth's day. Note the peculiar verb forms, punctuation, vocabulary, and sentence structure. Rewrite the statement so it would not seem strange if it appeared in a current magazine. Why do you suppose Wilkinson's language became dated?

5. Wordsworth wrote many excellent ballads. If you would like to give a dramatic reading of one of his ballads, please see me. I have mimeographed copies of "We Are Seven," "Lucy Gray," and several others.

F. Evaluation

To what extent did I achieve the goals I set for this lesson?

The student teacher did not ask all of the questions listed in his lesson plan. The first question—"Does the author do more than paint a word-picture of what he felt was a beautiful scene?"—led to a stanza-by-stanza analysis of the meaning of the poem. Then, without consulting his lesson plan, he asked about (1) the average person's insensitivity to beauty around him and (2) the differences between a poet's and an average person's sensitivity to surroundings and verbal skill. Having thought through twelve thought-provoking, rather than recall, questions, he was primed to make an interesting and worthwhile presentation. Had he plodded through all the questions, his students would have become bored with the inevitable repetition. Of course, one can pick flaws in his plan. Some teachers would object to twelve discussion questions for a four-stanza poem, deplore the lack of emphasis on the author's life and times, and urge that questions come mostly from students rather than the teacher.

Experienced teachers who use the poems in an anthology year after year rarely develop detailed lesson plans. Many of them do prepare mimeographed study guides listing thought-provoking questions that relate each literary selection to students' lives. For example, Questions 1, 3, 8, and 10 from Lesson Plan II might be included in a reading guide for "I Wandered Lonely as a Cloud." Such study guides help students appreciate assigned selections and provide examination questions superior to the completion, true-false, or multiple-choice types. But a student teacher or beginning teacher can profit from detailed lesson plans; they give him confidence and can insure variety in content and methods, which high school students welcome.

Some critic teachers claim rightly that when a class session ends, the student teacher should ask himself, "To what extent did I achieve my stated aims for the lesson, and why?" A conscientious teacher is rarely completely satisfied with the outcome of a particular lesson. He takes an objective look at what occurred during the period, then attempts to duplicate his successes and avoid his failures. This comes under the heading of *Evaluation.*

UNIT PLANS

How does a unit plan differ from a daily lesson plan?[6] A unit plan is also organized around *Aims, Methods,* and *Evaluation,* but it might cover a five-week study of modern American poets. Depending on daily lesson plans has one serious disadvantage: students may see five weeks of work as a series of disconnected experiences. If they are given an overview, including aims and methods, of the work that will be undertaken over a period of weeks, the daily classroom activities become parts that contribute to a whole. In most of his pursuits, man acts with purpose, intelligence, and interest when he has long-term goals that can be achieved by daily attention to specific activities. A unit plan may be defined as a series of coordinated daily lesson plans unified by overall objectives.

As a high school English teacher, I was impressed by my students' interest in the happy and unhappy people limned in poems by Edwin Arlington Robinson, Edgar Lee Masters, Carl Sandburg, and others. I developed a unit, *Portraits of Happy and Unhappy People,* that included one hundred short poetic portraits written between 718 B. C. and 1948 by well-known Greek, Roman, Chinese, Japanese, Indian, Hebrew, English, American, French, German, and Italian poets. An additional 150 poetic portraits provided students with a choice of supplementary readings. My aims for the unit were as follows:

1. To have students compare their ideas on happiness and unhappiness with those held by people of various times and places.
2. To help students understand why the values of man relating to family, love, death, nature, war, peace, wealth, poverty, country, and God have remained almost constant for over twenty-five hundred years.
3. To examine man's ideas about good and evil.
4. To help students define, develop, and defend a philosophy of life.

To introduce the unit, I spent a period reading and relating to the foregoing objectives a half-dozen poetic portraits which had been favorites

[6]See Virginia Alwin, "Back-Country America—an Illustrative Unit" in "Building Instructional Units," *The English Language Arts in the Secondary School* (New York: Appleton-Century-Crofts, Inc., 1956), pp. 70–111.

in other classes. I then distributed a reading guide listing one or two discussion questions on each of the hundred portraits. The next day we began reading and discussing the poems. We frequently compared poems expressing conflicting or similar points of view. We also compared similarities and differences among groups of poems representing different cultures. Throughout the unit, students gave brief written and oral reports on ideas in poems they selected from the supplementary list—explanations of why they accepted or rejected them wholly or in part. If I were teaching the unit today, I would have small groups of students give dramatic readings of some of the poems, exemplified by professional actors presenting poems from Edgar Lee Masters' *Spoon River Anthology.*

Students like the portraits of happy people (George Meredith's "Juggling Jerry," Emily Dickinson's "Some Keep the Sabbath," Edgar Lee Masters' "Lucinda Matlock," T. A. Daly's "Mia Carlotta," and Carl Sandburg's "Fish Crier" and "Happiness"); but they were attracted even more to the unhappy ones ("Lord Randal," William Shakespeare's "Tomorrow and Tomorrow and Tomorrow," Robert Browning's "Soliloquy of the Spanish Cloister," Thomas Hardy's "The Man He Killed," A. E. Housman's "When I Was One-and-Twenty," Edwin Arlington Robinson's "Miniver Cheevy," Edgar Lee Masters' "George Gray," and Carl Sandburg's "Mamie").

I taught a variety of poetry units to senior high school students, but none was so successful as *Portraits of Happy and Unhappy People.*[7] I believe it appealed to my students because the poems in the unit are short, clear, dramatic, and relate to concerns shared by many teen-agers and adults.

Although units of work organized by English teachers are usually somewhat similar in aims, content, and methods, the possible variations seem endless. Very common are units on written composition, oral composition (speech), grammar, usage, poetry, the short story, the drama, the essay, and the novel. Uncommon are units on listening, semantics, and the evolution of language. A unit commonly covers only a small part of what is called *drama, essay,* or *short story.* Some junior high school teachers will devote a week or two to a unit on Poe's short stories. Twelfth-grade teachers may develop a unit on Shakespeare's plays or recent Broadway plays. Many junior high school English teachers and some college teachers of freshman English courses have welcomed anthologies with

[7]Edgar Lee Masters' *Spoon River Anthology*—poetic portraits of mostly unhappy people—was a best-seller in 1915. Before him, Michael Wigglesworth's *Day of Doom* (undistinguished verse) became a best-seller; after Masters, Stephen Vincent Benét's *John Brown's Body* and Robert Frost's *In the Clearing* won similar acclaim. What other American poets wrote best-sellers?

poems, short stories, essays, and plays organized under theme headings: *Family Life, The Self, Education, Folklore,* and *American Traditions.* They feel theme units relate more directly to students' lives than units based on centuries, authors, or literary types.

Carefully planned units need not lead to compartmentalization of reading, writing, speaking, and listening. A modern American poetry unit could include writing, speaking, and listening activities; an oral composition unit could include reading and writing experiences. Some English teachers advocating unit plans see value in carefully alternating units to provide variety and logical continuity. They suggest that since most students would rather write essays than short stories, poetry, or plays, a unit on recent American essays should be followed by one on written composition. The unit on written composition would, of course, include work in grammar and usage. The English teacher, they feel, should not only favor unit plans over daily hastily improvised lesson plans; he should have a clear conception of how the units in various courses contribute to achieving overall departmental reading, writing, speaking, and listening goals.

Once a teacher has developed a carefully planned unit on modern American poetry, he needs to revise it during and at the end of the unit. Revision is as essential for the teacher as for the student who is writing compositions. And in making revisions, the teacher should encourage suggestions from his students. Most beginning teachers avoid teacher-student planning. They feel secure only when they determine course goals, content, and methods. But they lose little autonomy by providing alternate assignments that give students an occasional choice of activities, and they can get leads for future planning by asking students what they liked and disliked about a just-completed unit.

Two common criticisms of student teachers by critic teachers are: they do not know how to make effective lesson plans, and they do not know how to motivate students. A good lesson plan has motivation built into it because it has what students consider clear, worthwhile, and achievable objectives and logical, various, and interesting methods. Content and methods that reflect a direct approach to helping students achieve worthwhile objectives are usually logical and interesting. If improving written composition is the goal, most students are impressed by guided writing experiences, repulsed by illogical and uninteresting workbook and handbook exercises.

Lesson plans are, then, not so mysterious as many English methods students think. An effective lesson plan includes (1) clear, worthwhile, achievable objectives and (2) methods that lead directly (no dull, annoying detours)[8] to achieving the objectives. Whenever the course content is not prescribed by tradition, the teacher selects the content he believes will help students realize his goals. If English teachers have reasonable content mastery and a modicum of imagination, they should be encouraged to select the content and methods they think will help their students develop language skills and an appreciation of literature.

Although the beginning English teacher may be unenthusiastic about departmental syllabi stipulating spelling lists, vocabulary lists, objective usage and literature tests, workbook and handbook exercises, and sentence diagraming, he may not feel secure enough to reject them. But he can, at least, base spelling lists on the correct spellings of words students misspell in their compositions and examinations, and vocabulary lists on words taken from the literature they are asked to read. He can also select for individual students handbook and workbook exercises that relate directly to their serious errors in speech and writing. Also, he can supplement required objective usage and literature tests with essay tests. His revisions of departmental syllabi are unlikely to be questioned by colleagues or administrators if his students are making reasonable progress towards the goals set by the English department.

ASSUMPTIONS ABOUT PLANNING A LESSON

Prepare to explain why you accept or reject, wholly or in part, the following assumptions about lesson plans:

1. Syllabi developed by English departments should explain in detail what to teach and how to teach it.
2. A well-organized English program requiring identical content and methods in all tenth-grade English classes is desirable.
3. Written lesson plans take the spontaneity out of teaching.
4. A student's appreciation of literature can be measured by essay or objective tests.
5. Unit lesson plans based on themes are superior to those based on literary types.
6. Teacher-student planning is not a waste of time and energy.
7. The Aims-Methods-Evaluation lesson plan pattern is too simple.
8. A teacher's lesson plan exposes his philosophy of education.
9. A teacher should seldom stray from his lesson plan.
10. The two lesson plans on "I Wandered Lonely as a Cloud" are dissimilar in several significant respects.

[8]Handbook and workbook exercises, spelling lists, and vocabulary lists.

11. The learining principles exemplified in Lesson Plan II, p. 55–59, could be applied in teaching the short story, essay, drama, and novel.

12. The values of reading a poem, Robert Frost's "Stopping by Woods on a Snowy Evening," in depth are illustrated in John Ciardi, "The Way to the Poem," *Saturday Review*, Vol. 41, No. 15 (April 12, 1958), pp. 13–15+.

13. A carefully constructed unit plan provides for (1) worthwhile reading, writing, speaking, and listening experiences and (2) individual differences.

14. A detailed lesson plan gives the beginning English teacher confidence.

15. Some excellent suggestions on developing units are presented in The Commission on the English Curriculum, National Council of Teachers of English, "Building Instructional Units," *The English Language Arts in the Secondary School* (New York: Appleton-Century-Crofts, Inc., 1956), pp. 67–70 and 112–18.

16. A teacher should always give students an overview of a new unit.

IDEAS TO TEST

To increase your skill in lesson planning, complete one or more of the following assignments:

1. Observe a high school English class; state in three brief paragraphs the goals the teacher tried to achieve, the methods he used, and the extent to which the class session was worthwhile and why. If you cannot observe a high school class, substitute one of your college English classes.

2. Assume that after you have observed your critic teacher teach a sophomore English class for a week, he says:

> Next week I should like to have you begin teaching the following selections in a unit on the short story: Washington Irving's "The Legend of Sleepy Hollow," Nathaniel Hawthorne's "The Great Stone Face," Edgar Allan Poe's "The Pit and the Pendulum," Bret Harte's "The Outcasts of Poker Flat," Mark Twain's "The Celebrated Jumping Frog of Calaveras County," and O. Henry's "A Municipal Report."

Under *Aims* list your overall objectives for the unit, not specific objectives for each selection. Under *Methods* explain in some detail just how during the first class session you will give your students an overview of the whole unit, which would include (1) aims, (2) selections to be read in and out of class, (3) methods that will be used, (4) written and oral assignments based on the short stories and related material,

(5) total time allotted to the unit, (6) examinations, and (7) supplementary reading. Then make a detailed lesson plan for one of the short stories: list the *Aims,* and develop as part of *Methods* several thought-provoking discussion questions relating the story to students' experiences.

3. Since developing discussion questions relating a literary selection to high school students' experiences is one of the most difficult problems facing a student teacher, develop such questions for your favorite poem, short story, essay, novel, and play. Also, if your college or university has a teaching materials service, visit it to determine what audio-visual aids are available for your favorite literary selections.

4. If your college's Curriculum Laboratory has a collection of literature anthologies, browse through them; select a dozen poetic portraits suitable for a very brief unit on *Poetic Portraits of Happy and Unhappy People.* List your objectives for the unit and the poems to be included. Then select two of the poetic portraits, and develop under *Aims* and *Methods* a lesson plan for a single class session. Include several discussion questions under *Methods.*

5. Use the poems listed under "Supplementary materials," page 56, to develop a brief unit on *Noticing Nature.* State your objectives and methods for the unit. Then choose one or more of the poems, and develop under *Aims* and *Methods* a lesson plan for a single class session. Why would Thomas Hardy's "Afterwards" probably be an excellent choice to introduce the unit?

6. Develop a lesson plan for Appendix 13, 14, 15, 16, 17, 18, or 19.

4

Making Readers out of Students: Part I

Before reading this chapter, formulate clear, defensible answers to the following questions. After reading it, prepare to explain why you changed or retained your answers.

1. Why are there reluctant readers, slow readers, and nonreaders in almost every high school? How would you help them?
2. What is literature? What are the distinctive qualities of a literary masterpiece? of trash?
3. Why is literature included in the English program?
4. What are your goals for teaching literature?
5. As you recall them, what were the aims, methods, and personality traits of your best and worst high school and college literature teachers?

RELUCTANT READERS, SLOW READERS, AND NONREADERS

Even the unique English teacher who is assigned to teach only college-bound students faces the problem of (1) stimulating reading interests and (2) developing reading skills. The English teacher whose students' academic abilities are mostly average or below average usually considers "teaching students how to read and enjoy reading" among his most serious problems. Asked to classify students who have reading problems, he might label them reluctant readers, slow readers, and nonreaders. When you have the opportunity, test some of the following approaches to helping such students.

Reluctant Readers

Every high school has students who do well on objective and subjective tests designed to measure reading speed and comprehension, but who read only what is required by teachers. If they are acquainted with *Masterplots* or other sources which summarize fiction, they use them, especially for supplementary readings that culminate in book reports. Experienced English teachers sometimes conclude that 90 percent of their students are reluctant readers.

Teachers give many reasons why they can rarely make readers out of students. Some blame the home: "The parents' reading is limited to the local newspaper" or "The home lacks the quiet spot essential to the reader." Some blame the school: "Heavy curricular and extracurricular assignments leave little time for voluntary reading" or "The English teachers' preoccupation with literary analysis, biographical and historical information, recall tests, vocabulary lists, memorization, literary masterpieces, and covering ground makes reading a road with uninteresting detours every half mile."

How can the English teacher turn reluctant readers into avid readers? He cannot change his students' home surroundings, but he can change their school environment by testing some of the ideas on teaching literature illustrated in Chapters 4 and 5. Then, if he asks himself the following questions whenever he completes a unit on poetry, the short story, the novel, the essay, or the drama, he can develop plans which may help increasing numbers of students see literature as a source of pleasure rather than a plague.

1. Did I give students an overview of the literature unit—details about aims, selections to be read by all students, bibliographical material for individual reading, nature of discussions and other oral composition activities, written work, and examinations?

2. Why did students enjoy or reject the introductory selections I read to them?

3. Did the discussion questions I provided for selections read by all students stimulate their thinking or test their recall of what the author wrote? How many of the questions related the ideas and feelings of the author to the experiences of the students? Did I begin discussions with students' questions?

4. Was the biographical and historical material I presented to the students or required them to read indispensable in appreciating the assigned selections?

5. Did I (1) give students in-class time for free reading? (2) talk with individual students about their free reading? (3) devote an occasional period to group discussions of free reading students were doing? and (4) do everything I could to make free reading materials available to students?

6. Did I occasionally read to students selections not in the anthology?

7. Knowing that students' most common complaint is "I don't understand it!" did I read aloud and explain the difficult parts of selections before I assigned them?

8. Were class discussions dominated by me or by several students?

9. Did I discuss with students what they liked most and least about the unit? Did I revise the unit to accommodate worthwhile suggestions?

10. Did my quizzes and examinations measure appreciation of the selections read or merely check students' recall?

When adults gather voluntarily to discuss "great books," the able discussion leader does not resort to dissertations on biographical and historical data, quick quizzes, or recitation of memorized passages. He may briefly present information about the authors and their times that makes their work more meaningful. But he is more likely to get the discussion under way by asking, "Why did you like or dislike Dante's *The Divine Comedy*?" or "What was Dante's purpose in writing *The Divine Comedy*?" or "Why is *The Divine Comedy* included in lists of great books?" or "How does *The Divine Comedy* relate to our times?" The able discussion leader is a guide and resource person, never a dictator. The English teacher who approaches literature in the classroom as he does with friends in his own home will gradually convince many reluctant readers that literature can outdo television in providing entertainment and instruction.

Slow Readers

A slow reader is usually, but not always, a reluctant reader. Experienced teachers spot him quickly and try to determine whether his problem is rooted in poor eyesight, poor health, low I.Q., inferior instruction on the elementary level, or emotional problems.

Reading specialists who work with the slow reader are found in few schools, so the regular teacher has to assume the responsibility of helping such a student. Of course, the recommendations made above to help the reluctant reader will not go amiss with the slow reader, but the latter usually needs some individual instruction every day.

The teacher must first isolate the reason why a student cannot read rapidly enough to keep up with his classmates. Tests administered by the school nurse or family physician may show that physical causes may be ruled out, and I.Q. tests may show that he is capable of improving his reading speed and comprehension. In this case, the teacher should talk with the student to find out, if possible, his attitudes towards reading and how they originated. To discover at what reading level the student functions most efficiently, the teacher should have him react orally and in writing to reading materials of varying degrees of difficulty. The teacher must try to provide material the student is able to read and wants to read.[1] Reluctant and slow readers will often read difficult books when the content is sufficiently appealing.

Some help in selecting reading materials with high interest is available through the Educational Division, Reader's Digest Services, Inc., Pleasantville, New York 10570; George W. Norvell's *The Reading Interests of Young People*; G. Robert Carlsen's *Books and the Teen-Age Reader*; and the book clubs (see page 74). The teacher's best source of materials is a good school library, especially if he knows content well enough to help each slow reader select suitable material.

Helping the slow reader depends, then, upon the teacher's skill in (1) discovering the reasons for the student's difficulties and (2) developing a reading program which promises to eliminate them. But perhaps even more important to the slow reader is a sympathetic and patient teacher who is encouraged by the smallest monthly gains in reading speed and comprehension. Such a teacher mirrors one of Marcus Aurelius Antonius' pronouncements: "Be satisfied with success in even the smallest matters, and believe that even such results are no trifles."

How does one find time to help the slow reader? Teachers who do not ignore the problem provide some daily individual instruction while other students are busy with regular assignments. If there are a half-dozen slow readers in a class, teachers can save time by providing some group instruction. To repeat, the best way to salvage slow readers is (1) begin where they are, (2) set goals they can and want to achieve, and (3) help them daily to take a single short step towards the goals.

Nonreaders

Nonreaders need the attention of a reading expert who has the skill and time to determine why six or more years of reading instruction have been

---

[1]Charles Spiegler, "Give Him a Book That Hits Him Where He Lives," in *Improving English Skills of Culturally Different Youth*, ed. Arno Jewett, Joseph Mersand, and Doris V. Gunderson (Washington, D. C.: U. S. Department of Health, Education and Welfare, Office of Education, 1964), pp. 91–99.

in vain. Regular classroom teachers sometimes struggle for a semester or more with students who can sometimes learn to read a sentence in a primer today, only to forget how by tomorrow. Such patience and persistence is admirable, but it seems to be a waste of time and energy.

Fortunately, many modern school systems are fast reducing the number of high school students who are slow readers or nonreaders. How do they do it? They have special classes taught by reading experts who help all students from grades 1–12 who have reading difficulties. A nonreader is almost always detected before he reaches the third grade, but few teachers have the time and skill to help him. Most slow readers and nonreaders profit tremendously when they automatically receive individual attention from experts when they need it.[2]

DEFINING LITERATURE

When asked to define *literature*, high school and college students give a variety of answers: "Literature is the best that has been thought and said." "It is the writings that have stood the test of time." "It is an interpretation of life." "It is the novels, poems, short stories, essays, and plays we read in English classes." When asked, "What is good literature?" they repeat some of the foregoing definitions and make additional generalizations: "Good literature is honest, not sensationalism or sentimentalism for profit's sake." "It is the work of authors whose sensitivity and verbal skill enable them to share with readers their insights and feelings." "Good authors help a reader become more aware of his world—men, ideas, events." "Good writers are master psychologists who reveal why man behaves as he does." "Good literature reflects in moving fashion the history of man's sorrows, joys, and values." "It helps make man more humane." "It has universal appeal; and it is finally possessed by educated men everywhere."

The many definitions of literature and good literature are capped by Matthew Arnold's claim: the mission of poetry is to interpret life for us, to console us, and to sustain us. All types of good literature stir and refine the sympathetic reader's thoughts and emotions. They provide vicarious experiences that help him solve problems, and thus add pleasure and meaning to his life. Many people have been consoled and sustained— given perspective—in time of adversity by lines from literature which reflect the transitory nature of man and his perpetual crises.[3] Literature

[2]For ideas on teaching reading, ask The Reading Center, Southern Illinois University, Carbondale, Illinois 62901, to place your name on the mailing list for *The Reading Forum*, a free pamphlet published four times a year.

[3]A television program on November 25, 1963, the day of President Kennedy's funeral, was devoted to the reading of British and American poetry selected to console and sustain bereaved Americans.

has also caused man to fight for freedom and justice and, equally important, to laugh at himself and others.

GENERAL GOALS

Should a junior high school student—it would be a boy—ask you during your first day of student teaching, "Why do we have to study this stuff?" (Elizabeth Barrett Browning's "How Do I Love Thee"), what would you say? The answer of some teachers has been, "You'll be glad you had to when you grow up" or "You want to graduate, don't you?" When occasionally the latter answer is answered with a "No!" he may hand the student a detention slip demanding a private conference after school. The tête-à-tête rarely converts a student to Emily Dickinson's conclusion:

> There is no frigate like a book
> To take us lands away,
> Nor any coursers like a page
> Of prancing poetry.[4]

Literature is included in the language programs of schools of all nations. The seven liberal arts originated in ancient Greece; one of them, grammar, included the study of Homer's *Iliad* and *Odyssey*. During the Middle Ages, schools replaced the Greek and Roman classics with religious literature. The Renaissance brought these classics to the fore again, and they played a leading role in schools well into the twentieth century. The vernacular literatures—Italian, English, French, and German—rose in the early Renaissance, and over a period of five hundred years works in these languages slowly won supremacy over the Latin and Greek classics. Today most European secondary schools still offer Latin and Greek; but American high schools rarely offer Greek, and Latin is elected by fewer and fewer students.

As the vernacular literatures developed, Napoleon and other rulers realized that their native writings could be used in schools to promote nationalism. A nation's literature is, of course, part of its history, and can stimulate in students pride in and devotion to ideals personified by its heroes. The ancient Greeks worshiped the military heroes in the *Iliad* and the *Odyssey*. In this century the French, Germans, and Russians have used literature to build intense devotion to country. In addition to helping pass on a social heritage, literature provides models of effective writing which help students improve their written and oral English.

[4]Reprinted by permission of the publishers from Thomas H. Johnson, Editor, *The Poems of Emily Dickinson* (Cambridge, Mass.: The Belknap Press of Harvard University Press). Copyright 1951, 1955, by The President and Fellows of Harvard College.

We have noted why literature is included in the school curricula of all countries. However, specific problems for the English teacher are to determine what he expects to accomplish when he teaches literature and how he expects to accomplish it. In an ideal situation he would set goals and then, after studying the interests and abilities of his students, select the content and methods that promise to help him achieve his goals. Actually, he can usually choose supplementary literary selections only —departmental syllabi and state-adopted anthologies dictate much of the content.

Most English teachers admit they are successful only when their students use books for pleasure and profit all their lives. They feel they have failed with students who never read voluntarily a single book comparable in quality to those read in literature classes. If a student spurns literature after he completes the required courses in high school and college, he quite obviously considered it an obstacle to be removed forever by passing tests on certain books. An English teacher seldom knows how well he succeeds in making readers out of students because it is impractical to check their reading habits after they leave his classes. Furthermore, some students were avid readers when they entered his class, and it is difficult to determine whether their association with him increased or decreased their zest for literature. But an alert teacher can detect in students' responses whether they are developing favorable or unfavorable attitudes.

When sixty-five entering college freshmen were asked, "What were some of the desirable results of literature courses that you thought were well taught?" they gave many variations of the following answers:

1. I have learned to read for enjoyment rather than just because it was required.

2. I have learned why people from other countries and the United States live the way they do.

3. I have learned to read things with an open mind and form opinions after I finish the article or whatever I am reading.

4. Literature helped me to understand myself and others. It can sometimes give us our reasons for living and the pattern by which we are going to live.

5. Literature has given me some background for other subjects, especially history.

6. It helped me to use better words and better grammar.

7. It improved my reading speed and comprehension.

8. Reading aloud more or less took the shyness out of me.

9. I haven't gotten anything from literature.

10. I learned to like the works of dull writers.[5]

SPECIFIC GOALS

If an English teacher's purpose is to help students develop such a deep appreciation of literature that they will turn to it all their lives, he has set what most of his colleagues consider an indispensable ultimate goal. However, to achieve this goal, he must set subsidiary ones. His ultimate goal will remain a dream unless he demands specifics by asking, "In order to achieve my aim, what shall I teach and how shall I teach it?" The specific goals of English teachers vary, but most of them would probably approve of the following:

Upgrading Students' Present Reading Interests and Abilities

To determine students' present reading interests,[6] the English teacher might ask them to respond orally or in writing to two questions: "What have you read voluntarily in books, magazines, and newspapers during the last month?" "During the last semester, which required readings in English and other classes did you find interesting and worthwhile?" Although students' reading abilities are reflected in what they choose to read, they often read what is easily accessible in the home, classroom, and school library. Perhaps the best way to ascertain their reading skills is to have them read and react in the classroom to literature of varying degrees of difficulty.

Teachers have always been aware that reading interests and abilities will vary considerably even among students grouped homogeneously, but they feel compelled to devote most of their time to stock selections dictated by tradition. Since these selections are often too difficult or uninteresting for many students, they reject them completely, or accept them as they would a bitter medicine.

Upgrading students' reading interests and abilities is difficult when the curriculum demands that all students be subjected to the "best" literature. Although most English teachers cannot avoid teaching what is

---

[5]The English teacher who inspired this Olympian compliment deserves recognition in a book entitled *Peerless Pedagogues*, but he must remain anonymous forever. The completed questionnaires were unsigned.

[6]For a research study on the reading interests of junior and senior high school students, see George W. Norvell, *The Reading Interests of Young People* (Boston: D. C. Heath and Company, 1950).

demanded by tradition, some of them cater to their students' interests and abilities by providing a wide choice of supplementary readings. Paperbacks available through the Teen Age Book Club and Campus Book Club (902 Sylvan Avenue, Englewood Cliffs, New Jersey 07632); American Education Publication, Inc., Paperback Programs (Education Center, Columbus, Ohio 43216); Hertzberg-New Method, Inc. (Paperback Department, Vandalia Road, Jacksonville, Illinois 62650); and various publishers have made it easier for teachers to give students opportunities to read worthwhile literature they can appreciate.

If students are to develop the reading habit, they must enjoy reading. Once they become readers, they will probably gradually turn from the ephemeral to the permanent in literature. Most avid adult readers of good books read in high school some books labeled trash by their English teachers. Limiting in-class reading to "classics" written for mature, sophisticated adults may cause even conscientious students to conclude at the end of the semester, "I've had it; no more of that for me if I can help it."

Acquainting Students with Worthwhile Current Publications

In times past, English teachers rarely made available to students writings that supplemented textbooks. Today some teachers not only use the better newspapers and magazines in class but also arrange for class subscriptions to them. Keeping first-rate newspapers and magazines in the library and classroom is considered essential by the English teacher because he knows they are found in few homes. For example, in the homes of the upper, middle, and lowest ten per cent (Otis I. Q.) of 589 senior high school students there were (1) no subscriptions to *The Atlantic* and *Harper's* and only one subscription to the *Saturday Review*, and (2) three subscriptions to *The Wall Street Journal*, one subscription to *The New York Times*, none to *The Christian Science Monitor* or *The St. Louis Post-Dispatch*.[7] Much of the literature of the past is still timely today, but it was even more so when written. To ignore the best written interpretations and resolutions of today's problems is a common practice in schools, and is one reason why many students feel literature accents the irrelevant.

Showing Students What Literature Offers in Pleasure and Profit

A person who makes literature a part of his life does so because he enjoys

[7]Royal J. Morsey, *A College Seminar to Develop and Evaluate an Improved High School English Program* (Muncie, Ind.: Ball State University, 1961), p. 31.

it. When you ask him why he enjoys reading, you discover that he relates what he reads to his past, current, and anticipated experiences. He has many questions about these experiences—questions about family, friends, children, old age, death, love, hate, jealousy, free will, war, peace, ambition, work, God, nature, government, justice, and conformity. Literature may give him few final answers; but he does find honest discussions of man's quest to insure the ascendancy of good over evil, humaneness over animality, and knowledge over ignorance.

The man who turns to literature of the past and present has vicarious experiences that give him tools (ideas and emotions) to combat bad fortune and promote the good life for himself and others. Good literature instructs as well as entertains. Philosophers say their purpose is to pursue wisdom. The wisdom of the ages is found in works of authors skilled in interpreting the world they lived in. In most of his tragedies, Shakespeare depicts dramatically men dominated by the Machiavellian philosophy— that the ends justify the means and might makes right—a recipe for misery which, though attributed to Machiavelli (1469–1527), has been responsible for much inhumanity from primitive times to the present. Of course, in both his tragedies and comedies, Shakespeare juxtaposes good and evil because they have always appeared so in the lives of men.

Writers whose works deserve to be labeled literature appeal to the reader's intellect and emotions as they reveal their own ideas and feelings about man's basic problems. More often than not, they show the reader that to know all about a man (Clyde in Dreiser's *An American Tragedy*, for example) is to forgive all. But, except for a Leibnitz or Pope, writers seldom believe that whatever is, is right; they are often as partisan of the good, the ideal, as Isaiah. They are, however, not propagandists. Honesty is one characteristic reflected in the great literature of all times and places. Master writers rarely cater to the conditioned responses of their contemporaries—most of the great books have been censored at one time or another, from Homer's *Odyssey* to Twain's *The Adventures of Huckleberry Finn*.[8] Fortunately, some intelligent men have always prized the right of a writer to say what he thinks and feels. They have valued especially highly the writer who sees man's strengths and weaknesses clearly and possesses the verbal skill to share his insight.

Literature, then, can give the reader the pleasure and profit of partially understanding the nature of man's brief journey from womb to tomb. No one has surpassed Shakespeare, in *The Tempest*, in expressing an obsession of the world's finest writers—the impermanence of man and all his monuments:

[8]Anne Lyon Haight, *Banned Books*, Second Edition (New York: R. R. Bowker Company, 1955).

Our revels now are ended: these our actors
As I foretold you, were all spirits, and
Are melted into air, into thin air:
And, like the baseless fabric of this vision
The cloud-capp'd towers, the gorgeous palaces,
The solemn temples, the great globe itself,
Yea, all which it inherit, shall dissolve,
And, like this insubstantial pageant faded,
Leave not a rack behind: We are such stuff
As dreams are made on, and our little life
Is rounded with a sleep.

Likening man's span of life, his history, and his habitation to a five-act fantasy, a dream, does not lead to despair—it gives the thoughtful reader or listener perspective, enables him to see all men as partners in a brief pilgrimage on a transitory planet. In *Henry IV*, Act V, Scene 1, Shakespeare expresses, through Hotspur, a sentiment supported in most of the world's best writings, one which a devotee of literature usually comes to share:

O gentlemen, the time of life is short!
To spend that shortness basely were too long.

Literature is not a sermon, not a source of moral precepts. One who becomes addicted to it discovers that it helps him decide what to look for and do as he plays his part in the "insubstantial pageant," and he usually, like Disraeli, finds himself on the side of the angels.

The above and all other goals of the literature teacher can be condensed into "I want my students to appreciate literature." Again, appreciation of a literary selection depends on understanding and reacting sympathetically to what the author says. A teacher can best broaden and deepen a student's feeling for literature when he can help him select books that meet his interests and abilities. Since curriculum patterns rarely recognize differences in students, the teacher must do what he can to help perhaps 150 students appreciate a literary selection written for educated adults. But the teacher who realizes that this involves students' sympathetic understanding will make every effort to tie the selection to their experiential backgrounds.

In the next chapter individual attention will be given to ideas on teaching poetry, the short story, the novel, the drama, and the essay. Although many teachers prefer units limited to one literary type, the theme unit including all literary types (the novel and long play are sometimes excluded) has become increasingly popular, especially on the junior high school level. But a teacher who prefers theme units still has problems which concern teaching each one of the common literary types included in a theme unit.

ASSUMPTIONS ABOUT TEACHING LITERATURE

Be prepared to explain why you accept or reject, wholly or in part, the following assumptions about teaching literature:

1. Literature not only interprets life for us, consoles us, and sustains us but also challenges the dictum that whatever is, is right.

2. Good literature is honest, not sensational or sentimental for profit's sake.

3. Good writers are often master psychologists.

4. Literature reminds us that every man must be his brother's keeper.

5. Literature should be a source of instruction rather than enjoyment.

6. Making readers out of students should be the ultimate goal of one who teaches literature.

7. Helping students understand what literature can do for them is difficult.

8. All high school students should be subjected to the "best" literature.

9. Students who are avid readers of ephemeral literature will gradually upgrade their reading fare.

10. Newspapers and magazines should be included in English curricula.

11. American literature should be used to promote nationalism.

12. Two National Council of Teachers of English publications— William R. Wood et al., *Censorship and Controversy*, and N. C. T. E. Committee on the Right to Read, *The Students' Right to Read*—reflect a stand on censorship English teachers should support.

13. Parents should decide whether books like Hawthorne's *The Scarlet Letter* and Salinger's *The Catcher in the Rye* should be included in high school curricula.

14. Anne Haight's *Banned Books* proves that most of the world's leading literary masterpieces have been censored, many for reasons other than obscenity.

15. An English teacher has failed with students who never read voluntarily, after they complete his course, a single book that could be labeled literature.

16. A teacher can measure accurately his students' progress in developing an appreciation of literature.

17. . . . we read fine things but never feel them to the full until we have gone the same steps as the author (John Keats).

18. A man ought to read just as inclination leads him, for what he reads as a task will do him little good (Samuel Johnson).

19. The use of supplementary materials is indefensible when there is not enough time to cover adequately the material in the anthology.

20. Students will tackle hard-to-read literature if authors' ideas or stories interest them.

21. That only 50 percent of American adults read one or more books a year should be blamed on their unpleasant experiences with books in school.[9]

22. Educated readers never read trash.

23. There are literary selections all students must read.

24. Schools can make avid readers out of very few students.

25. Schools place too much emphasis on reading for enjoyment.

26. If an "A" student says at the end of a literature unit, "Thank God that's over," he and his teacher have failed.

27. Most literature in high school curricula was written for educated adults.

28. Teen Age Book Club paperbacks are of low quality, suitable only for slow readers. (I have heard many English teachers make this statement.)

29. Simplified editions of novels should be banned from schools.

30. Recommending specific methods for teaching the various literary types is ridiculous; whether it is poetry or prose, one can only read, explain, discuss, and think about it—nothing else.

31. A theme unit made up of short stories, essays, one-act plays, and poems all relating to "The Family" has weaknesses as well as strengths.

32. The traditional separate units on poetry and the short story, essay, novel, and drama are superior to theme units.

33. The classic literature is always modern (Edward Bulwer-Lytton).

34. A classic is something everybody wants to have read and nobody wants to read (Mark Twain).

35. The purpose of high school literature courses is to fill the student's mind with the best that has been thought and said.

36. Vicarious experiences provided by literature can influence a reader's actual experiences.

37. High school students who make the highest grades in English spend the most time on voluntary reading.

38. Reading literature can provide an escape from thought as well as provoke thought.

39. Reading to students selections that supplement material in their literature anthology will affect favorably their attitudes toward literature.

40. "An understanding of the spirit of the scientific method and its

---

[9]For surveys on reading of books by American adults, see Elmo Roper, "Lightly Traveled Road to Wisdom," *NEA Journal*, Vol. 48, No. 4, April, 1959, p. 9.

application to human affairs is the most fundamental social concept . . . the teacher of literature should possess."[10]

41. In *Literature Study in the High School*, Dwight L. Burton makes excellent suggestions on why and how literature should be taught.

42. In *The Reading Interests of Young People*, a research study, George W. Norvell reveals that many junior and senior high school students appreciate quality literature.

43. Giving literary selections the once-over-lightly treatment is as bad as dissecting them into bits.

IDEAS TO TEST

1. Ask students to write a brief definition of literature. Write several of the definitions on the blackboard and have students evaluate them.

2. Ask students to list what they have read voluntarily in books, magazines, and literature during the last two weeks. Discuss with students the reading interests reflected in the listings.

3. Have students write a brief paragraph on "Why I Like Literature" or "Why I Dislike Literature." Read aloud some of the paragraphs and discuss them with students.

4. As one measure of your students' reading ability, ask them to state in a sentence the theme or narrative thread of several brief poems of varying difficulty.

5. Compare the results of identical attitude-towards-literature questionnaires completed by students at the beginning and end of the semester.

[10]Louise M. Rosenblatt, *Literature as Exploration* (New York: D. Appleton-Century Company, Inc., 1938), p. 158.

5

Making Readers out of Students: Part II

Before reading this chapter, formulate clear, defensible answers to the following questions. After reading it, prepare to explain why you changed or retained your answers.

1. How do you define poetry? How would you teach it?

2. If you have any qualms about teaching poetry to high school students, what are they?

3. Can short stories do more than provide an escape from reality? Defend your answer.

4. How would you defend the inclusion of the novel in the high school curriculum?

5. What are your goals in teaching the drama?

6. Would you rather teach the essay than the other literary types? Defend your answer.

7. Which of the approaches used by your high school and college teachers in teaching poetry, the short story, novel, drama, and essay do you accept? reject? Why?

There are specific ideas on teaching (1) poetry, (2) the short story, (3) the novel, (4) the drama, and (5) the essay which deserve attention. Test the most promising ones.

TEACHING POETRY

English teachers frequently face this question: "What is the difference between poetry and prose?" Have you found a clear and convincing answer? Whenever we attach exclusive qualities to poetry, someone points them out in writings rightly labeled prose. We say that poetry (1) has fixed rhythms, (2) suggests rather than explains in detail, (3) features figurative language, (4) appeals to the emotions, and (5) sometimes rhymes; but the first four qualities can be present in prose, and the fifth quality can be absent in poetry. To show sharply the differences between poetry and prose, compare a prose paraphrase of "I Wandered Lonely as a Cloud" with the poem itself. The fixed rhythm, economy of language, emotional intensity, and rhyme of Wordsworth's poem will stand out clearly —an experience for the student which does more to define poetry than a dozen definitions.

Perhaps even more difficult than defining poetry is breaking down students' prejudices against it. Ask what they think of poetry, and some of them say: "It's all about love and nature." "It's okay for girls." "Poets are odd—Poe, for example." After you explain how ancient Greek and Roman rulers and soldiers valued poetry highly, knights of the Middle Ages wrote it, Renaissance men were as proud of their sonnets as of their prowess with a spear or rapier, and the educated and uneducated of all ages enjoyed the ballads sung or recited by the entertainers of their day, they remain unimpressed.

To offset their claim that poets are effeminate, you tell them about the extra-poetical activities of Dante, Chaucer, Shakespeare, Ben Jonson, Milton, Goldsmith, Whittier, Masefield, Frost, Masters, Sandburg, and many others, but all to no avail. Press further those who dislike poetry, and you expose grievances pointing to the way it has been taught: "I don't like to memorize poetry" and "I don't see why we have to learn all about the poets' lives and times." But the most common complaint is "I don't understand it."

Why is "I don't understand it" the most often-heard complaint of students who reject poetry? One reason becomes immediately clear to anyone who has the chance to watch English teachers in action. Quite frequently, the teacher's opening remark is, "How did you like the poems [usually from five to ten] assigned for today?" When the response is perfunctory, he hurries through five to ten poems in half an hour, telling students what the poems are about or raising some of the questions in the anthology. Covering ground so another five to ten poems can be assigned for the next day seems to be his objective. Since most English teachers like poetry, why do many of them hurry their students through a poetry unit? Perhaps they are pressured by syllabi, which may call for assigning an average of five poems each day, or by their consciences, which pain them when a class period is spent on a short poem. Covering ground, an obsession with some teachers, almost always leads to losing many students during the first few class sessions. "I don't understand it" will be heard less frequently in the classroom if English teachers turn a deaf ear[1] to "time's wingèd chariot hurrying near."

The most effective teacher of poetry I ever observed was Professor Philip Schneider, who taught a course in Browning in the Dayton Y.M.C.A.-Wittenberg College Evening School. His deep love of poetry was equalled by his desire to make it meaningful to students. Whenever he made assignments, he anticipated and cleared up difficulties he knew students would have with Browning's style and vocabulary, and he read aloud every poem he assigned during the semester. This helped us more than anything else to appreciate Browning, because very few of us knew how to read poetry. When Professor Schneider read "Fra Lippo Lippi," he became the tipsy Renaissance painter who explained so persuasively to the police why on a spring evening he deserted painting for a bit of riotous living. Although he frequently explained difficult lines, he never dissected poems. He knew what needed explaining, and because he welcomed all questions and answered them carefully, students were not afraid to expose their ignorance. He was delighted and polite when anyone ignorant on some point rose to speak. He avoided "Look it up," the refrain of teachers who do not understand that a questioner wants an answer, not a penalty.

Mr. Brown, a critic teacher, is consistently successful in developing in most of his students an appreciation of poetry. In discovering why he is so successful in teaching poetry, the following illustrations seem relevant.

1. To introduce a poetry unit, he spends a period or two reading aloud poems his students can appreciate: Martial's "How to Raise a Son," the ballad "Lord Randal," Lewis Carroll's "Father William," John Masefield's "Sea Fever," Dorothy Parker's "Resumé," Virginia Church's "Retirement" and "Not Mellin Food," Robert P. Tristram Coffin's "Tit for Tat," Ogden Nash's "In Far Tibet," Langston Hughes' "Freedom Train," Phyllis McGinley's "Lament of the Normal Child," Franklin Adams' "The Rich Man," and many others. He has a fat sheaf of such poems—a rich source of introductory readings. He makes brief comments about some of the poems and authors, and he encourages students to make comments and raise questions; but since most of the poems are simple, he spends little time on explanations and questions. His purpose is to demonstrate that there is poetry students can enjoy.

2. After spending a period or two reading poems to his students, he asks each one to read his favorite short (not over twenty-five lines) poem to the class, explain why it is his favorite, and answer questions

[1] Every experienced teacher has one.

his classmates and teacher may raise. Students who do not have a favorite poem are asked to find one they like in one of the anthologies available in the library and the classroom. Both anthologies and specific poems are listed on a mimeographed sheet he distributes. He said the first time he asked students to present a favorite poem, he failed to limit the length to twenty-five lines; and one girl recited all of Alfred Noyes' "The Death of the Highwayman" from memory, in a singsong soprano that caused him a spate of agony followed by intermittent nightmares for nine years.

3. After a week devoted to teacher and student readings of poetry, Mr. Brown and his students spend a period inspecting the section of the anthology to be used in the unit. They examine the table of contents, index, material accompanying each poem, and study aids. He distributes his own discussion questions for each poem, leaving spaces for students' questions. His discussion questions relate the poems to the experiential backgrounds of students. He then assigns several poems and reads them to the class.

4. He asks his students to assume several out-of-class responsibilities:
   a. Practice reading aloud all short poems.
   b. Write one-sentence statements of the theme of each lyric poem and the narrative thread of each narrative poem.
   c. Prepare to discuss the questions provided for each poem. Add your own questions.
   d. Choose from each poem a line or lines that you find especially appealing or effective. Prepare to defend your choices.

5. The in-class activities are organized as follows:
   a. All assigned short poems are read aloud by students or the teacher. Mr. Brown or his students often read supplementary poems that relate to the assigned poems.
   b. The class determines the theme or narrative thread of each poem. Sometimes a half-dozen students' statements of a poem's theme or narrative thread are written on the blackboard and compared.
   c. Students' questions are discussed, and some of the discussion topics provided by the teacher also receive attention.
   d. Students present and defend their favorite lines from the poems.
   e. After discussing short poems, Mr. Brown or a student rereads them aloud to restore their unity.

6. He encourages students to memorize lines they like. When, periodically, students present the lines to the class, they are also prepared to interpret and defend their choices. They are never given special credit for these presentations or required to memorize lines for examinations.

7. He calls attention to poets' specific skills as their poetry is read

and discussed. He never devotes time to exercises on stanza forms and metrics, but does make such materials available to interested students.

8. Knowing that authors are aware that a poem, short story, or play must stand alone, and that few readers will do historical or biographical research voluntarily in order to understand a literary work, he minimizes biographical and historical study.

9. He helps each student develop an individual reading program based on the student's interests and abilities as they are revealed through daily reading of poetry, class discussions, and brief questionnaires completed at the beginning of the unit. He requires no book reports—only a reading diary in which the student lists each book he reads and explains in a sentence or two why he can or cannot recommend it to classmates.

10. His examinations are never true-false, matching, completion, or multiple-choice. When, early in the unit, he issues a mimeographed list of discussion questions on assigned poems, he tells students examination questions will be taken from the list—a practice which startles the teacher who believes students should know all the details he himself has mastered by going over the same material several times a year for many years.

Mr. Brown has an enthusiasm for poetry, sympathizes with students who do not, avoids sarcasm, and seldom seems in a hurry. There are many reasons for his success; but he succeeds primarily because he makes certain students understand what a poet tried to say. Understanding usually comes to students who hear a poem read aloud by an expert who takes the time to explain troublesome words and allusions, and who relates the theme of a lyric poem and the narrative thread of a narrative poem to their experiences through thought-provoking discussion questions.

TEACHING THE SHORT STORY

If asked to choose between lyric poetry and the short story, most students pick the short story. The idea or mood limned in a lyric poem is often difficult for them to share, but a tale told in a dramatic narrative poem or short story includes conflict and suspense which relate closely to their own vicarious and actual experiences. Through the television play, most students experience daily the suspense that accompanies conflict between heroes and heels. This dissolves in the final scenes when the heels get their comeuppance—a beating, bullet, rope, or jail. Confronted early in a story with conflict between man and man, woman, animal, the elements, society, or himself, the student is anxious to see how it develops and is finally resolved. The conflict in a story not only creates suspense but also causes characters to show one or more qualities which are part of everyone's experience: courage, jealousy, hatred, loyalty, greed, rivalry, fear, love, or unselfishness.

What can short stories do for high school students beyond pro⟩
entertainment? They can (1) reveal why people behave as the
(2) show the effect of strong emotions on men's lives; (3) help ⟨
evolve worthy goals and ideas on achieving them; (4) help them αεν⟨
a sympathetic understanding of minority groups and foreigners; and
(5) give some conception of the history of human problems and values
from 1400 B.C. (the Egyptian period) to the present. The ultimate goal of
the English teacher is to teach the short story so effectively that his
students will continue to turn to short stories for entertainment and
instruction. A teacher has no positive check on whether he achieves this
goal, but a daily analysis of students' responses can inform him whether
he is succeeding or failing.

Once a teacher has developed aims for a short-story unit, he must
ask what content and methods will help achieve them. Content is often
prescribed by a departmental syllabus, but the teacher is usually free to
choose his methods, even though they may be restricted somewhat by time
limits set for the unit by the syllabus. Given the opportunity to observe
hundreds of experienced and novice teachers teach the short story, one
notes some practices which seem effective and some which seem ineffective
in teaching students to appreciate this literary form.

When you have the opportunity, test some of the following ideas on
teaching the short story. They have found favor with critic teachers and
student teachers.

1. At the beginning of a short-story unit, discuss with students the
kinds of stories they like or dislike and why; stories they read voluntarily; values they receive from reading stories; magazines which publish
interesting short stories; and stories dramatized on television. (Revise
your unit plan to reflect leads revealed by the discussion.)

2. At the beginning of a unit, tell students that the ancient Egyp-
tians, Greeks, Romans, Hebrews, Indians, Persians, Arabians, and Chinese
treasured short stories for the entertainment and instruction they provided.
Read to them a few ancient short stories. They will probably like "The
Cyclops" in Homer's *Odyssey*, Aesop's "The Country Mouse and the Town
Mouse," Phaedrus' "The Shipwreck of Simonides," and "The Prodigal
Son." All can be read in a single period if "The Cyclops" is cut somewhat.
Give students the names of anthologies in the school or classroom library
which feature the great short stories of the world.

3. At the beginning of a unit, read to students a short story from a
magazine to prove that not all short stories are in textbooks. If you also
read some ancient short stories, ask students to indicate similarities and
differences between ancient and modern stories.

4. At the beginning of the unit, discuss with students their use of

the editorial aids in the anthology, the story assignments in the anthology, required supplementary readings, sources of stories for free reading, the teacher's list of discussion topics (several on each assigned story), and the nature and frequency of tests. All of this material can be summarized in two or three mimeographed pages.

5. A reading guide listing several discussion questions on each required short story can help students relate short stories to their own experiences—a necessary step in developing appreciation. Why are the following discussion questions superior to the objective questions on page 89 in helping students appreciate "The Devil and Tom Walker"?[2]

> a. Literary critics claim that stories provide entertainment and instruction. Was Irving's primary purpose to entertain? instruct? both? Defend your answer.
>
> b. You have labeled *good* or *bad* the behavior of friends, relatives, classmates, and man in general. In a humorous way, the author is critical of man's evildoing. What does the author consider man's most evil traits? Why do you agree or disagree with him?
>
> c. Why do you agree or disagree with the common belief that good always triumphs over evil? Why was Tom unable to enjoy the wages (wealth and influence) of evil (usury)?
>
> d. Define and illustrate humor. Does Irving use humor effectively? Defend your answer. Select several of the most humorous lines in the story, and prepare to defend your selections.
>
> e. How does Stephen Vincent Benét's "The Devil and Daniel Webster" differ from "The Devil and Tom Walker"? Why do you suppose both stories have proved good drama material?

6. Once the unit is under way, a number of in-class activities can help students develop an appreciation of the short story.

> a. Determine, as a group, the central narrative thread of the story. Is the following sentence an acceptable statement of the narrative thread in "The Devil and Tom Walker"?

Tom discovers too late that his contract with the devil cannot be broken.

> b. Base discussions on students' questions and those distributed by the teacher. Relate material on character, plot, setting, romanticism, realism, local color, and style directly to the story being discussed and use it only when it helps heighten appreciation.
>
> c. Since students often reject literature because they cannot understand the author, the teacher should read aloud and explain

[2]See Washington Irving's "The Devil and Tom Walker," Appendix 16.

the beginnings of difficult stories. A teacher who assigns "The Devil and Tom Walker" might recall to students' minds "Rip Van Winkle" and "The Legend of Sleepy Hollow," then help them get under way by reading and explaining the two pages of descriptive material leading to Tom's first dialogue with the devil.

d. Have the class spend a minimum of two sessions out of five on the silent reading of short stories of its own choosing. While the class is so occupied, the teacher can discuss quietly with individual students what they are reading and also recommend future reading that matches their interests and abilities. A student who reads from one to three stories each free reading period will read ten to thirty short stories that he might not otherwise read during a five-week unit. By circulating among students during the free reading period, the teacher can determine the progress they are making without resorting to written reports and tests. However, some students may want to react in writing or orally to stories that stir them.

e. Some teachers ask students to prepare and present condensed dramatic versions of short stories. It is easy to change Hemingway's "The Killers" into dialogue because much of it *is* dialogue. Stage trappings and exits and entrances can be kept at a minimum without affecting the enjoyment of actors and audience. The dialogue-heavy short stories of Ring Lardner, William Saroyan, James Thurber, and Jessamyn West also lend themselves admirably to dramatization. There are students in most classes who enjoy converting a short story into a play and presenting it to the class.

f. An English teacher can provide students with a pleasant surprise by reading aloud a recent prizewinning short story.

Today teachers and students need not rely solely on a class anthology. If they spend thirty-five to ninety-five cents each on paperback volumes of the works of single authors and anthologies, they will have immediate access to perhaps five hundred short stories from a dozen countries and a hundred authors. The advantage of such a classroom library cannot be overestimated—having books easily available helps make readers out of students.

The ideas presented in the preceding paragraphs will not insure students' developing an appreciation of the short story. Their value can be ascertained only by testing them. They do indicate that the common routine of administering searching oral and written recall quizzes on each story in a unit can be varied in many ways. When sixty-five entering college freshmen responded in writing to "What are a few 'Dos' for literature teachers?" their answers revealed that they prized most highly high school English teachers who occasionally varied the daily pattern by presenting selections not found in the textbook. Here are several other "Dos" suggested by the entering freshmen:

1. Read aloud to us, have us read aloud, and have us listen to recordings of authors reading their own works.
2. Let the student express his personal ideas and feelings about something he has read before you, the teacher, explain your feelings and beliefs about the same selection.
3. The teacher should express his idea of a literary selection, but he shouldn't force the student to accept his way of thinking.
4. Relate incidents and ideas in literature to our lives.
5. Do tie in literature's importance with other subjects.
6. Let students lead discussions sometimes.

Here are several of their answers to "What are a few 'Don'ts' for English teachers?":

1. Don't lecture.
2. Don't dominate class discussions.
3. Don't have a few students dominate class discussions.
4. Don't go too fast.
5. Don't criticize modern-day literature—this is one of the most disgusting things.

Among the poor practices are two popular ones that can rarely be justly blamed on departmental syllabi.

1. When a unit on the American short story is announced, most students are enthusiastic. But their enthusiasm wanes when background material shoves the reading of stories into the future. Background material is featured in the dreary, fact-filled, terminology-laden "Introduction to the Short Story" which precedes the short stories in many anthologies and, unfortunately, gives some teachers subject matter to be analyzed and memorized. When one questions the value of the analysis, teachers ask, "How can students learn to appreciate the short story when they know nothing about *character, plot, setting, climax, romanticism, realism, naturalism, local color, surprise ending, conflict, single effect,* and *style?*" Some teachers mix with definitions of terminology data detailing the contributions of various authors to the development of the short story. A three-day obsession with the twelve terms listed above and twenty-five

authors (Washington Irving to John Steinbeck) is climaxed with an objective test. Typical test items are as follows:

1. Underline the title of the story Poe wrote: (a) *The Purloined Gold Bug*, (b) *The Purloined Pendulum*, (c) *The Purloined Heart*, (d) *The Purloined Letter*, (e) *The Purloined Amontillado*, (f) *The Purloined Bells*.
2. Underline the title of Stockton's famous story: (a) *Squire Patrick's Lady*, (b) *A Fickle Widow*, (c) *The Lady and the Wolf*, (d) *Lady Bird*, (e) *The Lady or the Tiger?*, (f) *Wolf Whistle*.
3. Underline the label frequently applied to Bret Harte's stories: (a) colorful, (b) local color, (c) off-color, (d) coloratura, (e) colorific, (f) coloramic.
4. Underline Samuel Clemens' middle name: (a) Langhorne, (b) Langston, (c) Langley, (d) Langtry, (e) Langland, (f) Langham.

If students do poorly on the test, another period is spent reviewing the "Introduction to the Short Story."

2. When the introductory material has been covered, the first story is assigned: "Read Washingon Irving's 'The Devil and Tom Walker' for tomorrow." The next day the teacher begins the questioning: "Where and when does the story take place?" "Whose wealth lay buried where?" "What did Walker and his wife quarrel about?" "What does Tom uncover at the fort?" "Whom does he meet there?" "How does Irving describe the devil?" "How did Deacon Peabody acquire his wealth?" "By what name does Tom call the devil?" "Was Tom afraid of the devil?" "What kind of an agreement did he make with the devil the first time he met him?" "What happened to Tom's wife?" "What did Tom find in the checkered apron?" "Did he feel good or bad about the loss of his wife?" "When Tom meet the devil a second time, what does Tom agree to do?" "What kind of customers did Tom have?" "What did Tom do with his wealth?" "How did Tom try to avoid paying the devil his due?" "What happens when Tom says to a customer, 'The devil take me . . .'"? "What happened to his bonds and mortgages? gold and silver? horses? house?" "What is the moral of the story?" "Did you like the story?" When the last question has been answered, another story is assigned, followed by another barrage of questions, and so on, until the last story has been processed. Short objective quizzes break the monotony somewhat, and a long objective quiz ends the unit.

Various verse and/or prose versions of many of the world's great short stories entertained and inspired listeners at family fireplaces and in banquet halls long before they were written down. For example, the narrative poems (short stories) about Greek heroes in the *Iliad* and *Odyssey* were sung by minstrels like Phemios Terpiadês for hundreds of years before they were finally recorded and became the core of the academic curriculum of Greek citizens' sons.

Let your students leave the textbook for a while and become listeners once again. Play a recording of an author reading his own short story. There are many choices: Robert Benchley, Erskine Caldwell, J. Frank Dobie, Shirley Jackson, Dorothy Parker, S. J. Perlman, Leo Rosten, Dylan Thomas, Eudora Welty, W. Somerset Maugham, Katharine Anne Porter, William Saroyan, and John Steinbeck. Or play one of the many fine stories of well-known authors recorded by Michael Redgrave, Burgess Meredith, Basil Rathbone, E. G. Marshall, Henry Morgan, Julie Harris, James Mason, Raymond Massey, Julie Haydon, Ralph Bellamy, or Jason Robards, Jr. (Recordings by these people are listed in *Listening Library*, a free catalog available at Listening Library, Inc., 1 Park Avenue, Old Greenwich, Connecticut 06870.)

TEACHING THE NOVEL

As when he handles other literary types, the teacher of the novel asks himself, "What should be my aims?" and "How can I best achieve them?" If his primary aim is to help students develop an appreciation of the novel which will persist throughout their lives, the selection of a novel becomes significant. In most schools tradition, exemplified by the class anthology, dictates the novel that gets five weeks or more of undivided attention. Most teachers, however, are free to choose novels for "outside" reading, especially if the school has a good library. If the school library has few novels, perhaps each student can buy one or more paperbacks to be shared with classmates.

In many schools, two novels receive the full treatment: *Silas Marner* and *David Copperfield*. In one school practicing homogeneous grouping, Esther Forbes' *Johnny Tremain* keeps "slow" tenth graders occupied for eight weeks. How can teachers and students spend two months on *Johnny Tremain* without reading it backwards? The teacher gives a quick daily quiz—five to ten objective questions—on several pages assigned the preceding day. The quiz is graded in class. The teacher then asks each student, "Your grade?" and enters it in his black book.[3] When the grades are recorded, oral quizzing begins in earnest. By the end of the period, a series of searching recall questions has led the students to paraphrase the several pages assigned the preceding day. Questions begin with *Who, When, What, Where,* almost never with *Why.* At the end of each chapter, students are rewarded with a twenty-five-item objective test.

[3]Many teachers use the same time-consuming technique after spelling tests have been graded in class.

Before *Johnny Tremain* is put to rest, they are subjected to a fifty-item review test that would have stumped Esther Forbes.

What are some alternatives to the full-treatment approach? If *Silas Marner* is listed in the eleventh-grade syllabus as *the* novel, the teacher can help students get under way with it by devoting a period to reading aloud the pedestrian parts of the first and second chapters. He can give them information about characters, setting, and plot (without giving it away) that will whet their interest. He can also provide for each chapter several discussion questions which highlight the narrative thread of the story and relate the characters and their behavior to the students' lives.

Instead of devoting each class session to discussions and tests, part or all of two or three periods a week can be spent in silent reading, with the teacher available to help students who are having difficulties. By being given class time for reading, almost everyone should be able to read *Silas Marner* in two weeks or less. Students who read the novel in a few days can meet with the teacher during a silent reading period to demonstrate their understanding of the novel, and can then be helped to choose additional novels by George Eliot or another author.[4] (The same procedure—excluding class discussions—can be followed with the supplementary novels students read.) Everyone will, of course, participate in the class discussions. And instead of the customary objective tests, students can be asked to write an answer to one or more discussion questions:

1. Why did Silas become, but not remain, a miser and recluse?

2. The author presents a contest between good and evil, with good the victor. (a) Explain how and why evil loses and good wins in the novel. (b) Why is it difficult to support the following statement: "Silas was completely good and Dunstan and Godfrey were completely evil"?

3. If you found yourself in Silas' predicament—unjustly accused of theft—would you do what he did? In defending your "Yes" or "No" answer, include an explanation of what Silas did.

4. Explain in detail why *Silas Marner* would or would not make an effective movie or television play.

Some senior high schools schedule courses in the novel that shun the daily assignment-test-discussion pattern. In one school which assigns students to academic, average, and slow classes on the basis of I. Q., reading, and mathematics scores, students placed in the average group spend one semester in an English class devoted almost exclusively to the silent reading of novels. Only Marjorie Kinnan Rawlings' *The Year-*

---

[4]They might enjoy reading an hilarious satirization of *Silas Marner* in Richard Armour, *The Classics Reclassified* (New York: McGraw-Hill Book Company, Inc., 1960), pp. 109–22.

ling and William Saroyan's *The Human Comedy* are read by all students, then discussed in class. During the remainder of the semester, class time is spent in silently reading books selected by students with the help of the teacher.

When a student completes a book, he meets with the teacher in a corner of the room or in the hall for a brief discussion of the book and his future reading. In helping with these choices, the teacher's primary concern is to match the student's interests and abilities with books worth reading. Teacher and students have the advantage of an excellent school library and a paperback bookstore within three blocks of the school. Grades are based on written tests on *The Yearling* and *The Human Comedy* and oral quizzes on the books the student selects.

The course contributes more to making readers out of students than the traditional assignment-test-discussion courses, because the students are relaxed. In the brief individual oral discussion of books students chose to read, the teacher, probably not having read many of the books and pressed for time, asks a question or two about the purpose of the author and the roles of the main characters, or just "Why did you like or dislike the book?" How many adults would continue to read novels if they were not only subjected to detailed objective tests on every chapter and on the whole novel, but had to write a ten-page report on the setting, plot, and characters?

When you teach the novel, you and your students may be restricted considerably by departmental requirements, but there are usually opportunities to borrow appealing supplementary novels from the school and city libraries. If there are no restrictions on students' buying paperbacks, you can quickly build an excellent classroom library. Once you have arranged for adequate supplementary material, quell the urge to demand book reports and to administer detailed quizzes, and do not feel guilty of neglect if students read silently in class. If your conscience needs easing, circulate among them to give them the help they request.

TEACHING THE DRAMA

Although the narrative poem, the short story, the novel, and the drama have characteristics in common—setting, character, and plot—the drama is unique: it comes to life only when effectively presented on stage or screen. Is there a high school student who has not seen hundreds of movies and television plays? Some teachers still ignore this experience when introducing the drama. The Westerns many students enjoy are so much alike that they can give an accurate, detailed description of the typical plot, characters, and setting. The plot of a Western could be compared with that of *King Lear* to illustrate that the worst and the best in serious drama usually present a contest between good and evil.

Of course, *King Lear* has a plot and subplot which seem complicated to most high school students; but the plots in both Westerns and Shakespearean tragedies feature conflicts that culminate in violence and death. In Shakespeare, the good frequently die with the bad—a touch of realism that would bring an abrupt halt to all Western and detective serials.

Most English teachers would probably agree that their biggest problem with the drama is teaching Shakespeare's plays. Shakespeare wrote his plays for money. He hoped his sonnets and a few longer poems would bring him immortality. But how wrong he was. His sonnets receive some attention in eleventh or twelfth-grade literature classes, but his plays are required reading in almost all junior and senior high schools. Some junior high school teachers read all of *Julius Caesar* and *The Merchant of Venice* to their students, a rather monotonous routine; but they claim most of the class cannot read the plays. Others read to their students, or have them read, the versions of *Julius Caesar* and *The Merchant of Venice* in Lamb's *Tales from Shakespeare*.

If common sense, rather than tradition, determined the drama offerings in high schools, one-act modern plays would be used in the seventh and eighth grades, and continued into the ninth grade with the addition of a few modern three-act plays suitable for fifteen-year-olds. In the tenth and eleventh grades some full-length plays by Goldsmith, Sheridan, Ibsen, Galsworthy, Shaw, and others could be attempted by classes that seemed ready for them. Shakespeare would be confined largely to twelfth-grade classes, although able students on all high school levels should be encouraged to do supplementary reading which includes plays too difficult for their classmates. Why do we compel teenagers to read plays written for mature adults? In all subjects except high school literature, we begin with the simple and work up to the complex.

Since you will be required to teach Shakespeare to high school students, you will learn quickly that the abrupt approach to Shakespeare, "Read the first two scenes in *King Lear* for tomorrow," is similar to assigning a problem in calculus to students who know only simple arithmetic. One critic teacher who has helped hundreds of high school seniors appreciate *King Lear* uses approaches to the play that are worth testing. Because he considers the play itself the most absorbing thing for his students, he spends little time on Shakespeare as infant, whining schoolboy, lover, sonneteer, playwright, actor, and squire of Stratford, and even less on the Elizabethan theatre and times.[5] Since the skillful playwright

[5]This teacher once declared, "There is 'a time to be born and a time to die, a time to plant . . .'; but there is no time to burden students with bardolaters' books brimming with guesses about the life of the "Sweet Swan of Avon,' 'Star of Poets,' 'who struck the second heat upon the Muses' anvil,' shook a lightning lance 'at the eyes of ignorance.'" (The paeanic phrases are the work of the first and perhaps most reliable bardolater, Ben Jonson.)

uses the first scenes to give necessary background information, the teacher reads most of Act I to his students, stopping frequently to make explanations and answer questions.

In the first scene of *King Lear*, Shakespeare introduces all of the leading characters except Edgar and explains why Lear plans to divide his kingdom among his three daughters, why he gives all of it to Regan and Goneril, excluding Cordelia, and how Regan and Goneril begin to plot their villainy. Since the critic teacher realizes that students frequently have as much trouble differentiating among the characters as they do determining the plot, he points up their identities and their relationships with other characters. He does an equally careful job with Scene 2, the subplot, which resembles the main plot outlined in Scene 1.

Once the critic teacher has introduced the play, he gives his students class time to read it, helping them at the beginning of each period with the plot and the character relationships. He urges them to read the play through as rapidly as possible. On the first day, he distributes mimeographed discussion topics—several on each act—designed to help them understand the narrative thread, the behavior of the characters, and the relevance to today of many of the play's problems. To illustrate his discussion topics, here are some he based on Act I:

1. Why is the relationship between parents and children a common theme in plays, novels, and short stories?

2. What causes friction among brothers and sisters? parents and children? Why was there friction between Cordelia and her sisters Regan and Goneril even before she was rejected by her father?

3. Explain why you agree or disagree with the fool when he says to Lear, "Thou shouldst not have been old till thou hadst been wise"?

4. How is the subplot (Scene 2) different from the main plot (Scene 1)? similar?

5. How and why do Goneril and Regan humiliate Lear?

6. When Lear curses Goneril, he speaks two frequently quoted lines.[6] What are they, and what do they mean? Are they true? Defend your answer.

7. What are the most impressive lines in Act I? Prepare to defend your choices.

8. State in a sentence or two the narrative thread of Act I.

When most of the class has finished *King Lear*, he and his students

---

[6]"How sharper than a serpent's tooth it is
To have a thankless child!"

make plans to read the play in cast.[7] Parts are assigned in advance, with a different cast for each act. He uses the Laughton-Boyer approach: the characters read their lines without benefit of separate entrances, exits, and stage trappings. When the reading in cast is completed, several days are spent in discussing the questions distributed at the beginning of the unit and those raised by the students. Students' favorite lines in the play are also presented and discussed. Grades are based on (1) the in-cast reading performance, (2) participation in class discussions, and (3) a written examination taken from the discussion questions distributed by the teacher.

Since the time devoted to *King Lear* rarely runs over two weeks, the teacher and students have an additional three weeks to read other plays. Sometimes groups of students read and present scenes from other plays by Shakespeare; sometimes all of the students buy a paperback edition of Thornton Wilder's plays, scenes from which are presented by different groups of students; and occasionally students select and present scenes from recent Broadway plays.

The reasons for the teacher's success in teaching *King Lear* are not difficult to pinpoint. (1) He does not devote too much time to historical and biographical backgrounds; (2) he helps students get under way with the reading of the play; (3) he has them read the play in cast, with everyone participating; (4) he bases discussions on thought-provoking rather than recall questions; (5) he avoids objectives tests; (6) he does not stay with the play too long; (7) he gives students an overview of what will be attempted during the five-week period; and (8) he provides annotated lists of plays from various countries and times available in the school library and inexpensive paperback editions. His methods work as well with *Our Town* as with *King Lear*.

TEACHING THE ESSAY

Most high school students are more familiar with the essay than with prose fiction—the novel, the short story, and the drama—because they read essays, usually called articles, in newspapers and magazines[8] and write compositions on "essay topics."

A beginning teacher may conclude that his students' acquaintance

---

[7]For excellent shortened versions of "Romeo and Juliet," "Julius Caesar," "Hamlet," "King Lear," "Macbeth," and five of Shakespeare's comedies, see Lewy Olfson, *Radio Plays from Shakespeare* (Boston: Plays, Inc., 1958).

[8]Of 589 senior high school students polled in May, 1960, 186 claimed they read newspaper editorials, and 212 claimed they read newspaper columnists. Yes, 536 read the front page and 477 the comics (Morsey, *Seminar . . .* , p. 64).

with editorials, columns, and articles in newspapers and popular magazines will cause them to greet an essay unit with enthusiasm. That is rarely the case, especially when the anthology begins with Washington Irving and carries on through Emerson, Thoreau, and William James. Most of the essays students read voluntarily relate directly to current events that interest them, while those in an essay unit seem detached from today's happenings. And the broad vocabulary and leisurely rambling style of early essayists are seldom savored by students with limited vocabularies and patience. But the content of the best early essays can be related to students' own experiences by using carefully framed discussion questions. For example, let us take Emerson's "Gifts."[9] Here the writer lauds gifts which are beautiful and those created by the giver, and suggests that purely functional gifts (food and clothing) are an obligation man has toward his fellows. He agrees with the leper in Lowell's "The Vision of Sir Launfal" that "The gift without the giver is bare."[10] This difficult essay can be made meaningful to students by using discussion questions such as the following:

1. What kinds of gifts does Emerson approve in the introductory paragraph? in later paragraphs? Why do you agree or disagree with him?

2. Would Emerson approve of our giving Thanksgiving and Christmas baskets to the poor? Defend your answer. What do you think of the custom? Why? What would Emerson think of our foreign aid program? Would he support the Peace Corps? Defend your answer.

3. Have you ever given a gift that you made to a parent or relative? If so, why did the receiver probably value it more than a present from a store? If you have received gifts made by the giver, what was your reaction? Why?

4. Give illustrations to clarify the meaning of the following quotations, and explain why you agree or disagree with what they say: "The gift without the giver is bare," "It is better to give than to receive," "Don't look a gift horse in the mouth," "Beware of Greeks bearing gifts," and "He bites the hand that feeds him."

Since the essay makes up a section or appears under various theme headings in all high school and college literature anthologies, you have had the opportunity to observe a number of English teachers teach it. Which of their approaches seemed to promote appreciation? prevent it? Check your answers to the preceding questions against the ways of

[9]See Appendix 17.

[10]Stanza VIII.

promoting and preventing appreciation of the essay discussed below, and decide which of the ideas deserve to be tested in the classroom.

The approaches illustrated below seem to promote appreciation of the essay. Test some of them to see whether they produce desirable results for you and your students.

1. One critic teacher introduces a unit on the essay by discussing briefly with his students unassigned essays they have been reading recently. He then asks them to define the term *essay*. The definitions reveal that an essay may be a prose presentation of the feelings and ideas of an author on any subject, and it may be serious or humorous in offering information, arguments, descriptions, and criticism. Students are often unaware that newspaper editorials and columns are usually essays; most speeches and some letters can be similarly classified; diaries may include essays on a wide variety of subjects; and Clarence Day's *Life with Father* and Hendrik Van Loon's *The Story of Mankind* are books of closely related essays. The teacher next reads a few essays to students, making comments and asking questions as he reads. These may be from *The Reader's Digest, The Atlantic,* or *Harper's*; or he may read a humorous essay or two by Mark Twain, Clarence Day, Robert Benchley, James Thurber, or Emily Kimbrough.

2. Another critic teacher gives his students mimeographed discussion questions, several on each essay in a unit. The questions help students spot and challenge significant assumptions made by the essayist. The questions begin with: "Why do you agree or disagree with . . .?" "What are your arguments for . . .?" "What are your arguments against . . .?" "Why do you accept or reject the following statement by the author?" Such questions encourage students to bring their experiences and thinking to bear on the ideas of the essayist, instead of merely repeating what he said. In short, "What do you think, and why?" exemplifies the questions he asks. He is convinced that merely asking students to repeat a writer's ideas or feelings emasculates their minds.

3. Another teacher departs radically from the common pattern of limiting the essay unit to paragraph-by-paragraph paraphrasings of selections in the anthology. He distributes mimeographed annotated lists of essays easily accessible in books (including paperbacks) and magazines. He and many of his students also make available for classroom use their own books and magazines containing essays. Then, instead of devoting all their time to analyzing those in the anthology, students spend at least half their class time silently reading essays from the aforementioned sources. Occasionally a class session is devoted to discussing the essays students have read during their free reading periods, a procedure which

stimulates many students to read what their classmates found interesting and worthwhile.

4. Another teacher makes free reading material available to his students by loading on a cart thirty or forty volumes of essays selected from the school library. He takes them to the classroom and "sells" them to his students by commenting on the nature of the essays in each volume. When he makes a "sale," he has the student fill out the charge-out card in the back of the book. The charge-out cards are given to the librarian, who assumes the responsibility of seeing that the books are returned when due. (This procedure works equally well with poetry, plays, short stories, and novels.)

Some approaches that seem to prevent appreciation of the essay are:

1. A teacher may introduce an essay unit with, "Tomorrow we shall begin a unit on the essay. Read Addison's 'Sir Roger at Church' and 'Sir Roger at the Theatre.' They are very short. Read them carefully. I may give you a quick quiz on them at the beginning of the period." Why is such an introduction greeted with groans?

2. In discussing a specific essay with students, a teacher may dwell too heavily on exposing his students' ignorance of small details. Such a teacher seems convinced that anyone who does not recall everything the author said has not really read the essay. He uses forthcoming tests to motivate students.

3. The once-over-lightly approach is not a rarity. A teacher using it assigns several essays on Monday, and on Tuesday opens the class session with "Are there any questions?" If there aren't any, and there usually aren't, he may continue with "What does Addison say in 'The Coquette's Heart'?" If there is no response, he summarizes in a sentence or two what Addison said and presses on to the next essay. Sometimes unanswered questions lead to the command, "Spend the period reading the essay!"

4. A teacher may ask students to buy workbooks that accompany some literature anthologies. He will assign an essay today and have his students complete workbook exercises on it during the first half hour of the next period. He then has them exchange workbooks and grade the exercises as he reads the answers from a key. He takes up the workbooks, makes an assignment for the next day, and, if there is any time left, asks about difficulties encountered in the exercises. Such a teacher will welcome teaching machines for literature.

Workbook and handbook exercises and objective literature tests can be programed easily on computer teaching machines; but if we must introduce machines, why not resurrect the less expensive pinball machine?

It will have no greater influence than the computer teaching machine on a student's ability to speak and write clearly, thoughtfully, and correctly and to appreciate literature.

5. Some teachers assign an essay and spend the next class period having students read it aloud. Perhaps that is the only way reluctant readers get any reading done, but the procedure quickly becomes a boring pattern and tempts students to substitute in-class for out-of-class reading.

TEACHING LITERATURE—A SYNTHESIS

In this chapter, dozens of ideas on teaching the common literary types have been presented; but the ultimate goal and many of the methods are the same for all types. The ultimate goal is appreciation. A student who appreciates a literary selection responds to it with his intellect and emotions because it relates to significant past, present, and/or anticipated experiences. When he discovers that literature is a sound source of entertainment, information, and instruction, he is apt to become addicted to it.

A teacher meeting 100–150 students a day soon discovers that literature is not quickly made palatable by the adoption of methods promoted by English supervisors and authors of books and articles. Should he test them, he discovers they may need to be modified to fit students and facilities that differ from class to class and school to school. But if he persists in trying some of the recommendations of others, he will soon have ideas of his own to test. His chances of success are enhanced if he is obsessed with the one big problem confronting all English teachers: How can I help students appreciate literature? If he has this problem clearly and constantly in mind, he can then spend a lifetime gathering data (from books, magazines, colleagues, conferences, experiments); developing hypotheses; and testing hypotheses. Such a problem-solving procedure is used by effective teachers. They are motivated throughout their careers by the conviction that by testing new or revised ideas they can do a better job the next semester. However, most such teachers would agree with Virginia Church, who suggests that a utopian situation, if it were attainable, would soon pall:

> When I get UP There,
> I hope God will give me some cherubim to teach.
> Not just the goody good ones,
> But boys that slip away to play
> At marbles with the stars;
> A wistful child perhaps,
> Who's just a little frightened with the There.
> Maybe He might even allow

One young devil to slip in
So I could bring him up to a front seat
And feel at home.[11]

You may have few "young devils" to contend with; but remember even a master English teacher's soul is tried by reluctant readers, slow readers, and nonreaders.

BOOK LISTS

1. American Library Association, 50 East Huron Street, Chicago, Illinois 60611: *Patterns in Reading*, $2.25.
2. R. R. Bowker Company, 1180 Avenue of the Americas, New York, New York 10036: *Paperbound Book Guide for High Schools*.
3. Fader, Daniel N. and Elton B. McNeil, *Hooked on Books: Progress and Proof* (200 Madison Avenue, New York 10016: Berkley Publishing Company, 1968), $0.75.
4. National Council of Teachers of English, 508 South Sixth Street, Champaign, Illinois 61820: Richard S. Alm, ed., *Books for You* (grades 9-12), $0.90; G. Robert Carlsen, *Books and the Teen Age Reader*, paperback $0.60, hardcover, $3.95; Raymond C. Emery and Margaret B. Houshower, *High Interest-Easy Reading for Junior and Senior High School Reluctant Readers*, $1.00; Robert O'Neal, *Teachers' Guide to World Literature for the High School*, $2.95; John S. Searles, "More Sources of Free and Inexpensive Material," an annual article in the September issue of the *English Journal*, includes names of many publishers who provide free lists of books (mostly paperbacks) suitable for high school students; and Charles B. Willard, ed., *Your Reading—1966 Edition* (grades 7-9), $0.75.
5. See page 74 for names and addresses of book clubs.

ASSUMPTIONS ABOUT TEACHING POETRY, THE SHORT STORY, NOVEL, DRAMA, AND ESSAY

Prepare to explain why you accept or reject, wholly or in part, the following assumptions about teaching poetry, the short story, novel, drama, and essay:

Poetry

1. One can easily help students understand the differences between poetry and prose.

2. One can break down students' prejudices against poetry.

[11]Virginia Church, *Teachers Are People* (Santa Barbara: W. Hebberd, 1945), p. 82.

3. A short poem should be read aloud by students or the teacher before and after it is discussed.

4. When a department syllabus calls for "covering" forty poems in two weeks, one should not spend a period on a single poem.

5. Several principles of learning are illustrated in Professor Schneider's teaching of Browning's poetry (see page 82).

6. Mr. Brown's ten approaches to teaching poetry (see pages 82–84) are worth testing in the classroom.

The Short Story

1. The short story is not an American invention.

2. Short stories provide entertainment and instruction.

3. Essential background material should be taught students before they begin reading short stories.

4. Students can profit from the quizmaster approach illustrated on page 89.

5. All of the six procedures described on pages 85–87 are worth testing in the classroom.

6. During a poetry, short story, novel, or essay unit, students should devote two or three class periods per week to silent reading.

The Novel

1. Most teachers devote too much class time to a single novel.

2. Most novels can be related to students' experiences by using thought-provoking questions.

3. The novel presents problems for teachers and students not encountered in the short story.

4. A course based on silent, in-class reading of novels should be included in high school curricula.

5. It is easy to defend the novel's inclusion in the English curriculum.

The Drama

1. In teaching plays, the teacher can use students' experiences as television viewers.

2. Shakespeare's plays present teaching problems not encountered in modern plays.

3. In a drama unit, plays which all students are asked to read should be read in cast.

4. All of the approaches used by the "critic teacher," pages 93–95, are commendable.

The Essay

1. Emerson's "Gifts" can be made meaningful to students.

2. The approaches to teaching the essay which "promote appreciation," pages 97–98, are not wholly good.

3. The approaches to teaching the essay which "prevent appreciation," pages 98–99, are not wholly bad.

4. Carefully selected essays from magazines and newspapers (editorials and columns) should be read and discussed in the classroom.

IDEAS TO TEST

1. Appoint interested students to produce a mimeographed class anthology of favorite short poems. Each student selects one poem and explains in a paragraph why the poem is his favorite. To keep down expenses, limit the favorite poem and paragraph of comment to one page. Have students select the cover page for the anthology from several created and submitted by classmates. Students are usually willing to bear the cost, approximately thirty cents, of such a publication.

2. Require each student to develop a personal anthology of ten or fifteen favorite poems, with no poem running more than a page or two. Poems could be accompanied by a paragraph of comment by the student.

3. Have students present, with or without comments, several of their favorite lines from poems they read during a poetry unit.

4. Accumulate a personal anthology of several hundred short poems to draw on when you need supplementary poems for classroom use. Such an anthology makes suitable supplementary poems easily accessible. Whenever you run across a short poem you think students might enjoy, add it to the anthology.

5. If a number of students voluntarily write poems, make a mimeographed anthology of their work available to them and their classmates. You must, of course, obtain permission to include their poems in the anthology.

6. Schedule a tape-recording session at which all students and the teacher record one or more of their favorite short poems. Should some students fear recording poems in front of others, provide privacy somehow. Let students hear the recording; then discuss with them how they can improve their reading of poetry.

7. If you read poetry well, tape-record your students' favorite poems with or without comments. Such a tape can prove useful when you cannot meet your classes. Furthermore, students can enjoy the master's voice even when he has an acute case of laryngitis.

8. Poems like "Lord Randal" and Robert Frost's "The Death of the

Hired Man" lend themselves beautifully to dramatization. Select effective student readers for the parts.

9. Choose poetic portraits of happy and unhappy people from William Shakespeare, Robert Browning, A. E. Housman, Edwin Arlington Robinson, Edgar Lee Masters, Edna St. Vincent Millay, Robert Frost, Carl Sandburg, and W. H. Auden; have small groups of students present them in the manner of the Broadway dramatization of Edgar Lee Masters' *Spoon River Anthology*.

10. Ask students to explain why they accept or reject, wholly or in part, the following assumption: In his "Seven Ages of Man" (*As You Like It*, Act I, Scene 7), Shakespeare draws an excellent portrait of Renaissance man; and in "The Unknown Citizen," W. H. Auden does the same for modern man.

11. Use the few minutes occasionally left at the end of a class period to read informally a short poem or two. Most students like poetry when there is no pressure to remember what the poet wrote.

12. Test in your own classroom the ideas on teaching poetry illustrated in Mr. Brown's ten techniques, pages 82–84.

13. Use the Teen Age, Campus, or American Education Publication book clubs.

14. Two critic teachers were given permission by their principals to use four-dollar book-rental fees to buy for each of their students paperback copies of a novel and one collection each of plays, short stories, poems, and essays. Both teachers and students appreciated the variety of material the four dollars provided. And the students were delighted to become book owners. A teacher whose principal permits experimentation could use four dollars from each one of thirty students to buy thirty different novels, thirty different collections of short stories, etc., i.e., build a classroom library of 150 paperbacks that would meet the interests and abilities of almost all his students.

15. Keep a display stand in your classroom filled with paperbacks suitable for high school students. Sell them at cost. (The book distributor will provide the rack.)

16. Ask students to place in the classroom chalk trough books they are willing to share with classmates.

17. Encourage students to clip from newspapers and magazines references to writers and their works. Select items from the clipped materials for comment and bulletin board displays.

18. Abstract from *TV Guide*, or a similar publication, a list of coming television programs which relate to literature, mimeograph it, and distribute it to students. Follow up in class to see how many students gave up a favorite program to listen to a prominent poet or a fine play. To

insure a good response to their recommendations, some teachers assign television programs.

19. A few teachers ask students to contribute towards class subscriptions to one or more of the following magazines: *Saturday Review, Harper's,* or *The Atlantic.* Some teachers encourage students to make available for classroom use some of the magazines received in their homes.

20. When available, occasionally use outstanding recordings of books, plays, poetry, essays, folk music, and folklore. A free catalog of recordings available for sale is published by Listening Library, 1 Park Avenue, Old Greenwich, Connecticut 06870. It lists recordings of (1) Louis Untermeyer's paperback anthology, *A Treasury of Great Poems*; (2) most of Shakespeare's plays (complete); (3) readings of their own works by many prominent authors; (4) full-length books (*The Call of the Wild, The Red Badge of Courage,* etc.); (5) famous speeches; (6) some of Emerson's essays, poems, and speeches.

21. Have students present a scene or two from each of several plays which had a successful run on Broadway within the last ten years. Have a narrator summarize the scenes not read.

22. Provide students with discussion topics on assigned readings. Both high school and college students have told me that such questions help them appreciate literature.

23. Some teachers write on the blackboard every day a famous line or two from literature. An inexpensive source of famous lines is Permabook's paperback *The Shorter Bartlett's Familiar Quotations,* which runs the gamut—from Edgar Guest's "It takes a heap o' livin' . . ." to Samuel Johnson's "A decent provision for the poor is the true test of civilization."

24. The best source of "Ideas to Test" is the *English Journal,* published ten times a year by the National Council of Teachers of English, 508 South Sixth Street, Champaign, Illinois 61820. Membership is three dollars per year for students, seven dollars per year for teachers. The Council provides a free pamphlet, *Resources for the Teaching of English,* which lists books, research reports, pamphlets, filmstrips, recordings, literary maps of many states, and annotated book lists for high school students. Most of the items are available to members at discount prices.

25. Instead of the usual teacher-student discussion of literature, divide students into groups of four or five, and have them discuss among themselves a selection they have read in common or report briefly to fellow students on their free reading.

26. Have interested students write epilogues for plays, short stories, and novels.

27. Ask students to write a paragraph explaining why they agree or disagree with a controversial idea in a literary selection. Read aloud and discuss the paragraphs.

28. Have a student imagine he is the leading character in a novel, play, or short story, and have him write a personal letter, humorous or serious, to the class giving interesting sidelights about his ideas, behavior, and experiences.

29. Ask students to write brief unsigned answers to two questions: "What is literature? In what ways has reading literature benefited you?" The answers will prove interesting and enlightening.

Since what students know and how they feel interests most teachers, more of them might ask questions which reveal such matters. Most students are flattered when asked for their opinions. Other questions that bring useful information are: "How much time did you spend last week voluntarily reading (1) books, (2) magazines, (3) newspapers?" "What did you read voluntarily?" "How much time did you spend last week watching (1) television, (2) movies?" "Which television programs and movies did you see?" "Which of the following newspaper sections do you read regularly: (1) front page, (2) comics, (3) ads, (4) women's page, (5) sports, (6) editorial, (7) financial, (8) theatre, (9) columnists?" "What are your favorite school subjects, and why?" "Which newspapers do you have in your home?" "Which magazines do you have in your home?" Whenever you feel the questions pry, have students hand in unsigned answers.

30. To replace the usual lengthy book reports on outside reading, have students keep a reading diary which includes the name of the literary selection and the author, a one-sentence statement of the theme or narrative thread, and a one or two-sentence evaluation. If diary items are recorded on 3″ x 5″ cards, they can be filed and made available to the class.

31. Give students occasional opportunities to discuss informally the unassigned books they are reading.

32. To determine quickly whether students have grasped the meaning of a short story, novel, or play, have them write a single-sentence statement of the narrative thread.

33. Ask students to share favorite short literary selections with classmates by reading them aloud and explaining why they are favorites.

34. Provide students periodically with opportunities to (1) present to the class lines from prose and poetry which they memorized voluntarily and (2) explain why they chose them.

35. Base a debate on a controversial issue presented in an essay.

36. Have a panel respond to a controversial essay.

37. Substitute for the popular many-item objective tests on literature one or two essay questions.

38. Give students an overview of the aims, content, and methods of each literature unit.

6

Helping Students Write Effectively

Before reading this chapter, formulate clear, defensible answers to the following questions. After reading it, prepare to explain why you changed or retained your answers.

1. Should you have thirty students in each of five classes, how would you go about teaching them to write clearly, thoughtfully, and correctly?

2. Why do you write? How did you learn to write well enough to maintain your status as an English major?

3. If you say to a high school student, "Your composition reflects originality and imagination," what do you mean?

4. What are your opinions about the value of handbook, wordbook, and workbook exercises in teaching written composition?

5. If you were asked to teach a five-week unit in written composition, what would be your aims, and how would you achieve them?

PROMISING PRACTICES

One teacher who uses effective practices is Mr. Johns, whose ideas on teaching written composition are illustrated in the following activties:

1. When Mr. Johns begins a composition unit, he asks his students, "Why do people write?" Their answers reveal that people write to influence, inform, keep records, share strongly-held feelings and ideas, clarify thoughts, make a living, and get reactions from readers. When he asks, "How did writing originate?" students share information about the sign

and symbol systems of American Indians and other early peoples. They also discuss why spoken language preceded written language; the great value of written language in passing on man's social heritage; the influence of the printing press in providing educational opportunities for more people; and the role of books, magazines, and newspapers in today's world.

Another question that Mr. Johns always asks, "When and why do you write?" is usually answered with, "I write only in school or when my parents insist I answer Aunt Lucy's letter." A few students correspond regularly with foreign students, some write an occasional letter to a newspaper or magazine editor, a few girls write notes in class to friends, and one or two girls keep a diary. When asked why they do little voluntary writing, most of them confess their troubles with spelling, punctuation, and capitalization. They feel inferior in written composition, resulting perhaps from seeing their papers bleed with red ink from teachers' pens.

When Mr. Johns asks how originality and imagination are reflected in writing, most of his students insist that the two qualities are unattainable by amateurs. They associate originality with something completely new, and imagination with science fiction, Poe's short stories, and horror movies. They seem skeptical when Mr. Johns tells them that their writing is likely to show imagination and originality when they express clearly and honestly what they think or feel about a topic. He asks why each generation takes a fresh look at the ideas in the literature of the past and decides that some of them need reinterpreting. Change, they discover, is as certain as death and taxes.

Furthermore, they learn that the writer whom critics compliment on his originality is usually the first to admit his debt to those who preceded him, just as Salk shared with his predecessors and colleagues the credit for developing a polio vaccine. When Mr. Johns asks, "Who has recently had a completely new idea on any subject?" students begin to understand that originality in writing can be achieved by one who personally interprets an idea that has very likely had a long history. Imagination seems less forbidding when they realize it is not necessary to equate it with what never has been or will be. They become aware, too, that there is no imagination and originality in the work of a writer who parrots someone else's ideas. The foregoing discussion injects confidence into students who had previously concluded that the terms are exemplified only by the writings of professionals.

2. Mr. Johns reads aloud some excellent, good, and poor compositions written by former students and asks why they are effective or ineffective. If his students are unable to evaluate them, he indicates the differences among the themes in organization, sentence structure, clarity, thought, originality, and style.

3. On the second or third day, Mr. Johns has his students write in class a mailable one-page letter to a friend, pen pal, or relative. He has discovered that the best way to uncover quickly his students' composition strengths and weaknesses is to have them write a letter, rather than take an English placement test. He assigns a letter because their familiarity with the form makes them unafraid of the assignment. By analyzing the letters, he determines quickly the classwide and individual instruction needed to improve content, organization, sentence structure, paragraphing, usage, spelling, punctuation, and capitalization.

4. Knowing that most students have trouble deciding what to write about, Mr. Johns spends a period or two discussing possible material for essays (articles, diaries, editorials, and columns), short stories, poems, letters, and brief dramatic sketches. He first asks them to list in their notebooks subjects from which specific material can later be drawn. The students quickly suggest thirty or forty subjects—sports, school, television, transportation, communication, girls, boys, jobs, books, etc.—but they slow down when asked to supply topics or titles which can be handled adequately in a paragraph or short theme. Previously suggested topics must be made more specific. For example, the student interested in air travel can be helped to narrow his subject to "A Rocket Ride to Rotterdam in 1990."

Since most students prefer to write essays rather than poems or short stories, he illustrates the essay's organization by reading essays of former students, magazine essays, and short traditional essays. Students are surprised that these writers normally follow a simple three-part organizational pattern: (1) an introductory paragraph revealing their purpose in writing the essay; (2) a series of paragraphs developing in some detail what the first paragraph outlined in the briefest fashion; and (3) a closing paragraph giving a summary, an apt quotation, a suggestion—anything impressing the reader as a reasonable, perhaps anticipated, conclusion.

Students are urged to select quickly a tentative topic for their first essay. Several topics volunteered by students are written on the blackboard, and each one is analyzed: (1) Why is it too broad, too narrow, or just right? (2) Why does or doesn't it attract the reader's attention? After a discussion of the questions, Mr. Johns suggests that students begin planning the introductory paragraph and the main body of their essays. While they are so occupied, he helps with necessary revisions students whose tentative topics were not discussed.

5. For the next few days, Mr. Johns' students work on their essays[1] in and out of class. He helps them as a group and individually. If, as he circulates among them, he discovers that most of them need help with

[1]Several may be working on short stories, poems, or dramatic sketches.

the introductory paragraph, he will involve the whole class in a discussion of this section. Effective introductory paragraphs written by students are placed on the blackboard to initiate discussion. But he usually spends most of his time helping individual students. Students are encouraged to use the tools of the writer—dictionaries, thesauri, handbooks—available in the classroom.

6. Early in the writing unit, Mr. Johns asks whether each student is willing to spend twenty-five to thirty cents for a mimeographed anthology of the class's essays, poems, short stories, letters, and short dramatic sketches. When students approve such a project, as they always do, he explains that (1) at the end of the unit each student will select from what he has written one page of material he wants included; (2) students interested in creating a cover for the anthology may submit unsigned covers (the one considered best by the class is used); and (3) an editorial board of three selected by the teacher will edit all contributions, develop an attractive format, and provide a typewritten rough draft to the class for final corrections and minor revisions.

7. Within a few days after his students write letters (see 3 above), Mr. Johns reads them and presents his findings to the class. First, he asks students to point up the strengths and weaknesses of a number of letters (excellent, good, and poor) that he reads to the class without identifying the writers. Second, he bases class instruction on common serious errors which interfere with clarity. Poorly organized paragraphs, involved sentences, sentence fragments, unsupported assumptions, and sentences omitting essential punctuation are placed on the blackboard and edited by students. Third, he puts on the blackboard sentences that illustrate the most common serious errors in usage: nonagreement between subject and verb or pronoun and antecedent, incorrect forms of personal pronouns, and double negatives. Fourth, as students revise their letters he helps them with their individual problems. Fifth, he calls attention to the notation "Rewrite" which he made on some of their letters. Letters to be rewritten, corrected, or revised are due the next day.

8. Instead of dictating or distributing spelling lists, Mr. Johns asks students to enter in their notebooks the correct spellings of words they misspell in compositions and tests. Once a week, while the class is working on their assignments, he asks individual students to spell certain words from their lists to see whether they have mastered them.

9. Mr. Johns requires all students to bring to class a rough draft of their compositions the day before the final draft is due. The class is divided into groups of four or five to check each other's papers for strengths and weaknesses in organization, content, sentence clarity and effectiveness, paragraphing, vocabulary, usage, punctuation, capitalization, and spelling.

He says that the first few times students make these evaluations, they detect only errors in the last four items. However, toward the end of the unit the favorable results of in-class emphasis on organization, content, and sentence effectiveness are apparent when the small groups edit each other's compositions. The advantages of small-group editing of rough drafts are that students do better work when their papers have a student audience, they improve their editing ability by observing capable classmates, and the teacher can read the final drafts quickly because many of the errors were corrected during the editing session.

10. Mr. Johns believes that giving students a wide audience is one of the best ways to motivate them to improve their composition skills. The small-group editing sessions increase the audience, especially when students are part of a different group each time rough drafts are edited, but he also reads to his class many of the final drafts. He does not make the mistake of reading only the papers of two or three outstanding students. During the writing unit, everyone has one or more of his compositions read to the class. Mr. Johns frequently interrupts his reading with, "Is this sentence (or paragraph) clear? accurate? supported with evidence?" Students learn that clarity, honesty, and supported generalizations are valued highly by their teacher.

11. Mr. Johns explains at the beginning of the composition unit that each student must keep a file of his compositions—rough drafts, final drafts, rewritten final drafts if any—so he and the student can check periodically the progress being made. A final short paper, written in class, is compared with the letter written under similar conditions early in the unit. The grade for the unit is based on the compositions in the file and the final paper written in class. Students like the emphasis placed on performance, not on their ability to place in proper places in workbook and handbook exercises single, double, and triple underlinings, S's, P's, T's, F's, X's, plus signs, minus signs, check marks, circles, and parts-of-speech labels.

After observing Mr. Johns a number of times, one is impressed by his students' enthusiasm and progress. When I asked, "How do you find time to read all their papers?" he replied, "Except for the short letter students write in class early in the unit, I don't spend much out-of-class time on their papers. I can tell from reading their letters what help they need. By reading and discussing the letters and compositions written by former students, the class soon understands that a composition must say something worth saying and say it clearly. But I save the most time by helping students plan and write. I see their compositions at various stages and offer suggestions whenever necessary. Also, the student editing sessions reduce errors in spelling, punctuation, and capitalization. By the time I read the final drafts, most of the minor errors and some of the weaknesses in content, organization, and sentence structure have been eliminated. It is surprising how quickly I can grade a set of papers when I can concentrate almost exclusively on content and organization. I often grade the final drafts in class while students are working on their next writing assignment. I write a brief comment on each paper praising the composition's strengths and calling attention to its weaknesses. Students are encouraged when their final drafts are not heavily marked with red."

Mr. Johns has an answer for teachers who say, "Yes, students cannot learn to write well unless they practice under the supervision of someone who can help them; but I just don't have time to grade the papers." It is "You can stop grading themes outside of class and still give students guided writing experiences—by limiting the length of the compositions to a page or even a paragraph, and by frequently evaluating papers the way teachers evaluate talks: as students read their compositions, the teacher grades them on content, organization, vocabulary, sentence structure, and usage."

In *The Reading Interests of Young People*, George W. Norvell contends that even students deficient in reading speed and comprehension will read difficult books when the subject matter attracts them. Similarly, students write best when they feel strongly about a subject or when their writing serves a purpose: a personal response to a controversial issue; a letter to a friend, relative, or pen pal; or a poem, essay, or short story for a school publication.

A senior high school class reacted in writing to a police-enforced ten o'clock curfew law for teen-agers. Students read their compositions with enthusiasm, and the audience was absorbed in the arguments for and against the law. When the subject was more controversial than it is today, equal interest was shown in compositions on teen-age dating. A teacher alert to teen-age problems can help students identify them and write about them. Some teachers have encouraged their students to correspond with foreign students. The names, countries, and ages of foreign students interested in writing to Americans appear frequently in *The Christian Science Monitor*.

One of the most interesting and worthwhile class sessions I ever observed arose from a student teacher's being interviewed by a group of senior high school journalism students. The student teacher had been a pianist with several name bands. The day before I observed his class, they had interviewed him about his experiences as a professional musician. The next day, several students read their feature articles based on the interview and had them criticized by fellow students. The writers were surprised most by the large number of inaccurate statements in their stories. All of them had listened and, they thought, recorded accurate notes the day before; but the variations (dates, names, events, and ideas) in the articles were alarming. In most composition classes, students' statements are rarely challenged. Too much attention is paid to form, too little to content. Should one attach more importance to the ribbon and wrappings of a package than to its contents?

Students spend many of their waking hours describing, explaining, arguing, asking, blaming, bragging, guessing, plotting, wishing, and daydreaming—communicating with others or with themselves. If a teacher can make communication in writing almost as satisfying as informal oral communication, the final compositions in a unit should elate rather than frustrate him. Remember, also, that students need an audience in addition to the teacher, and, certainly, failing a student because he misplaces a comma or misspells a word will turn his attention away from communicating something he wants to share with others to filling pages with inane error-free sentences.

QUESTIONABLE PRACTICES

When some junior high school English teachers are asked why their students spend many hours completing and checking handbook and workbook exercises, they say, "I want them to make a good showing on the objective English placement test they take when they enter senior high school." Answering the same question, senior high school English teachers say, "I want my students to do well on the college or university English placement tests." Heads of college and university English departments explain their use of objective English placement tests with "We don't have the time to read hundreds of themes"; or if they have been seduced by certain dispensers of objective tests, "The placement test tells us as much about a student's writing ability as a theme." If one suggests that knowing facts about English usage (many English placement tests are predominantly usage tests) does not guarantee writing ability, they resort again to the refrain, "Well, we just don't have time to grade hundreds of themes."

In some colleges, entering freshmen who place in the upper 25 percent on the English placement test are excused from a three or five-hour first course in composition. Many students so excused reveal themselves as "C" and "D" students in the second composition course. To excuse 25 percent of incoming college freshmen from a first course in English composition largely on the basis of what they know about English usage seems as illogical as freeing criminals who can recite from memory a minimum of seven and a half of the Ten Commandments. Even if knowledge about good usage did transfer automatically into speech and writing, is mere conformity to usage standards more important than clarity and thought in writing?

English teachers asked to explain why they avoid written composition activities in the classroom give one or more of the following replies: "If I tell students, 'Write a five-hundred-word theme for tomorrow,' I have over 150 papers to grade, which is impossible." "I believe the best way to prepare students to do well on objective college English placement tests is to have them master workbook and handbook exercises that approximate the content of the tests." "I don't feel qualified to teach composition; all of my college work, except freshman English, was in literature."

Although many English teachers conclude that devoting time to written composition is impossible because of heavy teaching loads or the need of workbook and handbook drills to prepare their students for a college entrance test, some teachers with 150–200 in five classes have students do considerable writing as shown above, while others keep them busy with workbook and handbook exercises. And they do not sacrifice clear eyes and pay astronomical light bills. Furthermore, their students do better on objective college entrance tests than those who are workbook and handbook addicts.

ASSUMPTIONS ABOUT TEACHING WRITTEN COMPOSITION

Prepare to explain why you accept or reject, wholly or in part, the following assumptions about teaching written composition:

1. Heavy teaching loads do not make it impossible for English teachers to test the assumption that students learn to write by writing frequently under the guidance of a capable teacher.

2. Weekly tests on spelling lists are an effective way of helping students eliminate spelling errors from their written work.

3. Instruction in grammar and usage should be based directly on strengths and weaknesses revealed in students' oral and written work, rather than on workbook and handbook exercises.

4. Errors students make in compositions should be tabulated and classwide instruction provided for the most common serious errors only.

5. Students' grades should be based on performance in written composition, not on skill in completing handbook and workbook exercises.

6. Individual instruction is indispensable in teaching written composition.

7. Content in written compositions is more important than form and usage.

8. Most students have ideas they enjoy sharing with others.

9. Colleges and universities should not blame high schools for entering freshmen's deficiencies in written composition.

10. People write primarily to influence others.

11. Some of the ideas on teaching written composition presented in this chapter are difficult to test in a high school classroom.

12. Diagraming sentences can help students improve their written composition skills.

13. People also communicate through painting, sculpture, woodworking, and sewing.

14. A composition teacher's work is done when he has marked students' errors in spelling, punctuation, and usage.

15. The basic assumptions in the following quotation are easy to defend:

> The Harvard Report *General Education in a Free Society* recommends "constant practice" as essential to improve writing in secondary schools. The experimental research of Lokke and Wykoff, reported in the *Review of Education Research*, measured the effect of increasing the amounts of writing practice: doubling it reduced failures 66% and improved grades 60%. The California Council survey collected the opinions of 430 experienced teachers and nationally known teacher-educators concerning the *approximate amounts* of writing practice that were considered necessary to develop the average pupil's competence in written expression in secondary school. These teachers believe that different grade levels require slightly different amounts of practice, from 150 words a week for freshmen to 350 words a week for seniors. They also observed that individual differences among pupils will justify more practice for some, less for others. *But the overall average amount recommended by most teachers is 250 words each week for each pupil.* Many recommend that some writing be done daily.[2]

16. "Ambiguous!" is the most serious adverse comment one can make about a written or oral statement.

17. Books on teaching English by Don Wolfe; Hans Guth; Abraham Bernstein; J. N. Hook; Walter Loban, Margaret Ryan, and James R. Squire; John S. Lewis and Jean C. Sisk; and Edwin H. Sauer (see Bibliography) include excellent suggestions on teaching written composition.

18. Everything has been said (Bruyère).

19. Some students have trouble with written composition because thoughts come faster than the pen can record them.

20. Most students deal in broad generalities when they write and speak, disregarding the dependence of effective communication on particulars.

[2]William J. Dusel, "Determining an Efficient Teaching Load in English," *Illinois English Bulletin*, Vol. 43, October, 1955, p. 4.

21. When writing came in, man's almost complete reliance on memory went out; but many teachers still teach as if there were no reference books.

22. Students should not be conditioned to believe that written and oral compositions can be easily classified under narration, description, exposition, or argumentation.

23. English teachers should have lay readers to help grade papers.

24. A careful evaluation of the paragraphs in Appendix 1, 2, 3, 4, or 5 will reveal to an English teacher what kinds of help the whole class and individual students need to improve their written composition skills.

25. There are reasons why students do not always believe a teacher who says, "Select composition topics that reflect your concerns, not mine."

26. Many teachers and parents find it difficult to take the ideas of young people seriously.

27. Making students' compositions bleed with red ink curbs their interest in writing.

IDEAS TO TEST

1. Have students submit a tentative topic before they begin developing it into a theme. Topics students choose are sometimes so broad they could not be covered adequately in a thick volume. There is a story of an ancient king whose writers produced a ten-volume history of mankind. The king, a busy man, told them five different times, "Boil it down!" He seemed satisfied when they finally gave him a one-sentence summation: "Man is born, he suffers, he dies."

2. Develop a file of good, average, and poor compositions written by your students. When you introduce a composition unit, read some of them to your students to illustrate different kinds of content, organization, and usage.

3. To discover your students' composition strengths and weaknesses at the beginning of a unit, have them write a brief composition in class.

4. Early in the unit, devote a period or two to helping students develop a list of forty or fifty subjects for compositions. Ask them to demonstrate how a dozen or more specific topics for compositions can easily be drawn from the subject "Space Travel." Illustrate on the blackboard how broad topics can be narrowed to permit a thorough treatment within the word limits set for the composition.

5. Since most students will choose to write essays rather than poems or short stories, base illustrations of the organization of typical essays on essays written by former students or those appearing in current magazines or the students' literature anthology. To save time, you may find yourself reading quite a few beginning and ending paragraphs and summarizing the material in between.

6. To motivate students, publish a mimeographed class anthology. Interest in such a project is heightened when every student's work is included. The cost can be kept down by allowing only one page per person and by having students edit, type, assemble, and distribute the anthology.

7. Make students reserve a page in their notebooks for the correct spellings of words they misspell in compositions and tests. Every week, quietly give an unannounced oral spelling test to each one of a half-dozen students while their classmates are working on assignments.

8. Give students a wide audience for what they write. Have them check each other's rough drafts in class, and devote considerable time to reading aloud compositions that illustrate their composition strengths and weaknesses.

9. Tabulate the errors students make in their compositions. Discuss with the class only common serious errors. Give individual attention to those whose errors are not classwide. Always turn to students' compositions—not workbooks, handbooks, and standardized tests—to discover the help they need with organization, content, sentence structure, vocabulary, usage, and mechanics.

10. Require students to keep a file of all rough drafts, final drafts, and rewritten compositions. Check each student's file periodically to measure his progress. But do not use the file as some college teachers do. They call it in at the end of the term to see whether the revisions requested on the final drafts were made. If students' revisions of final drafts are not due within a day or two, many of them will hurriedly make all of the revisions the day before the file is due—a practice that is of little, if any, benefit to them.

11. If your principal allows the purchase of paperbacks, ask students to buy a paperback dictionary; and, if shelf space permits, have them keep it in the classroom. An easily accessible dictionary is needed to develop the dictionary habit.

12. Ask students to double-space compositions and tests. Writing so spaced is easier to read, the teacher's marks and comments can be placed near the material that inspired them, and the students can easily insert revisions requested by the teacher. Book and magazine editors have long realized that single-spaced manuscripts do not give them room to work.

13. To achieve greater objectivity in grading students' compositions, use an essay evaluation form[3] that calls for an evaluation (poor, below average, average, above average, very good) of (1) usage, (2) punctuation, (3) sentence clarity and effectiveness, (4) vocabulary, (5) spelling,

---

[3]See example in Appendix 6.

(6) organization, (7) paragraphing, and (8) content. Such a form seems formidable, but teachers who use it claim it saves time. Students like it because it pinpoints their composition strengths and weaknesses. If each student were required to complete the form and attach it to the compositions he hands in, he might do more of the editing, leaving less for the teacher to do.

14. Check H. H. Remmers and D. H. Radler, *The American Teen Ager* (Indianapolis: The Bobbs-Merrill Company, Inc., 1957) as a source of issues of concern to teen-agers. The book is a mine of factual information about their feelings and thoughts about adults, schoolwork, marriage, religion, government, and delinquency—much of which can lead to excellent composition topics.

15. Students are pleased when a teacher occasionally submits for their evaluation something he wrote.

16. Begin a semester by having students write a letter to you on their interests, plans for the future, and academic problems. Write a letter to them on your educational background, teaching experiences, and academic and other interests.

17. Having students make daily one-paragraph entries in a journal or diary provides regular practice in writing which appeals to most students. Some teachers are able to check these brief entries in class while students are working on another assignment. An inexpensive shorthand notebook is suitable for such a journal.

18. Have some composition activities grow out of the students' required reading—evaluations, not rehashes, of literary selections.

19. Instead of teaching all of the grammar and usage in a handbook, give attention to serious usage weaknesses as they appear in students' speech and writing.

20. Require the careful revision of compositions. Too often students throw away compositions which took the teacher many hours to grade.

21. To save grading time, occasionaly ask students to read their compositions aloud; evaluate them as you would a talk.

22. Provide interested students with names, addresses, and ages of foreign students who want to correspond with them. *The Christian Science Monitor* is a free source of such names and addresses.

23. Examine an English placement test very carefully. Then ask yourself, "If I gave this test to a student, what would the results tell me about his ability to express himself clearly, thoughtfully, and correctly?"

24. At the end of a composition unit, give students an objective achievement test in English. Compare the scores on this test with the grades they made in the composition unit.

25. Have mimeographed, or copy on the blackboard, a student para-

graph dominated by primerlike sentences. Ask students to suggest changes which make for desirable sentence variety.

26. Write a subject and a predicate on the blackboard. Ask students to build a clear and interesting sentence by adding single word, phrase, and clause modifiers.

27. After grading a set of themes, ask yourself, "Have I done anything a proofreader could not have done?"

28. As you read a set of compositions, encircle sentences and paragraphs which illustrate composition strengths and weaknesses. Then mimeograph the encircled sentences and paragraphs exactly as the students wrote them. Devote a period or two to a discussion of the mimeographed material. Occasionally you may decide to mimeograph all the introductory paragraphs or closing paragraphs, and sometimes you may decide to mimeograph whole themes. (Numbering the sentences consecutively facilitates discussion.) The advantages of this method over the opaque projector or the blackboard are (1) it saves class time, (2) each student has before him a copy on which he may make notations and corrections, and (3) he can refer to it whenever he wishes. Its disadvantage is that most teachers do not have the necessary supplies, duplicating equipment, and time to type and run off stencils.

29. If you have the opportunity, ask a group of parents what they mean when they complain, "Schools should teach more grammar." You will find that their definitions of grammar are quite different from those of informed teachers.

30. To impress students with the value of spacing, punctuation, and capitalization, ask them to what extent the following passage simulating ancient Greek writing remains "Greek" to them.

youhavebeenexchangingletterswithapenpalwholivesineurope
youarealikeinageandsexinarecentletteryourpenpalmentioned
readinganarticleondatinginanamericanmagazineandheorsheis
verymuchinterestedinknowingmoreaboutwhatamericanteenagers
callgoingsteadywritealettertoyourpenpalexplainingwhatgoing
steadymeansamongamericanteenagersalsoexplaininyourletter
whatyouthinkaboutgoingsteadybesuretosupportyourideason
goingsteadywithreasonssinceyourpenpalprobablywouldnotknow
americanslangpleaseavoidusingslanginyourletter

31. Many teachers tap students' dormant writing talent by having them, once a semester, base a theme on a picture or pictures from newspapers, magazines, or collections of prints of art treasures of the world available in most college and city bookstores. While the whole class responds in writing to a single picture, some teachers provide music (a recording) that synchronizes with it. A student teacher was pleased with

the results of having his students write about his recording of sounds made by racing cars, a locomotive, an airplane, a power mower, the sea, animals, a baby, and birds.

32. Give students an objective look at paragraphs they have written by having the owner of a tape recorder tape them at home and play them back in the classroom.

33. Clip from newspapers and magazines sentences, paragraphs, or complete articles that decry or laud the behavior of teen-agers. Have interested students write responses.

34. If students' ideas seem completely illogical or distorted, quell the desire to demolish them. Submit them to the class for evaluation. Many students, especially the bright ones, are quick to sense and parrot the teacher's point of view.

35. If you have two classes quite similar in ability, give an attitude-toward-composition test and a diagnostic test (a letter) at the beginning of the unit. In the experimental class replace grades with written comments and students' evaluations. In the control class grade every piece of writing. At the end of the unit repeat the two tests given at the beginning of the unit. Compare the results and discuss them with your students.

7

Helping Students Speak Effectively

Before reading this chapter, formulate clear, defensible answers to the following questions. After reading it, prepare to explain why you changed or retained your answers.

1. What were the oral composition (speech) goals of your high school and college teachers? Why were they successful or unsuccessful in achieving them?

2. Why do you accept or reject, wholly or in part, the idea that separate units in oral composition are superfluous when written composition and literature units provide numerous opportunities for discussions and reports?

3. If you were to teach a unit in oral composition, what would be your aims, and how would you achieve them?

EMPHASIZING PERFORMANCE

A former colleague, a high school social studies teacher who taught one course in speech, always came back from speech contests toting trophies. I learned the reason for his students' good work when I substituted for him a few times. When I met his class the first time, I wondered whether his "You don't have to do anything; the class will run itself" was true. It was. The students spent the period giving and judging talks. The judgments were polite but frank. Criticism considered unjust was challenged by the speaker or his classmates.

At the first opportunity, I asked him whether his speech class was run by students throughout the semester. He said that he participated in evaluations of talks when he thought students had overlooked essentials or overemphasized nonessentials, and he provided those participating in debate with bibliographical items. He attributed their success in speech contests to classroom emphasis on performance rather than proficiency in passing tests on textbook material. No class time was spent in reading or discussing principles in speech manuals. Practice under the searching but sympathetic eyes of thirty students and one teacher stimulated everyone to do his best, then to improve upon it. They derived speech principles from a careful analysis of their own talks, then applied them.

Few English teachers teach even a single speech class, and winning events in speech contests is not the objective of those who once or twice a semester plan a unit in oral composition. But many teachers and their students would find an oral composition unit more interesting and worthwhile if the emphasis were placed on performance—not on learning the rules of effective speaking, which takes so much time that students seldom get more than one opportunity to speak.

INCIDENTAL INSTRUCTION OR SEPARATE UNITS?

Some English teachers believe oral composition units are indefensible. They insist that putting reading, writing, speaking, and listening into separate compartments is the most illogical practice ever contrived by man. They give evidence to support their belief that all writing, speaking, and listening experiences should be related to literature. But is that possible without seeming to have as one's goal making literary critics out of students? They could also insist that all high school teachers teach these four skills. Perhaps English as a separate subject might be expendable if social studies teachers included literature in history courses.

The arguments against categorization are convincing, but the trend is toward segmenting the traditional compartments. Many English teachers spend a week or more on each one of the following: (1) each part of speech; (2) punctuation; (3) capitalization; (4) the library, without visiting it; (5) handbook material on writing; (6) handbook material on speaking; and (7) précis writing. Most teachers spend an hour a week—totaling almost two months of class time a year—dictating and checking spelling lists consisting of words many students have been able to spell for eight years or more. Isn't it likely that students' language skills cannot be improved unless classroom emphasis is on practice guided by a competent teacher? This means one who measures carefully, through performance tests, their present ability to read, write, speak, and listen, and then bases instruction directly on the strengths and weaknesses revealed by the tests. Wasn't Sophocles right when he said, "One must learn by doing the thing . . ."?

Most teachers support traditional separate units in oral composition, assuming that students must occasionally give undivided attention to improving their ability to speak well. They admit that they limit oral composition in most literature classes to discussions and reading aloud, with attention normally centered on a literary selection—not on voice, posture, usage, and the content and organization of students' oral contributions. They claim that the idea of teaching oral composition incidentally appears impressive in discussions or on paper, but that it is difficult, if not impossible, to carry out in the classroom.

PROMISING PRACTICES

The oral composition goals and methods of Mr. Paul, a critic teacher who is now retired, impressed most observers. His students were highly motivated by his goal—to help them improve their ability to speak clearly, thoughtfully, and correctly—and the following content and methods which he used to achieve it:

1. Mr. Paul opened an oral composition unit by asking, "Why do people converse, debate, and make speeches?" Students' answers indicated that people use spoken language to inform, get information, influence, record, enjoy the sound of their voices, and curb loneliness. When asked what they notice about television and school convocation speakers, they mentioned physical characteristics, mannerisms, pronunciation, enunciation, vocabulary, poise, nervousness, sincerity, insincerity, posture, content, and "bad grammar." Asked why they listen to some speeches on television and turn off others, students said that they continue to listen when the content interests them, the speaker is a well-known person, or members of the family make the choice of another program impossible.

As the discussion continued, most students agreed that a speaker's enunciation, pronunciation, and usage distract a listener only when they do not conform to his standards of what is desirable. Others felt that what a person says, not how he says it, is of primary importance, although they admitted that even illiterate usage may sometimes increase a speech's effectiveness. Most of the students agreed that when a speaker is introduced as an educated man to an educated audience, he is handicapped unless he conforms to their language standards. One student pointed out, however, that a speaker who never duplicates his uneducated audience's illiterate usage does not make himself conspicuous. One is not handicapped by using standard usage among those whose speech is substandard.

At the end of one first-day session, an observer asked Mr. Paul, "I

IMPROVING ENGLISH INSTRUCTION

know you were trying to bring out the usefulness of speech skills, and I believe you were successful; but what if you had a class of slow students?" He replied, "Although perhaps 70 percent of the students in many high schools come from low-income homes where they seldom hear the dialect of educated people, many of them can be persuaded that clear, thoughtful, and correct speech has practical value even for those who do not plan to finish high school. In our downtown senior high school, many students with low academic ability elect speech. Their teacher attributes their interest to the minimum of book learning required; the emphasis on developing skills they may find useful in unions, churches, and other organizations; and the practice of basing grades on performance rather than essay and recall tests."

2. The second day Mr. Paul told his students he had prepared a five-minute speech on "How I Used the Scientific Method to Get the Family Car." He suggested that since they would evaluate his talk and the oral presentations of their fellow students, they might develop a code for criticism to remind them that criticism should be constructive and sympathetic. In thirty minutes, the following code was developed:

A Code for Criticism

1. Criticize others as you would have them criticize you. Avoid disparaging or offensive remarks.

2. Support favorable and unfavorable judgments with facts, and suggest how shortcomings may be overcome.

3. Do not repeat criticism made by others.

4. Do not overemphasize insignificant strengths or weaknesses.

Mr. Paul also distributed[1] the following mimeographed rating form (see page 124) which students could use if they wished.

Mr. Paul explained the five items in the rating form as goals to be achieved, and suggested that students be prepared to defend their check marks under *Excellent, Good,* and *Fair.* He then gave a humorous talk on how, as a teen-ager, he was influenced by a science teacher's clear illustrations of the scientific method (define problem, gather data, develop hypotheses, test hypotheses) to use the method to get his father's permission to drive the family car to a school dance. The students enjoyed the talk, especially the part where Mr. Paul's carefully developed hypotheses failed. In their evaluations, several students enjoyed telling about hypotheses which had produced permission to use the family car.

[1]Some teachers claim that having students themselves develop a rating form has a favorable effect on their talks.

Rating Form for Talks

	Excellent		Good		Fair	
	Talk 1	Talk 2	Talk 1	Talk 2	Talk 1	Talk 2
1. Choice of Subject (audience appeal; appropriate for time allotted)						
2. Content (stimulating and fresh; assumptions reasonable and supported with evidence; original; thoughtful)						
3. Organization (beginning, middle, ending; unity, coherence, emphasis)						
4. Language (clarity; pronunciation; enunciation; voice; vocabulary; usage)						
5. Physical Presence (posture; eye contact)						

3. Mr. Paul spent the third class session helping students develop a list of subjects for talks, panels, interviews, conversations, and dramatizations. He reminded them that in a written composition unit they had learned to select and narrow a subject so it could be presented effectively in the allotted number of words. After thirty or more subjects had been suggested, he asked whether anyone had decided tentatively on a specific topic for his talk. Several students had, and were asked to write their topics on the blackboard. Mr. Paul asked, "Which topics seem suitable for a three-minute talk? Why?" The discussion which followed involved the interest appeal and wording of the topics and why they were too narrow, too broad, or suitable. He then asked his students to select by the next day a tentative topic for the kind of oral presentation they were interested in giving.

4. At the beginning of the fourth period, Mr. Paul asked his students to write on 3″ x 5″ cards which he distributed their tentative topics and whether a talk, panel discussion, interview, or dramatization was con-

templated. When he discovered that eight students were interested in panel discussions, he assigned, considering choice of topics and students' abilities, four students to Panel 1 and four to Panel 2. He asked them to meet immediately to elect a chairman, select a topic from those they had submitted, and assign each panel member specific responsibilities. He then asked the class to plan a beginning, middle, and ending for their topics while he consulted with students whose topics seemed to require revision. He told them he would spend the remainder of the period and whatever time was needed the next day helping individual students and those who were involved in group presentations. He also asked for volunteers to give talks two days hence.

5. Before the first talk Mr. Paul asked his students to turn to the code for criticism they had developed and then to the rating form he had distributed. He did not require them to complete the rating form for each talk, but suggested they use it to guide their evaluations. He made one additional suggestion: "After a topic has been presented by an individual or a group, feel free to ask a speaker to clarify or defend what he said"—a suggestion which not only led to many worthwhile discussions but also made speakers more careful about supporting assumptions with evidence, something seldom done effectively even by experienced speakers.

After a speech had been given and questions, if any, had been answered by the speaker, Mr. Paul asked the class to evaluate the talk while the speaker remained in front of the room. If he wanted to respond to criticism, he could do so. Mr. Paul frequently called on students who did not voluntarily participate in the evaluations. After the student criticism had been completed, he explained why he agreed or disagreed with them and commented on points which were overlooked. Students learned quickly that unsubstantiated generalizations in talks or evaluations were immediately challenged by other students or the teacher.

6. Mr. Paul never lowered the grades of students who exceeded by a few seconds the allotted three minutes per speaker, and he set no time limit on discussions and evaluations that followed the talks. But on the day the first speeches were given, he wrote on the blackboard, "Blessed is the man who, having nothing to say, abstains from giving in words evidence of the fact" (George Eliot). As soon as students completed their talks, he urged them to begin out-of-class planning of second ones which excluded the weaknesses they had revealed in their first talks. As the second talks were completed and evaluated, he handed each speaker the rating form showing his rating of Talk 1 and Talk 2. Mr. Paul is convinced that at least two talks are essential if a speaker is to profit from the evaluations of his first one.

Much of Mr. Paul's success in teaching oral composition came from the care he exercised in helping students select a topic, adapt it to a time limit, and organize it. Students feel secure when the teacher takes time to help individuals plan, insecure when they are told, "Prepare a talk on any subject for the day after tomorrow." Other reasons why Mr. Paul succeeded are that he was not threatened by having students evaluate his own talk; he encouraged students to select topics they felt strongly about; he made certain that student-and-teacher evaluations were fair, sympathetic, and supported with evidence; and he gave students an opportunity to profit from their mistakes by having them give at least two talks.

When asked how he handled students who wanted to be excused from giving talks because they feared facing an audience, Mr. Paul said he usually had several such students each year. Some of them were willing to face the class if their first "talk" was reading a poem, a short-short story, an anecdote, or a brief essay. Others worked up enough courage to participate in a panel discussion. The few difficult cases were asked to prepare a written speech and told they would not be pressured to speak, but could volunteer when they were ready. He said he never threatened to fail such students, and in forty-three years of teaching had only five who did not participate fully in an oral composition unit.

Mr. Paul's students had an advantage over students in most schools because they sat on the outer side of tables arranged to simulate a horse-shoe, an arrangement which enabled each student to face his classmates and teacher at all times. Such a seating plan almost forces students to know each other, and results in more participation in class discussions. How can students communicate with each other when they are lined up in rows like worshipers in a church? Those in the fourth row see three rows of necks, those in the third row two rows of necks, those in the second row one row of necks, and those in the first row see the teacher or the blackboard. Students in many classrooms are even asked to demonstrate the significance of gestures and facial expressions in spoken communication while looking at the blackboard or at the teacher through a forest of moving necks.

Mr. Paul and a colleague were recalling one day the blunders they made as beginning teachers. Both had suffered through thirty seemingly endless rehashes of books or thirty presentations of unorganized excerpts from magazines, encyclopedias, and textbooks—all brought upon themselves by assuming that students needed no help in selecting, limiting, and developing a subject. And, feeling the pressure of time, stopwatch in hand, they had students pop up, recite, and pop into their seats with the precision of machine-powered pistons. They concluded that students profit little or not at all from the monotonous mouthing of copied material. (If you, too, are blunder-prone, see Emerson's essay "Compensation";[2] it may console and sustain you.)

[2]"Every sweet hath its sour; every evil its good."

Although most teachers schedule units on oral composition, they do not overlook other daily opportunities to help students improve their ability to speak English effectively. Many worthwhile activities in both written and oral English grow naturally out of a unit on literature. However, incidental experiences in oral composition have limited value when students and teachers place a premium on clear and thoughtful speech only during a formal speech unit.

ASSUMPTIONS ABOUT TEACHING ORAL COMPOSITION

Prepare to explain why you accept or reject, wholly or in part, the following assumptions about teaching oral composition:

1. Before students give talks, they should learn the principles of effective speaking from a teacher or handbook.
2. Only the teacher should evaluate students' talks.
3. Instruction in oral composition should be given incidentally, not in a separate unit.
4. All students who refuse to give talks should receive a failing grade for the unit.
5. A student speaker should have the opportunity to entertain questions and comments from his audience.
6. An unprepared student speaker should be asked to sit down.
7. A student speaker should not be permitted to use notes.
8. Shy students should be permitted to read their "talks."
9. A teacher can insure a sympathetic audience for student speakers.
10. A code for criticism of talks and a speaker rating form should be developed and used by students and teacher.
11. Students can learn the principles of effective speaking by observing and evaluating speakers at convocations and on television.
12. A teacher should help students with the content and organization of their talks.
13. Debate should be included in an oral composition unit.
14. What is said in a talk is more important than how it is said.
15. There are a number of reasons why student speakers rarely support their assumptions with evidence.
16. Talks on controversial issues should be encouraged in high schools.
17. All speaking, writing, and listening experiences in English classes should relate to literature.
18. Books on teaching English by Hans Guth; John S. Lewis and Jean C. Sisk; J. N. Hook; Walter Loban, Margaret Ryan, James R. Squire; Edwin Sauer; The Commission on the English Curriculum; Don Wolfe; and Abraham Bernstein (see Bibliography) have excellent ideas on helping students develop oral composition skills.

19. Basing an oral composition unit entirely on principles derived from a group analysis of talks given by the teacher, students, speakers on television, and convocation speakers will result in greater gains than if the unit were based on assignments in textbooks.

20. One can abstract from Hamlet's advice to the players—Act III, Scene 2—several worthwhile speech principles.

21. Speech is a mirror of the soul; as a man speaks, so is he (Syrus).

22. Students can be taught not to copy material from encyclopedias and other sources and pass it off as their own.

23. Quintilian was right when he said that a perfect orator must be first and foremost a good man.

24. Some of the ideas on teaching oral composition presented in this chapter are impractical.

25. Students need more help with spoken language than with written.

26. There are reasons why students who write sentence fragments never speak them.

27. No two people speak or write alike.

28. The mother usually has more influence on her child's spoken language than the father.

IDEAS TO TEST

1. The cry of most students asked to give a talk is "What shall I talk about?" Spend a period discussing with students their suggestions on possible subjects for talks. Then have them demonstrate how a broad subject —*College*, for example—can lead to a dozen specific topics which can be handled thoroughly in a three- or five-minute talk or a twelve- to twenty-minute panel presentation.

2. Once students have selected tentative topics, write several on the board and ask the class to judge them on the basis of (1) potential interest and (2) suitability in the light of the time limits set. Ask them also to suggest an effective beginning, middle, and ending for one or more of the topics. Write their suggestions on the blackboard under the headings *Beginning, Middle, Ending*, and then ask them to help organize the best suggestions into a proper sequence. Students whose topics are used in developing such tentative outlines should not be obligated to use them.

3. Help students develop a code for criticism of talks by asking them, "What kind of criticism would you welcome from your fellow students?" and "How should such criticism be offered?" Summarize their answers on the blackboard.

4. Have students develop a speaker rating form based on their observations while listening to effective and ineffective speakers.

5. Give a brief talk, and ask students to apply the code for criticism and speaker rating form in evaluating it.

6. Immediately after a talk has been given, allow the speaker a few minutes to answer questions and comments from the audience.

7. If each student has the opportunity to give at least two talks, he can show whether he has profited from the teacher's and classmates' criticism of Talk 1.

8. A senior high school teacher who asked students to base a three-minute talk on either the positive or negative version of one of the following topic sentences was pleased with the results.

    a. Science is (is not) a threat to religion.

    b. Minority groups are treated fairly (unfairly) at ———— High School.

    c. Status at ———— High School is (is not) determined by academic ability.

    d. Parents should (should not) be held responsible for the behavior of their children.

    e. High school students should (should not) go steady.

    f. I believe (do not believe) in restrictions on freedom of speech.

    g. The Bible as religion should (should not) be taught in our schools.

    h. All high school graduates (only those in the upper 50 percent of their graduating class) should be allowed to enroll in state colleges and universities.

    i. The United States should (should not) help ill-housed, ill-fed, and ill-clothed people all over the world.

    j. Honesty is (is not) always the best policy.

    k. High school grades should (should not) be abolished.

    l. ———— High School should continue (adopt or abolish) homogeneous grouping.

    m. Sports are (are not) overemphasized at ———— High School.

    n. All students in our community have (do not have) equal educational opportunities.

    o. High school students should (should not) be conditioned to believe that a college education is indispensable to success in life.

    p. The Bill of Rights is (is not) properly enforced by our local, state, and federal governments.

    q. Most Americans reflect (do not reflect) in their behavior acceptance of "Do unto others . . ." and "Love thy neighbor. . . ."

    r. The physical fitness program at ———— High School is (is not) adequate.

9. Give students an opportunity to analyze their voice qualities (enunciation, volume, and rhythm) by having them tape-record and play back a short poem, anecdote, or speech.

10. Discuss with students the difference between an assumption and a statement of fact. Then tell students that at the end of a one-minute speech you are going to read, you will ask them, "What assumptions did I make?" and "What statements of fact did I make?"

11. As a first assignment, some teachers have each student stand at the front of the class to read a very short poem. They claim the experience helps shy students overcome somewhat their fear of facing an audience.

12. Have students submit a tentative topic before they begin developing it into a talk. Topics students choose are often so broad that they could not be handled adequately in a three-hour talk.

13. Ask students to explain why a prominent speaker gave the following answer to the question, "How soon can you address an audience of educators?": "If you want a fifteen-minute talk, give me two months to prepare it. I shall need about a month for a thirty-minute talk; but if you want me to talk an hour or more, I can do it now."

8

Helping Students Listen Effectively

Before reading this chapter, formulate clear, defensible answers to the following questions. After reading it, prepare to explain why you changed or retained your answers.

1. Why do some teachers devote considerable time to helping students develop reading skills, little or no time to helping them develop listening skills?

2. Students are informed and influenced by talk coming from radio, television, and convocation speakers, ministers, parents, friends, acquaintances, politicians, and teachers. How can one help them to check the accuracy and honesty of such talk when it relates to economic, political, religious, educational, racial, international, and other problems? As you listen, how do you determine what is accurate and honest and what is propaganda?

3. Why is television and radio advertising of cosmetics, tobaccos, and patent medicines apparently accepted by many listeners as factual, when scientific tests prove it is mostly fictional and common sense suggests it is mostly nonsensical?

4. If confronted with teaching a unit on listening, what would be your goals, and how would you achieve them?

AN OVERVIEW

When, thirty years ago, some educators realized that typical students spend more time listening than reading, they delegated to English teachers the responsibility of helping them develop listening skills. Recently, the growth of television and rapidly rising enrollments in college and university lecture courses have justified increased attention to listening. However, Sam Duker's 725-item *A Bibliography on Listening*[1] lists seventy-three published articles and research projects relating directly to listening at the elementary level, only twenty-four at the secondary level—data which seem to show that concern with the development of high school students' listening skills has been less than phenomenal. Most English teachers want their students to become thoughtful listeners, but some do nothing specific to achieve the objective.

Skill in listening is inseparable from other skills and abilities. An attentive individual with perfect hearing may not appreciate a fine speech and may be an easy mark for a propagandist. What a person brings to a convocation, television speech, dramatic performance, or discussion in background, interest, and thinking ability determines, in large measure, whether his response is rational or not. An adult who separates a speaker's facts from assumptions and notes how voice qualities, physical characteristics, and audience color his words is likely to have read widely and thought much. In a classroom, the teacher's skill in selecting, presenting, and analyzing subject matter largely determines how discriminatingly his students listen.

Many teachers blame their students' listening inadequacies on poor manners, lack of interest, the weather, or undesirable physical surroundings. But the reader has undoubtedly noticed that whenever classroom activities relate directly to student concerns, the class not only listens but is anxious to question and comment as well. The most effective teacher of listening skills emphasizes performance in written and oral composition, prizes thoughtful interpretation of literature, encourages questions from students, provides variety, relates instruction closely to goals students consider worthwhile, believes in academic freedom for students, and considers himself a student[2] among students. Such a teacher is likely to motivate even reluctant individuals to listen almost as avidly as Juliet did to Romeo's love talk or as gossips do to slander.

One teaching principle supported by all effective teachers was used by Socrates and Jesus: relate instruction to goals students consider worthwhile. Socrates' students were good listeners because he directed discussions concerned with issues related to the good life which were then, as now, significant and of current interest. In his parables, Jesus gave sharp, clear

---

[1]Sam Duker, *A Bibliography on Listening* (New York: Office of Testing and Research, Brooklyn College, 1961).

[2]Chaucer said of such a teacher, "And gladly wolde he lerne and gladly teche."

pictures of moral problems related to his listeners' lives. For example, in what critics have called a perfect short story, "The Prodigal Son," he promoted forgiveness as an essential part of the good life. Both Socrates and Jesus knew that to make people listen, the content of a discussion or parable must support or challenge in a dramatic way ideas which are unsettled in men's minds. The effective teacher in today's classroom, like Socrates and Jesus, knows that (1) intelligent listening is predicated upon the clear, thoughtful, dramatic presentation of subject matter students consider relevant to their own experiences and (2) irrelevance puts students to sleep as surely as sleeping pills.

Although some teachers insist that effective instruction in reading, writing, and speaking leads automatically to the development of listening skills, others defend giving special attention to three specific problems discussed in dissertations on listening: (1) getting and holding students' attention (a primary worry of student teachers), (2) stimulating them to evaluate what they hear, and (3) helping them recognize and record significant points made by speakers.

GETTING AND HOLDING STUDENTS' ATTENTION

In most high schools, the beginning-of-the-period bell brings quiet—an essential response in a well-ordered classroom. Such a response built up by an experienced teacher is frequently broken by student teachers who have not learned that (1) conferences with individual students must stop when the bell rings and (2) careful planning can cut the time required for taking roll, returning and accepting written work, and writing assignments on the blackboard.

Once the inevitable clerical work at the beginning of a class is completed, the student teacher relies on his lesson plan to insure interest and full attentiveness. The second lesson plan in Chapter 3, on Wordsworth's "I Wandered Lonely as a Cloud," is likely to interest students; the first lesson plan may cause a quick loss of attention, accompanied by discipline problems ranging from boredom to bedlam. However, a good lesson plan can lose much of its force when the teacher (1) becomes mesmerized by a window, wall, or ceiling; (2) calls only on volunteers; (3) sits behind a desk, preventing eye contact with students seated beyond the first two rows; (4) dominates discussions; (5) makes oracular pronouncements; (6) takes verbal detours that lead nowhere; and (7) if a woman, wears skin-tight sweaters, too-short skirts, ponderous ear pendants, dangerous heels, jingling jewelry, bizarre hairdos, or masklike makeup. The student teacher (usually a woman) who demonstrates startling departures from good taste in dress is rare, but she presents a problem to critic teachers and college supervisors—criticizing a person's appearance is equated with attacking baseball, motherhood, and Uncle Sam. Even rarer is the male student teacher who amuses high school students with a conspicuous fraternity emblem, embryonic beard or mustache, or exceptional hairdo.

HELPING STUDENTS EVALUATE WHAT THEY HEAR

The high school English teacher concerned with helping his students evaluate what they hear, an ability indispensable in a democracy, is uncommon. Is any listening skill more necessary than competence in separating a speaker's statements into fact and fiction? In both high schools and colleges, students usually write and speak to convince teachers that what they read in assigned books or heard in class has properly informed and influenced them.

Why is the ability to ask pertinent, thought-provoking questions—a skill possessed by all intelligent listeners—seldom consciously developed in students? Teachers laud students who can paraphrase an author or speaker. But shouldn't a teacher be constantly on the defensive trying to answer students' questions? After all, he is the educated, experienced one, presumably with ideas which may help them find defensible answers. If students pump him for facts only, they might as well go to books; but if they are encouraged to challenge his assumptions—"What do you mean?" "How do you know?"—class sessions may sometimes be as exciting as basketball games. Of course, the teacher should not hesitate to turn these questions back onto his class.

In only two of my university courses, both in philosophy, did the instructor encourage students to challenge his assumptions. Students were on the offensive (without being considered offensive) most of the time. The instructor was never disturbed by blunt questions, and seemed delighted when he had to say "uncle." To meet a teacher who did not know all the answers was a pleasant experience, perhaps because we had so few answers ourselves. Many of us discovered for the first time the difference between a statement of fact and an assumption. When we were asked to underline the statements of fact in a book we were reading, we were surprised to find that two or three underlinings per chapter sufficed. Unhampered discussions led by an articulate, informed, and thoughtful teacher made students aware that (1) learning involves more than carrying the "learned lumber" of authorities in one's head until it can be unloaded at examination time and (2) most "knowledge" is assumption, a comforting and stimulating discovery because it brought release from many absolutes.

Why don't all teachers help students identify and weigh assumptions about economics, politics, race, religion, and government voiced in their own written and oral compositions and in literature? Why is the student with unorthodox views unpopular in many classrooms? A colleague reported recently that a high school student in a "Bible as literature" course compared the Bible with the *Odyssey*, implying that both were a mixture of history and folklore. He was a pariah from then on, helped to become one by a teacher who refuted "heresy" with vigor.

Academic freedom for the student has never been an issue in American education, but it should be. Intelligent listening is best promoted when all sides of questions are freely investigated by students and teachers. However, in some high schools a student who challenges authorities is likely to alienate both classmates and teachers. This situation seriously limits students' opportunities to learn to evaluate unorthodox views they will meet elsewhere. Listening in and out of the classroom which is punctuated with "What do you mean?" "How do you know?" can reduce the influence of the drivel that dominates much political and advertising talk on television. Practice in asking these questions is stimulated in classrooms where free discussion is considered a right by students and teachers. Both should be able to raise questions and present ideas without being suspected of subversion.

Some high school teachers discuss controversial issues in the classroom without angering fellow teachers, administrators, students, parents, or pressure groups. They try to make issues clear, not to convert students to their own convictions. All students are permitted to present and support their beliefs without censure, and are free to accept or reject the assumptions of classmates and teacher. There is no reason why a teacher should not present his position on controversial topics, provided he acknowledges that his beliefs are not final answers and that other responsible people differ with him. He should, of course, habitually support his stand on issues with reasons, and should insist that students do so as well.

HELPING STUDENTS RECOGNIZE AND RECORD SIGNIFICANT POINTS

Many high school students seldom take notes on classroom lectures and discussions. However, an increasing number of high school English teachers are explaining to college-bound students how careful listening and note-taking will help them realize that (1) the teacher who equates recalling facts with learning will at examination time convert his favorite subject matter into true-false, multiple-choice, and completion statements, and (2) the teacher who consistently asks thought-provoking questions in class will usually follow that pattern in examinations. When queried about their concern with examinations, English teachers reply that college-bound seniors are grade-conscious because high grades mean scholarships and admittance to status colleges and universities. Whether lectures on listening and note-taking are worthwhile is debatable. Most students, especially the bright ones, are already masters at detecting the subject-matter prejudices of teachers. And listening and note-taking skills are best learned through guided practice, not lectures.

Some high school English teachers periodically require college-bound students to take notes during a class session. The next period is devoted to analyzing the notes to see whether they are clear, accurate, and significant. Students do learn quickly that the temptation to record everything a teacher says interferes with intelligent listening. It seems doubtful, though, whether this occasional attention to note-taking develops skills which will transfer to the college classroom.

More high school speech teachers than English teachers prepare students prior to a convocation speech or television address to (1) relate the speaker's topic to their own experiences and (2) analyze the speaker's delivery and summarize and evaluate the content of his speech. Such an assignment seems to produce the best results when students are provided with rating cards that indicate what they should evaluate.

One critic teacher occasionally asks his students to record, as he reads a brief essay, the gist of the author's statement of purpose in the first paragraph, his development of his purpose in the middle paragraphs, and his summary or conclusions in the final paragraph or paragraphs. After he has read the essay, he asks students to read aloud and evaluate their notes on each of its three parts. He sometimes varies the procedure by providing several specific questions which alert his students to the main points made by the author. A teacher who thus helps his students to abstract what is significant from an essay presented orally might also ask them to explain why they accept or reject, wholly or in part, the essayist's assumptions.

The note-taking activities presented above would be more valuable if they were a regular part of the English program of college-bound students. Of course, whenever a teacher reads a literary selection or explains a composition principle to students, he can test and develop their listening skills by asking them questions which get at essentials and stimulate thoughtful responses. He should never equate effective listening with attentiveness. Certainly attentiveness is indispensable. But it must be coupled with the desire and ability to judge the accuracy, significance, and validity of (1) students' and teachers' assumptions in themes, speeches, and discussions, and (2) radio and television speeches, news programs, and advertising. The effective listener can repeat what he hears, but he can also separate facts from assumptions and weigh both.

In the classrooms where more value is attached to recalling subject matter than to analyzing it, students listen because it is a duty rather than a way of enjoying the discovery, defense, and refutation of ideas. Merely reciting a writer or speaker's ideas produces mental stagnation; challenging them can lead to new ideas, and eventually to discoveries which make intellectual pursuits exciting. In the past, few men and women challenged tradition and rid themselves of the bad habits ingrained by a memoriter-type education. In today's new science and mathematics courses, students are encouraged to ask "Why?" Would not such a question produce insight, understanding, and excitement if applied consistently to language and literature?

Since units on literature, oral composition, and written composition usually provide many in-class listening experiences, perhaps listening skills should be developed incidentally rather than in separate units. But even though separate units on listening are rare, a conscious effort must be made to help students recognize, record in writing, recall verbally, and evaluate lectures, speeches, discussions, dramatic performances, news programs, and television and radio advertisements. In most English classrooms students have many opportunities to record and report what they hear in and out of the classroom, but few chances to judge it. Questions beginning with *Who, What, When, Where* should, whenever feasible, be followed with *Why* questions.

Since the English teacher has ways of checking his students' competence in listening through written and oral tests and responses during class discussions, he becomes alarmed only when their proficiency drops. Whenever that happens, he might ask himself the following questions:

1. Do I relate subject matter to goals students accept as worthwhile?

2. Do students feel free to express ideas not commonly held?

3. Do I welcome all questions from students, even those previously asked?

4. Do I introduce variety in content and methods into the daily classroom routine?

5. Do I accent improved performance in written and oral composition rather than extraneous exercises, thoughtful interpretation of literature rather than recall of what an author said?

6. Do I give special attention to students who have hearing losses or personal problems serious enough to prevent successful participation in classroom activities?

There are many problems in doing experimental research on listening.

A teacher would have to match (by I. Q., scholastic ability, sex, age, economic background, etc.) students in an experimental group with those in a control group. A valid, reliable listening test which measures the ability of students to recall, interpret, and evaluate what they hear would have to be developed and administered to both groups at the beginning and end of the experiment. It would be no small problem to introduce into the experimental class activities that involve recalling, interpreting, and judging oral presentations of various kinds. Should the test results show that the experimental group made greater gains than the control group in developing listening skills, skeptics might ask: "Is it possible to achieve accuracy in matching students and measuring their gains in listening proficiency?" "What kind of instruction did the accentuation of listening activities in the experimental class supplant?" "Did you administer, at the beginning and end of the experiment, standardized English achievement tests and subjective tests designed to measure performance gains in writing, speaking, and appreciation of literature?"[3]

Although experimental research on listening involves solving formidable problems, the experienced English teacher should test (1) content and methods which promise to improve listening skills and (2) instruments designed to measure these skills. He should recognize, however, that no matter how successfully he segregates listening skills from those of reading, writing, and speaking, many experienced English teachers develop skilled listeners without ever saying, "Boys and girls, we shall now devote two weeks to listening. Are you listening?" They give daily attention to promoting effective listening.

ASSUMPTIONS ABOUT TEACHING LISTENING

Prepare to explain why you accept or reject, wholly or in part, the following assumptions related to teaching listening:

1. Most students are influenced more by what they hear than by what they read.

2. We often "read" our cherished beliefs and feelings into what we hear.

3. Politicians try to inform rather than influence an audience.

4. In politics, the spoken word has proved more powerful than the written word.

5. Effective note-taking can be taught.

---

[3]An experimental class which outshines a control class in listening gains could lag behind it in reading, writing, and speaking gains, a development a researcher cannot ignore.

6. Listening skills can be taught.

7. Listening skills should be taught incidentally, not in separate units.

8. Most English teachers merely pay lip service to the idea that helping students develop listening skills is worthwhile.

9. Students should learn how to separate a speaker's statements of fact from his assumptions.

10. Radio and television advertising of toothpaste, cosmetics, patent medicines, soap, and cigarettes is based upon scientifically arrived-at facts.

11. Listening skills cannot be isolated from reading, writing, and speaking skills.

12. Doing experimental research on listening presents insurmountable problems.

13. In their books on teaching English, Lou LaBrant, Don Wolfe, J. N. Hook, The Commission on the English Curriculum, and John S. Lewis and Jean C. Sisk (see Bibliography) agree on how to help students develop listening skills.

14. An attentive student is not necessarily an effective listener.

15. A student with an I. Q. of 140 is unquestionably an intelligent listener.

16. It is much more difficult for an English teacher to teach teenagers listening skills than for a driver-training teacher to teach them driving skills.

17. It is easy to understand why some scientists are quick to challenge the assumptions made by fellow scientists at professional meetings, and equally quick to accept without question those made in sermons by a fundamentalist preacher and political speeches by an extremist.

18. It is difficult to list the characteristics of an intelligent listener.

19. A teacher who can give "Yes" answers to the six questions on page 137 is very likely helping his students to improve their listening skills.

20. Listening skills are not so easy to demonstrate as skills in golf, typing, the fine arts, or the practical arts.

21. It is easier to deceive with the spoken word than with the written word.

22. Most teachers talk too much, listen too little.

23. Ambrose Bierce's definition of a *bore* is cutting but apt: a person who talks when you wish him to listen.

IDEAS TO TEST

1. While disagreeing with others about what a speaker said, we sometimes suddenly realize that we have read into a speech our cherished

prejudices. Try to test the extent to which students do this by reading to them a short controversial speech from *Vital Speeches* or a popular magazine. Then ask them to write one-sentence answers to each one of the following questions:

    a. What was the speaker's or writer's purpose?

    b. What were the speaker's or writer's main points?

    c. What were the speaker's or writer's conclusions?

Compare the answers, and have students account for the variations. Return the papers with a mimeographed sheet giving what you consider objective answers to the three questions. Give students the opportunity to challenge your answers. If possible, provide each student with a copy of the speech or essay.

    2. Follow the procedure in "1" above, but use a student's or convocation speaker's speech or a short poem students have not read.

    3. Most students have difficulty in differentiating between statements of fact and assumptions. Ask students to explain the difference between the two kinds of statements made in the following radio report of a football game by a partisan high school student.

    a. Seven hundred sad spectators saw North get beaten by Central.

    b. The final score was 28 to 6.

    c. North would have won if Smith had been able to play.

    d. North would have won on a dry field.

Detecting the difference between b and a, c, and d (above) is easy for most students. Have them try the more difficult task of separating statements of fact from assumptions in a brief talk made by the teacher or a student. In the discussion that follows, ask students to illustrate the value of supporting assumptions with evidence.

    4. Ask students to help you define, illustrate, and detect the following propaganda devices:

        a. Name-calling. (Currently common name-calling words are: *radical, racist, liberal, conservative, Bircher, hippie, yippie, beatnik, hawk, dove,* and *Communist.*)

        b. Glittering generalities. (The following words and phrases are favorites of politicians who want to arouse emotions and cloud issues: *liberty, motherhood, patriotism, American way, economic security,* and *equality.*)

        c. Transfer. (An idea or program is labeled good because it is supported by church, lodge, political party, school, community, state, or nation.)

        d. Testimonials. (A product or idea is good because it is used or recommended by a movie star, sports figure, socialite, housewife, cowboy, or comedian.)

        e. Plain folks. (A few years ago politicians were born in log cabins; indulged in hunting, fishing, and farming; and kissed babies. How do they project the plain folks image today?)

f. Card-stacking. (Hitler lauded his free elections but did not emphasize that there was only one candidate for each office. A crooked politician avoids answering accusations by pointing up his war record, church membership, and devotion to the poor.)

g. Bandwagon. (Many people follow the majority in whatever they do; they support the popular cause or product.)

You might ask students to bring to class illustrations of how the above propaganda devices are used by advertisers, politicians, school organizations, and teachers. Also, ask students to (1) illustrate their use of propaganda devices in dealings with parents, friends, and teachers; (2) try to prove or disprove the assumption that all propaganda devices have a common purpose; and (3) differentiate between good and bad propaganda.

5. Ask students to take notes during a class session. At the next session, help them analyze their notes for accuracy, clarity, significance, and completeness.

6. Ask students to check a television soap, cosmetic, or patent medicine ad against the scientific analysis of the product made in *Consumer Reports* or *Consumer Bulletin*. Have them present their findings to the class.

7. Ask students to complete the following questionnaire:

a. Which radio programs do you listen to regularly? occasionally?

b. Which television programs do you watch regularly? occasionally?

c. Which current motion pictures did you see during the last month? Which one did you like best?

d. If you have a phonograph, what are your favorite records?

e. Approximately how much time do you devote each week to radio _____ ? television _____ ? records _____ ? current motion pictures _____ ?

The results of the questionnaire can be used in many ways: (1) to stimulate in-class written and oral evaluations of students' listening habits, (2) to make assignments that call for evaluations of programs popular with students, (3) to compare students' listening habits and the quality of their schoolwork, and (4) to make the teacher aware of how students spend their out-of-school hours.

8. Require students to listen to a televised political speech. The next day, ask them to write a very brief paragraph in answer to each of the following questions: "What were the main points made by the speaker? Why do you accept or reject, wholly or in part, the main points?"

9. Ask a student "reporter" to interview the teacher or a classmate

in front of the class. Have students write a brief feature based on the interview. The next period, have some students read their stories aloud to the class. Compare the stories for completeness, relevance, and accuracy.

10. Ask students to explain orally or in writing why sometimes they listen and sometimes they do not during class sessions.

11. Have each student record a brief poem or anecdote on a tape recorder. Play back the recordings, and have students explain why certain recordings are easy and interesting to listen to and why others present difficulties.

12. Write the following topic sentence on the blackboard, and ask students to develop it into a paragraph: *To become an intelligent listener is not easy.* Base a class discussion on the paragraphs.

9

Helping Students Understand the Nature of Language: Part I

Before reading this chapter, formulate clear, defensible answers to the following questions. After reading it, prepare to explain why you changed or retained your answers.

1. What is your definition of linguistics? What is new about the new grammar? Why do you accept or reject, wholly or in part, the new grammar?

2. Assume that one hundred infants could be isolated on a thereafter inaccessible planet, and could survive and multiply. What kind of language might they develop after several thousand years? How would it evolve?

3. How did the English language originate? How has it changed since Chaucer (1340?–1400) wrote *The Canterbury Tales?*

4. How did American English originate? Why and how has it changed in the last three hundred years?

5. What should a high school student know about the evolution of the English language? How would you teach it to him?

6. What is grammar? What should the high school student know about grammar? Why? How would you teach it to him?

7. What is the difference between grammar and usage? How would you define standard, colloquial, and illiterate English? How would you teach English usage to high school students?

THE NEW GRAMMAR

From the seventeenth century until recently, compilers of English grammars seemed obsessed with "correct" usage. However, Edward Sapir,

Language, 1921, and Leonard Bloomfield, *Language*, 1933, paved the way for a change in emphasis, a concern with structural grammar; and since the early 1950's generative or transformational grammar has been developed by Zellig Harris, Kenneth L. Pike, Noam Chomsky, and others.[1] Today's grammarians are interested in what makes languages tick, their structures or systems. They seek linguistic theories that will prove useful in discovering, explaining, and evaluating the grammars inherent in languages. They concentrate on phonetics, phonology, morphology, accent, syntax, philosophy of language, the connections between writing and speech, and sometimes semantics. Since languages are complicated, they try to simplify, without sacrificing accuracy, their descriptions of how languages function. Definitions of the parts of speech by traditional grammarians seem simple but are sometimes inaccurate or incomplete. For example, *thing* in "A noun is the name of a certain person, place, or thing" is a catchall label that covers words as diverse as *horse, buggy, inauguration, rest, democracy*, and *beauty*.

The English sentence is the dominant concern of researchers and those who illustrate the principles of the new grammar in high school textbooks. In describing the sentence, they begin with basic sentence patterns, frequently labeled *kernel sentences*, from which an indefinite number of transformed sentences can be generated by the addition of single words, phrases, and clauses. For example, additions to the following kernel sentences other than simple determiners *(a, an, the)* are called transformations:

1. NOUN   VERB

   Teachers   teach.

2. NOUN   VERB   NOUN

   Teachers   test   students.

3. NOUN   LINKING VERB   ADJECTIVE

   Teachers   are (become, seem, appear)   learned.

4. NOUN   LINKING VERB   NOUN

   Teachers   are (become, seem, remain)   friends.

[1]For an account of the evolution of grammar, see Charles C. Fries, "Linguistics: The Study of Language" in *Linguistics and Reading* (New York: Holt, Rinehart, and Winston, Inc., 1962), pp. 35–92.

5. NOUN	LINKING VERB	ADVERB
The teachers	are	here.

Without using pencil and paper, carry one or more of the preceding sentences through several transformations by adding (1) nouns or pronouns, (2) adjectives, (3) adverbs, (4) verbs, (5) phrases, or (6) clauses. How can one transform sentences 3 and 4 to make them reflect reality more closely?

In high school textbooks on transformational grammar, nouns, pronouns, verbs, adjectives, adverbs, phrases, and clauses are given detailed individual attention to show how they can systematically transform basic sentence patterns. Two of many textbooks that illustrate this process are Paul Roberts, *English Syntax*, Alternate Edition (New York: Harcourt, Brace and World, Inc., 1964) and Harold B. Allen, and others, *New Dimensions in English* (Wichita: McCormick-Mathers Publishing Company, Inc., 1966).

Today high school English handbooks are gradually being revised to reflect reality more closely, a process that will undoubtedly continue indefinitely. Reality is revealed by researchers using the scientific method. They define language problems, gather data related to them, develop hypotheses that promise to solve them, and subject the hypotheses to thorough tests. They use the method as vigorously and rigorously as scientists seeking to improve transportation, medicine, agriculture, and communications. In an age of science, questions about old linguistic theories snowball. Researchers have for many years questioned the traditional grammarian's modeling English grammar on Latin grammar, emphasizing written rather than spoken English, promoting rigid rules about correctness, and defining grammatical terms inexactly. But until recently compilers of grammars for schools were seldom influenced by them; they adopted patterns established by their predecessors. Today's makers of handbooks give recognition to the findings of linguists who provide new insights into language systems through scientific analyses of . (1) the spoken and written language of the people who use it and (2) the linguistic theories of associates.

The authors of high school handbooks that feature recent linguistic theories developed by research rarely claim that students learning the new grammar will possess the key to improved speaking, writing, reading, and listening skills. However, most of them suggest that as students climb the educational ladder the cumulative insights provided by the new grammar will enable them to understand better the nature, structure, and function of the language, a development considered good for its own sake. A few hypothesize that students who learn to illustrate intonation patterns will achieve greater accuracy in punctuation; and those who master the system behind transforming basic sentence patterns will gain insights into language structure that will improve their sentence clarity and style.

One natural outcome of the new points of view provided by students of language systems is questions from English teachers. Two teachers who recently attended linguistics institutes asked, "Should the theories in a new-grammar handbook be presented in formal, chapter-by-chapter fashion?" "Can one help students *discover* the new-grammar theory as they speak, write, read, and listen?" "How can pragmatic-minded students be induced to become enthusiastic about the nature of a tool (language) rather than its everyday use?" "What kinds of research designs might reveal the outcomes of various approaches to teaching the new and old grammars?" "Is generating sentences from basic sentence patterns new?" "What can be abstracted from traditional and transformational grammars that will help students improve their performance in speaking and writing?" "Can transforming kernel sentences be taught so that students will make reasonable progress toward (1) using the dialect of educated people and (2) presenting ideas clearly and thoughtfully?"[2]

Perhaps such questions imply demands beyond the ken of any grammar; but students and teachers are seldom motivated by theories that do not promise to help them improve reading, writing, and speaking skills. Furthermore, asking questions should not be interpreted as a refusal to entertain new ideas but as an opportunity to give them a fair hearing. Questions should stimulate further inquiry. A new grammar is arising from questions that exposed the weaknesses of traditional grammar. Questions about the new grammar may lead to research that will give it a currency and usefulness it might otherwise not achieve.

Four of my student teachers experienced satisfying class sessions, not by transforming systematically kernel sentences fabricated for the occasion or taken from a handbook, but by informally transforming sentences in paragraphs their students had written. They copied three paragraphs (one excellent, one average, one fair) on the board, numbering the paragraphs and lines for easy reference and leaving wide spaces between them for easy editing.

One student teacher wrote the paragraphs on the board before she met an eight o'clock class. Students spied them as they entered the classroom and began discussing them with each other. After the bell sounded, she opened the discussion by asking, "Why do you suppose I copied some of the paragraphs you wrote yesterday on the board?" Each one of the other three student teachers opened the session with one of the following questions: "What are the strengths and weaknesses of paragraph 1?"

[2]See Neil Postman and Charles Weingartner, *Linguistics* (New York: Holt, Rinehart, and Winston, 1967).

"Could paragraph 3 be improved? How?" "Which one of the three paragraphs is the most effective? Why?"

Suggestions and questions from students came so fast they were difficult to handle. The student teachers spent the period fielding questions and comments, and some wisely tossed them back to students for answers and evaluations. When a consensus was reached about the efficacy of certain suggestions, the student teachers made the revisions.

I discussed the procedure with the four student teachers. They enjoyed their students' enthusiastic responses but were upset by the avalanche of suggestions and questions. A farm girl likened the class session to going through a cornhusker. She was also worried about her inability to separate the wheat from the chaff: not having anticipated the questions and comments that arose, she could not make instant decisions about their value. Another was apologetic about not "covering" even one of the three paragraphs. All felt it was less hectic to work on a page in a workbook but concluded that the enthusiasm the approach evoked and the quality of the questions and comments warranted trying it again. At a meeting of student teachers at term's end one student teacher reported that she repeated the technique with improved results because she had foreseen the nature of her students' questions and comments. (At this juncture I squelched an impulse to extol or stress to her fellow students the scoutmaster's pet precept, "Be prepared!")

The above approach led not only to proofreading for mistakes in spelling, punctuation, and capitalization but also to editing that produced much-needed revisions in sentence structure, content, and usage. After such a session or two, high school students might regard favorably lessons in transformational grammar. Students could be helped to abstract kernel sentences from their paragraphs and then generate new sentences by the addition of nouns, pronouns, adverbs, adjectives, determiners, phrases, and clauses. Once they became familiar with the terminology of transformational grammar, it might be used in discussions of sentences in student paragraphs placed on the board or dittoed. Such a procedure may seem too unsystematic for teachers accustomed to workbook and handbook exercises; but it would appeal to students. They enjoy improving their own sentences through transformations suggested by themselves or classmates.

Editing paragraphs placed on the blackboard palls when used too often. Classwide instruction in composition and grammar should be supplemented with much individual instruction. However, if during a composition unit rough drafts are edited by groups of students (see page 109) and then several final drafts are edited by the whole class, students are likely to develop editing skills rather than just proofreading skills. Why do publishers pay editors much higher salaries than proofreaders?

As a supervisor of student teachers, I have usually found traditional or transformational grammar taught in a formal fashion, as a subject apart from speech and writing. The arguments that grammar study is good for its own sake do not impress the increasing number of teachers and students who are pragmatists, products of an age of inquiry. Grammars of the present and future must contribute directly to improving students' language skills, or their roles in the curricula of American elementary and high schools may become as inconspicuous as the study of Greek. Perhaps when the interest in the problem of making the new grammar functiona₁ leads to research on how it can be done, students will be helped by English teachers *to discover* the nature of their language system as they speak, write, read, and listen.

TEACHING LANGUAGE HISTORY

Many English and American writers and scholars have worried about their changing language. Edmund Waller (1606–1687), an English poet, concluded that a writer who expected to be read centuries later should write in Greek or Latin. Alexander Pope (1688–1744) predicted that the works of Dryden (1631–1700) would soon be as difficult to read as Chaucer's. Joseph Addison (1672–1719), the English essayist, suggested appointing a government agent to enforce stability in language. His agent appeared in the garb of the grammarian who in the eighteenth and nineteenth centuries forced a square peg (the English language) into a round hole (Latin grammar). The grammarian slowed change in language considerably, but not so much as did Samuel Johnson in the field of spelling with the publication of his dictionary in 1775.[3].

Although prominent writers have for several centuries provided conclusive proof that living languages Change, *Webster's Third New International Dictionary* (1961 edition) was severely criticized for recording certain changes in language, and such criticism will probably continue to flare up every time a new dictionary makes its debut.

Anyone who glances at the history of the English language sees that change is certain, but final answers to when, where, why, and how language originated may never come. A common guess is that a language based on gestures and facial expressions preceded the time when early man produced combinations of noises which gradually became associated with individual objects. The development of classificatory terms like *baby, man,* and *woman* probably took place thousands of years after labels for individual objects became commonplace. Abstract terms like *truth, beauty,* and *goodness* are presumed to have arrived late in the history of language.

[3]Albert C. Baugh minimizes Johnson's influence in fixing spelling: *A History of the English Language*, p. 256.

Chaucer is often called the father of the English language. However, he adopted a London dialect, one of three major English dialects, and used it so effectively in *The Canterbury Tales* and other works that it achieved status in the eyes of some educated contemporaries. They, of course, still placed Chaucer's English on the fourth rung of the language ladder: Latin, Greek, and French remained on the top three rungs. The language used by Chaucer was of Germanic origin.

This Germanic origin of early English is more evident in Chaucer's vocabulary than in that of twentieth-century Englishmen or Americans, because his vocabulary is five hundred years closer to the primitive Germanic language which produced today's German, Swedish, English, and Danish. Of course, even in the fourteenth century Vulgar (spoken) Latin and some of the Romance languages (French, Italian, and Spanish) derived from it had contributed to the dialect Chaucer chose for his writings. But the most frequently used English words, then and now, evolved directly from those brought into England between A.D. 400 and 700 by invading Germanic tribes: Angles, Saxons, and Jutes. Since Chaucer's day, the Romance and Teutonic tongues, because of faster transportation and communication, have borrowed freely from each other, with perhaps no language borrowing more words than American English.

Soon after the American Revolution, British visitors to America and British contributors to magazines viewed with alarm verging on horror the American defilement of a language which had been corrupted continuously by Britishers. They seemed unaware that the language of Chaucer[4] had been defiled unashamedly by Shakespeare and his contemporaries. The Elizabethans' vigorous experimentation with language, especially vocabulary, was matched only by the Americans'. British purists were not alone in reviling Americans for their linguistic radicalism. Benjamin Franklin (1706–1790) took a Tory attitude towards innovations in vocabulary equaled in fervor only by the nineteenth and early twentieth century English teacher's crusade against slang.

For Britons and Americans who have supported the *status quo* in language, no century has proved satisfactory because change appears in every century. Fortunately, they are usually alarmed only by current changes in language; the good old days are but twenty-five to fifty years in the past—easily accessible for comparison with the bad new ones. Policing only today's "crimes" against language makes the purists' assignment easy and topical. Yesterday's "crime" becomes today's personification of virtue, i.e., standard English.

[4]Thomas Occleve (1370?–1450?) called Chaucer "The firste fyndere of our faire language." To Edmund Spenser (1552?–1599), Chaucer was the "well of English undefiled."

Polonius' "Neither a borrower nor a lender be" was ignored by those who helped develop American English. They adopted words from many sources with ever-increasing vigor. They borrowed freely from the Indians (*pone, papoose, powwow*), the French (*bureau, prairie, portage*), the Spanish (*creole, alligator, quadroon*), and the Germans (*zwieback, kindergarten, sauerkraut*). Some of the words were Americanized in pronunciation and spelling.[5] Early Americans demonstrated exceptional talent in creating hundreds of graphic compounds (*sweet potato, catfish, bluegrass, prickly heat*) which described objects and conditions not found in their homelands.

Can and should we give high school students some insight into how and why American English has changed from colonial times to the present? I shared with high school students H. L. Mencken's lively *The American Language.* I read and discussed with them excerpts which pictured the curious, sometimes hilarious, euphemisms used by members of various occupations;[6] the fascinating metaphors of hoboes and prison inmates;[7] the surprising differences between American and British English; the startling variations in pronunciation of American English; the fixity of spelling; the picturesque names of American towns and states; the evolution, inevitability, and verve of slang; and the changing fashions in vocabulary and usage. Mencken promotes pride in a language which is as virile as the Chicago pictured by Carl Sandburg, a far cry from its anemic counterpart embalmed in staid handbooks and workbooks. Although *The American Language* has recently been revised and condensed into one volume (see Bibliography), the original three-volume edition is still an excellent source on the evolution of American English for the student and teacher who enjoy an avalanche of illustrative material.

If your senior high school students read English and American literature in the typical carefully-edited anthology, consult early editions (most libraries have them) for excerpts from the following authors in the language they used: Chaucer, Shakespeare, Milton, Pope, Wordsworth, Tennyson, and John Masefield.[8] Writers of prose could be substituted or included. Analyze the excerpts for changes in spelling, pronunciation,

---

[5]Today *dachshund* is evolving into *dashhound*, an abomination to the purist but inevitable because *dachs* and *hund* present pronunciation difficulties for Americans. Many young Americans unceremoniously call the dachshund *wiener dog* and *sausage dog.*

[6]See those relating to exequies on pp. 287–288.

[7]Their use of *calf-slobber* for meringue on a pie was appreciated by farm boys; and "Pass the sand (sugar) and red-lead (ketchup)" became commonplace in our school cafeteria, abetted by a teacher attracted to the terminology.

[8]Ask interested students to compile a sampling of excerpts.

capitalization, sentence structure, vocabulary, and usage. Many excellent excerpts showing changes in language from Chaucer to the present appear in George H. McKnight and Bert Emsley, *Modern English in the Making*. A more recent analysis of the evolution of English is made by Albert C. Baugh, *A History of the English Language* (New York: Appleton-Century-Crofts, Inc., 1957).

TEACHING GRAMMAR AND USAGE

The connotations of *grammar* and *drill* may account for their popularity among parents, teachers, and administrators. They are austere terms— punitive, Puritan, Rock-of-Gibraltar-like. *Usage* seems a vapid term— anarchic, laissez-faire, footprints-in-the-sand-like. Most parents, English teachers, and students avoid the label *usage*. To them, one who speaks and writes by the handbook uses good grammar and one who does not uses bad grammar. Parents who notice their children's linguistic mistakes—"I seen it," "He done it," "I ain't going," and "She knowed him" —conclude that English teachers should dispense substantial doses of grammar. Teachers respond to the parents' conclusion by concentrating on handbook and workbook exercises, not realizing that editing and diagraming someone else's sentences, completing usage exercises, and memorizing rules have little or no effect on students' written and spoken English. Through their addiction to objective entrance tests, colleges and universities abet the illusion that knowledge about English usage is inevitably accompanied by the ability to speak and write effectively.

Attempts to differentiate between grammar and usage have not been successful. One definition of grammar which allows the label *usage* a separate existence is based on the assumption that the grammar of a language is reflected in certain fixed patterns which one who wishes to communicate successfully must follow. Fortunately, a child learns the patterns through imitation before he enters school. The Low German language has roughly the same patterns as English. Although in America it is purely a spoken language, it is an effective communication tool.[9] Some use it more skillfully than others; but during the sixteen years I used it daily, I never heard anyone correct another's usage. We did notice that the Low German spoken by the natives of a nearby community varied somewhat from ours in pronunciation of certain words. But the variations were only amusing, not confusing.

Language patterns which are as inescapable as politicians' speeches

[9]The twentieth-century revolution in transportation and communication will make it a dead dialect before the end of the century. Such a dialect can survive only in isolated communities.

can be observed in one's daily speech. The following basic patterns were taken from talks by seventh graders on "Why I Want to Go to College":

1. NOUN   VERB

   Graduates   succeed.

2. NOUN   VERB   NOUN

   I   train   dogs.

3. NOUN   LINKING VERB   ADJECTIVE

   Veterinarians   are   useful.

4. NOUN   LINKING VERB   NOUN

   Brothers   are   pests.

5. NOUN   LINKING VERB   ADVERB

   The cheerleaders   are   here.

In the English classes I have observed, I have only occasionally seen the language-pattern approach to teaching grammar. One teacher asked students to supply words (which made sense) for the following patterns which he had written on the blackboard:

1. Noun (subject)—verb.
2. Noun (subject)—noun.
3. Noun (subject)—linking verb—adjective.
4. Noun (subject)—linking verb—noun.
5. Noun (subject)—linking verb—adverb.

With some help, the students were able to produce simple sentences illustrating the patterns. The teacher then told them that written and spoken English is based on the five language patterns they illustrated and have been using most of their lives. They seemed pleased to learn that all the millions of people who use English are compelled to operate linguistically within five patterns.

The teacher next asked a a boy to write a sentence on the board illustrating Pattern No. 1. He wrote

Dogs howl.

The teacher then told them they usually use modifiers when they speak and write. He asked them to add single-word modifiers, then phrases, and finally clauses to the student's statement. The sentence passed through the following stages, with many additional unrecorded variations:

1. Dogs howl.
2. Stray dogs howl mournfully.
3. The stray dogs in our neighborhood howl mournfully at night.
4. The stray dogs in our neighborhood that I feed on the sly howl mournfully at night whenever the moon shines.

The teacher told me that the above demonstration of transforming basic sentences shows students that a subject and verb usually provide only the skeleton of a sentence, and that modifiers are commonly needed to communicate clearly an idea or feeling. He added, "The approach also helps them understand the functions of the parts of speech which they rarely acquire through completing labeling exercises in handbooks and workbooks." When I asked him how much time he devotes to the five sentence patterns he had written on the board, he said, "I use the rather formal approach you saw today at the beginning of the term, along with some material on the evolution of British and American English. Thereafter I relate instruction in language patterns, functions of modifiers, and historical and current changes in language directly to their work in written and oral composition and literature."

One can easily illustrate that these language patterns have persisted over the centuries. It is also easy to illustrate that many of the usages most English teachers label bad grammar were considered acceptable among educated people in Shakespeare's day;[10] and some of them (see 4, 5, 6, 8, 9 below) are still apparent in the speech and writing of educated Americans. All of them are represented in handbook and workbook exercises as departures from standard English.

1. I will *not* budge for *no* man's pleasure (*Romeo and Juliet*, III, i).
2. *More* larger *(Antony and Cleopatra*, III, vi).
3. *worser* (*Romeo and Juliet*, III, ii).
4. To speake *plaine* (*Much Ado About Nothing*, II, iii).
5. between you and *I* (The Merchant of Venice, III, ii).
6. *Who* does he accuse *(Antony and Cleopatra*, III, vi)?
7. twentie *mile* (*The Merry Wives of Windsor*, III, ii).
8. These *kind* of knaves (*King Lear*, II, ii).

[10]Before Wordsworth published his preface to the *Lyrical Ballads* in 1800, writers rarely gave the uneducated significant roles in their writings.

9. God send every one *their* hearts desire (*Much Ado About Nothing*, III, iv).

10. My old bones *akes* (*The Tempest*, III, iii).[11]

One can also easily find historical and current examples of changes in spelling, punctuation, pronunciation, capitalization, vocabulary, usage, and even subordination (compare the eighty-word sentences of seventeenth-century prose writers with sentences in today's *Harper's*). All of these changes take place within the framework of the sentence patterns (subject-verb, subject-verb-predicate adjective, etc.) illustrated above. The sentence patterns remain the same whether one says, "I laid down for a nap" or "I lay down for a nap"; "The data is correct" or "The data are correct"; "Everybody did their work" or "Everybody did his work"; "It is different than mine" or "It is different from mine"; "Can I be excused?" or "May I be excused?"; "I have got it" or "I have it."

To claim that the first sentence in each of the foregoing pairs is ambiguous or wrong seems ridiculous. Is there evidence that the usage in the second sentence of each pair is favored more frequently by educated people? One can argue, and most high school English teachers do, that educated people can be wrong. If one answers that almost all linguists support the idea that correct usage should be abstracted from the speech and writing of educated people, an English teacher could reply: "Defining *educated* is difficult; a person with a diploma or degree is not necessarily educated." And he is right if he claims that the first sentence in each pair would attract attention if used in addressing an audience of English teachers. However, Presidential candidates in the United States, even those who graduated from status schools, are apparently not handicapped by using "different than," "everybody . . . their," "have got," "Who are you looking for?" "I felt badly,"[12] "everyone . . . they," "data is," and "The reason is because. . . ." But the workbook maker usually insists the usages are unbecoming to educated people, assigning a zero (in his key) to the student who fails to label them incorrect.

In recent years, linguists have successfully introduced into many colleges and universities courses on the nature and development of English and the application of structural linguistics to writing, reading, speaking, spelling, and listening. Linguists have checked the English

[11]George H. McKnight and Bert Emsley, *Modern English in the Making* (New York: Appleton-Century-Crofts, 1928), Chapter 10. Copyright 1928 by Appleton-Century-Crofts.

[12]Some prominent television personalities unwittingly add to the comedy of their performances by accenting *badly* in "I felt badly" so emphatically that it seems clear that they are not only entertaining the peasants but even "educating" them.

language against the folklore disseminated in some handbooks and dictionaries. They have applied the scientific method to the study of language. Through historical research, they have revealed how and why the English language has changed. And through observing, recording, and analyzing English as it is spoken and written in various parts of the United States today, they are fast providing factual data which may overthrow some of the language absolutes preserved in many handbooks and defended by many English teachers.

Linguists have accumulated incontrovertible evidence that (1) the English language has changed and is changing; (2) there are different levels of usage; (3) the dialect of educated people is not pictured accurately in most handbooks; (4) most educated people shuttle between standard and colloquial levels; (5) certain specific sentence patterns are used by all who speak English and are learned before they enter school; (6) acceptable or unacceptable usage is finally determined by society (not grammarians) and influenced by time and place; (7) the levels of usage in a community can be revealed only through analyzing the language habits of the people; and (8) improved language habits are more likely to be achieved by students through guided reading, writing, speaking, and listening experiences than through the memorization of rules and completion of workbook and handbook exercises.

Since the "good-grammar" teachers advocate the dialect educated people use in formal writing and speaking, one should ask how this differs from the "bad grammar" of uneducated people. W. W. Charters, who tabulated the speech and writing errors of thousands of elementary school children in 1914, discovered that their unorthodox use of verbs accounted for approximately 57 percent of the errors made, pronouns 14 percent, double negatives 11 percent, mixing of adverbs and adjectives 4 percent.[13]

A high school English teacher asked to isolate the most common serious errors in English usage will mention first the misuse of verbs, particularly the past and past participle of *lie, lay, sit, set, do, see, rise, raise, hang, drink, run, go, burst, know,* and *write.* A speaker presumed to be educated addressing an educated audience can cause an epidemic of eyebrow lifting with "He don't . . . ," "I seen . . . ," "You was . . . ," "I learned him," "I knowed," "He should of wrote,"[14] or "I don't know no. . . ." No response of similar epidemic proportions would greet his

---

[13]Henry L. Mencken, *The American Language*, Fourth Edition (New York: Alfred A. Knopf, Inc., 1962), p. 420.

[14]A colleague claims when he marked an "F" on a student's one-page term paper ("Religion in the *Odyssey* Compared with Modern Catholicism") and added the comment that although brevity is not a vice, it is not always a virtue, the student came in to lament, "If I had knowed you wanted it, I would of wrote more."

use of "I can't hardly . . . ," "He stepped off of . . . ," "He is different than
. . . ," "They planned to invite Hilda, Julius, and I," "It was him," "He
was afraid of we men," "I promised to help whomever wins," "Neither
of them did their assignments," "Not one of the women were," "There's
two or three acts," "Those kind are good," "They had a real good turn-
out," "I felt badly," "He left it go," "Between you and I," "He walks like
his father does," "Can I be excused," or "Who are you working with?"
Departures from standard English which jolt educated people are those
involving certain irregular verbs, but the intensity of the jolt varies with
the verbs misused. "He laid there for an hour" and "They have drank[15]
more than they should" are more likely to go unnoticed than "I seen him
there an hour ago" and "I should have went sooner."

Charters' discovery that verbs (mostly irregular) accounted for over
50 percent of the serious mistakes in elementary students' usage does not
surprise one who examines the principal parts of certain pairs of verbs:
sit-set, rise-raise, and *lie-lay.* Some English majors become confused when
asked to list the principal parts of the foregoing verbs, although very few
of them use them incorrectly in their speech and writing—except that for
the past tense of *lie,* many of them used *laid.* Memorizing the principal
parts of irregular verbs does not guarantee improvement in their use.

The next most common serious error discovered by Charters is also
easily explained, because many students have difficulty in choosing between the objective and subjective case forms of personal pronouns (*I-me,
he-him, she-her, we-us,* and *they-them*) and relative pronouns (*who-whom*).
Once a student has entered school, he rarely uses the objective case form
of a personal pronoun as the subject when it occurs singly at the beginning of a sentence ("Me want to go"), but he may say, "Mary Jo and
me went." And he seldom uses subjective case forms of personal pronouns
when they occur immediately after a preposition ("Go with I") or a verb
("You will see I tomorrow"). But some students use the subjective case
forms of personal pronouns as the object of a verb or preposition when a
number of words intervene between the preposition or verb and the pronoun: "The prizes were divided among Al, Loretta, Bill, Frances, and
I" or "They invited Annette, Gisela, Jerry, Andrew, and I."

The average student has trouble when personal pronouns are linked
to the subject by linking verbs. He is likely to say, "It's him, her, us,
them"; and he probably shuns the relative pronoun *whom* like the plague.
If the distinction between *who* and *whom* is taught in the classroom, he
may, for a day or two, recognize the existence of *whom* by saying, "*Whom*
are you?" or, if he possesses leadership qualities, "I'll give the back of

---

[15]Some shun *drunk* because of its unpleasant connotations.

my hand to *whomever* uses *whom* incorrectly." Should he, as a cheerleader, clap his hands thrice and call for, "One, two, three, four, *whom* are we for?" his English teachers might have mixed feelings—compliment him for replacing *who* with *whom*, whisper a boo for ending a cheer with a preposition—but his classmates might terminate his tenure as cheerleader.

A really radical revision of "One, two, three, four, *who* are we for?" occurred to me: "One, two, three, for whom are we?" The cheer, above reproach in its usage, presented tempting possibilities of a tremendous sales potential and financial gains. But I give it free to humanity. Introduce the cheer in your school. If it gains acceptance, you might next attempt to convert cheerleaders to "Two, four, six, eight, *whom* do we appreciate?" and win even more hysterical plaudits.

Many linguists have labeled various usages standard, colloquial, and illiterate; it is interesting to note that those labeled illiterate involve mostly irregular verbs and unadulterated double negatives (not "I can't hardly" but "I don't have no"). English teachers should take a hint from such data and strive to eliminate illiterate usages from students' speech and writing. But most of them assume the impossible task of converting students completely to standard English as defined in handbooks and workbooks—a language used by comparatively few educated people, and then only, as a rule, in formal situations.

Most student teachers usually teach usage, spelling, punctuation, vocabulary, or capitalization as separate subjects. When asked about the weaknesses of their piecemeal approach, which often excludes written composition, most of them say they fear penalties when they depart from the critic teacher's pattern. A few admit they need the security which accompanies limiting the day's activities to a page or two in the workbook, a spelling list, or a vocabulary list. They say that basing instruction in grammar and usage on excerpts from students' compositions encourages questions and comments not covered in workbook and handbook keys.

Some of the student teachers who cannot afford to antagonize critic teachers by experimental grammar and usage instruction become critic teachers free to choose their teaching methods; but by then, unfortunately, they have become permanently addicted to the handbook and workbook exercises and spelling and vocabulary lists. Furthermore, even student teachers who accept enthusiastically the logic of scholars' conclusions about different levels of English usage seem relieved to rid themselves of a lot of hard work by accepting the verdict of some critic teachers that high school students are confused unless all usage is lumped under two labels: standard and illiterate, or right and wrong.

The rational approach to detecting the usage strengths and weaknesses of students is to analyze their speech and writing. Since such an analysis will reveal that some students need very little instruction in usage and others a great deal, why should those with few, if any usage problems waste many hours completing usage exercises in handbooks and workbooks? (Also, there is no evidence that students who need a great deal of instruction in usage profit from completing these exercises.) Furthermore, even though students must understand the various levels of usage and learn to operate on the standard level when the occasion demands it, the teacher's job is primarily to help them communicate clearly and thoughtfully rather than merely "correctly." Of what value are flawless table manners to one who has nothing to eat and acceptable usage patterns to one who has nothing to say?

Anyone who reads and listens does discover that mistakes in usage can interfere with communication. A speaker or writer is handicapped when his departures from acceptable usage draw attention away from what he is saying. Moreover, a supposedly educated person is classified otherwise, and sometimes penalized severely, for slipping to a usage level presumed to be reserved for the uneducated. For example, a professor of business education seemed proud to say that as he went through a stack of applications (letters) for a graduate assistantship, he threw away all which did not hew closely to standard English usage. He may have passed up the most capable person for the appointment, but he was convinced that any deviations from standard usage would make functioning effectively as a graduate assistant impossible. Many employers feel the same way; but, fortunately, most of them do not have the professor's eye or ear for detecting an applicant's amendments to the laws of standard English.

ASSUMPTIONS ABOUT TEACHING
LANGUAGE HISTORY, GRAMMAR, AND USAGE

Prepare to explain why you accept or reject, wholly or in part, the following assumptions about the nature of language:

1. Languages change.
2. High school students vary their language to suit the situation in which they find themselves.
3. There are different levels of language: standard, colloquial, and illiterate. (Some English teachers use *unacceptable* in place of *illiterate*.)
4. To avoid confusion, the teacher must convince students that only standard English is acceptable among educated people.
5. Good English usage is determined by analyzing the dialect of educated people.

6. One can justify a comparison between language levels (standard, colloquial, illiterate) and eating etiquette levels (formal, family, picnic).

7. A child's sentence patterns have become established when he enters kindergarten or the first grade.

8. There are differences between American English and British English.

9. American English has borrowed heavily from other languages.

10. Chaucer was the "first fyndere of our faire language" and "the well of English undefiled."

11. There is a difference in meaning between *grammar* and *usage*.

12. Serious mistakes in usage interfere with communication.

13. Usage, spelling, punctuation, vocabulary, and capitalization should be taught as separate subjects.

14. Educated people use only standard English.

15. Drill exercises in usage are indispensable in developing good written and oral usage.

16. Language habits are acquired from people with whom we associate.

17. Many English teachers broadcast half-truths and falsehoods about the nature of language.

18. Instruction in usage should be based on the usage errors students make in their speech and writing.

19. Slang has had a long and interesting influence on the English language.

20. Words can acquire new meanings and lose old ones.

21. A simplified system of spelling would save teachers and students many hours of work and worry and reduce the costs of printers and publishers.

22. There are excellent arguments for and against a teacher's correcting his students' oral usage errors as they make them in the classroom.

23. Practically all students make the same mistakes in usage.

24. The plain people, hereafter as in the past, will continue to make their own language, and the best that grammarians can do is to follow after it, haltingly, and not often with much insight into it.[16]

25. In the National Council of Teachers of English's Monograph No. 7, *Facts about Current English Usage*, presenting separate usage studies by (1) Sterling A. Leonard and (2) Albert H. Marckwardt and Fred G. Walcott, the conclusions reached in both studies were the same.

26. Arthur G. Kennedy's *English Usage* reflects more conservatism on questions of usage than Robert C. Pooley's *Teaching English Usage*.

[16]Henry L. Mencken, *The American Language*, p. 473.

27. Charles Carpenter Fries' analysis of letters addressed to a bureau of the Federal Government reveals some useful facts about the usage habits of people with varying amounts of education.[17]

28. Writers who contribute serious articles to *Harper's* and *The Atlantic* use standard English (as defined in handbooks) exclusively.

29. H. L. Mencken, in *The American Language*, provides many interesting and worthwhile facts and conclusions about the evolution of American English.

30. A comparison of brief excerpts from early editions of the writings of Chaucer, Shakespeare, Milton, Pope, Wordsworth, Tennyson, and Masefield reveals evolutionary processes in spelling, capitalization, vocabulary, punctuation, and usage.

31. Linguists apply the scientific method to the study of languages.

32. The social-pressure approach ("good English is the dialect of educated people") is effective in motivating students to improve their usage.

33. Knowing the derivation of words adds nothing to one's ability to communicate clearly and effectively.

34. A speaker or writer is not seriously handicapped if he limits his use of verbs to the following verbs in C. K. Ogden's "Index to Basic Words": *be, come, do, get, give, have, keep, go, let, make, may, put, say, see, seem, send, take,* and *will.*[18]

35. Millions of American children who cannot define *good usage* or *good grammar* speak the dialect of educated people.

36. Mastery of the principles of structural linguistics or formal grammar should not be considered a desirable substitute for practice in writing and speaking under the guidance of a competent teacher.

37. We are justified in making students whose speech and writing reflect pronounced linguistic aberrations feel inferior.

38. The dialect of educated people allows differences in the pronunciation of *been, amen, art, either, neither, can't, creek, rodeo, greasy,* and *Cuba.*

39. That some words still have a magic quality for some people is recognized by hotels which avoid 13 in numbering floors.

40. To determine "correct" usage, we should go back to the "goode olde dayes," spelling excepted.

41. *Ain't* will never make the dialect of educated people.

42. To master a language, eschew practice—describe, analyze, and categorize its individual structures.

[17]Charles Carpenter Fries, *American English Grammar* (New York: D. Appleton-Century Company, Inc., 1940), Chapter 3, etc.

[18]C. K. Ogden, *The System of Basic English* (New York: Harcourt, Brace and Company, 1934), pp. 309–318.

43. If the new grammar achieves separate-subject status—replete with handbook and workbook materials which students must master—it will soon become as successful as formal grammar in preventing students from developing speaking and writing skills.

44. Dictionaries are like watches; the worst is better than none, and the best cannot be expected to go quite true (Samuel Johnson).

45. In an age of specialization, some English teachers should teach only grammar, others only literature.

46. English usage in the literary selections in Appendices 13, 15, 16, and 17 is dated.

47. Words are like leaves, some wither ev'ry year,
And ev'ry year a younger race succeeds (Horace).

48. For evil . . . as well as good, words make us the human beings we actually are. Deprived of language we should be as dogs or monkeys (Aldous Huxley).

49. Students can be helped to discover the nature of their language system as they read, write, speak, and listen.

IDEAS TO TEST

For your convenience, the following "Ideas to Test" are listed under *History*, *Grammar*, and *Usage*.

History

1. Play a brief passage from a recording designed to duplicate the sounds of Chaucer's language. Providing each student with a mimeographed copy of the passage while he listens will help him get its meaning and some understanding of the relationship between Chaucer's spelling and the sounds. Mimeographed passages from Shakespeare, Milton, Addison, Johnson, Scott, and Dickens could be compared with Chaucer's language to reveal some of the changes in the English language over a span of five hundred years.

2. Abstract material from H. L. Mencken, Chapter I, "The Two Streams of English," *The American Language*, that demonstrates how American English evolved from a British English base.

3. Abstract material from Frederick Bodmer, *The Loom of Language*, to show the similarities among Teutonic languages, among Romance languages, and between Teutonic and Romance languages.

4. Ask students to illustrate and evaluate the contributions to communication of (1) gestures, (2) facial expressions, (3) sounds of nature,

(4) sounds of animals, (5) pictures, (6) sculpture, (7) architecture, (8) music, and (9) wordless signs and signals.

5. Ask students to use pantomime to convey an experience or feeling to their classmates.

Grammar

1. Ask students to write definitions of what they call *good grammar* and *bad grammar*. Compare, illustrate, and discuss the definitions.

2. Help students provide, underneath the following sequences of the parts of speech, words which make sentences:

  a. Noun or pronoun—verb
  b. Noun or pronoun—verb—noun or pronoun
  c. Noun or pronoun—linking verb—noun or pronoun
  d. Noun or pronoun—linking verb—adjective
  e. Noun or pronoun—linking verb—adverb

Ask students whether they can provide other basic sentence patterns.

3. Ask students to add single word modifiers, then phrase modifiers, and, finally, clause modifiers to "The dog bit the boy" which will provide details about dog, boy, and time. Also, ask the students to illustrate how using auxiliary verbs with *bite* and *bitten* changes the meaning of the sentence.

4. Ask students to demonstrate under what circumstances the following single words may be complete sentences: *John, fine, good, yes, no, quickly, jump, again, so,* and *perhaps.* Then ask them to demonstrate how the meanings of the one-word sentences can be changed in speech by intonation and in writing by the use of punctuation marks. (Example: John? John! John.)

5. Ask students to illustrate the versatility of the word *well* by using it as a noun, adjective, adverb, verb and interjection.

6. Ask students to illustrate why they accept or reject the following assumption: What you say is found not in the noun but in what you add to qualify the noun. . . . The noun, the verb, and the main clause serve merely as the base on which meaning will rise. . . . The modifier is the essential part of any sentence. (From John Erskine, "Note on the Writer's Craft," *Twentieth Century English* (New York: The Philosophical Library, 1946), p. 255, William S. Knickerbocker, editor.)

Usage

1. Ask students to explain how they feel about having their written and oral English corrected by teachers and other adults.

2. Ask a few interested students to demonstrate regional differences in pronunciation and usage. There may be students in your class who exemplify natural differences in speech.

3. Present students with facts illustrating differences in usage and pronunciation among different social levels. Ask students to check the facts by observing usage levels in their own community.

4. Encourage interested students to read George Bernard Shaw's *Pygmalion* and report why they agree or disagree with Shaw's thesis in the play.

5. Keep a written record of your students' most common departures from standard usage in their speech and writing. Then ask the class to (1) list them under *colloquial* or *unacceptable* and (2) be prepared to defend their decisions.

6. To help students develop an ear for the different levels of usage, read to them a short list of their own oral and written statements which reflect standard, colloquial, and unacceptable usage. Give them enough time between each statement to label the usage and jot down a brief defense of the label. In the discussion that follows, (1) compare the labels applied to the statements and (2) try to reach a consensus on the proper one for each statement.

7. The National Association for the Advancement of Colored People objected to including Paul Laurence Dunbar's "New England" and "Negro" dialect poems in high school literature anthologies, even though both dialects originated in England. Ask students whether they can explain why the NAACP objects to including these dialect poems in anthologies, when the objection has led to the elimination of the once-famous Negro poet's work from almost all literature anthologies. (The NAACP apparently concluded that the "Negro" and "New England" dialects used by Dunbar picture the Negro as illiterate and thus degrade him.)

8. Give your students an objective usage test, and compare their scores with what you have observed about their usage in written and oral composition. (I have occasionally recorded student teachers' oral statements containing usage errors, then asked them to take a test involving correcting the statements and defending the corrections. Some of them make a hundred on the test but fall into the same errors the next day. Even though they know the rules, they do not use them in their speech.)

9. Determine the usage instruction your students need by analyzing their speech and writing. You will discover that many students need little, if any, instruction, others a great deal. By determining this, you will immediately find that editing usage errors in workbook and handbook exercises is carrying coals to Newcastle for many of them.

10. Have small groups of students help each other eliminate from

their compositions errors in usage, spelling, punctuation, and capitalization. Also, give instruction which will enable them to help each other improve theme organization, paragraphing, sentence structure, and content.

11. To point up interesting vocabulary differences between American and British English, ask students whether they can give the American equivalents (given in parentheses) of the following British nouns: *hoarding* (billboard), *biscuit* (cookie), *chemist* (druggist), *lift* (elevator), *stores* (groceries), *black treacle* (molasses), *draughts* (checkers), *bonnet* (automobile hood), *flickers* (movies), *minerals* (soft drinks), *hood* (automobile top), *lorry* (truck), *bank raider* (bank robber), *parking pitch* (*parking place*), and *dustman* (garbage collector).

12. Convince students there are no true synonyms by asking them to insert the most suitable word—*fat, corpulent, portly, stout, chunky, heavy, obese, large, big, chubby,* or *huge*—in the blank space in the following advertisement: "We have a complete line of suits for_____men."

13. Ask students to add to the following list additional old words which have taken on new duties since football became a popular sport: *Statue of Liberty, block, blitz, roll out, back, clipping, red-dog, bomb, gridiron, pigskin,* and *punt.* Students might also list some of the old words that have been given new meanings since baseball and basketball players, writers, and fans began building special vocabularies for the two sports.

10

Helping Students
Understand the Nature
of Language:
Part II

Before reading this chapter, formulate clear, defensible answers to the following questions. After reading it, prepare to explain why you changed or retained your answers.

1. How do you define *semantics*?

2. *Language is a system of symbols or labels* is a common semantic principle. When an American child sees a bird, he may say "bird." A French child would say "oiseau." The object (bird) which triggers the response "bird" or "oiseau" is called a *referent*. What are the referents for *pen, shoes,* and *watch*? What are the referents for fictions, words like *democracy, communism, justice,* and *truth*?

3. *Language must reflect reality* is a second common semantic principle. What is reality? How does one ascertain reality? Describe a drop of water. Then place it under a microscope and describe it. Which description, if either, reflects reality?

4. *One cannot say all about anything* is a third common semantic principle. Whenever you say something you abstract, leave out details. Which details do you omit when you say "John, one of my students, isn't very bright"? Why is abstracting inevitable whenever you speak, write, or think?

5. How can you help students read and listen critically, and speak and write clearly and thoughtfully?

DEFINING SEMANTICS

The word *semantics* was derived from *sémantique*, coined by Michel Bréal, a Frenchman, in 1897. To Bréal, semantics was principally the study

165

of the evolution of languages, an analysis of "the intellectual causes which have influenced the transformation of our languages."[1] He traced the evolution of many words: how *species*—standing for *saffron, cloves, cinnamon, nutmeg* in the vocabulary of druggists in the Middle Ages—changed to *spices*;[2] how *gain* originally meant *harvest* to Frenchmen and gradually was extended in meaning until it included "produce obtained by all kinds of work and even that acquired without work";[3] and how many words, through a process of evolution, came to mean almost the opposite of what they originally meant.[4] He also illustrated how metaphor contributes to the expansion of language and how synonyms are an impossibility—"either they are differentiated or else one ceases to exist."[5]

Bréal's work resembles that of modern semanticists—Ogden, Richards, Korzybski, and Walpole—when he demonstrates that metaphor increases the meanings of a word, abstracting is inevitable (the "amount of truth which can be contained by a name . . . is of necessity small in proportion to the reality of the object"),[6] and words are not objects but represent objects (words "have no more existence than the signals of a semaphore, or than the dots and dashes of Morse telegraphy").[7] Bréal also emphasized that language is composed primarily of words which do not point directly to objects in our environment:

> We have only to take the page of any book, and to suppress all the words which, not corresponding to any objective reality, must be the result of an operation of the mind. Of a page so treated hardly anything will remain.[8]

Recent writers on semantics largely ignore what concerned Bréal most—the transformation and evolution of language; they devote their attention to what he mentioned incidentally—abstracting, finding referents for fictions, and reflecting reality in language.

Alfred Korzybski's *Science and Sanity* (first edition, 1933) did much to stimulate interest in semantics. In its over seven hundred pages, semantic principles are applied to man's social problems. Korzybski emphasized the necessity of making language reflect the world's structure, things as they are: "Any map or language, to be of maximum usefulness, should, in structure, be similar to the structure of the empirical world."[9]

---

[1]Michel Bréal, *Semantics: Studies in the Science of Meaning*, trans. Mrs. Henry Cust (London: William Heinemann Ltd., Publishers, 1900), p. 5.

[2]*Ibid.*, p. 109. [5]*Ibid.*, p. 28. [8]*Ibid.*, p. 247.

[3]*Ibid.*, p. 116. [6]*Ibid.*, p. 172.

[4]*Ibid.*, p. 145 [7]*Ibid.*, p. 249.

[9]Alfred Korzybski, *Science and Sanity*, Fourth Edition (Lakeville, Conn.: The International Non-Aristotelian Library Publishing Company, Institute of General Semantics Distributors, 1958), p. 11.

He believed the structure of the empirical world is most likely to be revealed to man through applying the scientific method to current problems.

Korzybski's main thesis—we should use the scientific method to reveal reality—is illustrated in the life of Copernicus (1473–1543). Copernicus felt the words *The sun moves around the earth* did not reflect the structure of the universe. He was intrigued by the hypothesis of ancient Greek astronomers: the earth moves around the sun. After years of tests and investigations, he was convinced our universe is sun-centered rather than earth-centered. Tycho Brahe (1546–1601), Johannes Kepler (1571–1630), and Galileo (1564–1642) made further tests which verified, refined, and expanded Copernicus' conclusions. Eventually the Copernican theory was accepted by the Church, which had pronounced it heresy because it seemed to relegate man from the center of the universe to its fringes.

The label *general semantics* is used by some semanticists to differentiate their emphasis on making language a more effective tool in human affairs from Bréal's emphasis on the evolution of language. However, most speakers and writers use the term *semantics* instead. The concerns of general semanticists are reflected in the titles of books written by Korzybski and his interpreters (*Science and Sanity* is difficult reading): Stuart Chase's *The Tyranny of Words*, S. I. Hayakawa's *Language in Thought and Action*, Irving Lee's *Language Habits in Human Affairs*, and Wendell Johnson's *People in Quandaries*. The four books, original contributions even though influenced by Korzybski, should appeal to English teachers because they illustrate clearly and interestingly how semantic principles can be applied to today's language problems.

Prior to the twentieth century, Englishmen John Locke (1632–1704) (*An Essay Concerning Human Understanding*) and Jeremy Bentham (1748–1832)[10] and an American, A. B. Johnson (1786–1867) (*Treatise on Language: or the Relation Which Words Bear to Things)*[11] illustrated clearly and dramatically, without benefit of the term *semantics*, that words are symbols which label ideas and objects inexactly. Locke and Bentham were especially concerned with abstract terms (fictions) because their referents are not easily found in one's environment and are, consequently, interpreted differently by everyone. In the twentieth century Bertrand Russell in *An Inquiry into Meaning and Truth*, P. W. Bridgman in *The*

[10]See C. K. Ogden's *Bentham's Theory of Fictions* (New York: Harcourt, Brace, and Company, 1943).

[11]Published in 1836, the book is superior to some written over a hundred years later. Only two copies of *Treatise . . .* are in public libraries; but in 1948 Irving Lee edited one of A. B. Johnson's later works (originally published in 1854): A. B. Johnson, *The Meanings of Words Analyzed into Words and Unverbal Things, and Unverbal Things Classified into Intellections, Sensations, and Emotions* (Milwaukee: John Chamberlin, 1948).

Intelligent Individual and Society, and Thurman Arnold in *The Folklore of Capitalism* demonstrated an awareness of semantic principles without relying on the term *semantics.*

Before and after the word *semantics* came into general use, many high school English teachers urged underlining critical reading and listening and clear, thoughtful speaking and writing in English curricula. The general semanticist agrees with them, but believes that the skills are more likely to be mastered if students become keenly aware of the implications of three semantic principles: (1) the inevitability of abstracting (omitting details) in speech and writing; (2) the necessity of checking language against reality; and (3) the necessity of finding referents for words they read and hear and providing them for words they speak and write.

Some teachers believe that semantic principles should be taught incidentally, as students read, write, speak, and listen. Others believe that incidental instruction must be reinforced by devoting, once or twice a year, a week or more to applying these principles to carefully selected language activities.

In the following pages are presented (1) definitions and illustrations of three semantic principles, "Abstracting Is Inevitable," "Language Must Reflect Reality," and "Find the Referent" and (2) suggestions on applying semantic principles to students' reading, writing, speaking, and listening activities.

"ABSTRACTING IS INEVITABLE"

No one has been able to say all about an object, feeling, or idea; details are always omitted by man's every label, description, or inference. When a mathematics teacher says, "John is dumb," he may imply he is saying *all* about John, but he has left out perhaps dozens of significant details. John may be a fine student in one or more academic subjects, an excellent artist or musician, and a superb athlete. Furthermore, the mathematics teacher may be suffering from indigestion or lack of sleep; or he may be comparing John's work with that of John's mathematically gifted brother.

Why is it impossible to say all about anything? Words are not what they label; they are symbols that stand for objects, ideas, and experiences. When a person calls a pen a writing instrument, it is obvious that a pen is more than the words *writing instrument*; it is an object on the nonverbal level—words alone cannot reveal all of its characteristics. The inability of words to do more than roughly represent experiences is made clear when one attempts to describe the flavor of red pepper, the aroma of roasting peanuts, or the feel of a razor's edge.

Although semanticists say that only a few details can normally be abstracted from a total situation, a few details presented by an able

168   IMPROVING ENGLISH INSTRUCTION

poet can sometimes convey more meaning to readers than their actual experiences. During World War I, thousands of hurrying citizens saw a laughing young man move buttons one inch west or east on the war map in front of a newspaper office. They probably said "Good" or "Too bad," depending on the direction the buttons were moved; but Carl Sandburg portrayed vividly in "Buttons" the cost in American, French, British, and German lives which preceded the moving of buttons one inch east or one inch west. Sandburg saw beyond the territorial gains or losses on the Western Front, and was able to abstract from what he saw a word picture which caused many of his readers to understand for the first time that newspaper headlines announcing victories and defeats are written in the blood of soldiers.

An anecdote in Lesage (1668–1747)'s *Gil Blas* reveals how dislike of an individual can cause people to abstract from an experience an indefensible conclusion. A known braggart told a throng he could impersonate a pig's squeals more realistically than a competitor who had just won its approval. He was shouted down, but finally gained the platform. His impersonation was soundly booed. Imagine the discomfiture of the crowd when he produced a live pig from underneath his coat—the pig whose grunts and squeals it had so vigorously booed. Another story impugns the judgment of a more sophisticated audience: Whenever Enrico Caruso sang a leading role, he was called out for encore after encore; but when occasionally he sang long arias behind stage, the applause was perfunctory.

Many evaluative words are abstractions that semanticists say reflect a *two-valued orientation*; i.e., some individuals choose evaluative labels which almost always mirror one of two extremes: good or bad, sane or insane, bright or dumb, rich or poor, high or low, hot or cold, democratic or undemocratic, happy or miserable, white or black. Such two-valued judgments are purely verbal; they cannot be defended if checked with the object level. For example, psychologists have classified individuals as idiots, imbeciles, morons, dull, normal, bright, very bright, and geniuses. Each one of the classifications can be particularized; no two idiots or geniuses are alike. Many people conclude that they must be either superior or inferior. Students sometimes say they have inferiority complexes. One reason is that they abstract from the behavior of others only what is good and from their own behavior only what is bad. They forget that no one is superior or inferior in all respects.

"LANGUAGE MUST REFLECT REALITY"

Man has always sought answers to questions about reality. Primitive man was terrified by lightning and thunder (see Robert Browning's "Caliban upon Setebos") and perplexed by birth, sickness, dreams, and death; so he formulated theories designed to provide peace of mind. He gradually became aware that his theories were not always correct—a significant step in the development of the scientific method. However, unlike today's scientists, he did not consciously and persistently test them.

No one can ascertain the world's structure with finality. The scientist is continuously revising his always tentative conclusions about it. His structure of the universe (reality), he states a problem, gathers data related to the problem, formulates hypotheses he hopes will solve the problem, and tests the hypotheses. He continues this procedure until the problem method is to observe, experiment, and test. To discover facts about the is solved or deemed unsolvable. Reliance on the scientific method has brought success in the treatment of tuberculosis, some cancers, yellow fever, diphtheria, polio, and other once "incurable" diseases, but has also produced weapons that threaten man's survival.

The scientific method has been widely used during the last four hundred years, but it cannot be credited to one man or a hundred. It grew out of the history of the human race. Primitive man's crude theories were steps in the gradual refinement of the scientific method. Even the farfetched diagnostic and prescriptive folklore about human ills—mental and physical—quoted by Robert Burton (1577–1640) in his *Anatomy of Melancholy* are attempts to account for and cure all the ills flesh is heir to. They are hypotheses which over the centuries were gradually rejected and replaced with new hypotheses. However, today many people still profess a faith in astrology, phrenology, numerology, and some kinds of advertising which equal in naïveté the faith in medicines catalogued by Burton made up of hair, excreta, roses, violets, precious stones, capon and dormouse grease, and the earwax of dogs.

The modern scientist's beliefs about the structure of the universe are easily summarized: Observation and experimentation have led him to assume that the universe and everything in it is constantly changing, Heraclitus' (sixth-fifth century B. C.) conclusion; matter is extremely complex; there are no absolutes—theories must be revised as additional data become available; valid experimental results can be duplicated by others; and many questions cannot be answered, at least not at present. He realizes that the label *knowledge* shelters assumptions useful only when they help man gain increasing control over his environment. Einstein believed his theory of relativity was the best current explanation of the structure of the universe and would serve as a problem-solving tool, but he conceded it might eventually be supplanted by a more versatile theory.

When a student looks at a drop of water, he sees transparent liquid. Should he examine it under a microscope, he might find it teeming with life. Should he ask a scientist about the structure of water, he might hear that water is a flow of electricity. This illustration indicates that what we see when we look at a drop of water, the bark of a tree, a blade of grass, or a grain of sand with the naked eye is quite different from what we see of them under a microscope. What we see with a microscope may be little compared with what we might see should its power be doubled. And there may always be a submicroscopic or inferred level which man's instruments cannot reach.[12]

Faith in absolutes makes the language of most people primitive in structure. When Jean Valjean, the leading character in Victor Hugo's *Les Misérables*, was released from the galley, he was given a yellow passport. The yellow passport meant *criminal* to almost all who saw it, so most doors were closed to him. Today many people distrust anyone who has served a prison sentence even though many former lawbreakers lead exemplary lives. An individual's faith in absolutes dissolves when he understands that all things change and most of what we call knowledge is made up of suppositions (theories, assumptions) which are accepted tentatively and replaced with more versatile ones.[13] In colonial times, followers of John Calvin (1509–1564) believed all men were predestined at birth to heaven or hell; but Michael Wigglesworth, a stern Calvinist, softened somewhat when it came to sentencing the child—to the infant predestined to eternal damnation he assigned the "easiest room in hell."[14] Today some people still insist our Constitution is a sacred document good for all time and should not be changed, even though the many amendments are called to their attention. The individual who would avoid absolutes must revise his theories whenever new data justify such revisions.

Perhaps the primitive structure of many people's language can be attributed to their unfamiliarity with the scientific method, or, if they are acquainted with it, their conviction that it can be applied only to problems relating to the physical universe. They feel that in solving economic, religious, governmental, and other social problems, it is best to draw upon the absolutes of our ancestors, the founding fathers.[15]

[12]See Wendell Johnson, *Language and Speech Hygiene: An Application of General Semantics* (Chicago: Institute of General Semantics, 1939), pp. 15–21.

[13]Note the labels used for two celebrated theories: *theory of evolution* and *theory of relativity*. Both theories have been used to reveal more of reality.

[14]See Michael Wigglesworth's *Day of Doom*, a verse summation of the Puritan creed. (The first time the author taught *Day of Doom*, he asked his students, high school sophomores, "What beliefs do all Christian creeds hold in common?" A boy answered, "All Christians believe in God and immorality.")

[15]However, the appellation "founding fathers" is usually earned by those who challenge successfully the absolutes of their ancestors.

People are not born with absolutes. Children are usually inquisitive; but as they grow older, they are often conditioned so thoroughly to accept what is that their curiosity (the trademark of the scientist) disappears. If they relied on the scientific method to solve problems, their ideas and behavior would be controlled less by conditioned responses.

"FIND THE REFERENT"

There is no inherent connection between a word and its referent.[16] When one of two friends walking in the woods sees an object (referent), a certain bird, he thinks (reference), and then labels the object with the word (symbol) *oriole*. His friend who hears him say *oriole* reverses the order—he hears his friend say the word, thinks, and if possible, looks at the object. If their references (thoughts) about the object result in different labels, *oriole* and *cardinal*, they can perhaps study the referent (*bird*) further and agree on the correct label. If the two friends were Germans, the labels would be different. This further demonstrates that there is no inherent connection between symbol (word) and referent (object).

The emphasis on finding the referent seems superfluous if one accepts the claim of some semanticists that words which do not label a specific object are meaningless noises. But the emphasis seems justifiable when we recognize that words both with and without observable referents seem to have definite, through variable, meanings for most people. When the curator of an art museum says to an art expert, "This picture is a Rembrandt," the expert can analyze the referent (*picture*) and explain why he agrees, disagrees, or chooses to suspend judgment. When Politician I says to an audience of factory workers, "My opponent, Politician II, has betrayed you," the referent for *betrayed* is not so easily ascertained. Could Politician I prove to his audience that Politician II voted against every bill designed to benefit labor, explaining also the main provisions of each bill, he might be justified in asking them to conclude that Politician II voted against the worker's interests. Even then, referents provided by Politician II—the good of the country as a whole, undesirable long-term results of pro-labor legislation, etc.—might provide a logical refutation of the "betrayed you" accusation.

The words of a speaker or writer must be related definitely to referents which have been part of the experiences of his listeners or readers, or the words will be Greek to them. For example, a bookkeeping teacher's lecture on assets, liabilities, proprietorship, income, costs, gross profit, expenses, and net profit is likely to lack meaning for students unless the

---

[16]See the "Ogden and Richards Triangle" in C. K. Ogden and I. A. Richards, *The Meaning of Meaning* (New York: Harcourt, Brace, and Company, 1927), p. 11.

teacher relates the bookkeeper's terminology to familiar words and experiences. Students asked to subtract their debts (liabilities) from the money value of their belongings (assets) can easily ascertain what they are worth (proprietorship); and they begin to understand the bookkeeper's terminology in the process. Similarly, students who sell newspapers can list what their customers pay them under income, what they pay the publisher for newspapers under cost, and subtract the cost from income to give them their profit before expenses are deducted, i.e., gross profit. They can then subtract their expenses from their gross profit to give them the amount they actually made, net profit. If the bookkeeper's terminology is not related to students' experiences (to referents familiar to them), they can only parrot it.

Some students fail in algebra, literature, and science because they are not helped to find referents for the subjects' key words. Finding and checking the referents for a newspaper's vital statistics section, cooking recipes, results of athletic contests, and weather reports is usually fairly simple. However, when an editor editorializes about political happenings, labor organizations, or economic conditions, his referents may mirror personal bias or the policies of the newspaper's owners.

Finding the referent for a word is usually fairly simple when the referent can be tasted, felt, heard, smelled, or touched—discovered by the senses. Primitive man's language was probably made up mostly of nouns which labeled specific referents: *tree, stone, animal, water, boy, girl, fish,* and *sun.* But when man began asking "Why?" about the universe, other men, and himself, began to formulate hypotheses about things he did not understand, he coined words semanticists call *fictions.*

What are fictions? In one sense all words are fictions, even words with obvious referents, because all words are symbols used to label objects, ideas, sounds, and behavior. But the label *fiction* is reserved for words which do not point to an object in the environment, words like *justice, truth,* and *loyalty.* One who is skeptical about the emotive power of most fictions should ask friends to define *democracy, socialism,* or *communism.* Furthermore, many people fictionalize (overrate) the worth of movie stars, athletes, politicians, and pets. People unmoved by movie stars may worship builders of verbal Utopias: Plato, More, Bacon, Butler, Bellamy, and others.

An individual who is aware that words are merely symbols pointing to objects or ideas will, whenever possible, check words against what they represent on the nonverbal level. He realizes that (1) his interpretation of a referent will not be the same as anyone else's because no two individuals ever have identical experiential backgrounds, (2) he must find the other person's referent for communication to take place, and

(3) he must exercise exceptional care in checking the referents of fictional terms. For example, if an organization claims to be democratic, he may check whether its policies and procedures are (1) determined and carried out by all of its members or just a few and (2) in conflict with the Constitution. If most men applied "Find the referent!" to a writer's or speaker's name-calling, glittering generalities, and unsupported assumptions, he would have little, if any, influence on them.

APPLYING SEMANTIC PRINCIPLES

Test the following assumptions to see whether they help students learn to apply semantic principles as they read, write, speak, and listen:

1. High school students can learn to recognize the injustice of speakers' and writers' using classificatory terms with complete disregard for differences. A discussion based on the all-inclusive labels found in literature, newspapers, and magazines and in students' talks and written compositions might include these questions: "Why do some speakers and writers imply that people who can be classified as *Republicans, Democrats, Negroes, Jews, teachers, policemen, Russians, Englishmen,* or *Frenchmen* are exactly alike?" "Why are no two objects, animate or inanimate, ever exactly alike?" "Why are blanket labels, carefully qualified, sometimes necessary?" "How can they be qualified so they approximate reality?" "If there are sixty teachers in a school, why should one think of them as individuals: Teacher 1, Teacher 2, Teacher 3, . . . Teacher 60?"

2. To acquaint students with the nature of abstracting, ask them to (1) write a single-sentence or brief-paragraph interpretation of a literary passage, editorial, or speech and (2) compare and evaluate their interpretations. Such an exercise can lead to a discussion of why students abstract what they do, why words have personal meanings, and how prejudices of various kinds originate. They may discover the significant role conditioned responses play in determining what they abstract from an event, idea, individual, or object.

3. Assumptions (sometimes called hypotheses, theories, hunches, guesses, or opinions) are legion in speech and writing. Ask students to underscore the assumptions and encircle the statements of fact in a short mimeographed newspaper editorial or column. Compare and discuss their decisions. Also ask them to explain whether the assumptions are adequately or inadequately supported with evidence.

4. Students should discover that finding referents for concrete terms is much simpler than finding them for fictional terms whose referents are often quite vague. They can easily see that *book, pencil, clock,* and

automobile point directly to objects in their immediate environment, but that the relationship to objects, events, behavior, or ideas of *hope, freedom, courage,* and *equality* is often difficult to detect. Ask students to explain (1) how fictions in Patrick Henry's "Speech in the Virginia Convention" (*patriotism, freedom, truth, liberty,* and *love*) are made meaningful through context, (2) why the terms have different referents for each student in the class, (3) why some of the terms are highly emotive, and (4) to what extent his assumptions are supported with evidence.

5. Ask students to bring to class an advertisement from a magazine, newspaper, or mail-order catalog or a written reproduction of a television ad. Ask them to (1) explain why they consider the ads accurate or inaccurate and (2) estimate the educational and economic backgrounds of subscribers to each magazine and newspaper. How, for example, do the subscribers to *Harper's* and *The Reader's Digest* probably differ? How are the differences reflected in the advertising of the two magazines?

6. Your students' ability to read and listen critically depends to a considerable degree upon their sensitivity to the context of words. To show them how context affects the meaning of words, write the following sentences on the blackboard:

The *bat* circled the street light.
He did not *bat* an eye.
The pitcher is at *bat.*
He may *bat* the ball into left field.
The word *bat* has many meanings.
I'll use your *bat* in this inning.
He went on a *bat.*
He threatened to *bat* his ears down.
The *bat* will fill the hole in the plaster.

An analysis of the sentences should convince students that a word can have many meanings which are not only influenced by their verbal context but also by time, place, and the mood of speaker and listener. For example, with the bases filled in the last half of the ninth, "The pitcher is at bat" might be said in a tone of voice conveying, if the pitcher is a weak hitter, a note of despair.

7. When students read newspapers and magazines or listen to television programs, they should try to understand the context in which statements are made. Discussing the following questions might help students understand the larger context: "What is the official position of the writer or speaker?" "Why are owners of newspapers and radio and television stations often accused of giving biased views of the news?" "Why has it been said that advertisers influence news?" "Do owners of newspapers and radio and television stations (usually wealthy men) influence

the news published on political, economic, and international events?" "Why are they likely to support the status quo, or a return to an era which for them approximates Utopia?" "Why do many newspapers play up the sensational?" "How would you determine what to print if you owned a newspaper or magazine?" "Why would you be accused, no matter what your publishing policy might be, of distorting the news?"

8. Ask questions about students' stereotyped statements. For example, why is Charles' assertion that "Girls are smarter than boys" open to question? What does he mean by "smarter"? How can his statement be checked for accuracy? What findings of educators and psychologists seem to refute his assumption?

9. Students can better understand the label *liberty*, a favorite of most politicians and one used loosely by most of us, by answering the following questions: "Why is *liberty* a favorite word of many speakers?" "What does it mean?" "What are some of the liberties we enjoy?" "What restrictions must be placed on liberties?" "What liberties are guaranteed by the Bill of Rights?" "Why does our government find it difficult to enforce the Bill of Rights?" "Why are rights guaranteed in the Constitution denied to some minority groups?" "Why, during World War II, were children of parents who came from Japan placed in American concentration camps and children of parents who came from Germany left free?" "Why are liberties not carefully guarded easily taken away?" "Why are liberties curtailed during wars?" "Why do certain groups want to limit the liberties the majority may enjoy?" "What fears prevent some of us from openly supporting minority groups that are denied rights guaranteed by our Constitution?" "Why is it difficult to define *liberty* without using the term in the definition?" "Why does it seem impossible to point out all the referents for the label *liberty*?" "Why is the dictionary definition of *liberty* incomplete?" Another approach to arriving at a better understanding of *liberty* would be to have students write a one-sentence completion of "Liberty is . . ." and then compare their statements.

The foregoing exercises will be of little value to students unless the teacher helps them apply semantic principles whenever they speak, write, listen, and read in the classroom. Students need daily practice to (1) become conscious of their own and others' abstracting, (2) seek out the referents of writers and speakers and choose words to represent their own referents exactly, (3) develop a sensitivity to context and connotation, and (4) check their own and others' communications against reality. Many of them can be helped to take a more objective look at their own and others' language habits by reading S. I. Hayakawa's *Language in Thought and Action*, Stuart Chase's *The Tyranny of Words* and *The Power of Words*, Irving Lee's *Language Habits in Human Affairs*, Wendell Johnson's *People in Quandaries*, or Hugh R. Walpole's *Semantics*.

ASSUMPTIONS ABOUT TEACHING SEMANTICS

Prepare to explain why you accept or reject, wholly or in part, the following assumptions relating to semantics:

1. Whenever a person makes a statement, he abstracts (omits details).

2. The scientific method has proved to be the best tool in revealing reality.

3. The origin of the scientific method cannot rightly be ascribed to one or a hundred men.

4. Helping students find the referent in written and spoken language is a must for the effective teacher.

5. The "Ogden and Richards Triangle" (see C. K. Ogden and I. A. Richards' *The Meaning of Meaning*, p. 11) is a useful device for the student of semantics.

6. Korzybski's belief that a language reflecting the findings of science would introduce sanity into man's dealings with his fellow men is sound.

7. The referents for the label *semantics* are easy to find.

8. Fictions such as *Democrat, Republican, Socialist, Communist, liberal,* and *conservative* do not have the same meaning for any two people.

9. A conservative is one who worships dead radicals.

10. When using the labels *teacher, Catholic, Jew, Protestant,* and *artist,* writers and speakers usually place too much emphasis on similarities, not enough on differences.

11. The meaning of a word is fixed by other words in a sentence. The meaning of a sentence is fixed by other sentences in a paragraph. The meaning of a paragraph is fixed by other paragraphs in a theme. The meaning of a theme is affected by a context that stretches beyond the classroom.

12. The accuracy of Heraclitus' observations that (1) no man can step into the same river twice and (2) there is nothing permanent except change are easily illustrated.

13. The scientist does not agree with Ecclesiastes' "There is nothing new under the sun."

14. The context of a speaker or writer's statement is complex.

15. A person's experiential background determines whether the following terms have pleasant or unpleasant connotations for him: *hippie, hawk, dove, beatnik, college student, gambler, policeman, teacher, Democrat,* and *Republican.*

16. Euphemisms are an essential part of language.

17. There is some truth in Alexander Pope's couplet:

> The hungry Judges soon the sentence sign,
> And wretches hang that jury-men may dine.

18. A word is not the object that it symbolizes.

19. It is easy to separate statements of fact from assumptions in a newspaper editorial or advertisement.

20. The three semantic principles presented in this chapter can be taught successfully to high school students.

21. "I may say, that we should have a great many fewer disputes in the world, if words were taken for what they are, the signs of our ideas only, and not for things themselves."[17]

22. ". . . poetry often conveys in a few sentences more of lasting values than a whole volume of scientific analysis."[18]

23. "The words that we use never exhaust all we could say about a sensible experience."[19]

24. "The inmates of colleges are just as credulous as the inmates of slums."[20]

25. "The word is but a symptom, a symbol, a sign, pointing not only to an object or a concept, but to a subject and conceiver."[21]

26. Language is often used to deceive the reader and listener.

27. Metaphors are born almost every day.

28. The magazine *ETC: A Review of General Semantics* (540 Powell Street, San Francisco, California 94108) is a useful source of ideas for the English teacher interested in semantics.

29. Instead of spending a lot of time describing semantic principles, the English teacher should help students apply them to (1) materials he has gathered from newspapers, magazines, and television programs and (2) similar materials he urges students to gather.

30. A word like *well* has many meanings until other words used with it make its meanings specific.

31. The classroom should be a place where the pronouncements of newspaper editors, radio and television commentators, politicians, and magazine writers are questioned to see whether they reflect reality.

32. S. I. Hayakawa's *Language in Thought and Action* is an excellent source of ideas for the English teacher interested in helping students

[17]Alexander Campbell Fraser, editor, John Locke's *An Essay Concerning Human Understanding* (Oxford, England: Oxford, Clarendon Press, 1894), p. 135.

[18]Korzybski, *Science and Sanity*, p. 437.

[19]Bertrand Russell, *An Inquiry into Meaning and Truth* (London: George Allen and Unwin, Limited, 1940), p. 66.

[20]Arthur Ponsonby, *Falsehoods in Wartime* (New York: E. P. Dutton and Company, 1929), p. 25.

[21]Isaac Goldberg, *The Wonder of Words* (New York: D. Appleton-Century Company, 1938), p. 315. Reprinted by permission of Appleton-Century.

apply semantic principles as they read, write, speak, and listen. (If you wish, substitute another book on semantics in the preceding statement. Several are listed in the Bibliography.)

33. Many individuals seem unaware that their behavior does not match their verbal support of racial tolerance and civil rights.

34. To understand semantic principles is easy; to apply them is difficult.

35. Beliefs are acquired, never inborn.

36. Many of the masterpieces of world literature do not reflect reality.

37. Adults' statements beginning with "Young people are" and young peoples' statements beginning with "Adults are" rarely reflect reality.

IDEAS TO TEST

1. Ask students to explain why the following statements do not reflect reality.
   a. High school students do not study as hard as they used to.
   b. Women drivers are responsible for most automobile accidents.
   c. Athletes are poor students.
   d. Few sons are like their fathers, most worse, a few better than the father (Homer).
   e. Teachers do not grade fairly.
   f. Paperbacks sold in drugstores are trash.
   g. Straight-A students are bookworms.

Ask students to add to the above list additional similar statements they have heard recently.

2. When Stuart Chase asked one hundred people to define *fascism*, no two definitions were alike.[22] Ask your students to define *democracy*. Compare the definitions, and help them determine why their definitions vary.

3. Ask students to explain why the following words have pleasant, unpleasant, or somewhat neutral connotations for them: *aardvark, Catholic, Protestant, labor union, Wall Street, Jew, Negro, Cuban, Puerto Rican, Russian, policeman,* and *teacher.*

4. Ask students to explain why no Christian parents would name a son *Judas* and why American parents seldom name a son *Jesus.*

5. Have students explain why for most people one label in each of the following pairs has pleasanter connotations than the other: janitor-maintenance man, beauty operator-beautician, officeholder-public servant, hearse-funeral coach, cop-officer, pupil-student, student union-student cen-

[22]See his *The Tyranny of Words,* pp. 186–93.

ter, preacher-minister, boss-employer, worker-employee, saloon-tavern, undertaker-mortician, pawnshop-loan office, hamburger-ground beef, politician-statesman, old man-senior citizen, truant officer-attendance teacher, and insane asylum-mental hospital.

6. Proverbs are usually "allness" statements which leave out many details. Sometimes proverbs on a specific subject conflict: "Out of sight, out of mind" and "Absence makes the heart grow fonder." Ask students to explain why the following proverbs are assumptions which should not be taken at face value:

    a. Good fences make good neighbors.
    b. Strong back, weak mind.
    c. Money is the root of all evil.
    d. The good die young.
    e. Figures don't lie, but liars figure.
    f. Don't look a gift horse in the mouth.
    g. Two heads are better than one.
    h. A cat has nine lives.
    i. One hour's sleep before midnight is worth three after.
    j. Familiarity breeds contempt.
    k. God helps those who help themselves.
    l. Don't count your chickens before they are hatched.
    m. The pen is mightier than the sword.
    n. There will always be wars.
    o. There never was a good war or a bad peace.
    p. He who hesitates is lost.
    q. Make haste slowly.
    r. Early to bed and early to rise makes a man healthy, wealthy, and wise.
    s. A bird in the hand is worth two in the bush.

7. Ask students to write a strictly factual one-paragraph auto-biographical sketch. After a group analysis of the paragraphs to see whether they are completely factual, ask students to both entertain and enlighten by inserting a few inferential statements in the sketches.

8. Carl Sandburg's poem "Elephants Are Different to Different People" illustrates that what three men abstracted from a scene at a zoo was determined by their individual physical natures and backgrounds. Read the poem to students, and ask them why they prefer one of the three descriptions of the elephant over the others.

9. Ask students why they agree or disagree with Emerson's attack on the verbal nature of education:

We are students of words: we are shut up in schools and colleges for ten or fifteen years, and come out at last with a bag of wind, a memory of words, and do not know a thing.[23]

10. Ask students to explain why they accept or reject, wholly or in part, the following assumptions: All men acquire their economic, political, religious, and other beliefs along with their language. A German, Russian, French, or Italian infant brought up in an American family would automatically absorb the family's beliefs.

11. Ask students to illustrate to what extent the following propaganda techniques recommended and practiced by Adolf Hitler (see *Mein Kampf*) are used by advertisers, politicians, and pressure groups of various kinds:

(1) arguments must be directed to the least intelligent of the people; (2) avoid "scientific ballast" as much as possible; (3) give the simple points "thousandfold repetition"; (4) seek to hold the attention of the great masses; (5) seek not "the many-sidedness of scientific teaching"; (6) restate the few points as slogans; (7) never try to become versatile, altering the methods, for the masses will not retain the idea; (8) never permit the faintest suggestion that there is right on the other side; (9) no halfway urgings will do; things are either "positive or negative, love or hate, right or wrong, truth or lie"; and (10) regardless of all else, keep focused on the fundamental principle, limit the program, and repeat it eternally.[24]

12. Ask students to compare Tennyson's purpose in "The Charge of the Light Brigade" with Siegfried Sassoon's in "Counter-Attack." Such an assignment can lead to a discussion of what determines poets' abstractions from an object, event, or thought.

13. To help students understand the nature of abstracting, ask them to write a brief interpretation of a controversial literary selection, editorial, or speech; then ask them to compare and evaluate their various abstractions. Such an exercise can lead to a discussion of why students abstract what they do and how prejudices originate.

14. To demonstrate how inferences can arise from an accumulation of facts somewhat obscured by unusual metaphors, ask students to infer what Emily Dickinson is describing in "I Like to See It Lap the Miles." The facts in the poem imply that she is describing a locomotive. Students might then participate in the more difficult ask of separating inferences from facts in Edwin Markham's "The Man with the Hoe" or "The Right Kind of People."

15. In the late 1930's and early 1940's the Bible of semanticists was

[23]Ralph Waldo Emerson, *Essays and English Traits*, Harvard Classics (New York: P. F. Collier and Son, 1909),V, p. 226.

[24]Irving J. Lee, *Language Habits in Human Affairs* (New York: Harper and Brothers, Publishers, 1941), p. XVIII.

Korzybski's *Science and Sanity*. Korzybski's thesis is that use of the scientific method can lead to sanity in human affairs. Ask a student or students to read Paul DeKruif's *Microbe Hunters* and then explain to the class how scientists go about solving problems. Then demonstrate how almost everything inanimate (spectacles, pens, lights, purses, ceiling, blackboard, chalk, erasers, windows, cosmetics, and watches) in the classroom owes its origin to the scientific method.

16. Ask students to account for the happy-ending fetish in the dramatic offerings of radio, television, and motion pictures.

17. Most students accept the proverb, "You get what you pay for." Ask them to present evidence from *Consumer Reports* and *Consumer Bulletin* magazines which challenges the proverb.

18. Having students compare the referents of words in a simple ballad with those in a fairly difficult lyric poem—"Lord Randal" with Edgar Lee Masters' "Ann Rutledge"—will illustrate that finding meaning in referents provides the key to understanding poetry.

19. I have discovered that over 90 percent of the perhaps two thousand high school and college students to whom I have read Edwin Arlington Robinson's "Reuben Bright" cannot answer the question, "Why did Reuben Bright tear down his slaughterhouse?" Try the poem on your students. If they are stumped by it, ask them why; and you will be surprised why it does not relate to their experiential backgrounds.

20. Read Robinson's poem "Richard Cory" aloud to students. Ask them to supply a context larger than the poem itself to explain the surprise ending: "And Richard Cory . . . put a bullet through his head."

21. Perhaps the most violent poetic denunciation of an individual is Carl Sandburg's "To a Contemporary Bunkshooter." Before you read it to students, ask them whether (1) invective is ever more effective than logic and (2) an author can ever appeal strictly to a reader's reason. After reading the poem, ask them to explain why they accept or reject the following assumptions:

    a. The poem is all feeling, no thought.
    b. Sandburg's tactics are as intemperate as the bunkshooter's.
    c. He is justified in hating the bunkshooter.
    d. His purpose was to annihilate the bunkshooter with words.
    e. Invective is a weapon that should never be used.
    f. All evangelists should read the poem.

For other examples of language designed to arouse emotions, see Langston Hughes' "Freedom Train" and Jonathan Edwards' "Sinners in the Hands of an Angry God."

22. When students hear a convocation speaker, they have an opportunity to analyze a "total" context—the speaker's accent, appearance, race,

voice, gestures, and message and the audience, time, place, and occasion. When students analyze the speech in class, the various factors can be evaluated by discussing these questions: "How does a speaker's voice affect listeners?" "How does the reaction of an audience to a speaker's address influence an individual listener?" "Why do audiences often applaud a political speaker who ridicules his opponent?" "Why can some speakers say nothing and please an audience?" "What criteria should be used in evaluating a political talk? a sermon?" "Why is the 'total' context never the same for even two listeners?" "To what extent should good usage, neatness, and oratorical skill be discounted by a listener?" (Why do you suppose David Garrick, the famous British actor, was able to make an audience laugh or cry by the way he spoke a single word: "Mesopotamia"?)

23. Ask students to explain why the first metaphor in each of the following statements has pleasant connotations, the second one unpleasant. Then have them write sentences which give the second metaphor in each statement pleasant connotations.

> You may call a woman a kitten, but you must not call her a cat.
> You may call her a mouse, but you must not call her a rat.
> You may call her a chicken, but you must not call her a hen.
> You may call her a duck, but you must not call her a goose.
> You may call her a vision, but you must not call her a sight.[25]

24. A study of the connotations of words can be based on materials from literature, newspapers, radio and television talks, magazines, and advertising. Having students underline the words with definitely pleasant or unpleasant connotations in newspaper editorials, stories, columns, and letters to the editor can help create an awareness of how and why such words are used. A group evaluation of the underlined words of individual students can form the basis of an enlightening discussion on (1) how and why connotations of words differ for individuals and (2) how words with pleasant or unpleasant connotations can be selected by a writer or speaker to win over his audience.

25. A group analysis of paragraphs on "A Definition of a Happy Life" will clearly demonstrate that what individuals students abstract from an object, event, or idea is determined largely by their past experience. Ask students to account for the differences and similarities in the paragraphs.

26. To reveal that words about words, dictionary definitions, for example, are frequently not closely related to the object level, ask students to draw a picture of a gnu based on the dictionary definition ("any of a

---

[25]*The Phi Delta Kappan*, Vol. 29, No. 5, January, 1948, p. 244.

genus of African antelopes with an oxlike head, short mane, downward curved horns, and a long tail") and then compare the picture with one in the dictionary or, better still, with a zoo gnu. After viewing the gnus in the zoo, students would probably conclude that even though dictionary definitions are often helpful, they carry more meaning when the dictionary user has had direct experience with the referents of the words.

27. A worthwhile activity, once students understand the nature of assumptions, is for individual students to question the unsubstantiated assumptions made by classmates in oral discussions and written compositions.

28. Comments on written compositions such as "Defend!" "Where are the facts to support this statment?" "Why?" "Every?" "All?" "Always?" "Never?" can stimulate students to qualify sweeping statements and defend assumptions.

29. Ask students to underline, in their most recent composition, all of the words which do not directly represent objects. Then ask them what the underlined words represent, and why their definitions do not always agree with their classmates'. They will discover that the referents of abstract words (fictions) are hard to find.

30. Write the following incomplete statements on the blackboard: "Teachers are . . . ," "Americans will . . . ," "Politicians believe . . . ," and "The French people feel. . . ." Ask students to complete them so that they will reflect reality.

31. To develop students' sensitivity to language-fact relationships, have them record their own and others' semantic blunders in a notebook. Such a notebook can help them (1) develop a sensitivity to language which does not reflect reality and (2) practice applying semantic principles as they read, write, speak, and listen.

11

Evaluating
Students' Work

Before reading this chapter, formulate clear, defensible answers to the following questions. After reading it, prepare to explain why you changed or retained your answers.

1. Why and how is a teacher's philosophy of education revealed in the tests he gives?

2. When you face a new class, how can you determine quickly how well your students can read, write, speak, and listen?

3. As you work a semester or more with students, how will you measure their progress in the above fields?

4. What are some strengths and weaknesses of objective tests? essay tests?

5. To what extent do students' grades indicate a teacher's success or failure?

6. What are some advantages and disadvantages of homogeneous grouping? Do you prefer homogeneous or heterogeneous grouping? Why?

7. When should tests be given? What kind of test follow-up is desirable?

One who observes student and critic teachers daily sees hundreds of tests, but seldom a question which measures insight, understanding, or appreciation. Essay questions begin with *Who, What, When,* and *Where*, almost never with *Why, Compare, Support, or Defend*. Testing takes up a lot of time in most English classes. Should you visit fifteen classes in five days, you are likely to see written tests being administered in over half of them. Spelling tests lead all the rest in frequency. Publishers' objective tests on selections in literature anthologies are becoming popular (with teachers) in some schools. There are also tests on vocabulary lists featuring words teachers never use and objective tests on novels, plays, poems, essays, and short stories so searching that teachers need keys to grade them. (The author's scores on the literature tests hover around 28 percent.)

If an English teacher wants to help students appreciate literature and express ideas clearly, thoughtfully, and correctly, why doesn't he use tests which measure progress towards these goals rather than recall of facts about literature and usage? Research does not support the assumption that objective test scores will match students' speaking and writing abilities. A 1961 research study revealed that the scores of 589 senior high school students on the grammar part of *The New Purdue Placement Test in English* showed little correlation with scores on an essay they wrote.[1]

DIAGNOSTIC TESTS

When you face a new group of students, explain to them that you want to find out quickly how well they read, write, speak, and listen so you can help them improve. Students are motivated by worthwhile objectives and logical approaches to achieving them. To discover how well students can read, ask them to write a one-sentence statement of a lyric poem's theme or a one-paragraph interpretation of an essay. Such an assignment, supplemented with questions about literary selections they read in class, can help you find out how well each student understands a printed page.

To measure their writing ability, give students a simple assignment and plenty of time to complete it. Having them write a two-page double-spaced letter in class will inform you about their strengths and weaknesses in content, organization, sentence structure, paragraphing, vocabulary, usage, spelling, punctuation, and capitalization. Composition problems common to all students should be taken up with the whole class; those not classwide should be discussed with students who have them. The most serious problems should be faced first.

The help students need in oral expression can be detected during class discussions and oral composition units. Most of the instruction needs to be individual and based, if possible, on the teacher's written profile of students' speaking performances.

Qualities affecting skill in listening are many: hearing, intelligence, vocabulary, experiential background, interest, and thinking ability. A teacher's questions can expose how well students can abstract what is significant from various oral presentations: readings, reports, panels, and

[1] Morsey, *Seminar . . .*, p. 46.

lectures. Questions can also reveal whether students appraise thoughtfully what they hear.

Once a teacher has specific information about students' problems in English, he should select relevant content and methods. If, for example, students are deficient in written composition skills, he does not take them on a detour through handbooks and workbooks; he spends class time helping them write, revise, and rewrite. "Composition" accenting niggling, irrelevant exercises will be kept at a minimum.[2] Every composition is a test, and the final examination on a composition unit should be another composition, to be compared with the others students wrote.

In many English classes, every day is test day. Most of the tests are informal. A teacher who discusses with students a poem he has just read to them knows almost immediately whether they appreciated it. Sometimes he knows their degree of appreciation before he finishes reading it. The effective teacher is testing hypotheses—his objectives and the content and procedures he uses to achieve them—almost every minute he is in the classroom. His goals—helping students appreciate literature and become effective writers, speakers, and listeners—enjoy almost universal acceptance, but ideas on achieving them are often controversial. Continuous testing is necessary to see whether his methods are producing results.

OBJECTIVE TESTS

What are the advantages of using objective tests? They are easy to grade, especially if they can be machine scored, and the results can be compared with national norms. A principal's announcement to the P.T.A., "Our students are above national norms in English," is greeted by a warm glow all around, even though many of the students cannot write a simple letter free of sentence fragments, run-on sentences, involved sentences, and misspellings of one and two-syllable words. After standardized achievement tests in English are given in the spring, some critic teachers greet each other with "Half of my students have made gains of two years since last fall!" a feat frequently resulting from their constant concentration on workbook and handbook exercises resembling those in the achievement tests.

Another reason many teachers favor objective tests is that they seldom lead to arguments with students. This is because students have been conditioned to accept as infallible the sometimes indefensible assumptions of teachers and handbook and workbook authors about usage. Nevertheless, teachers are right when they claim that students seldom contest objective test grades.

Many teachers use several objective questions at the beginning of a

[2]Perhaps sixty seconds every four semesters is enough.

class session to check whether students have read an assigned selection. The purpose of the test is specific, and the results usually reveal what the teacher wants to know. Such instant quizzes do cause some laggards to read assignments, a necessary prelude to worthwhile class discussions. However, since objective tests measure only recall of facts about literary selections and related data, as well as what a student knows about grammar and usage, punctuation, spelling, and capitalization, rather than his ability to express ideas orally and in writing, they should be used sparingly by teachers who profess to want to help students appreciate literature and improve their compositions.

The experience of a member of the Board of Education of a large city school system with by far the most popular of all objective tests is strikingly revealing. At a board meeting, he asked why his daughter Elizabeth always received "A's" in spelling when she made a dozen spelling errors per page in her letters to Aunt Mary. He felt teachers were not maintaining high standards. The superintendent of schools discovered that Elizabeth's spelling grades originated in perfect scores on weekly spelling lists. Few teachers and parents understand that "A's" on spelling lists do not insure correct spelling in compositions.

ESSAY TESTS

What are some strengths of essay tests? They require more than recall of information. Some essay questions elicit parroting rather than the weighing of facts and ideas, but they can pose problems which require students to develop, organize, and support ideas. For example, to answer the following essay test on "The Prodigal Son,"[3] a student must recall and weigh the message in the story.

Essay Test on "The Prodigal Son"

Assume a jury has been assembled to judge the merits of the grievance of the brother of the Prodigal Son. You are the lawyer chosen to present his case to the jury. Present detailed, clear, and logical arguments to the jury supporting your client's complaint and offsetting the opposing lawyer's contention that the father was right in what he did.

The student's answer to the test should reveal whether he appreciates the story. He has to know what happened in the story, place himself in the position of a character who is usually condemned for his selfishness and unforgiving nature, and organize his arguments so they will influence the

[3]See "The Prodigal Son," Appendix 15.

jury. A satisfactory completion of the test requires thinking, not just recalling facts.

The most frequent objection to essay tests is that they take too much grading time. One cannot ask students to grade them; but for the teacher who grades his own tests, an essay test need not take more time than an objective test. Assume that he spends an hour developing a fifty-item objective test on a dozen short stories. He could probably write three essay questions in ten minutes. If he asks students to answer only one or two of the three questions, he will cut grading time considerably. Why must an examination comprise five or ten essay questions? One good essay question is superior to fifty objective questions for measuring students' appreciation of literature.

HOMOGENEOUS GROUPING

Since homogeneous grouping is again being promoted as a way of improving instruction, you will probably teach homogeneously grouped classes, especially if you are employed in a large school. (Why can't small schools afford homogeneous grouping?) Such grouping became popular in the 1920's, stimulated by the rise of standardized tests which ranked students from idiot to genius. Many schools dropped it in the late 1930's, but some reintroduced it after Sputnik.

A common argument for homogeneous grouping is that bright, average, and slow students placed in separate classes will learn more.[4] Bright students competing with peers will work up to capacity. Slow students will make haste slowly, not get lost in the rush. Average students will cover more ground than the slow group, less than the bright group. Education is a horse race: the fast are entered in the Kentucky Derby, the average run at county fairs, and the slow pull surreys in Central Park. Those who question the arrangement may be reminded that physical education departments daily demonstrate the wisdom of homogeneous grouping: the best play on the first team, the next best on the second team, and the rest participate in intramural sports or cheer the first team on.

How do schools identify bright, average, and slow students? One large school uses I. Q., mathematics, and reading scores. Another has students choose, after counseling, the academic or the regular course. Most schools classify students into two or three groups on the basis of I. Q. scores; some use their previous grades as well as their scores on one or more standardized tests.

[4]Research does not support this theory. See James S. Coleman, and others, *Equality of Educational Opportunity* (Washington: U. S. Government Printing Office, 1966).

What are some arguments against homogeneous grouping? In some senior high schools, students in slow sections are told or learn from experience that they cannot make grades higher than "C." The logic behind the ruling is that giving grades higher than "C" enables some slow students to make "B's" and "A's" while some academic students make "C's" and "D's." Such a situation is considered unfair, since slow students could top academic students in honor lists published periodically in newspapers and class rankings determined at the end of the senior year. Furthermore, careless prospective employers and college registrars could be misled by "A's" and "B's" in the transcripts of slow students. But can you imagine the reaction of conscientious slow students who learn "C" is the summit for them?

Students in slow groups are often apathetic, sometimes resentful. Although labeled "S" (slow), they apply the label "D" (dumb) to themselves.[5] An average or bright student mistakenly placed in a slow section can be conditioned into believing he is inferior. A student who discovers that his best efforts cannot win academic success cannot be very highly motivated. Some teachers defend the placement of students in "S" sections with the argument that they might as well learn early that they are below par mentally. Others claim that students do not know whether they are in a slow, average, or academic group—a conclusion that takes the first prize for naïveté. Few share the philosophy of a teacher who said one should be especially kind to slow students because "You can't blame them for being behind the door when the brains were passed out." But even student teachers, with few exceptions, want to teach the academic classes. Some experienced teachers say slow groups waste the taxpayer's money and should not be in school. But the professional teacher is unimpressed with the clincher, "You can't make a silk purse out of a sow's ear." He has over the years seen a number of such transformations, and suspends judgment when a colleague's "sow's ear" appears in his classroom.

The decision to group students is usually made on the basis of standardized tests, with the I. Q. test carrying most weight. How dependable are such tests? To maintain faith in I. Q. and other standardized test scores, you must believe that all your students have had (1) the same educational opportunities, (2) the same motivation to profit from the same educational opportunities, and (3) identical attitudes toward taking tests. If a student has had inferior schooling or has lacked drive to do well academically, he may be placed in a slow group even though he has average or superior innate ability. If a student has been conditioned to fear tests which may decisively affect his future, he may not be able to do his best, especially on timed tests.

[5]Some students claim the "S" really means *Stupid*.

IMPROVING ENGLISH INSTRUCTION

A student teacher who examines the cumulative record cards of students in slow classes often finds that the I. Q. scores of 90 percent of them dropped from one to fifteen points between the third and sixth grades, with another similar drop between the sixth and ninth grades. Why do their scores drop? They are almost always slow readers with limited reading vocabularies, and I. Q. tests are primarily vocabulary tests which become increasingly difficult as such students are shoved up the educational ladder. Some of the students' I. Q. scores fall below 50, but one has only to talk to them to know that they are not feebleminded. Giving a slow reader a timed, written I. Q. test is as unfair as expecting a Percheron to win the Preakness or a gardener to cultivate a concrete expanse.

First-grade students are frequently tested and assigned to a slow, average, or fast group. First-grade teachers say that a student in a slow group might be transferred to an average or bright group, i.e., if he can cover the academic ground, he can progress from the lowest group, "Snails,"[6] to the middle group, "Tortoises," to the top group, "Antelopes." But what happens to students who accept decisions by school authorities as infallible? Do they conclude they are where they belong? Psychologists have discovered that if enough people tell a physically fit person "You look ill today," he is likely to become ill.

When you have the opportunity, try to determine whether a group of high school English students you are observing is an average or an academic group. Your guesses may well be wrong as often as they are right. One can always spot slow groups in some schools because they have that beaten-down look and get heavier doses of formal grammar.

One teacher who questions homogeneous grouping says he has taught bright groups that were less highly motivated than average groups. They had been conditioned by former teachers to expect "A's" and "B's" even when they did little or nothing. A group of thirty students with I. Q.'s above 120 should make mostly "A's"; but, unfortunately, a high I. Q. is not always accompanied by diligence. But many critic teachers have complete faith in I. Q. scores. When one visits their classes, they immediately display these scores in the first column of their grade books with the comment, "You can see what a poor class this is," or "This is a really good class." The students nearby who hear the remark either beam or turn away embarrassed.

In some schools, once a student is branded with standardized test scores, he thrives or becomes a scapegoat. A social studies teacher at a large city high school, asked why so many teachers were buzzing around

[6]When slow groups are labeled "Bunnies," students quickly supply a modifier. Should we bring our classificatory terms up to date: Rockets, Jets, Bullets?

the permanent record card files the day before grades were coming out, said, "Oh, they're checking to see whether they've made any mistakes; they don't want to give "F's" to geniuses and "A's" to morons. They're getting aboard the bandwagon."

One teacher who likes to work with slow students claims it takes her six weeks or more to help them overcome their defeatist attitude and become convinced they are of some worth after all. On a Monday she asked one such group what they had done over the weekend. Most of them had seen from one to six movies. Some had spent six hours in a movie house on a single day. When asked after class why moviegoing was a weekend vocation for many of her students, she said, "Well, they can identify themselves with a hero or heroine and enjoy success for a while, escape the daily failure they experience in school." What would you do if you never really succeeded at anything for six hours a day, Monday through Friday, for nine to twelve years?

Many experienced teachers are aware that students with high I. Q. scores have no monopoly on good judgment, good character, and high motivation. They also admit that (1) some mediocre students suddenly "find themselves" and become top students, and (2) some "A" students make a profession of earning good grades and building an image which charms teachers. Too often, the classroom's doubting Thomas is conditioned into conformity by his teachers and fellow students. In some classes there is nothing quite so hilarious as a person with an unusual idea. Intellectual nonconformity in the high school is rare because such tendencies are spotted and treated in the elementary school as manifestations of poor adjustment, i. e., bad manners, recalcitrance, belligerence, exhibitionism, or hostility.

After revealing a prejudice against standardized tests, I should probably not use them to illustrate a point, but I will anyway. The correlation between the scores on the Otis I. Q. test and Remmers' Socio-Economic Scale of 589 senior high school students was negligible, .12.[7] But it is easy to find slow classes comprised of students exclusively from families with low incomes. The aspiration level of these disadvantaged students is often low. They and their families attach little value to books, magazines, and newspapers and the special dialect of educated people.[8]

Arguments for heterogeneous grouping sound woefully weak to some nationally known critics of American education. They look enviously at European schools, many of which send only 15 to 20 percent of their academically able eleven-years-olds to secondary schools, the others to

[7]Morsey, *Seminar* . . . , p. 46.

[8]See Patricia C. Sexton, *Education and Income: Inequalities of Opportunities in Our Public Schools* (New Haven: Compass, hardcover, 1961; New York: Viking, paperback, 1964).

IMPROVING ENGLISH INSTRUCTION

upper elementary or technical schools. Of course, they do not recommend that compulsory education be abolished, but they do have faith in numbers, a combination of either two or three numbers which supposedly signify whether a student is academic, average, or slow. And they are certain that educational progress is accelerated by homogeneous grouping. Their opponents argue that the primary objective of education is to make students out of pupils and that covering subject matter more rapidly in academic classes does not necessarily help bring this about. They also argue that in adult life people are seldom judged on the basis of scores on I. Q. and other tests. They ask, "Could Darwin, Einstein, Edison, the Wright brothers, and Churchill, who were not good scholars during their younger years, have risen above the handicap of being placed in slow classes or trade schools?"

Proponents of heterogeneous grouping insist that intelligence is many-faceted—social, academic, and mechanical. They argue that sometimes the seemingly nonacademic student shows more good judgment than one who is reading the ninety-ninth book on the list of one hundred best books. And they urge that equal opportunities for all can best be maintained in American high schools by not shunting anyone into a group labeled *slow*. They accept the idea of counseling a student to help him discover his interests and abilities, but reject the idea of using numbers on a standardized test to place him in a slow, average, or academic slot.

When I taught in a small community where homogeneous grouping was impractical, I never felt that bright students were shortchanged. Differences among students were great when measured by standardized tests (which were fortunately filed and forgotten a few days after they were administered) but were not so noticeable in classroom discussions and extracurricular activities.

Many "A" students are skillful at ingesting and regurgitating textbook material, a skill usually rewarded only in classrooms and on quiz programs.[9] Some educators claim an intelligent person is one who can solve the economic, governmental, social, and vocational problems that confront him. Terman did discover that people with exceptionally high I. Q.'s have a better record in problem solving than the general run of the population.[10] But a high percentage of people whose scores on standardized tests are average or below function effectively in their jobs and as citizens.

[9]Quiz programs, now temporarily defunct, brought the typical high school and college social science, English literature, geography, and science routine to the television screen and caused many viewers to conclude that memorization of an encyclopedia and an almanac equaled education.

[10]See L. M. Terman and M. H. Oden, *The Gifted Child Grows Up* (Stanford, California: Stanford University Press, 1947).

Some colleges have honors classes, assuming that gifted students will coast in heterogeneous freshman and sophomore English and social science classes. But some faculty members are convinced that covering more ground (books) will not guarantee a better product. Many students who have an honors reputation to maintain have no time to think or to read unassigned books and magazines. They are sometimes stuffed the way Germans used to force-feed geese; they are fattened with facts. Perhaps it is better to read one book slowly and thoughtfully than ten in a hurry, always wondering, "Will this be on the test?" Socrates' dictum "Know thyself" is hopelessly incompatible with Professor Schnell's dictum, "Know Homer's *Iliad* and *Odyssey* and Euripides' *Antigone, Oedipus Rex,* and *Philoctetes* by next Tuesday!" (The tutorial system at Harvard University features individual conferences and much writing, rather than merely heavier reading assignments.)

There is no final answer to the question, "Is it best to group students homogeneously?" Those who push such grouping seem now to be in the majority, and those who do not are sometimes pronounced opponents of the "pursuit of excellence." To label a student *slow, average,* or *academic* seems so fair and logical to some teachers and administrators that it may take a long time before they recognize the abuses which currently accompany such labeling. The biggest crimes are assuming that (1) the effect of a student's environment on his I. Q. score is negligible and (2) a student with a low I. Q. score does not deserve the finest teachers and school facilities.

Another serious mistake in evaluation is made by teachers who delegate their decision-making responsibilities to students, causing many of them to conclude that leadership and dependency qualities are fixed at age thirteen. The nonaggressive, especially those without social status, are often squelched in such an environment. Students do learn best to make decisions through practice; but at times the shy student should portray an assured leading character in a class play and the "leader" should discover that a subordinate role can be dull and lonely. No professional teacher allows aggressive, uninhibited students to take over all school activities.

For the English teacher, the significant immediate questions in evaluation are, "What goals should my students and I strive to achieve?" and "How can we determine the progress we are making toward them?" If the goals are developing appreciation of literature, intelligent listening, and an effective command of written and oral English, tests of progress toward them have to measure more than recall of facts. Whenever you develop or buy a literature test, ask yourself, "Does it measure appreciation?" Whenever you develop or buy a written composition, oral composition, or listening test, ask yourself, "Does it measure performance?"

ASSUMPTIONS ABOUT EVALUATING STUDENTS' WORK

Prepare to explain why you accept or reject, wholly, or in part, the following assumptions about evaluating students' work:

1. A teacher's philosophy of education is revealed in the tests he gives students.

2. The reading, writing, speaking, and listening abilities of students can be measured with objective tests.

3. Students' grades also indicate their teachers' successes or failures.

4. Homogeneous grouping is highly desirable in a modern school.

5. The outcomes of research studies on homogeneous grouping have been inconclusive (see *Encyclopedia of Educational Research*).

6. The fairest way to group students homogeneously is on the basis of previous grades, not standardized-test scores.

7. Some objective tests measure thinking ability.

8. A student in a slow class should not be given a grade higher than "C."

9. A student in an academic class should not be given a grade lower than "C."

10. Essay test grades are highly subjective.

11. Diagnostic tests given at the beginning of a unit are as essential as tests given at the end.

12. A student's appreciation of a literary selection can be measured.

13. The accurate measurement of a student's progress is one of the English teacher's most difficult problems.

14. In his book *The Brain Watchers*, Martin L. Gross proves that personality tests are misused by some schools and business corporations.

15. The contents of Banesh Hoffman's *The Tyranny of Testing* illustrate that he gave his book an appropriate title.

16. The following quotation proves that essay tests should be used sparingly by the English teacher:

> Early in the second decade of this century, Starch and Elliott performed one of the most famous pieces of pioneering work in educational research. They took two English themes of equal merit and had them graded by 142 English teachers on the basis of 100 percent. Grades on the first paper ranged between 50 and 98 with a median of 80.2 and on the second paper between 64 and 99 with a median of 88.2. The variability of the two sets of grades was about the same.[11]

17. Dorothy Adkins Wood's five "Rules for Evaluating Essay Test

[11]N. M. Downie, *Fundamentals of Measurement: Techniques and Practices* (New York: Oxford University Press, Inc., 1958), p. 172.

Papers" (see her *Test Construction: Development and Interpretation of Achievement Tests*) should be observed by English teachers.

18. Miss Barstow's "A Twelfth-Grade English Test for Diagnosing Common Errors in Usage and Spelling" (see Educational Testing Service's *Making the Classroom Test*, pp. 12–13) is the best approach to determining a student's usage strengths and weaknesses.

19. Hillel Black's *They Shall Not Pass* tells the tale of the valiant stand taken by the ancient Greeks at Thermopylae.

20. In grading a set of thirty papers, one should give three "A's," five "B's," fourteen "C's," five "D's," and three "F's."

21. Mathematics Teacher A always gives a student full credit for a problem when the only error is a mistake in addition. Mathematics Teacher B always penalizes such an error with a zero. Mathematics Teacher B is right; A is wrong.

22. Our tests penalize too severely students who come from an environment where illiterate English is common.

23. There is an obvious reason why there is a high correlation between vocabulary tests and I. Q. tests.

24. Personnel directors should not hire college graduates who make serious mistakes in English usage.

25. Men dress their children's minds as they do their bodies, in the prevailing fashion (Herbert Spencer).

26. It is easy to develop and administer an effective teacher-rating form.

27. Half the ability in this country goes down the drain because of the failure of intelligence tests to measure the real mental ability of the children from lower socio-economic groups, and because of the failure of schools to recognize and train this ability (Allison Davis).

28. Robert Browning's "prize the doubt" should be part of every teacher's creed.

IDEAS TO TEST

1. Early in the semester, give your students an objective usage test. Then ask students to write a brief essay. Grade both and compare each set of individual scores. The results of the two tests will indicate that a high score on an objective usage test is not always accompanied by the ability to write effectively. By having students write their names on the back of the essay, you can avoid having names influence grades.

2. Devise ways of measuring performance in speaking and writing. Knowledge alone does not necessarily change behavior. For example, a researcher checked for one month the food selections of university seniors majoring in dietetics as they went through a cafeteria line. He discovered

that the meals they chose were no better nutritionally than the choices of other students.

3. If you assign spelling lists, compare students' scores on the lists with their spelling ability in written composition.

4. Most teachers who use the word list approach in teaching spelling do not seem to realize that many of their students can spell the words in their lists correctly. If you must use spelling lists, dictate the list as a test rather than a study list; then hold students responsible only for the words they misspell.

5. Since research has shown that spelling is an individual problem not solved by using traditional spelling lists, have each student list in his notebook the correct spellings of words he misspells in themes and tests. Check with individual students every week or two to see whether they have mastered the words in their lists.

6. If you are required to administer annually the typical achievement tests in English, check the scores against the students' grades in written and oral composition. Remember that objective achievement tests measure knowledge about grammar and usage, not performance in composition.

7. Encourage students to ask questions. Convince them that every question is welcome, even though it was asked by another student a minute ago. In too many classes, students conclude that asking a question reflects ignorance rather than intelligence. Students' questions can often tell a teacher as much about their progress as formal examinations. They also tell the alert teacher whether the content and methods he has chosen are proving effective in achieving his objectives.

8. Discuss with students (1) why people who specialize in mathematics are often as naïve about interest rates on installment purchases as those who shun mathematics, (2) why high grades in social studies do not necessarily mean good citizenship, (3) why knowledge about grammar and usage does not guarantee good written and oral usage, and (4) why the ability to recall facts about literature is only one ingredient of appreciation. Ask them what they think of educational practices which seem to have little or no effect on a person's behavior.

9. As a change of pace from the traditional essay questions, ask students to explain why they agree or disagree with certain assumptions about literary selections. Example: Explain in detail why you agree or disagree, wholly or in part, with the following assumptions about Robert Frost's "Stopping by Woods on a Snowy Evening":

    a. The author does more than paint a word-picture of a beautiful scene.

    b. The line "But I have promises to keep" has a single specific meaning.

12

Using and Doing
Research on Teaching
English

Before reading this chapter, formulate clear, defensible answers to the following questions. After reading it, prepare to explain why you changed or retained your answers.

1. You have seen research produce spaceships, curb polio, and inundate us with gadgets of all kinds. How does a researcher solve problems?

2. Assume you have in mind an approach to teaching reading, writing, speaking, or listening which you think is superior to one you are now using. How could you determine scientifically whether it is superior?

DEFINING RESEARCH

Research has been defined as the search for truth; the collection, organization, interpretation, and presentation of data; common sense verified; and the use of the scientific method in solving problems. Illustrations of common types[1] of research may give substance to these definitions.

Historical research is illustrated by the work of scholars who have cast light on the educational aims and methods of ancient Athenian and Spartan schools, the evolution of British and American English, and the status of American teachers from colonial times to the present.

The *survey*, a type of research popular among graduate students in colleges of education, centers on questionnaires resembling those of census takers, pollsters, and agencies which rate radio and television programs.

---

[1]For individual chapters on the common types of research, see John E. Wise, Robert B. Nordberg, and Donald J. Reitz, *Methods of Research in Education* (Boston: D. C. Heath and Company, 1967).

Teachers sometimes use questionnaires to find out students' attitudes, opinions, and knowledge. (See Appendix 10, "A Survey of Students' Fears. . . .")

Activity analysis or job analysis research is promoted in industry by time-and-motion-study experts who, for example, isolate and analyze every motion made by a printing press operator in setting up and running off a job. If some of his motions can be eliminated or accelerated, production can be increased and costs cut. The work of the English teacher has also been studied to determine how much time he devotes to teaching writing, speaking, listening, and literature, and to directing extracurricular activities.

Case study research is done by social workers, psychologists, psychiatrists, and guidance counselors, who may need to isolate hereditary and environmental influences which produced an individual's behavior. The case study pattern was developed by Sigmund Freud and his followers, but Robert Browning also did case study pioneering in "Fra Lippo Lippi" and other poems. Case studies have been made of families (the Jukes, Kallikaks, and Edwardses), and Robert S. and Helen M. Lynd made case studies of Muncie, Indiana, in *Middletown* and *Middletown in Transition*. Few high school teachers licensed in the last twenty-five years have escaped making a case study of a problem child. Perhaps such studies should be made of teachers high school students consider outstanding.

Experimental research may draw upon historical, survey, activity analysis, and case study research; but its key procedure, testing hypotheses under carefully controlled conditions, presents unique problems. For example, a researcher who has developed a pill which he thinks will halt the common cold usually gives his pill to an experimental group and an inert pill (placebo), identical in appearance to the medicated one, to a control group. After a period of perhaps a year, he compares the cold histories of the two groups, hoping that the medicated cold pill takers caught substantially fewer colds than the control group.

All of us are aware of the accomplishments of researchers in improving transportation, communication, agriculture, and medicine. And we are confident that within a decade or two cancer will be controlled as effectively as polio. Why are we less certain that substantial breakthroughs will be made in solving problems related to education in general and to teaching English in particular?

EVERY TEACHER A RESEARCHER

Alert teachers and ministers discover that talking at people rarely results in behavior changes. But authors of books and articles on teaching English often tell teachers what to do, rather than involving them in the quest for answers to teaching problems. Even the reports on carefully designed and controlled research studies seem to be ignored by most English teachers. For example, dozens of studies in the last fifty years have exposed the ineffectiveness of the word list approach to teaching spelling, but all except one of the forty critic teachers I observed within the last year dictate word lists once or twice a week. As a part of an extensive study of instructional practices of teachers in 179 junior and senior high schools in Colorado, Tovatt found that most of the teachers used classroom procedures in teaching language and composition that have been either disproved or made seriously questionable by research.[2] (We need research on why research in English is seldom consulted by English teachers.)

Research in English will lead to improvement in instruction only when large numbers of English teachers are somehow motivated to check in their own classrooms the validity of research done by others. Once they begin checking such research results, they may eventually develop projects of their own. Perhaps the best approach to developing researchers among English teachers is to involve in research activities students in college and university teacher-preparation programs. This approach demands a radical departure from the conditioned-response instruction accented in most of their classes.

SPECIFIC RESEARCH PROBLEMS

What are some of the hypotheses about teaching English which need to be tested through research? Proposals can be derived from the following statements taken from the "Assumptions About . . ." sections at the ends of chapters in this book:

1. A well-organized English program requiring approximately identical content and methods in, for example, all tenth-grade English classes is desirable.

2. Essay or objective tests can measure accurately students' appreciation of literature.

3. Teacher-student planning is not a waste of time and energy.

4. One can break down most students' prejudices against poetry.

5. Students will read what is for them hard to read literature if the authors' subject matter interests them.

6. Most literature in the high school curriculum was written for educated adults.

[2]Anthony Tovatt, *The Dispersion of Selected Recommended Procedures in Teaching High School English in Colorado* (Ed. D. dissertation, The University of Colorado, 1951), pp. 179–83.

7. Students who read a lot will gradually upgrade the quality of their reading.

8. Paperbacks distributed by the Teen Age Book Club are of low quality, suitable only for slow readers.

9. Heavy teaching loads do not make it impossible for English teachers to help students learn to write by writing frequently.

10. Instruction in grammar and usage should be based directly on the strengths and weaknesses revealed in students' written work, rather than on handbook and workbook exercises.

11. Listening skills can be taught successfully in high school English classes.

12. There is a difference in meaning between *grammar* and *usage*.

13. Practically all high school students make the same mistakes in written and spoken usage.

14. Writers who contribute serious articles to *Harper's* and *The Atlantic* use standard English (as defined in handbooks) exclusively.[3]

15. The principles of semantics can be taught successfully to high school students.

16. High school English teachers are not interested in using or doing research.

17. The reading, writing, speaking, and listening abilities of students can be measured accurately by objective tests.

18. Homogeneous grouping is indispensable in a modern school.

19. The use of an "Essay Evaluation Form" (see Appendix 6) can (1) help English teachers achieve greater objectivity in grading themes and (2) help students edit their themes.

20. An oral composition unit based entirely on principles derived from a group analysis of talks given by the teacher, students, speakers on television, and convocation speakers will be more effective than one based on mastering principles in textbooks.

21. The frequent reading to students of literary selections which supplement material in the literature anthology will favorably affect their attitudes toward literature.

To test any one of the preceding twenty-one hypotheses about teaching English requires an experimental design. The design for testing Assumption 14—"Writers who contribute serious articles to *Harper's* and *The Atlantic* use standard English (as defined in handbooks) exclusively"—would be fairly simple. Included in the statement of the experimental design should be definitions of *standard usage* and *serious articles*.

[3]See Harold Allen, editor, *Applied English Linguistics* (New York: Appleton-Century-Crofts, Inc., 1958), pp. 269–75.

One could decide arbitrarily that the definition of *standard usage* as presented in a popular high school handbook would be the yardstick used. To get a good sample, one would have to determine how many issues of the magazines should be combined for departures from standard usage. The researcher would, of course, have to be experienced in detecting nonstandard usage. Furthermore, he would have to admit that the usage policies of the editors of *Harper's* and *The Atlantic* would color the results of the study.

Many of the assumptions in the above list can be tested satisfactorily only if matched experimental and control groups are used. The following two research projects illustrate (1) the experimental-control group approach and (2) the type of research which can be undertaken with a limited expenditure of time and money. In each instance, it would be highly desirable for the teacher to have two classes on the same grade level with approximately the same ability—one class to be called the experimental class, the other the control class.

Action Research on Two Ways of Teaching English Usage

Assume you are interested in testing the hypothesis that students are more likely to improve their written usage if instruction is based on usage problems revealed in their writing, rather than on those featured in handbooks and workbooks. To determine the beginning-of-the-semester usage strengths and weaknesses of students in the experimental and control classes, have them write a two-page double-spaced letter and take an objective diagnostic usage test. Score the letters and tests and file them.

Throughout the semester, use workbook and handbook exercises in the control class. In the experimental class, base instruction in usage exclusively on the strengths and weaknesses shown in students' compositions and essay tests. At the end of the semester, administer the same tests given at the beginning. Score the tests, then subtract the beginning from the end-of-semester test scores to determine whether the gains made by the experimental class in knowledge about usage and the ability to reflect good usage in their writing exceeded those made by the control class. (Also, note the correlation between the diagnostic test scores and letter-writing scores. Only the letter-writing scores reflect changes, if any, in performance.)

You should, of course, not devote any more of your time to the experimental class than to the control class, which may necessitate grading most of the experimental group's papers in class. You could divide the students in the experimental class into small groups to proofread each other's rough drafts. Classwide instruction could be limited to the most common serious mistakes in usage, and you could spend the remainder of your time helping individuals with their usage problems. By following this procedure, you can help experimental students eliminate most of their usage errors as they write, revise, and rewrite their themes in class. To reduce grading time further, have students devote an occasional class session to reading their rough drafts aloud and explaining how they might be improved. Measurement experts would recommend that the beginning and end-of-semester tests should be coded, mixed together, and graded by a teacher who does not know the students; but who has the temerity to ask a colleague to assume such a task?

The foregoing research project might be broadened by testing the following hypothesis: A control class which devotes class time to hand-book and workbook exercises, spelling lists, vocabulary lists, and dia-graming sentences does not make the gains in written composition that are made by an experimental class which devotes class time to writing, revising, and rewriting themes.

Action Research on the Influence of Paperbacks on Students' Attitudes Toward Literature

A second research project—on the influence of paperbacks on attitudes towards literature—presents a serious problem because it is difficult to measure these attitudes objectively. Assume you are interested in testing the hypothesis that the use of paperbacks is more likely to help students develop favorable attitudes towards literature than the use of a single literature anthology. Using a single anthology in the control class presents no problem, but you may have to get the permission of your principal to use the students' book-rental fees to buy for each member of your experimental class a paperback novel and separate anthologies of essays, short stories, poems, and plays—five volumes in all. The cost would be approximately four dollars per student.

Getting the money to buy the paperbacks may be difficult, but it is simple when compared with determining at the beginning and end of the semester each student's attitudes toward literature and then abstracting from the data the changes, if any. The survey approach seems simplest. Develop a questionnaire that includes the following questions, or better ones if they occur to you: (1) What unassigned books and magazines have you read within the last month? (2) How many books, other than textbooks, do you own? (3) What is literature? (4) What have you liked most about literature courses? (5) What have you liked least about literature courses? (6) What, if anything, have you gained from reading literature? (7) What have you liked about literature anthologies used in your classes? (8) What have you disliked about such anthologies? (9) If paperbacks have been used in your English classes, why did you like or dislike them? (10) List your school subjects in order of preference: 1. _____ 2. _____ 3. _____ 4. _____ 5. _____ 6. _____. At the end of the semester, administer the same questionnaire; then compare the beginning and end-of-the-semester answers of the experimental and control students. (Convince students that their answers to questionnaires will not affect their course grade.)

Desirable variations could be introduced into the experimental class; membership in a book club could provide suitable supplementary reading. Another possibility would be to use the book-rental fee to buy, not five paperbacks for each student, but thirty different novels and thirty different anthologies of short stories, poems, plays, and essays—150 volumes in all. Students could, then, spend three or four periods a week on free reading and the remaining time on several literary selections which all are required to read.

If you are unfamiliar with research procedures, the two research studies outlined above may seem complicated. You might prefer to begin by testing informally an idea which promises to improve English instruction. The outcome would not be a research report buttressed with statistics, but a statement: "It worked" or "It did not work." A researcher would challenge such a conclusion with "Prove it!" or "How do you know?" and if one's answer were, "I can't prove it, but . . . ," he might counter with a benign smile or begin shaking like an indignant parent. Perhaps after testing informally some of the twenty-one hypotheses listed above or additional research projects listed at the end of this chapter, you may want to test them again under formal research conditions, aided, if possible, by someone conversant with the methodology of research.

To illustrate in detail a common research pattern and the work involved in a fairly simple research project, a summary of *A Common-Sense Approach to Teaching Spelling*[4] is presented below. The study was designed to test this hypothesis: Students whose instruction in spelling is confined to mastering the correct spellings of words they misspell in their writing will make greater gains in spelling over a period of one year than students whose instruction is based on weekly or twice-weekly word lists.

A Common-Sense Approach to Teaching Spelling

Each one of fourteen high school English teachers (hereafter called participants) involved in the study had as part of his teaching load a tenth,

---

[4]Vivian B. Maine and Royal J. Morsey, *A Common-Sense Approach To Teaching Spelling* (Muncie, Indiana: Ball State University, 1962.) See Appendix 7.

IMPROVING ENGLISH INSTRUCTION

eleventh, or twelfth grade experimental class and control class selected at random. The participants agreed that in their control classes spelling would be taught the traditional way, i.e., by using a weekly or twice-weekly list of twenty or twenty-five words obtained from wordbooks, handbooks, and workbooks. The participants first dictated the list of spelling words as a study list. Within a week, it was dictated again as a test, and a third time as a part of the in-class grading procedure. The three-part pattern usually took an hour or more of the control students' time.

In the experimental classes, the participants administered in September a seventy-five word diagnostic test composed of spelling demons abstracted from lists of words most frequently misspelled by high school students and college freshmen. Experimental students recorded correctly in their notebooks the words they misspelled in (1) the diagnostic test and (2) their compositions and essay tests. They were urged to use a dictionary whenever they wrote in-class or out-of-class themes. From two to four times a month (while other students were working on an assignment), the participants used class time to check individual students' mastery of the words in their spelling lists.

In July, 1960, Mrs. Vivian Maine, an English teacher at Anderson Senior High School and a graduate student in English at Ball State University, Muncie, Indiana, asked whether she might check for spelling errors the letters which had been written by 589 students in the fourteen control classes and the fourteen experimental classes in September, 1959, and again in May, 1960. She was interested in discovering which group of students would reveal a greater achievement in spelling. The September and May letter-writing assignments were identical:

> You have been exchanging letters with a European pen pal. You are alike in age and sex. In a recent letter your pen pal mentioned reading an article on teen-age dating in an American magazine, and he (or she) is very much interested in knowing more about what American teen-agers call "going steady."
> Write a letter to your pen pal explaining what "going steady" means among American teen-agers. Also explain in your letter what you think about "going steady." Be sure to support your ideas with reasons.
> Since your pen pal probably would not understand American slang, please avoid using slang in your letter.
> You now have exactly thirty minutes to write the letter.

The decrease between September, 1959, and May, 1960, in the total number of misspellings made by 304 experimental students (a decrease of 184 misspellings) was compared with that of the 285 control students (a decrease of 166 misspellings). Both groups misspelled an average of 0.6 fewer words in May than in September. But when one notes that the control group devoted many more hours of class time to spelling than did the experimental group, one seems justified in urging English teachers to test the experimental approach in their own classrooms. Furthermore, the 3498 misspellings made by 589 students (experimental and control) involved only 942 different words. Of these words, only 412 were misspelled more than once. The most frequently misspelled word, *too*, was mispelled only 217 times in 1178 themes, an average of 0.37 misspellings per student or 0.18 per theme. Only two additional words were misspelled over a hundred times: *all right*[5] and *you're*. These facts point up the most significant conclusion which can be drawn from the study: since spelling is an individual problem, students need spelling instruction based on their personal spelling demons.

EVALUATING RESEARCH CLAIMS

The authors of a recent research study claimed the following hypothesis was tested and found to be correct: high school students who devote the time normally spent on written composition to reading literature will, over a period of one school year, make gains in written composition equal to those of students who write compositions regularly. The study left one important question unanswered: Did the teachers whose students wrote compositions merely proofread the papers, or did they help their students edit them? In most English classes, students' compositions are returned with marks indicating mistakes in spelling, capitalization, punctuation, and usage, and marks identifying comma splices and sentence fragments. Most students throw the returned papers away. They do not revise or rewrite them unless required to do so, and they rarely are. If English teachers merely proofread their students' themes for errors, perhaps reading literature would be a good substitute for writing. However, if the composition teacher indicates weaknesses in content, organization, and sentence structure and insists on necessary revisions, there is no substitute for writing. "Writing is a skill that can be improved by practice under the guidance of a competent teacher" is a hypothesis some of you might care to test.

One should always be very critical of claims made by researchers. Many ideas on teaching English are supported by research, but the only way to find out whether they will improve instruction in your classroom is to test them. If possible, consult a qualified researcher about drawing up an experimental design, collecting and analyzing data, and maintaining experimental conditions.

[5]The predominant misspelling, *alright*, is considered acceptable, not preferable, by *Webster's Third New International Dictionary*.

MAKING A START

When you engage in research for the first time, select a problem that is significant and specific, and that lends itself to a simple experimental design. Many of the "Ideas to Test" and "Assumptions About . . ." at the end of chapters in this book can be expanded into simple research proposals. Carry out an experiment at least once a year; it will not only add zest to your teaching but will also help you build skill in introducing and controlling experimental conditions. Do not hesitate to repeat in your classroom research projects completed by others. Competent researchers are as critical of the claims of others as are doctors of the claims of patent-medicine manufacturers.

U.S. OFFICE OF EDUCATION AND THE N.C.T.E. RESEARCH FOUNDATION

Should you wish to submit an idea for a research project to Division of Elementary-Secondary Research, Curriculum and Demonstration Branch, U. S. Department of Health, Education and Welfare, Office of Education, Washington, D. C. 20202, or to Research Foundation, National Council of Teachers of English, Champaign, Illinois 61820, you should develop a proposal which includes (1) a clear statement of the problem, (2) data showing your familiarity with related research, (3) the hypothesis you are planning to test and how you are going to test it, and (4) a detailed statement of money needed for supplies, equipment, and salaries. Before you mail the proposal, ask someone skilled in research to check it.

To acquaint you with the kind of research projects which have been approved by the Division of Elementary-Secondary Research, U. S. Office of Education, ten typical projects under way in January, 1967, are quoted below.

1. Teaching English as a second language to pupils of elementary school age.

2. Program to extend curriculum materials in English for the able to a wider student group.

3. The development of a sequential and cumulative program in English for able college-bound students in the senior high school, grades 10–12.

4. A curriculum study center to develop and test sequential approaches to English in junior high school.

5. Developing competency in written composition in children from kindergarten through elementary school by means of curriculum materials.

6. The development of reading and language materials for grades 7–9.

7. An articulated program in composition, grades K to 13.

8. Materials and methods for teaching structural and generative grammar to high school students and their teachers.

9. Development of composition programs based on generative grammar and psycholinguistic theory for grades 7–9.

10. An integrated curriculum in literature, language, and composition for junior high schools.[6]

ASSUMPTIONS ABOUT DOING RESEARCH

Prepare to explain why you accept or reject, wholly or in part, the following assumptions about doing research:

1. The scientific method plays a vital role in experimental research.

2. Historical research on the evolution of British and American English has provided English teachers with valuable information.

3. Survey research can be used by the classroom teacher to discover students' knowledge and attitudes.

4. Activity analysis research revealing the nature of the English teacher's daily routine provides useful information about the English curriculum.

5. Case study research should be conducted by every English teacher.

6. Experimental research promises to produce more worthwhile information for English teachers than historical research.

7. The experimental-control class research design is highly suitable for determining whether one teaching method produces better results than another.

8. Worthwhile research by an English teacher is unlikely unless he has clear, defensible goals for teaching English.

9. Maintaining experimental conditions is one of the most difficult problems a researcher faces.

10. Research results are often disproved soon after they are published.

11. It has proved easier to develop more effective means of transportation than more effective ways of educating high school students.

12. Most English teachers are not interested in using or doing research.

13. The professional English teacher should feel obligated to undertake at least one simple research study annually.

14. Research in education is as easy to justify as research in agriculture, medicine, and industry.

[6]U.S. Department of Health, Education and Welfare, Office of Education, *A List of English Curriculum Development Centers and Research for Elementary and Secondary Schools*, Washington, D. C. 20202, January, 1967.

15. High school English teachers are seldom influenced by research studies and books and articles on teaching English.

16. Most teachers resist change in their daily teaching routine.

17. Most of us teach the way we were taught.

18. Few teachers rely on the scientific method (the researcher's tool) in solving problems related to teaching.

19. In *Action Research to Improve School Practices*, Stephen M. Corey says that classroom teachers should leave research to highly skilled researchers.

20. Some of the research projects in English described in the *Encyclopedia of Educational Research* are so simple that they could be duplicated by teachers with little teaching experience.

21. A teacher can determine what students think about him as a teacher by having them complete a teacher-rating form.

22. Research studies in English have not produced results so conclusive as research studies in agriculture and medicine.

23. Developing dependable experimental designs and controls for research in English is so difficult that the results of research studies in English should be viewed with skepticism.

24. The following quotation from Plato must be part of a researcher's creed:

> But that we shall be better and braver and less helpless if we think that we ought to inquire, than we should have been if we thought that there was no knowing and no duty to seek to know what we do not know;—that is a theme upon which I am ready to fight, in word and deed, to the utmost of my power.[7]

25. Developing experimental designs to test the twenty-one assumptions on page 200–201 would be easy in some instances, difficult in others.

26. More English teachers would be interested in doing research if their teaching loads were reduced to a total of one hundred students in four classes.

27. A superior English teacher can be identified by administrators, students, parents, and colleagues.

28. One can easily illustrate in detail how the researcher's use of the scientific method has enabled him to solve problems in medicine, agriculture, transportation, and communication.

29. Most educational research can be accurately defined as a statistically straight line drawn between an unwarranted assumption and a predetermined conclusion.

[7]B. Jowett, *The Dialogues of Plato*, Fourth Edition (Oxford: Clarendon Press, 1953), Vol. I, p. 285.

30. The N.C.T.E. report on *Research in Written Composition* should be read by all English teachers.

31. Research could help solve problems relating to war, poverty, and crime.

32. Walter Loban's *The Language of Elementary School Children* reflects attitudes towards research that should prove useful to an English teacher planning a research study. His Chapter 3, "Conclusions," pp. 81–89, illustrates that research is "common sense verified."

ADDITIONAL RESEARCH PROJECTS

Carry out an experiment at least once a year. Perhaps one of the following suggested research projects will appeal to you.

Literature

1. To determine the reading interests of your students, ask them to rate (A, B, C, D, or F) assigned poems, short stories, essays, plays, and novels. (See George W. Norvell's *The Reading Interests of Young People.*)

2. To determine what your students read voluntarily, have them enter periodically on 3″ x 5″ cards answers to the following question: "What unassigned books did you read during the last month?" (Questions about voluntary reading of magazines and newspapers also reveal worthwhile information about students' reading habits.)

3. Determine the response of students to paperback book club selections by keeping a record of books they buy and following up to see whether they read them and react favorably or unfavorably to them.

4. Ask students to write a one-sentence statement of the theme of a short, unfamiliar lyric poem you have written on the board. Then read the poem to them without comments. Next, ask students to write beneath their original statement a second one-sentence version of the theme of the poem. Compare the two statements to determine to what extent your reading the poem aloud helped the class to understand it.

5. If you have been using the analysis approach ("What did the author say?") in discussing literature, continue it in one class; in another class, use discussion questions which relate the literary selections to students' own experiences. (See discussion questions for Lesson Plan II, page 56). Compare the quality and frequency of the students' oral responses to questions in the two classes.

6. If the number of poems listed in a poetry unit in the departmental syllabus makes the once-over-lightly approach unavoidable, ask permission

to use in one class a leisurely approach which includes (1) reading all short poems aloud before and after discussion, (2) discussing thought-provoking questions which relate the poems to students' experiential backgrounds, and (3) reading aloud in class supplementary poems which relate to the ones in the syllabus. Use the traditional approach in another class. Administer attitude-toward-poetry questionnaires in both classes at the beginning and end of the unit. Compare the results.

You might limit the experiment to one class by using unannounced the traditional approach during the first half of the unit, the more leisurely approach during the second half. At the end of the unit, ask students which approach helped them most, and why, in developing an appreciation of poetry.

7. Use objective tests in one literature class, essay tests (drawn from discussion questions distributed at the beginning of the unit) in another. Administer attitude-toward-literature questionnaires in both classes at the beginning and end of the unit. Compare the results.

8. Have a dependable student record, as inconspicuously as possible, over a period of a week or more, the number of times each student participates in class discussions. (I did this in a university class, and discovered that six of thirty students dominated the discussions. But after calling on nonvolunteers over a period of two weeks, I was able to raise the number of regular participants to fifteen.)

9. Many teachers equate "discussing literature" with "telling." Ask a student to use a watch to determine over a period of one week how many minutes in each period are consumed by teacher talk.

Written Composition

1. Chart errors (kind and frequency) that your students make in themes. See William Miles Thomas, "Technical Errors in Compositions of the Average High School Senior," *The School Review*, Vol. 71, No. 2, Summer 1963, pp. 188–207.

2. Read to your students a half-dozen brief themes written by former students—two excellent, two good, and two poor. Have them rate the themes to see how well they can recognize effective and ineffective writing.

3. Have students write, at the beginning of a composition unit, a brief letter to a friend or relative. Analyze the letters carefully to determine what class and individual work needs to be done in organization, sentence structure, paragraphing, usage, spelling, punctuation, and capitalization. At the end of the unit, have students complete an identical assignment. Compare the two sets of letters to ascertain the progress made by (1) the class as a whole and (2) individual students.

4. If you require themes from students and grade them outside of class, continue the procedure in all except one experimental class. In this class, have students work on their themes in and out of class, but devote all class time to (1) helping individual students with their themes and (2) having students edit each other's papers. Evaluate all themes during the class session only. Compare the progress in composition made by students in the experimental class with one of your other classes—the one which most closely approximates this class in ability.

5. Parents frequently complain that schools do not teach enough grammar. Ask fifty parents, fifty teachers, and fifty high school students to spell out what they mean when they say "Schools should teach more grammar." Compare the answers of the three groups.

Oral Composition

1. In one of your classes, use your customary approach in the first oral composition unit, Mr. Paul's approach (see Chapter 7) in the second unit. Ask your students to explain in writing which of the two approaches they preferred, and why.

2. Take an inventory of the most common usage errors (kind and frequency) made by your students during an oral-composition unit.

Listening

1. Make a survey to determine (1) how much time your students devote to television and (2) the kinds of programs they prefer.

2. Develop and mimeograph a list of one hundred assumptions and statements of fact made on television by politicians, news analysts, panelists, and advertisers. To see how well your students can differentiate between the two categories, have them write an "F" (fact) or "A" (assumption) in a slot preceding each item. Tabulate the results.

Nature of Language

1. Analyze your students' speech and writing to determine each student's serious usage errors (kind and frequency). Develop and administer a test made up of their usage errors in context. Compare each student's test results with his recorded usage profile. The foregoing procedure will reveal whether there is a high or low correlation between a student's knowledge about usage and his usage in speech and writing. (I have frequently discovered that a student can make high grades on a usage test made up of sentences from his speech and writing.)

2. Check Arthur G. Kennedy's *English Usage*, Charles C. Fries'

American English Grammar, Albert H. Marckwardt and Fred Walcott's *Facts About Current English Usage*, Sterling Leonard's *Current English Usage*, and Robert C. Pooley's *Teaching English Usage* to determine to which usage levels they assign the expressions *everybody . . . their, can I be excused?, come quick!, different than, he don't know, it is me, that is him, etc.*

3. Make a survey of the slang used on the college campus where you are a student or in the high school where you teach.

Evaluation

1. Duplicate a theme written by a high school student. Ask several of your colleagues to grade the theme as carefully as possible. Compare (1) the grades given and (2) the usefulness to the student of the corrections and comments made by the various graders. Several months later, duplicate another theme similar in quality to the one above. (You could use the same one.) Attach to it a copy of the "Essay Evaluation Form," Appendix 6. Ask each teacher to grade the paper as heretofore, but to score the theme by using the form. Compare the teachers' scores on the two essays to determine whether the use of the "Essay Evaluation Form" makes for closer agreement on grades given.

2. Ask several of your colleagues to give you a copy of the test they administer on *Silas Marner* or some other long literary selection. Have students in one class take all of the tests so collected. Compare scores made by each student to determine the range of grades. Analyze the tests to determine colleagues' objectives in teaching the selection.[8]

[8]For a summary of recent research in English, see Nathan S. Blount, "Summary of Investigations Relating to the English Arts in Secondary Education: 1967," *English Journal*, Vol. 57, No. 5, May, 1968, pp. 710–724.

13

The Professional English Teacher: A Summary

Before reading this chapter, formulate clear, defensible answers to the following questions. After reading it, prepare to explain why you changed or retained your answers.

1. Why must achieving content mastery be a lifelong goal? In which areas of English do you feel inadequate, and what are you doing about it?

2. Why did you decide to become an English teacher? What do you wish to accomplish most as an English teacher? Why?

3. Why and how are you going to gather information about individual differences among your students? Give specific illustrations of how you will use the information.

4. Why are many students not interested in the fare offered in English classes? How do you plan to motivate such students?

5. Why do you accept or reject, wholly or in part, the procedures used by high school and college teachers to measure your progress in English? How will you measure your students' progress? Why?

6. Why and how do a teacher's tests reflect his educational aims (philosophy of education)?

7. What kinds of research are needed in English? Why? Why do many high school English teachers avoid using and doing research? What kinds of research projects in English require a minimum of time and money?

The professional English teacher (1) strives to master content, (2) develops defensible goals and methods, (3) recognizes individual differences, (4) knows how to motivate students, (5) relates his evaluative techniques (tests, discussions, etc.) to clear, defensible goals, and (6) conducts research and uses the research of others.

MASTERING CONTENT

Probably most high school English teachers elected to teach English, rather than another subject, because the content appealed to them. As high school and college students, they appreciated literature and saw value in written and oral expression. They felt that they could share interest and ability in these areas with students. But even though most beginning English teachers have devoted their high school and college years to mastering content, they are aware that their preparation in literature and composition is incomplete. During their first year of teaching, they sometimes find it difficult to keep a step ahead of students who have been conditioned to expect that a teacher has all the answers. But one who burns midnight oil during student teaching and his first year or two as a regular teacher is likely to change from a pupil into a student who sees mastering content as a lifelong project.

Beginning teachers sometimes feel inferior when they compare their understanding of language and literature with that of some of their own high school and college English teachers. They seem unaware that the teachers who impress them have had the advantage of many years of study time and teaching experience. The same beginning teachers may impress other beginners ten years hence, especially if they are acquainted with more than a few novels, short stories, plays, essays, poems, and a handbook and workbook—the core of many high school English curricula. Mastering content is a goal no one realizes completely, but the pursuit of it is one joy of teaching for the professional English teacher. He gradually acquires a knowledge of language and literature which impresses even reluctant learners. (Aesop said, "Little by little does the trick.")

A teacher who is also a student reads to his classes literary selections not in the class anthology, and recommends some of the current books and magazine articles he is reading. He makes it easy for students to buy appropriate paperbacks, and he advertises the resources of the school and community libraries. His students are impressed most by his concern with the present. He does not restrict his reading to the established masterpieces of world literature. He is not only familiar with the best in recent books but also with the articles, book reviews and theatre, music, and art news featured in the *Saturday Review, Harper's,* and *The Atlantic.* He keeps abreast of current affairs by reading a good newspaper (*The Christian Science Monitor, The New York Times,* or *The St. Louis Post-Dispatch*) and news magazine (*Newsweek or Time*).

A beginning teacher is probably aware that the finest in world literature, past and current, is available in inexpensive paperbacks. But does he know he can buy a useful library of paperbacks on the history and nature of language for less than ten dollars? Furthermore, by subscribing to *The English Journal* he can keep up to date on books and articles concerned specifically with content, goals, and methods for teaching language and literature.

The professional English teacher develops, then, a broad background of understanding in economics, religion, government, philosophy, science, history, the fine and practical arts, and education. Since the milestones of all the academic disciplines are recorded in literature, the English teacher who strives for content mastery does not remain a narrow specialist for long.

DEVELOPING GOALS AND METHODS

The professional English teacher demonstrates daily that all students deserve help in improving their language skills. He begins a new semester by measuring their present ability to read, write, speak, and listen, then provides carefully guided experiences which build on the skills they have. He eschews standardized tests, workbook and handbook exercises, spelling lists, vocabulary lists, and the quizmaster approach to literature. He helps students write and edit themes, he relates instruction in grammar and usage directly to their speaking and writing assignments, and he helps them relate literature to their own experiences. His goal is always improved performance, not merely increased knowledge.

RECOGNIZING INDIVIDUAL DIFFERENCES

The professional English teacher knows that even homogeneously grouped students' proficiency in reading, writing, speaking, and listening varies widely. He discovers their varying speaking and writing abilities by analyzing their performance in these areas—not by testing them with identical spelling lists, vocabulary lists, and handbook and workbook exercises. By analyzing their oral and written English, he learns that some group instruction is necessary, but that he must devote much of his time to helping individual students.

In literature units, he provides opportunities for the whole class to read and discuss certain literary selections, but also affords students a chance to pursue personal literary interests. He caters to students' varying literary interests by making them aware of the resources of the school and community libraries, the paperback book clubs, and the many paperback publishers. He keeps informed on what is available in paperbacks by coercing the school librarian to subscribe to *Paperbound Books—*

published monthly by R. R. Bowker, 1180 Avenue of the Americas, New York, New York 10036—which lists over forty thousand paperbacks, hundreds of which are suitable for high school students.

MOTIVATING STUDENTS

The professional English teacher relates instruction in reading, writing, speaking, and listening to students' own experiences. He knows that requirements in English classes must seem worthwhile goals to students today, not barriers to be overcome in order to insure a bright future. He does not motivate students with incessant testing which threatens failure to the uncooperative. He tries to provide learning experiences which are intellectually stimulating and enjoyable, as well as related to students' concerns. He is convinced that his success depends on his ability to convert students to a lifelong interest in books and learning.

GRADING

The professional English teacher realizes that (1) evaluative techniques designed to help students improve their performance in composition are easy to justify and (2) those largely confined to measuring students' abilities to complete handbook and workbook exercises are difficult to justify. In teaching literature, he assumes that his students' appreciation is not furthered by an emphasis on the popular recall-type tests. He emphasizes discussions and explanations which help students relate literary selections to their interests, problems, and ideas. Although he consistently uses thought-provoking questions to measure their feelings about literary selections, he also relies on many other ways of determining these feelings: (1) informal discussions, (2) the quality of oral reading, (3) their questions and comments, (4) their interest in other selections by the same author, and (5) voluntary writing which reflects the influence of an author.

The professional English teacher does not see tests as instruments to fill grade books. He uses them at the beginning of the term to discover what kind of help students need, and during the term to see whether the help being given them is producing results. He considers test results a measure of his own success as well as of his students'. If his students are not making the progress he expected of them, he does not exclude himself as a possible cause of their failure.

USING AND DOING RESEARCH

The professional English teacher does some experimenting, with or without benefit of a lighter teaching load and a foundation grant. He tests some of the many hypotheses about teaching literature and composition presented in books on teaching English and magazines like the *English Journal*. He also tests his own hypotheses. If, for example, he has two English classes roughly alike, he labels one *control class* and the other *experimental class*. He teaches the control class approximately as he has in the past; he introduces a new approach in the experimental class. He administers tests in both classes at the beginning and end of the term, and compares the results to see which group made the most progress.

The professional English teacher does not always have time to introduce and maintain experimental conditions when he tests a new idea. He frequently tries to ascertain its value by noting how his students respond to it. For example, he may try one of the paperback book clubs to encourage voluntary reading and decide—on the basis of the number of books ordered in a semester, not statistical studies—whether a club stimulates reading. He knows such informal testing of ideas fails to impress an experienced researcher, but is egotistical enough to assume that his guesses about the outcomes of certain changes in classroom procedure are intelligent ones. If he were challenged by his principal or colleagues to prove this, he would probably begin collecting data to see whether he could sustain his judgments with enough evidence to convince the skeptics.

CONCLUSION

The professional English teacher takes students as they come and does as much for each one as he can. He does not ask, "Why are they here?" but "What can I do for them?" He is always interested in developing and testing hypotheses which promise to help him solve problems involving content mastery, goals, methods, individual differences, motivation, measurement, and research. In our changing world, problems seldom remain static long enough to be solved once and for all. In education and most other areas of human endeavor, the scientific method appears to be the only tool immune to obsolescence. Professional English teachers have many characteristics in common, but the one which promises most for their students is their persistence in testing new ways of teaching reading, writing, speaking, and listening.

ASSUMPTIONS ABOUT THE PROFESSIONAL ENGLISH TEACHER

Prepare to explain why you accept or reject, wholly or in part, the following assumptions about the professional English teacher.

1. A lifelong pursuit of content mastery is a must for the professional English teacher.

2. Content mastery includes an understanding of past and current developments in the fine and practical arts, history, politics, economics, religion, science, and literature.

3. Goals in English must be related to students' concerns.

4. Methods used must lead directly to improved performance in reading, writing, speaking, and listening—not merely knowledge and recall of facts in these fields.

5. Individual differences among students in ability to read, write, speak, and listen can be ascertained and provided for by the competent teacher.

6. Gains made by students in language and literature can be measured accurately.

7. Students can be motivated to make progress in reading, writing, speaking, and listening.

8. Doing and using research are responsibilities of every English teacher.

9. The professional English teacher takes students as they come and does as much for each one as he can.

10. English methods courses offer more than the "tricks of the trade."

Essays on
"My Easter Vacation"
Written by
"Slow" Eleventh Graders

Sixteen "slow" students[1] segregated on the basis of scores on standardized mathematics, I. Q., and reading tests were allowed fifty-five minutes to write an essay on "My Easter Vacation." The following six essays represent the best and poorest work of the class:

1

I went to Teneensee on my Spring Vacation And I head more fun than if I stad at home in _____ I went to the Show at Teeneensee.

2

One thing I did on my vacation was I went to show and saw Steel Helmet. it The meaning of show was give you the idea of what are boys are going through. I liked the show it was about Keara. when the story show lots of men died and their feet were tied and they had tied a piece of rope in the opening of their mouth. All of them were died but one they had him tied. He was trieding get lose when he hear some one walk he stopped and play like he was died again. It was a boy he was a South Keara. After this boy help this man

[1] Almost all came from families with average or below-average incomes.

and boy went on. Later on they met a color Doctor and after that they met some boys. They going to a place that they went with because it had not even they would have been killed At the end all of the got killed but the color Doctor and made was tied and one them he met after—

3

The sunday after school was out Jack and Fred and myself. went on a fishing trip to tennese. It was small town named Dale Hollow while we were there we caught 82 fist between us. We were just up there three days it rained the first day and had to sleep in a pup tent.

One night while fred and I were running the trot line fred got his leg cut on a chock I could not get it out in the water and had Jack to bring the boat out so we could put fred in it and I had to cut the net that the hook was fasened onto.

We fished all night the second night we was there the next morning we life fot home about ten o'clock.

4

On Sunday April. My boyfriend and I went to —————— to meet his parents. They are very nice people. After we all got introduced his father took me and showed me around the farm. They have ten cows and a lot of pigs.

After that he was showing me how to milk a cow. It looks easy but I really think it is hard. He took the shears and sheared the cows for me.

My boyfriends little sister named a cow after me. That day after I got home I told my family about having a cow named after me they teased me. I have been have fun by have a cow named after me.

5

My vacation was a very pleasant vacation. The same Friday of my vacation I went to a dance at the armory. I know this will sound queer by Mister

Clean Head and his band was playing. I had a nice time at the dance, because every time I looked up some one was coming for me to dance. I danced so long my legs and my feet began to hurt. Saturday a bunch of us girls and boys went biciyle ridding. We had a very nice time. Some of the following days I went to the show with my sisters and friends. Tuesday I went roller skatting and met a bunch of girls and boys from out of town. Sunday I went to the show and saw a very good picture. After the show I went bowling with my father. I had a nice time bowling. Of course I didn't have the highest score all of the time but sometimes I was ahead until the end of the game. I was close to the losser of the game at the end. Then Monday school. I'm sore all over.

6

As school ended on the twenty-third I knew Spring was right around the corner and that we would have a whole week to find that out as our Spring vacation was due. We had lots of things the last two weeks. This was going to be a real vacation as I thought I was going to sleep late everyday. My sister had been staying for a couple of weeks to recover from having a baby. Judy and Lynday my two neices had come over all so. Mornings I wouldn't get much sleep as my nieces would come in and jumb on the bed until I threw them out or gave them some candy then lock the door. The nights I worked I would go home and try to get some sleep but the alarm clock would end all that the two o'clock feeding was just starting and would leave me with out any sleep the next morning.

ASSUMPTIONS ABOUT THE ESSAYS

Explain why you accept or reject, wholly or in part, the following assumptions related to the preceding six essays:

1. The six students should be required to devote a month or two to completing handbook and workbook exercises.
2. Essays 1 and 2 are hopeless.

3. Teaching composition to the six students is a waste of taxpayers' money.

4. Among Essays 3, 4, and 5, one is superior to the others.

5. The best way to help the students would be to mimeograph (double or triple space) the essays, distribute the copies, and then spend class time (1) discussing how the content, organization, sentence structure, usage, vocabulary punctuation, capitalization, and spelling of the essays might be improved; (2) having them make on the mimeographed sheets the revisions they and the teacher suggested; and (3) rewriting the themes the next day, with the teacher circulating to answer questions and make suggestions.

6. The students would appreciate having copies of a mimeographed class anthology of their rewritten essays on "My Easter Vacation."

Paragraphs on
"Why I Want to Go to College"
Written by
"Slow" Seventh Graders

Thirty "slow" students[1] segregated on the basis of standardized English achievement and I. Q. tests and their sixth-grade teachers' recommendations were allowed twenty minutes to write the following paragraphs on "Why I Want to Go to College":

1

Why I want to go to college is because I want to become a secratary. And this is why. I like to type and work-out shorthand such as (.) which means A. I like to wright which needs improved on. And it is a very study job.

2

Why I want to go to college. I want to go to college to be eathier a veterunarian or a constructor. this may seem strange But I want to be a veterunarian because I like animals. And I want to be a constrictor because my father is and I like to read. Anyway I havn't made up my mind yet. Who nose I may be a Doctor.

[1] Almost all came from families with average or above-average incomes. The principal of the school told me that most of the parents of these "slow" seventh graders hope their children can qualify for college.

I want to go to a air force acadmey because cause I want to be a flier. I want to become a flier because I want to have a militry career and also my father and his father were both fliers. To become a flier you have to learn how to fly a plan, gust how to work the gun and how to doge other plans. To be a flier you have to have much courage.

4

I want to go to college because of a Doctors curear. I learned that you have to go to college for four years. I am not afraid of work cause work can be fun. I am real friendly with the people over at —————— hospital. My aunt and Grandfather work at —————— Hospital. I know the pharmists real well and when the head isant around they let me inside. I think a doctors life is fun, its exciting, and sad. Bringing people in the amblance sounds fun, but not when they say D.O.A.[2] Those 3 letters are not funny. So here's why I want to go to college.

5

Some people don't like animals, but I love them well enough to go to college to learn about them. Even though the last few years of science have not been the best, I have decided to learn to like it so I can become a veterinarian. When animals are lost or are hurt some way I feel real sorry for them, but I can't really help them any way because I haven't been able to learn that much about them. I'm not sure what college it will be but what ever it is I'm sure I will be a veterinarian.

6

I want to go to college to be a modle. I want a college that will help me

[2]Dead On Arrival.

to have better poise, have a better appreciation of designs, etc. I think I have these two things now, but I would like to improve them. I would like to be a "free" lance modle." I'd like to meet people, and maybe go to a foreign country and modle. These are my reasons for wanting to go to college.

7

Can you guess why I want to go to college? I want to go to college because I want to be a chemist so I can make new cures for people who have ilnesses that can't be cured at this moment.

8

The reason I want to go to college is because I would like to explore numbers more and the different ways of using them. The College I would like to go to is ————, because it's a teachers college and are noted for the mathmatics course they have. This way I could get quite a few jobs, like engineering, manufacturing, industries and many more. This is the main reason I want to go to college.

9

Why? So I can design cars. Where? At General Motors Institute. I think I have a good chance at it and if I study hard I can make it. I'll work at it till I make it. Sometimes I get an inspiration. I sit down and draw what I feel.

10

Why do I want to go to college? I love children and I want to be able to understand and work with them. By going to college I feel I can learn the things I want to know and do with them.

11

My reason for wanting to go to college is that I want to be a Physical Education teacher. I want to attend ————. I will try to work hard. I think it would be fun to show exercises and acrobatics. I like to do things like that. I would like it if a shared a room with a girl in the Dormatoy. I know studing won't be a breeze. So I will get as much out of college as I can. After I graduate I want to go to a Junior High and teach it. That's my reason for wanting to go to college.

12

I want to go to college to study for the air force. When I get out of college I want to get a job at my dad's store and you have to have a college degree to get it. I want to be in the swimming program and swim on the teem. The college I want to go to is the most famous of all colleges, ————.

13

Why I want to go to College. Because I waunt to be a Music teacher and conduct an orcraster. I want to go to ———— College.

14

Why do I want to go to college? I want to go because I like sports that they have and the subjects. I would like to go to ———— because of its sports. In basketball I like it because of their good record and their coaches, and football because of good coaches and a good staff and its record. Baseball is also a good sport. They have good coaches and a good team. ———— has a good athletic director.

I want to go to college to become a veterinarian. My reasons are I love animals and love to care for them. The college I am going to is _____ for Pre Med and _____ for the rest of my seven years.

I want to be a veterinarian. I have always been interested in science. I have already planned to have a clinic. I love animals and always have. We have two dogs and are planning to have eight or nine more very soon. I want to cure dieses of all animals and attend _____.

We should all go to college, to get the satisfaction out of it. Another reason when you want to apply for a job anymore you have to have a college education. The reason for wanting to go to college is I want to be a nurse, because I have a cousin who is a nurse and goes to _____ University, and she says it is the best college for nursing. Another reason is I like to care for people. So that's my reason for wanting to go to college.

I want to go to college because of my ambition of being a teacher. I want to learn as much as I can about the world and it's people. I'm not sure what kind of teacher I would like to be, but I have considered being a gym, art, music, or science teacher.

I want to go to college to be a teacher. You hear all the time on T. V. about not having enough teachers. I like children and the way school run. I'll go to _____ or _____ for my schooling.

Engineering for Fun and profit is what I told my Mom when I asked here if I could go to —————. I told her it is one of the highest rating colleges in the U.S.A. for engineering but this is not the only reason that I want to go to college. Another reason is the high standings in sports ————— has. It has one of the most complete lines of subjects like engineering and science and has a very up to date colleges. These are the main reasons I want to go to college at —————.

21

The college I prefere to go to is ————— University. The reason for this is because it is a well known school and they have a good reputation in sports. Another reason is because if you don't go to college it is very hard to find a job. Also many people I know that have gone to ————— are doing very well in life.

Why spend four years supposedly working as a secretary when you have to work to make a living any way. I would like to go to college for future use. You can get a better job if you are a college graduate. I would like to go to ————— for many reasons. One, it has a good reputation, good teachers, and complete instruments for your future use. I think going to college is a very good idea.

23

Why I want to go to college is very plain to see and is reasonable. I want to go to college to get good school grades so I can help my children with their school work and be a good housewife and if in need of money I could get a

PARAGRAPHS WRITTEN BY "SLOW" SEVENTH GRADERS

job to help with our problems. I think you can all see why I want to go to college.

24

I have always wanted to be a veterinarian, even in my childhood. I have wanted to have a better understanding of animals. I will probably go to —————— since I have been there many, many times. After I take my years there I will start training dogs for police or army.

25

I want to go to college because I want to be a teacher. I would like to teach in elementary and somewhere in —————— because I have lived here all my life. I would like to be a teacher because I think it would be very exciting and I would like to be around kids and teach them things I learned when I was a girl.

26

I want to go to college to be a typest. Cause if you could type you could probly get a good job in an office, and usually a steady job. I would be a good thing to stay with.

27

I want to go to college so that I can be an engineer. I want to design cars for G. M. C. (general motors co.) I want to go to —————— for the first two years and I want to go to —————— for the rest.

28

I want to go to college because I would like to be a physical ed. teacher or coach and play baseball. I would like to go to ——————. They have had

230

a good baseball team for several years. My reason to be a teacher or coach I like to work with kids and I like all sports and I would enjoy coaching boys to go through defeats together and the wins.

29

Why do I want to go to college? This I've often debated with myself. But the best reason I have to want to go to college is to be a nurse. I feel that by nurses training I can learn to help people, and learn to be able to take care of them.

30

I would like to go to college for a good Education and when I graduate, I can get a good job and earn good money and I would like to go to Military Acedeny to try and make an officer to make my Dad pround of me.

ASSUMPTIONS ABOUT THE PARAGRAPHS

Explain why you accept or reject, wholly or in part, the following assumptions related to the preceding paragraphs.

1. A detailed inventory of the students' strengths and weaknesses in content, organization, sentence structure, usage, spelling, punctuation, capitalization, and vocabulary indicates that their teacher should devote most of his time to classwide rather than individual instruction.

2. The composition problem that cries most for immediate attention is spelling.

3. Selecting the three best and three worst paragraphs is easy.

4. Paragraph 5 ranks highest in content, organization, sentence structure, usage, spelling, punctuation, vocabulary, and capitalization.

5. The paragraphs reflect unrealistic hopes for "slow" students.

6. If all of the students in a methods class grade all of the paragraphs and then tabulate the number of "A's," "B's," "C's," "D's," and "F's received by each paragraph, the results will show considerable agreement in the grades given.

7. A teacher should find a more suitable topic for seventh graders than "Why I Want to Go to College."

Paragraphs on
"Why I Want to Go to College"
Written by
"Academic" Tenth Graders

Thirty-three "academic" students[1] segregated on the basis of standardized mathematics, I. Q., and reading tests were allowed thirty minutes to write the following paragraphs on "Why I Want to Go to College":

1

Going to college means alot to some people. To me it means having fun and meeting people. If I go to college it will be for that reason alone. To be what I want to be you don't have to have a college education. I'm not saying that if I go to college I will not study, because I know I will have to do alot of that. I will try my best to get through and I will not quite trying untill I susceed.

2

Those big old bullies! That's what they are! They won't let you in unless you are just the way they want you. They would rather make you poor than let you keep your money. Yes, those sheriffs can sure take everything away that you have "worked" for. Oh, about college? I will try to get in!

[1]Almost all came from families with average or below-average incomes.

232

Do I or don't I. If I do go, what course do I want to take and where do I want to go. I could take science, math, and histry and go to _____. Or maybe I should be a teacher and go to _____. But then, if I went to _____ that would mean living at home; that is out of the question. If I don't go to college I won't have to worry about any of this. Since I want to be a nurse I think this would be the best idea. But then it may not. Well I have three years yet to decide whether I want to go or not. Of course, I'll still have to keep my grades up, so if I do decide to go I can get in. I still don't know if I do or do not want to go to college.

4

One day in the near future, I will be starting to the college of my choice, I hope. I can see myself on that eventful day, the first day of school. I will be walking down the marble steps that lead from the Science Building, and all of a sudden I will have slipped on a banana peeling that some brainy person had carelessly thrown there. Boy, the book will fly. After picking myself up and gathering my books, I will head for home. Crossing the street, I will accidentally run in to someone. Will I ever get home without another accident? Another question enters my mind. Will all of my college days be filled with accidents? With my luck I might not get through the first week alive.

5

College, a place for work and fun, is a place where you can get a good education and be able to get a good job. Jobs anymore are few and far between for people who do not go to college or even finish high school. College can also get you jobs in the sport field. College is also a place for fun. There are many

PARAGRAPHS WRITTEN BY "ACADEMIC" TENTH GRADERS

good looking girls in college these days. Many girls and boys these days, are getting married in school and working there way through school. I plan to go to college, get married and have some children, and have a good enough job to support my family.

6

Why do I want to go to college? well because I want to get all the knowledge I can before my life is over. Of course, I have certain subjects that are more interesting than others, but I still would like to gain knowledge in generally everything. "Why do I want to gain knowledge?" well because, I need it to put it shortly, and college is my key to knowledge, so it's off to college for me when I graduate from highschool.

7

College is a place at which your ambitions are made much easier to obtain. Today the high school graduate would not have a chance of getting a certain job if there was a college graduate who also wanted it. This means that the high school graduate would be smart to go on to college where he could explore the field that he has chosen to be his occupation. In this I feel that it would be foolish to pass up the opportunity of going to college.

8

When we graduate from high school; are we grown-up? I fervently believe we are not. We only think we are, for college is the institution in which we must grow up. It is either sink or swim. For the first time we are away from our parent's "watchful eye." Being on our own is one of the most important things on the road to adulthood. In college we meet new people, learn the facts that will bring us to the peak of our formal education, and take care of ourselves. When we have accomplished these things, then we are on the way to an intelligent and mature adulthood.

9

"Help! I'm out of school," I screamed. Then I awoke. I had been dreaming but it seemed so real. There I was; out of school for good. Just the thought of it made me shudder. Would I really end up as I did in my dream, stranded. No, I decided. When I get out of High School I'm going on to College. I don't want to wind up like many of todays teenagers do, stranded. Because of my dream I decided that College would be my best bet. There I could learn a profession of some sort and when I go out into the world I won't be lost. I'm going to College so I won't be yelling for help.

10

I really don't know why I shall go to college. School has never been my favorite pasttime, but it was always all right. _____ would not be my choice of colleges, but I shall probably end up there. By going to _____ I would have to live at home, and I definitely do not want that. The colorful campus of _____ has always appealed to me. After graduation from _____, if I still want to be a teacher, I shall probably go to _____, after all, it is a teachers' college.

11

To me, college is a challenge that I must accept. College is not a place that you have to attend. If I attend college the teachers will not force me to do all of my assignments or try to make me pay attention in class; all they would do is flunce me. But why would I go there on my own, if not to study and get good grades? The grades I make will be important in later life when I go out on my own into the world and try to earn a living.

12

I have a good reason, believe it or not. To start out with, if I went to college I would want to become a teacher. Whats wrong with this. I don't want to have to clean the chewing gum and thumbtacts off of my chair everyday. One day I just might forget to do this and have to go home all of a sudden. There is another reason to. All of my pupils might be two or three times bigger than me. Of course they all know it all and who's going to argue, I don't want to be shown the way through the floor. For these reasons I don't want to go to college. I want to live a little longer.

13

Why should I? Why would anyone want to? People must be made out of money, or they want to work all the time just to go to college, so they can get a little piece of paper saying that they are able to make more money, because they have a higher education. Who needs money, who wants to have a comfortable life when they get older? Why should anyone want to go to college, when they could get married and let their husband support them? If everyone depended on the other person, no one would be very comfortable. Everyone needs an education, and should obtain one, if possible. It does not matter what you want to be, get a good education. An education is necessary in this age and time. A person that has a good education is very fortunate no matter what is said.

14

I am walking down the hall-ways of good "ole" ———— High. I am thinking of the day I will graduate from this school, but who isn't thinking of it. After high school, I don't plan to stop, short, my education, at least as of now. I plan to stay on the old weariness of homework everynight and calling teachers names which I am afraid to mention, except behind their backs. I am now thinking way ahead into the future. The day of entering college. I can see my classmates and myself on the first day of future sweating over this subject and that subject. May be it doesn't sound very inviting, but somehow, I look forward to it; I think!

15

The score is 69–68, with two minutes remaining in the game. The crowd is tense and excited. This is the first game of the season for the _____ and they are one point behind. If we loose this game I might as well drop this college. After all, basketball is the only reason I came to this college and if we aren't going to win any games, I'll just go to another one.

16

Supporting your husband can only be accomplished by going to college; that is, if you want to live in financial wealth. When your husband-to-be will not receive the amount of money you want for life, your only resort is to go to college. During your years at college, you won't be able to be married before you finish, unless your parents don't mind furnishing you with money; therefore you, more than likely, will lose your husband-to-be to a female who doesn't care about financial wealth, or to a female that has established her financial wealth.

17

Colleges, those over crowded schools of higher education give me cold chills. Some people attend college because their parents make them, they go, occupy space and deprive some poor inocent soul of the privilege of learning which he probably desires very much. For these so called space occupyers these are specialized schools where you can graduate from in four weeks to one year. By going to a specialized school your able to earn money while the poor inocent soul with the desire to learn more slaves away at text books. He will probably do something marvelous while you'll just do something good, but if college is not for you don't go.

18

Man is a herd animal. By herd animal I mean he does what everybody else does. That's why I plan to go to college. Why should I be the only one who doesn't go? Everyone else is going these days; they say so on T.V. I can go and join clubs, cheat on exams, and push beds up and down the highway like anyone else. But then again, every herd has it's individualists. Maybe I shouldn't go.

19

There are many places in this world that are just in a wreck. The people are hungry, not only for food but for God. They have no clothes to wear, no bed to sleep in, no purpose in life. These people need help, and they need faith. I want to be one of the people who will help them; a missionary. To be a missionary one has to study hard and go through a lot of red tape and letters. He must go to college and specialize in one certain area, but at the same time he must be a Jack-of-all-Trades. After he has struggled through college he is sent to some far-off country to put to use his college training.

20

Here it was, the last game of the season and I had to make good. This was not the night for mistakes and there weren't any. I did everything perfect, not one mistake was made. This was what I was hoping for. All the college coaches were here and they had their eyes on me. If I wanted to go to college I had to look good tonight and I did.

21

The main reason I want to go to college is not to play football, not to look at girls, but to learn something. Many people think learning is like a disease, once you start you're gone. This disease may strike at any time and the only ones immune are the "idiots." So, you "idiots" have nothing to worry about, but you others better watch out. Don't get me wrong, I am not criticizing learning, but I am saying that once you start you never stop, because there is so much to learn.

22

I have two main reasons for going to college when and if I graduate from —————. My first reason is that college seems so mysterious, and I wonder if it is like anything I have ever imagined. I decided to go to college and find out what it is like. My second reason is that I want to be a teacher, and I found out you must have a real good college education to be a teacher. So these are my two main reasons for going to college.

23

A few years of my life I hope to be spending in a laboratory, working as a medical technician. The only way I can possibly hope to achieve this is to attend college. While I am in high school I want to take as many courses as I can that deal with science. Then, when I do enter college; I will be more experienced and know more about what I hope to accomplish. Maybe, if I am lucky, I will be able to advance to some higher degree than a medical technologist.

24

Going to college is a real asset to anyone. It makes getting a job so much easier. No matter how bad they need someone, if you don't know what you are doing you are more of a handicap. A year or two of college can even help a new bride or mother. How? Special courses can help her in childcare, home decoration and maintenance, cooking, and maintaining a budget. These courses give her better ways of handling such necessities. It is true you can learn a lot up to high school, and training schools teach you your trade, but college offers you much more because it is much more.

25

The desire to learn can become a molegout disease which is incurable. To lease its ever present point a victim will allow himself to become entangled in a web of education. Although many people feel that high school is the end, but the true victim, of the molegout disease, finds himself thrown irrestable onwards and is no longer master of himself. He will eventually find himself knocking on the door of his last resort, college.

26

Although this question has been asked many times, and each time I answer it different, I think that the question requires some thought. Some of my college going friends have made the statements that college has many attractive female attendants, if coeducational, and that there is some sort of a mark of distinction when you attend a college. Personally, the thought of going to college just to be with attractive women seems stupid and very childish. Afterall, I have been going to school with beautiful girls almost all my life. The college graduate will not only have a mark of distinction but a key to almost any field they desire in later life. That key is why I want to go to college.

27

Going to college sounds like fun, until you think about it. What could be more boring that going to class everyday; listening to boring dryed up old speeches given by professors, who have grandchildren driving up to see them every week. Just think of those long study hours. Doesn't it sound like fun? But just think of all the girls. Well, that goes to show that there is some good in everything, including college.

28

The world rests upon the shoulders of the educated man. Our government, our cities, our entire civilization is dependent on knowledge. Without education there is no knowledge; without knowledge, we are as primitive as the lowest animal. Considering this, one can easily realize that education—as much as possible—is necessary. Elementary and high school are only stepping stones to education. Real education begins in colleges and universities. Therefore, if possible, I will certainly attend college.

29

College, the place of "egg-heads" and "all-Americans," the place where a boy becomes a man, and life becomes worth living, is the direction in which I am pointing my big toe. I can see it all now; boring professors talking as though they have a motor in their jaw; running an 80 yard touchdown; or having an A+ average. Fantastic, yes; Impossible no; all of these can come to true in a college of Jet Age America.

30

As I walked into the high school classroom, I felt a sickening feeling in my stomache. It was another boring class just like I had come into everyday, for the last three months. As I sat down the teacher began to lecture on "Why We Should Go To College." The more I listened to him, the more bored and discouraged I became. If this was a taste of how it would be for four long dreary years, I didn't want anything to do with college.

31

A man! Thats why I plan to go to college. Where else on this wonderful earth can a girl find an eligible man with a good education? Sure, there are other places but the odds are for me if I go to college, where the campus is just crawling with men. So you ask me what if I marry a plumber? Will your education be wasted? No, because if I marry a plumber I will probably have to get a job and help support him.

32

This may not be the why I want to go to college, but why everybody should go to college. If it is anywhere humanly possible, I think, everyone should have a college education. Why should anybody not want a college education; except, maybe, they just don't want to get right down to extremely hard work. After all college, it's true, takes a great deal of your time, but there still is time to meet new girls or boys, which ever the case may be. College is the last stepping stone to maturity. You might say that if a person is just out of high school; and he doesn't plan to go to college; then in my eyes, he is mentally immature to face the problems of the outside world. If you have a college education you are physically, mentally, and morally apt to face the world. In college you may join fraternities, and also, you may not agree, meet some fine teachers. Also, a person may go to college on an athletic scholarship and find that he would rather study than play in sports. So just keep up your grades, for those ivy covered walls are waiting.

College: a place of big monsters. They all seem to be about 6′5″ tall. You can see them almost everywhere. In the halls you must jump to stay out of their way. If you don't watch out, you might be flatened out! You don't want to get rid of them because when you see them you just don't know which one to choose. They're all so good-looking and you don't know which one to choose because of the great number of them. These good-looking fellows seem to make me want to go to college.

ASSUMPTIONS ABOUT THE PARAGRAPHS

Explain why you accept or reject, wholly or in part, the following assumptions related to the preceding paragraphs:

1. A detailed inventory of the students' strengths and weaknesses in content, organization, sentence structure, usage, spelling, punctuation, capitalization, and vocabulary indicates that their teacher should devote most of his time to individual rather than classwide instruction.

2. The grade distribution for the paragraphs should be as follows: three "A's," five "B's," seventeen "C's," five "D's," and three "F's."

3. If all of the students in a methods class grade all of the paragraphs and then tabulate the number of "A's," "B's," "C's," "D's," and "F's" received by each paragraph, the results will show considerable agreement in the grades given.

4. Several of the students see the purpose of a college education as more than preparing for a vocation.

Paragraphs on
"Why I Want to Go to College"
Written by
"Academic" Twelfth Graders

Twenty-four "academic" students[1] segregated on the basis of scores on standardized mathematics, I. Q., and reading tests were allowed thirty minutes to write the following paragraphs on "Why I Want to Go to College":

1

In this modern age the educated man is going farther in the business field. By educated I am refering to men or women with college educations. Many employers are looking for employes with college diplomas. This is why your chances of a getting a good job are good. This is also another outlook for college. This is the interest. You shouldn't go to college just to pass courses and graduate, you should go and take a personal interest in all your courses. This interest will help in later years.

2

I want to go to college to learn more, and I want to go to get a diploma. Today more than ever it is important to have a college education to get a job.

[1]Almost all came from families with average or below-average incomes.

After I get out of college I want to go west and start some kind of a business. A college diploma will help me to learn about the responsibilities, and the work involved in running a small business. Also, if I have to work for someone before I can work for myself I'll be able to get a better paying job with a college diploma.

3

By attending college I believe I will benefit in many ways. For example, college will prepare me for my future occupation in the best way possible. I will gain the background and knowledge needed for the future field I choose. Also, I will have an opportunity to learn more about people, culture, and the more serious aspects of life which I will have to face later on. College is a wonderful opportunity to prepare any young person for the future. Because from the time a person graduates until the time one is considered an adult, the person is not actually ready for adult life.

4

The main reason that I want to go to college is to be able to have a nice and suitable job. And to become a very skilled mechanic.

I feel that as the world is going, that everyone will need to have one, for our econommy is rising fast.

5

To me, a college education is not only important, but necessary. I plan to be a psychologist, and this field of work definitely requires a college education. I think that people who can go to college should by all means go. Anyone who has a chance to go, and refuses, is not planning to make much of their life. I want to go because I do plan to learn as much as I can in order to reassure my security in the future.

The principle reason I want to go to college to extend my education. By doing this I will be assured of better job offerings.

College will give me a fuller adult life. When things happen in "the world of tomorrow" I will have a better background on the subject.

I think that college is important in the lives of everyone. In going to college you can prepare yourself for nearly anything. With a college education you can support yourself easier because of the better jobs and pay offered. Aside from this, you also gain the higher grade of learning, just for personal use. College also is fun. There are many social activities in which you meet all varieties of people. These are the reasons I want to go to college.

8

College is where I can learn to put to use the things I have been studying for nearly all my life. Skills and basic fundamentals that were taught me in school will come to life and have a greater meaning in college. I will be taught a trade, and will also learn to live in the "grown-up" world. By learning these things I can be a better person for myself and my country.

I want to go to college to develop myself into a better citizen of my community. I would like to have more knowledge about my country, other countries and world affairs. I want to be intelligent and learn all I can for my chosen profession. If I have children I want to be able to explain things to them in the best possible way. More and more people are attending college each year and I want to keep up with the inteligence of the world.

10

I would like to go to college because it is a chance of higher education. I will have a much better chance of getting a higher paying, better job if I do.

It is important socially as well as educationally to go to college. You meet many new people, of which some will become lifetime friends.

College is also a part of your life that you will always remember. It can be fun. There are many parties and other social activities on the campus.

These are just a few of the reasons I would like to go to college.

11

In the present world the possibilities for getting a good job without more education than that of high school are becoming less and less. The jobs that are available, often do not pay as well and the working conditions are not as good as they could be.

Also, I would like to be able to choose my career. And with out a college education, a great limitation would be put on my choice.

A college education would help me in my personal life. A person just out of high school is seldom ready to take the responsibility of supporting a family or even being responsible for his or her own living. The few years spent in college give a chance for the much needed maturing. It is during this time that several ideals, goals and standards are set. The decision for the years ahead is made here, among the people you go to college with.

These people have much to offer you since they too want to learn. They are usually a good influence on you. (Didn't get finished)

12

I want to go to college, mainly, because I want to make something out of my life and its work. I think that the very thorough educational, as well as social, background one obtains at college, will be very valuable through out one's life. Our political and governmental leaders, doctors and nurses, and all the occupations that have very good wages, steady employment, and that are important in our complex nation, and the people who fill them almost must have a college education. College is very valuable, indeed; I want to go to college very much.

13

My main reason for wanting a college education, of course, would be, such a furtherment of education is necessary for my chosen vocation. Aside from this, however, a college degree, or even two or three years of such work, would give me the advantage in job seeking over the student who completed only high school. Most of the better, and important jobs today are held by men and women having a college education. I feel to be successful in the complicated life of today, just high school training is not enough if one intends to advance.

14

I want to go to college because I want to study to be a nurse. If I'm not able to be a nurse, I would still like to go to college to further my education. I believe that in order to really achieve what you want to in life you should have a college education. I think that it helps you a lot in life.

15

Because college gives you an opportunity to extend your education, to the demands of life in this world of vast wealth. Today college is an allmost necessity in this world because, of the great achievements in science & other fields of this type. With a college education you have higher degree of learning and therefore you can live a better life, tomorrow.

16

Most young people go to college to both further their education and the job they are seeking cannot be attained without going to college.

Take teaching, for example. Young persons cannot teach without four or five years of college background. Take a secretary, for another example. ———— has a two year secretarial course. The same two year course is also offered at ————. You can take either one, but alot of people go to ————. The job I am seeking must have a college background.

17

A college education is one of the most valuable assets any person can attain. Any amount of college training is much better than none at all. Practically all jobs of any merit require at least two years of college. College is also a very good place to meet and make new friends. There are also many social advantages gained through college. These are but a few of many reasons for attaining a college education.

18

I have a very good reason for wanting to go to college. I want to be in the field of medicine and the only way I can do this is to go to college and then continue on into medical school. Although if I did not have any plans in the future I would still want to go to college. The person who goes to college is better trained for many jobs in the world to day. Due to the fact that he is trained so much more than the average person he will have a lot better chance of getting a job in the field of work he likes. If a person goes to college and studies hard and gets good grades while there, he will not have any trouble finiancially in the future.

19

I want to go to college because I feel that everyone should get as much of an education as possible. I plan to be a teacher. I know that before I can teach I must go to college. Without a college education I could not be a teacher. I probably could not do many things I would want to do. If a person doesn't get a college education, he is limited in what he can do in the future. I want to go to college, you might say, to secure my plans for the future.

20

In today's complex world a college education is very important. It teaches you in the field of your choice, thus increasing job opportunities. Besides material factors, a college education is important in other ways. It helps you think for yourself, thereby helping you develop into a mature adult.

After high school, I would like to attend college. Aside from bettering my education and preparing for me for the future, college would give me the chance to meet new people. I would learn many interesting and helpful things from the people I meet as well as the knowledge I acquire while attending classes.

22

I really and truly would like to go to college, for several reasons. The most important is that I would like to make teaching my vocation. This, of course, requires a college diploma. Another important reason is that I want to get all the education I can before I am "turned loose in the world", so to speak, in order to become a useful, well-adjusted citizen of our modern world. I also feel that because ours is a constantly changing world, and new ideas and discoveries are no longer laughed at or discouraged, that any education I can obtain beyond that of high school will help me get a basic understanding of these new ideas.

23

I believe the reason most people go to college is for prestige. Frankly, if I were to leave school now and go to work, many years from now I would still be getting the same wage and same position. College would provide a position that with hard work would be advanced into a responsible one. Statistics show that people who go on to a higher education reap the benefits of hard work more than a lesser education.

24

Everyone wants to be successful regardless of their goal. To acquire success one must take advantage of the opportunities given him. College is perhaps one of the best opportunities offered to those want to obtain real success. Social activities help him to achieve the character that will necessary to be really successful. I, like everybody else, want to be a success in whatever I do. I know that college will give me the experiences I need to obtain success for my life.

ASSUMPTIONS ABOUT THE PARAGRAPHS

Explain why you accept or reject, wholly or in part, the following assumptions related to the preceding paragraphs:

1. A detailed inventory of the students' strengths and weaknesses in content, organization, sentence structure, usage, spelling, punctuation, capitalization, and vocabulary indicates that their teacher should devote most of his time to individual rather than classwide instruction.

2. The most serious weaknesses in the paragraphs are in content and organization.

3. Most of the paragraphs begin with an effective topic sentence.

4. Fifty per cent of the twenty-four "academic" students should receive "A's" and "B's" on their paragraphs.

5. The three best and three worst paragraphs are easy to isolate.

6. If all of the students in a methods class grade all of the paragraphs and then tabulate the number of "A's," "B's," "C's," "D's," and "F's" received by each paragraph, the results will show considerable agreement in the grades given.

7. All the paragraphs in Appendix 4, written by "academic" twelfth graders, are superior to all the paragraphs in Appendix 3, written by "academic" tenth graders, in content, organization, sentence structure, usage, spelling, punctuation, capitalization, and vocabulary.

8. The "academic" twelfth graders reveal a better understanding of the purpose of a college education than the "academic" tenth graders.

Letters on "Going Steady" Written by Tenth Graders

A heterogeneous class (slow, average, and academic students, mostly from average-income families) was allowed fifty minutes in September and fifty minutes the following May to write letters answering an imaginary foreign student's query: "What does 'going steady' mean, and what do you think about 'going steady'?" The students had no advance warning about the assignments. To conserve space only the bodies of letters are given.

Girl 1 (September)

I received your letter and was glad to hear from you. In your letter you asked about "going steady." I'll try to tell you what "going steady," means to me. Here in america "going steady," is the going of a boy and girl together. The boy dates no other girls and the girl likewise dates no other boys. Although some boys and girls go steady for the fun of it. Many people go steady because they really like each other and wish to be with no one else. I am sure many teen-agers all over America have gone or will go steady during at least their last year of junior high or high school years. Many of my friends have gone steady before.

Going steady although has its advantages and disadvantages. Some are when going steady with one, you really like it has its advantages. A disadvantage is by going steady with one certain boy you'll not have the chance to date other boys. When boys and girls go steady they are in a world of their own. As I mentioned earlier I said some go steady for no reason. The reason I say that is because I know a girl who went steady with a boy and they had an argument and broke up. The girl I believe only went steady with the boy because no one else would date her.

I will tell you my opinion of "going steady." I think "going steady" is all right. I see nothing wrong in going steady. I hope I have helped you a little on my opinions of "going steady." If a boy ever asks you to go steady and you have known him quite a while, you like him, and you share the same interests then I would or might consider going steady with him. I hope my little bit of information has helped you.

Girl 1 (May)

How are you and your family? I am quite well.

In your recent letter you asked, "going steady" what does it mean and how I feel toward it. Here in America we teen-agers very often go steady. It is the steady dating of one boy and one girl. The boy dates no other girls and the girl likewise dates no other boys. Here at high school there are many steady couples.

I feel that going steady is just fine because I see nothing wrong in it. There are many students and parents who object to going steady. Here are some opinions of my friends on "going steady." (1) You can be sure of a date. (2) Companionship, always know that he or she is around to go someplace together. You may think awful of the first opinion, you can be sure of date. I don't agree with that because if that's the situation the girl is just relying on steady to take her places. And apparently is not well-liked by the other boys.

Here is an opinion on "not going steady." The boy wants to play the field, date as many girls to find out what they are like. This is fine too. So as you can see, "going steady" is up to the individual person. For some people it is just fine, others object, think its silly. Like I said before its up to the individual.

I hope that I have given you some information about "going steady." You may be wondering, have I gone steady myself. The answer is no. I have had two dates recently with a boy named Eddie. I like him in a way but I'm not sure. So you see I'm having a problem myself. I hope to hear from you soon and tell me your ideas now on "going steady."

Girl 2 (September)

In your last letter you mentioned you had read an article in an American magazine on dating and "going steady."

When you asked my opinion on "going steady" I was quite surprised.

Jane, in my opinion there is nothing wrong with "going steady" in fact it can be quite nice.

In America to most boys and girls "going steady" means "togetherness." Someone of the opposite sex to have fun with.

Like I said before, "going steady is fine as long as it doesn't get too serious. But when your "going steady" gets to the point where you feel like you can't be without your steady or can't have fun with anyone but them than this is the time to break it up or quit "going steady."

The reason I say this is children our age are too young to get involved in anything so serious.

I, myself, am "going steady" and truthfully say it is loads of fun. Most American boys and girls are "going steady" and at least 50% of them never get seriously involved in this way everything is alright.

Well Jane, I hope this little talk has cleared some of the thoughts up in your mind and that now you have a better view on "going steady."

Well have to go now.

Bye! Bye!

Girl 2 (May)

Hi!

I received your letter this morning and thought I would answer it now while I'm not too busy.

Sara, in your letter you ask about "going steady." Well, although I'm far from being an authority on "going steady" I'll try to explain it the best way I know how.

In America "going steady" is an agreement that a boy and girl make after dating for a while which means than neither one of them is allowed to date anyone else. Now, you are probably think that this isn't fair Well, to some people it is and it usually works out all right. You see, Sara, when your "going steady" your always sure of having a date for a dance or party or what ever comes up. Sure, I know there are several disadvantages of "going steady" such as, while "going steady" you don't have a chance to meet new people and your always with the other person, which sometimes gets pretty boring. But the boy and girl take this under consideration before they start "going steady." Oh sure, sometimes it doesn't work out and the couple are constantly getting into arguements and finally "break-up", but on the whole it works out all right.

As for my real opinion, I think "going steady" is fine, if the couple is mature enough. I've gone steady four times, and always after breaking up we have remained good friends. Really I think that's the whole idea of "going steady" it's a close "friendship" in which you grow to know each other quite well.

Well, Sara, I'd better close for now. I hope I've cleared up a few questions in your mind. "Going Steady" isn't really so bad, if you ever get a chance, try it.

Write, real soon! God bless you!

Girl 3 (September)

I was glad to receive your letter this morning before starting to my classes.

In your letter you mentioned the article you read on "going steady." "Going steady" in America means, in general, that a girl is known to be a *curtain* boys girlfriend. Most of the boys are alittle leary on paying any great amount of attention on this girl. Oh! of course, it doesn't stop a girl and boys relationship altogether.

Many of the parents opinion on "going steady", I believe to be alittle worped. They think that "going steady" leads into marriage, it curtaing does not. Also parents think us going steady "as a cerious emotion of a girl and boy, again I don't believe this to be true.

My opinion of "going steady" isn't that a girl (or boy) is locked to one boy. She has maney boyfriends, but one boy who is special. One who she feels she can depend on. If she has a problem, they can work it out together. Also I believe a girl will pick a boy she isn't going to be embarressed at curtain tense moments. Of course, maybe in some cases there are some special things included in the agreement. Maybe an exchange of rings or a promised date on every weekend etc.

I hope I have helped you understand a little more fully about this subject. Ask more questions if nesseccary. Kaareh, I would recommend that you read more articles on this subject before you judge "going steady" entirely for yourself. There're many writen that I could send you if you would like. Many good ones that I have been reading are writen by Dick Clark.

Girl 3 (May)

I was happy to receive your letter the other day. It seems that I just can't get enough letters to read. I enjoy getting your letter every month so much.

In your letter you ask me about the term "going steading". To the American teenager this term does vary in meaning, but in the area I live "going steady" means an agreement between a boy and girl that usually consists of many things. The boy and girl usually exchange rings. The boys main duty is to funish the girl with transportation if he has a car and doing little things for her. The boy usually expects the girl to save all her dates fer him. In many cases I think "going steady" is wise, and in others I don't believe in it at all. One good thing about "going steady" is that you have someone you can talk to who is of the opposite sex, whom you can exchange your ideas and oppinions. One of the reason I stay to very close is the idea that I like to met different boys and go out with many different kind. I have gone steady, and I do reccommend every girl to try it once at least. It helps you understand others and how they feel about this idea.

There are many acticle in the American magazines, I will sent you some of the acticles in my next letter. I think you should read many different oppinions before you decide your concusion on "going steady", as I say es has its good and bad points.

In Teen for Today there usually are some good acticles. Also in Seventeen, Teen and many fashion magazines.

After you have read severael acticles I would like to hear your opinion of "going steady"

Girl 4 (September)

I received your letter asking my opinion on going steady. In my opinion there is nothing wrong with going steady, as long as you don't get carried away.

To me going steady is when two people have an agreement that they will go together and be the best of friends. While they are going together neather of the two are to date another person.

Some people don't do the wright thing when they go steady. After a while he or she gets accoustomed to the other one being around when ever he wonts to go out and etc.. They get bored at having the same person around all the time. So instead of tilling the other person that he or she feal that it would be better if they were to brack up and that they can still be friends and date once in awhile, he goes out on the other person. He thanks he has pulled some thing over on his steady. So he will try it over and over agin as long as the other person doesn't find out. But sooner or later the other person finds out and they don't part good friends.

I also thank that if another person is willing to go out with someone who is going steady (if they know it) this person might do the same to you if you were going steady with her.

I don't know why but when two people go steady they argue most of the time.

When I said he (she) I was just useing the turm.

Hope you will write soon.

Girl 4 (May)

Going study is fairly the same all over America. A lot of kids say the don't like to go steady, but the usually end up as one of the many.

Going study is the exchangeing of rings, which somehow shows thier effection tward one anotherr. They deside between each other what they can do and what they can't do. For instance nither one may be allowed to talk or flurt with another boy or girl as the case may be.

My opinion is that going study is getting out of hand. Some of the rules are not nessacary or good for the couple. They usually cause a lot of arguments. Which lead to break ups. After which they are the best of enimies. You can lose a lot of good friends that way.

Then there are the people who go steady because everyone else is. Then, because they don't really like each other will enouph they go out on one another. This can not do either any good. It might even hurt their reputation. Others will not trust them to be fair to them.

Although there is a form of going study that is good. That is when they have an agreement. They like each other: But they are alowed to date other, if they wish to. Usually they date each other the most. This causes less arguments and usually turns out good.

So please write soon. I do hope this has answer your questions.

Girl 5 (September)

When teenagers say they are going steady they mean that they are dating one and only one boy for a period of time. It doesn't mean they are engaged.

They usually don't date steady for very long at a time. It varys from a couple of weeks to a few months.

When a boy and girl are going together the boy gives the girl his Class Ring or Identification Braclet. She in turn gives him her ring or Identification Braclet. Usually the ring is worn on a chain around the neck.

If the boy doesn't have a ring or braclet he gives her something to show that they are going steady.

It doesn't mean that they have a date every night. It means that they have a date for week-end activities. If there is a ball game or dance or something like that, they go together if they want to. Maybe instead of the dance, they will go to a movie. But they will be going together to the movie, not one going with another boy or girl and the other staying home. May be I didn't state that last answer clearly. If so I shall explain it a little more clearly. What I meant was that the girl might have a date with another boy. If she went through with it they wouldn't be going steady for much longer. Only until he found out about it. Then they would break up and start dating other people until they found some one else they liked well enough to go steady with.

I hope I have answered your question.

I think it is okay to go steady. There isn't anything wrong with it if you don't get serious. Most teenagers are having to much fun to get serious. P.S. We teenagers here in America usually date in a croud. I mean a few couples get together and go somewhere.

Going steady is just a general meaning that you have a date for that big dance Friday night or something like that.

Girl 5 (May)

In your last letter you asked about "going steady," so I'm going to try to explain it.

"Going steady" means different things to different people. To most teen-agers "going steady" means that one will have a date whenever he or she wants one. Other teenagers go steady because they don't care to date anyone else. "Going steady" doesn't usually last very long, but sometimes it does. Most teen-agers don't "go steady" longer than a couple of months, if that long, but others take it more serious.

The boy and girl should decide for themselves if they want to "go steady." Nobody else can decide for them.

I haven't formed a special opinion on "going steady," but I don't think there is anything wrong with it.

In explaining what "going steady" means I forgot to tell you one other thing. While "going steady" the girl wears the boys class ring, pin, or something of that sort to show that she is "going steady." The boy also as something of hers, it could be a friendship ring or something like that. In different parts of the United States, people have different methods of showing they are "going steady."

Next time you write tell me if I have explained it so you understand.

Girl 6 (September)

In your recent letter you were discussing "going steady," and asked me to express my thoughts on it. To me "going steady" only means one boy which you date, and only him. This entitles you to ask him on social affairs and the same for him. In, and while you are "going steady" you only date him. We find that hard to do here in the U. S., because there are too many boys to be tied down to one. I have gone "steady" and I think I am personally better off without it. This sometimes helps the girl and the boy, but it most cases I feel that it hurts them. It also gives the right for the boy to expect you not to do any flirting or talking that leads other boys to you.

Couples who go steady get tired of seeing each other after a period of time, and it is sometimes a harsh blow to the other person envolved. This means a break-up of the couple and then dislike between them. Sometimes the couple gets back together and the same thing happens all over again.

A lot of the parents of the boys and girls who go steady feel that it is a teen-age engagement and this I feel is true. They also feel that this is the cause of a lot of our teen-age marraiges which don't work out.

The boy and the girl who reach the age that they feel that they must prove themselves as adults is the time when they want to go steady.

A lot of times the idea of going steady envolves a class ring or a car which enfluences the decision of going steady. In this case the boy is being used and when he realizes this he is very hurt again.

When a lot of teen-agers go steady, they have only been out with the boy a few times and they don't even know them, when after a few more dates they realize that they don't want to go with the boy after all.

I have been talking a lot about the boy and sometimes the fault isn't the boys' and instead it is the girl who wants and leads the boy on to the point of going steady. This is going to be unpleasant for all of them and I feel that we are and would be better off with out "going steady".

I am very happy to discuss the American way of life with you and if this doesn't help you in the idea of going steady, I'll try to answer some more of the questions that you have on the subject.

Girl 6 (May)

I just recieved your letter today and found it as interesting as all other's that you have written.

"Going Steady" in the U. S. means merely that a girl has a date whenever she wants one. There are, of course, advantages and disadvantages to going steady. The main disadvantage is that the girl and the boy are together too much. This has been one of the major topics that all people here find interesting to talk about.

Recently in our English Class we had class discussions envolving from "Going Steady" to "Teen-age" Marriages. We had a very interesting talk on the do's and don't's of this relationship. We really came to the conclusion that if you were not ashamed to have your parent's know or see what you're doing then it would be right and the rest wrong.

Here in the U.S.A. we usually think that once you become thirteen, you're old enough to stand on your own two feet and need no pariential help, so usually we don't want our parents around us.

My personal opinion about going steady is that I don't feel that it is necessary to have a good time. If you want to go to a certain place and feel that you need a date, usually most girls hint around and eventually get one.

I certainly hope that my view has helped you get some idea on the teenager's here in the U.S., and if you have anything else that you would like the American view point on, I certainly will be glad to help.

I will be looking forward to your next letter as I always am, and hoping that you and your family will stay in the best of health.

Girl 7 (September)

To be able to answer your question about going steady will be a very hard task because people have different meanings.

To some it means a security. The two going steady can always realy on each other for a weekend date, a party, and the big social events of the year such as a formal dance.

To others it means something more serious. Something that leads up to an engagement of merrage, and later merrage.

When people go steady they usually exchange rings. Sometimes it is identification bracelets, and then again it could be a class pen.

Although most of the people that go steady exchange rings, braclets, or pens there are some who feel they don't need anything to "Show" they are going steady.

You may not agree with me on this, but I don't think people should go steady. At least not until their last year at high school.

I think, in a lot of cases, when you go steady you see too much of your steady boy friend or girlfriend and not enough of your other friends.

When you go steady you don't date other people and widen your friendships with persons of the opposite sex.

If you like a person, you don't have to go steady with him to prove it.

I hope when you write back you will tell me what you think about going steady.

Girl 7 (May)

Since you were wondering about going steady, I will try to explain what it means.

If a girl has been dating the same boy for a few months, and they like each other for more than good friends, they usually exchange rings, class pens, or identification bracelets. This is a sign that they will not date anyone else.

When my parents were teen-agers going steady was the next thing to engagement. This is not true today; it is just a sign that the girl and boy will not date anyone else.

The next thing to going steady is going steadily. This is just an expression for dating the same person all of the time.

Personally, I can not understand why anyone needs to go steady. I feel that if the boy has a ring or pen to wear he should wear it and not give it away to someone.

I'll have to admit, I have tried going steady before. It worked out for a while but then the newness of it wears off and a great deal of the fun is lost.

Any teen-ager is too young to throw his life away by staying with one person. It is his time to meet more people and mix with a large group of people, instead of pairing off and loosing interest in his environment.

I can not even understand why anyone would want to go steadily. To me, it seems one would be too tied down and not be able to do as many things with more people.

I guess I have a great deal of growing up. My friends do not feel as I do about going steadily. I like to date, but through a little experience I would rather have a date only occassionally and with different people.

Well, from my viewpoint you might be able to understand going steady. I do have a great deal of growing up but I have a few years to do it in so I don't want to get too old, too fast.

Girl 8 (September)

How have you been? I was so glad to get your letter. How is your family?

To answer your question about dating, it is lots of fun. When we date one another, we go to shows, dances, parties, football or basket ball games. Some kids just go out for a ride or out to eat.

Another thing you asked about was "going steady". Going Steady has its good points, and there are some bad points too. But first you want to know what "going steady" means. It just means that you, and the boy like each other. It means that you are his girl, and he is the only one you date.

There is another meaning of going steadily. This means you like the boy, you go places, but you do date other boys too.

There are good parts of going steady. You like the boy, you have fun and some parents like it.

But just because there are good points, there are bad ones too. You may get tired of the same boy, you want to date other boys. Sone boys and girls think can tell the other what to do.

Going Steady can be fun, if you and your boyfriend agree on the different rules. I don't have anything agnist it, but I think it is beater to play the feild, date all the boys you want, and then go steady. If you go steady in the seventh, eighth, or ninth grade, what do you have to look forward to? Some people just want to act older.

Well, I have done most of the talking. "I hope you, and your family is fine." Thanks for your letter. Bye for now and write soon.

P.S. How do you like school? I like it very much, and I am having lots of fun too.

Girl 8 (May)

I was very happy to receive your letter. I am glad you want to know about dating and "going steady." I will try to tell you about it the best I can.

Right now most teanagers are going steady. There are some good and bad points about both? First, when you go steady, you date only that one boy. You can not date anyone else. If he does not take you out any where you have to stay at home, unless the girls ask you out. As you can see, the chance of meeting more and possibly better liked people is less when you do go steady.

Of corse, there are two sides to the story, just like there are two sides to a donkey. There are some advantages to going steady. You are sure of a date every week end. There is also a feeling of belonging.

When you go steady, there is usually an exchange of rings to show the other people you are going steady with someone. Right now the fad is (for the girl) to wrap the boys ring with angora, so it wont be too big on her.

Talking about going steady the is also another kind of dating. It is called "going steadlly." There is a difference. When you go steadlly, you can date more then just this one person but you date a certain person most. You do not have this person's ring, but you date him most of the time.

You also said you wanted to know about dating, where we go and what we do. Most kids start dating when they are fifteen (15), and sixteen (16) years of age. Some teanagers date before this if they are mature enough. This depends mostly on the parents. When you go on a date most people go to dances, shows, skating, out to eat, or just for a ride. As you can see, dating is a lot of fun. "We enjoy it.

Please write back and tell what you have been doing. How school is there, and what teens in Europe do to pass time, things for enjoyment too.

I must sign off now, write soon.

Girl 9 (September)

In your last letter you asked about going steady. Well I'd know to much about it because everyone seems to have different ideas.

When your going steady it usually means that your dating just one boy and he will only date you.

In my oppinion it has several good points. One is that your always sure of a date. If there is a big dance at school you wouldn't have to worry if your going to be asked, because if your steady can go, he take you.

I also think it has a few bad points too. I don't think that you can have as much fun because you have to go out with the same boy or he'll get mad. I think it's fun to date a lot of different boys.

One of you may get to bossy and think he owns you and you must jump at every command.

You may get tired of each other.

I think it really depends on the individuals involved.

You may talk to others, Judy, they'll all fell differently. I have never gone steady, so I cann't tell you what it is really like.

I hope everyone at you house is as well as they are at mine.

Girl 9 (May)

In your last letter you asked me what I meant by going steady with a boy. If you would ask ten different people you would get ten completely different answers.

Going steady is dating one and only one boy. Sometime a boy will give the girl his ring and she may give him hers.

I use to think going steady would be terrible but I have been going steady for almost five month with Dave and he is moving in a few weeks and breaking up with him will be murder.

If a boy askes you to go steady and you say yes, you are promising that you will not date others boys. This is good because your alway sure of a date on the weekend for all the big advents.

In some cases one or other may get too bossy or too posesive. But this has never happen to us. Dave does, though, say "I wish you wouldn't talk so much with other boys" but I just do it to make him jealous.

In several cases girls have gone with a boy so she could say they were going steady. this cases many heart achs and lots of trouble.

In my opinion the only reason a girl should go steady with a boy is because she rather go to dance, movies and etc. with him and no one else.

Some people go steady with somebody different very to week in these cases going steady mean very little but in other cases people have gone steady although high school and then got married.

I have probably been going encircles and you don't know any more than you did, but if a boy asks you to go steady ask him how he means it. I hope I have helped you somewhat in finding the meaning of going steady.

I hope very one is well and that you'll write soon.

Girl 10 (September)

I hope to explain to you the meaning of "going steady." Going steady simply means that you only go places with the boy of your choice and giving him a token of your friendship. He in return does the same. Most of the time it really isn't a serious friendship but that depends on who the boy is. A ring or a bracelet is the common token given to each other. You don't start to think of going steady until you are in your teens. Some relationships last for a long time some a very short time. I think that going steady gives you a better chance to know the other person. It also gives you confidence and reasurance. It's not a bad idea to go steady but don't take it to serious. You usually go together to games, dances and many places for enjoyment. It's good to go steady with different boys and not just one. I hope you have a general Idea of what "Going Steady" means?

Girl 10 (May)

I am glad you have ask such a question because going steady is sort of a style or a fad among American teen agers. Going steady depends on you, your parents and the boy you are going steady with. It is sort of a security among some teen-agers and a more serious situation to others. Going to dances and other places or just seeing each other at home is the generall meaning of going steady. A girl or boy don't usually think of going with anyone else if they are going steady. The couple may have an understanding of this or they might exchange a ring, bracelet or chain. In many cases going steady may last from one day to many weeks, months and years. Playing the field or going out with other boys or girls, as the case may be, is better than going with one all the time at first. Going steady usually starts when you enter high school. Some teen-agers start earlier and some a little later on in life.

Girl 11 (September)

You wrote and ask me to tell you about "going steady." I really don't know how to tell you about it. "Going steady" is kind of like a pre-engagement I would say. If you like a boy a lot but not well enough to get married you "go steady." Some people "go steady" because they are too young to do anything else. I've heard other people say they "go steady" for security. By that I mean if there was a big dance coming up and you were "going steady" you would be sure to get a date.

When a girl is "going steady" I think the main idea is that that person is taken for the time being and your suppose to keep away. I've even heard of some couples breaking up because the girl spoke to another boy. I think that is stupid. Some boys think if you are "going steady" with them you have to quit being friendly to other boys. Sometimes I think "going steady" is just a fad and soon will go out of style.

I don't know what the article said about it in the magazine but I know some parents don't agree with some younger people about the meaning of "going steady." Some parents won't even allow the word in the house.

One of my girlfriends isn't allowed to "go steady" so she does it behind their backs. I think parents should allow it because most boys and girls will do it anyway. Myself I think "going steady" is O.K. and it's allowed in our house. I have an older sister who has "goen steady" many times. Me not so many. It has its disadvantages and advantages so you have some idea of it now. I hope you could understand me. Please write soon.

Girl 11 (May)

Although I'm not too good at explaining things, I'll try my best to give you an idea about "going steady."

To most people our age "going steady" is just a fade and they do it because everyone else does. I don't know exactly how this started, but to me it means a pre-engagement. You really shouldn't "go steady" with a boy unless you really like him. It's almost the same as if you wouldn't date another boy if you didn't like him.

As I said before most people "go steady" because their best friend is or all the kids in their class is. In one article, in a magazine I read, a lot of the kids in a school were running away and getting married for no reason other than a popular couple did it. So as you can see, this fade can led up to serious things.

On the other hand many students have goen steady all through school and finally gotten married after graduation. I think they were alot happier this way.

Some couples who "go steady" take it too serious sometimes. For instance if a boy talks to another girl the girl he is going with gets mad. Or the other way around, the boy gets mad. Just because you're going with a boy is no reason you can't at least be nice to other boy. I think this is carrying things too far.

As you can see "going steady" has its good and bad points like everything else so you can draw your own conclusions. In some respects I like it and in others I don't. A great deal of deciding depends on the boy!

Boy 1 (September)

You have written me concerning an article in an American magazine about dating. You wanted to know what is ment by "going steady."

"Going steady" means that you have a girl friend or boy friend with whom you can go places with, such as the movies. If they're is a dance coming up you can count on going with her (or him). Uusually when two people are "going steady" they trade rings or something similar to that.

My opinion of "going steady" is this. I think it is all right because it gives the person a feeling of security to know that he has someone to go places and to do things with.

Boy 1 (May)

"Going steady" means different things to different teenagers; it can mean you are sure of having a date for Saturday night and other social affairs, or some teenagers go steady just to be accepted by the "crowd."

Teenagers in America use different things to symbolize "going steady." It may be a pin or another similar object. Most of the time though the boy gives the girl his ring and she wears it on her finger or around her neck on a chain.

Ther're many pro's and con's to going steady. I personally believe that going steady hurts the social life of the teenager because when he is going steady he is stuck with the same girl all of the time, and he does not get to mix with the other young people of his age group. As I have stated above, the reason that most teenagers say they go steady is so that they can be sure of having a date for the various social affairs and this *is* a good reason. I have stated my opinion and the opinions of others but wether you agree or disagree with it is entirely up to you.

Boy 2 (September)

This is your old buddy Bob from across the ocean. It's been along time since my last letter, but I've been aufly buisy with school and all starting, now that I'm in the grove of things I thought I would answer your last letter. Let me see you asked somthing about dating, I believe. You said you read an artical in Teen Time about going steady. Well here it means that you have one and only one girl. You are supose to be true to. When school is out for the day you are expected to carry her book home for her. When that big dance comes your supose to take her. It's really a trap you get your self into where ever you go, practically or what ever do, you have got to take her, or your on thin ice. But when you stop to think about it, it's not so bad, that is if you really like the girl, you won't mind doing these things one bite.

Parents will be parents where ever you go, you see they object very strongly to going steady. They don't see how tine's have changed since they were children.

Well I better be closing up. I hope I have straightened you out on going steady, write soon.

Boy 2 (May)

I received your letter just yesterday, after reading it I decided to write back right away. How are things in jolly old London? This past week has been a rough one, in school we had tests every day. I see here from your letter that your interested in dating here in America, well I'm pretty interested in it to. I can only tell what little I know from my own experiences and what I read in magazines. First I should like to point out going steady is not for me.

It means being tied down to one girl all the time, this I don't like I want selection and vairety when I date. You might think going steady will always
asure you of a date, but who needs it when all the abigations of a steady are
pesented, such as phoning your girl every evening, and going out at least
once a week. Some weeks you just aren't able to go on a date maybe because
of money or because your buisy every evening with school work or some other
project. This presents a problem, because your girl might think your tired of
her because you didn't take her anywhere this week.

As I said before I don't approve of going steady, however I guess some
people like it or they wouldn't go steady. To some it up going steady means
being tied down to one girl, this is only my opinion mind you so don't think
every teenager in America disapproves of going steady for this shurly isn't a
just opinion.

Boy 3 (September)

I received your letter today and found it interesting. It was good to hear
from you again and that your doing fine in school. I'm doing okoy also.

In your letter you said you had read an article on "going steady" in an
American magazine and you wished to know more about the subject. So I'm
going to try to tell you more about it.

First of all going steady is something which all boys and girls have been
acquainted with. It means that a boy dates only one girl and not any other.
There has been a lot of discussion about it in America. Some people feel it is
right others feel it is wrong, but I think it is up to the boy and the girl to
decide whether they should go steady. If so it means each person should live
up to their part of the deal, that is they should go places together and not
with soneone else.

I feel as if it is not a good choice to go steady because of several reasons. One is that if you go steady you usually don't get to take part in social gathes with other girls such as dancing with them. You always have to go on dates with the same girl and I don't think it should be this way. I think that while in your teenage years you should date different girls and not go steady. I also feel that sone people are too young to go steady. I feel you should be at least 14 yeas old to go steady. To sun it up I feel you shouldn't go steady.

Write again soon.

Boy 3 (May)

I received your letter yesterday and enjoyed hearing from you. In it you stated you wished to know more about going steady so I will give you my ideas

Going steady is something which two persons must decide. It mean that the boy should take the girl to dances and other social gathers and the girl shouldn't ever be without a date.

I disapprove of going steady for my own reasons.

To begin with I think teenagers shouldn't go steady because they should try to meet new people. If they do go steady this eliminates the chance. During the time two persons are going steady neither one can have a different date.

After reading this letter I hope you won't get the wrong idea about going steady. This is my own personal opinion.

I hope things are all right at your home.

Boy 4 (September)

Don't go steady because it is more fun to date all the girls. Going steady means that you date one girl and you give her a ring, pin, or something like that and she gives you a ring too. Any party or dance you go to you haf to take the girl you are going steady with. I don't thing you should go steady until you ar ready to get ingaged and I don't think you should get ingaged until you are ready to get married. I ain't gonna get married for a long time from now. Also when yo go steady you can't go out with the boys any more on Saturday night she want what your doing where your going every minute of the day and night.

Boy 4 (May)

I just received your letter, in which you want to know about going steady. Going steady means that you just Date one person all the time. It doesn't make any difference to me, wheater I go steady or not.

Boy 5 (September)

How are you. I got your last letter two days ago and I would be happy to explan what going steady means. This is when a boy and girl go out together quit often (usually at night) to have fun. They like each other a lot and have a great deal of fun together going to dances, moves, drive-in moves, and etc. I think going steady is alright. Sometimes parents don't want you to go steady, but I can see no good reason not too. I am going steady with a nice girl and we have a lot of fun together. The other night we went to the pig skin dance at high school after our football team was beaten 19 to 13 by an ———— team. It is a lot of fun going steady and I think if possible most young people should go out on dates.

I had fun on my vacation this year when my family went up to Canada for a few weeks. My dad and I went fishing and hunting together quit a few times. We were out in the middle of the lake and our motor wouldn't start. It took us about three hours to row the boat back to shore.

After returning from are vacation it was time for school to start. I've been in school about two weeks now and it is a lot of fun.

Boy 5 (May)

Going steady is something just about every teen-ager has a different oppinion on. Actually it means the two people don't go out with anyone except each other.

When two people go steady they usually like each other. But sometimes people just go steady to make sure that they will have a date when they want it.

In going steady the people usually trade rings, sometimes they don't though. When they do trade rings the boy usually wears her ring on a small chain around his neck. The girl wears his ring on a small chain around her neck or wraps yarn around the base of the ring and this makes it small enough she can wear it on her finger.

Its common around here to see a boy and girls going down the hall of the school holding hands and walking very slowly.

This is what I think about going steady. If you ask someone else you would probley get a completely different answer, that all in all means the samething.

Boy 6 (September)

The only thing I know about "going steady" is that a boy and girl have dates with each other and no one else. As to my opinions on the subject, I thing that any teenager up to the age of 18 shouldn't even be dating. My reason for this statement is that up to this age most teenagers are entirely to young. This is all I know about the subject and all I care to know about it.

Boy 6 (May)

You inquired in your last correspondence about that very curious American custom known amoung children in their teens as "going steady. What I don't know about "going steady" would fill an extremely large volume if there is that much information on such a trivial, childish matter as this one. Since you asked for an explanation of the term I will try to come as close as I possibly can. "Going steady" means that one male and one female, either because of affinity for each other or because "its being done", will come to the agreement that they will have no dates with anyone else except themselves. If it is affinity than causes a boy and girl to "go steady" in their teens it is a bad habit and shouldn't be practiced except by an adult and mature person at least over the age of twenty-one. As for "going steady" because "its being done" is just a way of seeking popularity amoung other students and practicing conformity to such a degree that a person needs no intellect of his own but just follows the herd movement.

Boy 7 (September)

I have just finished reading your letter and thought that I would answer it right since it is on such an interesting subject.

"Going steady" to me means that when you go steady with one girl you do not date any other girls. The first thing I would make sure is that I liked the girl very much, have several dates with her and walk her home from school. Don't ask her to go steady right away, but wait for maybe three weeks or a month.

After you start going steady do not pay any attention to any other girls. If you are at a dance or party, have a good time, but just with whom you are going steady with. Dance with your own girl only, even if its a "girls choice" dance and another girl asks you to dance with her. Explain to the girl why you cannot dance with her though.

I think that if you go steady you can have a lot of fun. You learn to know a girl very well. You can go over to your girl's house maybe and play cards or a game like bad mitton or tennis. You could also collect records together.

Another good reason for going steady is that you will always have a date for a dance or a party.

When you have your dates always make sure that you use very good manners.

I hope that this letter will give a better understanding of what going steady is like here in America.

Write soon and good luck with the girls.

Boy 7 (May)

I have just finished reading your letter and since you wanted to know more about "going steady" I decided to sit down and write to you right away. I myself am against going steady.

To begin with I will give my reasons why I am opposed to going steady and then some reasons for it.

If you do go steady it takes about all of your time. You should call up your girl almost every night after school unless your out for a sport and then you should call her up after practice. By the time you finish talking to her there is no time for any homework. Over the weekend you should spend some time with her also.

When you start spending your time with her you start losing out with the boys you run around with. You have to start going to more activities too. She will expect you to take her to some of the big dances which you will need money.

You could become to serious about the girl which to me is not very good.

Now for some good points of going steady. If you do go to some big dances you will be sure to always have a date or even a date to a school activity.

Suppose you are a shy guy, going steady after a while will pull you out of this when you get into some group activities. It may also get you interested in some new hobby which your girl enjoys very much.

Thats about all the information which I can give you for now. I will send you some magazine on going steady for some extra information.

If you are planning on going steady wait until you read the magazines. My tip to you is no don't do it!

Boy 8 (September)

You have written to me about a word going steady and you would like to know that it means. Will I think going steady means this; going steady is a slang word for teen-agers and I think going steady is a girls idea in the first place. Going steady is realy just boys and girls going togother you know boy friend girl friend.

Going steady mean not a thing to me at all and I never use the word. You ask me if I want with a girl. Yes I have about two or three. I think I might be over next year if I save enough money. Then we can realy have a singing time, see you next year maybe. write soon.

Boy 8 (May)

So you are interested in knowing more about what American teen-agers call go stedy. Teen-agers are funny people, and they use funny words to express thereselves. These funny words were call sang and thats what the teen-agers now in there speech; going steady is a sang word for going together that is all, their is no different from the magazine you read it is still the same.

What I think about going steady? Nothing I don't even use sang words any more and hardy use sang words in my speech. Will I have to stop writing now because its almost time for the bell to ring and I'll be late for my second class this is the only time I can write to you because I have homework after school all the time. Write back as

ASSUMPTIONS ABOUT THE LETTERS

Explain why you accept or reject, wholly or in part, the following assumptions related to the preceding letters:

1. The girls' letters show more originality than the boys'.
2. Only a few of the students' May letters are better than their September letters.
3. A detailed inventory of the students' strengths and weaknesses in content, organization, sentence structure, usage, spelling, punctuation, capitalization, and vocabulary indicates that their teacher should devote most of his time to classwide rather than individual instruction.
4. Selecting the three best and three worst letters is easy.
5. If all of the students in a methods class grade all of the letters and then tabulate the number of "A's," "B's," "C's," "D's," and "F's" received by each letter, the results will show considerable agreement in the grades given.
6. The letter writers need to spend more time on workbook and handbook exercises and vocabulary and spelling lists.
7. The following data on the nineteen letter writers would help you if you were to be their teacher next year.

DATA ON THE NINETEEN LETTER WRITERS

		GRADES ON LETTERS[1]		I.Q. OTIS	NEW PURDUE ENG. PLACEMENT		AVERAGE ENGLISH GRADES[2]		REMMERS' ECONOMIC SCALE HIGH 7; LOW 0
		SEPT.	MAY	SEPT.	SEPT.	MAY	GR. 9	GR. 10	SEPT.
Girl	1	71	64	100	96	106	3.0	2.0	3
"	2	62	72	97	97	88	3.5	3.0	4
"	3	60	65	101	79	89	2.5	1.5	4
"	4	37	40	102	79	76	2.0	1.0	4
"	5	71	80	95	85	91	2.0	1.5	3
"	6	60	65	112	77	104	3.0	2.0	4
"	7	64	86	120	98	96	2.0	2.5	4
"	8	70	70	104	83	107	2.0	0.5	4
"	9	68	67	115	93	98	3.0	1.5	4
"	10	56	61	93	95	101	2.0	2.0	5
"	11	76	76	103	83	96	3.0	1.5	4
Boy	1	70	67	119	105	130	3.0	2.5	3
"	2	71	63	110	99	89	2.0	2.0	4
"	3	72	70	120	104	100	2.0	2.0	5
"	4	53	59	104	83	91	2.0	0.5	5
"	5	61	67	104	83	107	2.0	0.5	4
"	6	71	79	121	131	148	2.0	3.0	4
"	7	68	74	113	86	96	2.5	2.5	4
"	8	38	31	79	73	75	2.0	1.0	3

[1]The nineteen September and nineteen May letters reproduced above and 1140 other letters on "going steady"—*most of them written in academic classes*—were stripped of their identity, mixed together, and then graded by fourteen high school English teachers.

[2]4.0, "A"; 3.0, "B"; 2.0, "C"; 1.0, "D."

Essay-Evaluation Form [1]

	VERY POOR	POOR	BELOW AVERAGE	LITTLE BELOW AVERAGE	AVERAGE	LITTLE ABOVE AVERAGE	ABOVE AVERAGE	GOOD	VERY GOOD	SCORES
I. GRAMMAR AND USAGE (Subject-verb and pronoun-antecedent agreement, tense, case, distinction between adjectives and adverbs, etc.)	1	2	3	4	5	6	7	8	9	——
II. PUNCTUATION (Comma splice or comma fault, etc.)	VP 1	P 2	BA 3	LBA 4	A 5	LAA 6	AA 7	G 8	VG 9	——
III. SENTENCE CLEARNESS AND EFFECTIVENESS (Sentence fragment, excessive coordination, faulty reference of pronouns, dangling modifiers, faulty parallelism, wordiness, etc.)	VP 1	P 2	BA 3	LBA 4	A 5	LAA 6	AA 7	G 8	VG 9	——

[1]Morsey, *Seminar* . . . , p. 17.

		VP	P	BA	LBA	A	LAA	AA	G	VG	
IV.	VOCABULARY	1	2	3	4	5	6	7	8	9	———
	(Right word, breadth, variety, adequacy.)										

		VP	P	BA	LBA	A	LAA	AA	G	VG	
V.	SPELLING	1	2	3	4	5	6	7	8	9	———

		VP	P	BA	LBA	A	LAA	AA	G	VG	
VI.	ORGANIZATION	1	2	3	4	5	6	7	8	9	———
	(Unity, coherence, and emphasis in whole theme, etc.)										

		VP	P	BA	LBA	A	LAA	AA	G	VG	
VII.	PARAGRAPHING	1	2	3	4	5	6	7	8	9	———
	(Unity, coherence, and emphasis within paragraph, etc.)										

		VP	P	BA	LBA	A	LAA	AA	G	VG	
VIII.	CONTENT	1	2	3	4	5	6	7	8	9	———
	(Stimulating and fresh content, assumptions reasonable and supported with pertinent evidence, more than emotional reactions, etc.)										

TOTAL SCORE .... ———

NOTE TO THE ENGLISH METHODS TEACHER

You might test the usefulness of the "Essay-Evaluation Form" by (1) discussing it with your students and (2) having them use it in grading the essays in Appendix 4.

NOTE TO THE EXPERIENCED ENGLISH TEACHER AND STUDENT TEACHER

You might test the usefulness of the "Essay-Evaluation Form" by (1) completing and attaching a mimeographed copy of it to each composition you return to students and/or (2) having students complete it and attach it to compositions they hand in.

ESSAY-EVALUATION FORM

Words Frequently Misspelled by Students

THE SEVENTY-FIVE WORDS MOST FREQUENTLY MISSPELLED BY 589 SENIOR HIGH SCHOOL STUDENTS IN 1178 LETTERS

This table, the seventy-five most frequently misspelled words,[1] shows that the 589 students' spelling demons (accounting for 52 percent of the total misspellings in 1178 letters) are simple and/or common words. Perhaps the words seemed so easy to many students that they felt no compulsion to consult a dictionary when they used them. Undoubtedly one of the reasons the following words in this table were misspelled eighteen or more times was that the nature of the assignment (a letter on "going steady") stimulated their frequent use: *steady, girl, marriage,* and *boyfriend.*

Seventy-Five Most Frequently Misspelled Words

WORD	TIMES MISSPELLED	WORD	TIMES MISSPELLED	WORD	TIMES MISSPELLED
too	217	doesn't	17	then	12
all right	112	experience	17	answer	12
you're	107	break	16	another	11
receive	96	explain	16	argument	11
a lot	81	feel	16	occasion	11
steady	58	your	16	meant	11
they're	52	among	15	and	10
their	49	dating	15	engaged	10
there	43	friend	15	I'm	10
truly	40	other	15	probably	10

[1] Maine and Morsey, A *Common-Sense Approach to Teaching Spelling*, p. 7.

WORD	TIMES MISSPELLED	WORD	TIMES MISSPELLED	WORD	TIMES MISSPELLED
sincerely	40	well	15	sense	10
opinion	37	decide	14	since	10
usually	33	girl friend	14	surprised	10
until	28	that's	14	writing	10
girl	27	magazine	14	letter	10
think	25	really	13	allowed	9
marriage	24	to	13	always	9
it's	22	week-end	13	article	9
whether	21	else	12	bracelet	9
quite	21	involved	12	definitely	9
together	20	parties	12	opposite	9
believe	19	serious	12	seem	9
boy friend	18	supposed	12	teen-ager	9
know	18	themselves	12	want	9
they	18	write	12	yours	9
Totals	1226		352		248

GRAND TOTAL 1826

NOTE TO THE EXPERIENCED ENGLISH TEACHER AND STUDENT TEACHER

You might be interested in (1) dictating this list to your students to see whether the words are "demons" for them and/or (2) developing a similar list from the spelling errors you find in your students' writings.

GRADE-LEVEL COMPARISON OF THE TWENTY-FIVE WORDS MOST FREQUENTLY MISSPELLED BY 589 SENIOR HIGH SCHOOL STUDENTS IN 1178 LETTERS

This table, grade-level comparison of the twenty-five most frequently misspelled words,[2] seems to indicate that the twenty-five words are approximately equally difficult for tenth-, eleventh- and twelfth-graders. By converting into percentages the data relating to the first five words in this table, one sees that an eleventh-grade teacher should not assume that the spelling of certain simple words was mastered on the tenth-grade level by all of his students.

[2]Maine and Morsey, *A Common-Sense Approach to Teaching Spelling*, p. 12.

	GRADE 10	GRADE 11	GRADE 12
too	.33	.39	.38
all right	.20	.19	.13
you're	.27	.16	.13
receive	.25	.10	.13
a lot	.32	.15	.28

Grade-Level Comparison of the Twenty-Five
Most Frequently Misspelled Words

WORD	MISSPELLINGS GRADE 10 (226)*	MISSPELLINGS GRADE 11 (323)*	MISSPELLINGS GRADE 12 (40)*	TOTAL
too	75	127	15	217
all right	45	62	5	112
you're	50	52	5	107
receive	57	34	5	96
a lot	33	37	11	81
steady	15	41	2	58
they're	20	30	2	52
their	12	34	3	49
there	12	26	5	43
truly	13	27	0	40
sincerely	11	22	7	40
opinion	17	20	0	37
usually	10	22	1	33
until	6	21	1	28
girl	2	25	0	27
think	13	10	2	25
marriage	11	11	2	24
it's	10	12	0	22
whether	9	11	1	21
quite	3	16	2	21
together	1	17	2	20
believe	4	13	2	19
boy friend	5	13	0	18
know	6	11	1	18
they	3	12	3	18
Totals	443	706	77	1226
Average Misspellings	2.0	2.2	1.9	2.1

*Number enrolled in class.

Statistics on
Senior High School Students

STATISTICS ON THE I. Q., ECONOMIC STATUS, BOOKS IN THE HOME, MAGAZINE SUBSCRIPTIONS, GRADES, ETC. OF THE UPPER, MIDDLE, AND LOWEST 10 PER-CENT (OTIS I. Q.) OF 589 SENIOR HIGH SCHOOL STUDENTS[1]

	MEANS		
	UPPER 10 PERCENT	MIDDLE 10 PERCENT	LOWEST 10 PERCENT
I. Q., Otis	127.1	108.2	85.1
Socio-Economic Status (7 highest possible score, 0 lowest possible score)	4.5	4.2	4.0
Books in the Home	235.0	182.0	67.0
Magazine Subscriptions	4.8	3.4	1.9
Newspaper Subscriptions	2.2	1.8	1.6
1959-60 Grades*	3.1	2.2	1.3
Boys	2.9	1.9	1.1
Girls	3.3	2.5	1.6
Previous Grades in High School	3.3	2.5	1.4
Boys	3.1	2.3	1.1
Girls	3.5	2.7	1.7
Total Hours Devoted to Voluntary Reading (Three Weeks)	25.8	21.5	16.7
Books	10.4	8.6	6.0
Boys	8.9	9.3	5.0
Girls	12.7	8.1	7.3
Magazines	7.3	6.2	4.3
Boys	8.2	7.4	4.4
Girls	6.2	5.1	3.9
Newspapers	8.0	6.7	6.5
Boys	9.0	7.1	6.9
Girls	6.4	6.3	5.7

*4.0 A; 3.0, B; 2.0, C; 1.0, D.

[1]Morsey, *Seminar* . . . , p. 31.

The following data . . . show that few out-of-state newspapers and "prestige" magazines are found in the homes of the upper, middle, and lowest 10 percent:

Out-of-State Newspapers

	NUMBER OF SUBSCRIPTIONS		
	UPPER 10 PERCENT	MIDDLE 10 PERCENT	LOWEST 10 PERCENT
New York Times	1	0	0
Cincinnati Enquirer	4	3	0
Pittsburgh Press	1	0	0
Detroit Free Press	1	0	0
Wall Street Journal	2	1	0

"Prestige" Magazines

	NUMBER OF SUBSCRIPTIONS		
	UPPER 10 PERCENT	MIDDLE 10 PERCENT	LOWEST 10 PERCENT
The New Yorker	1	0	0
The Saturday Review	1	0	0
National Geographic	3	1	1
The Atlantic	0	0	0
Harper's	0	0	0

NOTE TO THE EXPERIENCED ENGLISH TEACHER AND STUDENT TEACHER

You might be interested in determining how your students compare with the 177 senior high school students whose I.Q.'s, available reading materials, school grades, etc. are summarized above.

Comments on Literature
and Teachers of Literature
by Sixty-Five Incoming
College Freshmen

You may be interested in analyzing some of the answers given by sixty-five incoming college freshmen to the following questions. (Before you analyze their answers, see the assumptions on pages 295–96.)

I. *What were some of the desirable outcomes of literature courses that you thought were well taught?*

A. Reading Habit
1. I have grown to like reading. My senior high school teachers taught me to like Shakespeare as well as outside reading.
2. I have acquired a great interest in literature as a whole.
3. I learned to like the works of dull writers.
4. I have learned to read for enjoyment rather than just because it was required.

(A total of eighteen students claimed that one or more of their literature courses helped them develop a liking for literature.)

B. Insight and Understanding
1. I enlarged my view of the world in general.
2. I learned to see the author's purpose and deeper meaning of selections.
3. I have learned to evaluate selections I have read.
4. I have been able to better understand the author's motives in writing the work and what he wants the reader to get out of it. I have learned to understand human beings through poetry and prose.
5. I have learned why people from other countries and the United States live the way they do.

6. I have learned to read things with an open mind and form opinions after I finish the article or whatever I am reading.
7. Literature helped me to understand myself and others. It can sometimes give us our reasons for living and the pattern by which we are going to live.

(A total of seven students claimed that literature helped them develop an understanding of themselves and of others.)

C. Transfer
1. Literature classes helped me in creative writing.
2. I learned to express myself orally.
3. Literature has given me some background for other subjects, especially history.
4. It helped me to use better words and better grammar.
5. Literature increased my vocabulary.
6. I have learned to appreciate reading and it has helped me a great deal in other subjects.
7. It improved my reading speed and comprehension.

(A total of seven students claimed that literature helped them do better work in other subjects.)

D. Miscellaneous
1. Reading aloud more or less took the shyness out of me.
2. I have learned to recognize good reading and good authors.
3. I haven't gotten anything from literature.
4. I learned the different styles of authors.
5. There was only one book, *Macbeth*, which I thoroughly enjoyed.

II. *What were some of the teaching methods that were used in literature classes that you thought were well taught?*

A. Variety
1. Most important to teach a literature class effectively is a change and variety of activities.
2. We studied a great variety of authors of every nationality—English, Scottish, French, American, Welsh, Irish, German.
3. The teacher suggested outside readings but didn't insist on any certain selections.

(A total of three students prized variety in literature classes. See III-A.)

B. Difficult Literature
1. Teacher read parts that are hard for students to understand.
2. The teacher explained difficult selections very thoroughly.
3. Discussing literature hard to understand.
4. Going over parts of plays and stories to see exactly what the author meant.

5. The teacher read right along with us in class and explained everything that wasn't clear to us.

(Five students said they valued explanations of difficult passages.)

C. Dramatization
1. Sort of walking through them (plays) together.
2. Acting out or at least walking through plays being studied.
3. Plays were acted out.
4. One method I enjoyed especially in high school was acting out a play in class, using sound effects and making it as real as possible.

(Six students suggested that plays should be acted out.)

D. Tests
1. Having ten questions a day over what we were reading, this really kept us on our toes.
2. Short tests often.
3. We were given short answer tests after each selection and then a six-weeks test over all the material covered.
4. In high school teachers are worried more about our grade rather than what you could get from the story.
5. If we knew there was going to be a quiz, we would read the assignment; otherwise we wouldn't and would hope we'd get something from her explanation.

E. Miscellaneous
1. We studied one selection, *Macbeth*, and analyzed it word for word. This way I really learned to like Shakespeare.
2. Often an attempt was made to bring some application of the work to everyday life.
3. The teacher gave the class credit for having a little sense, and the class even acknowledged that maybe the teacher knew what he was talking about.
4. Movies were shown of outstanding selections.
5. The method I liked best in literature classes was open discussion.
6. Read aloud to us, have us read aloud, and have us listen to recordings of authors reading their own works.
7. One advantage of the lit class was that it was all in chronological order.

III. *What are a few "dos" for literature teachers?*

A. Variety
1. Do give a choice for outside reading.
2. Use a number of ways to study a selection so that the class will not get monotonous from using the same method constantly.
3. Have enough variety so the class won't expect the same thing day after day.

4. Have a variety in selections.
5. Offer a wide variety of literature to the student.
6. Bring in little outside things to break the monotony.
7. Do have a few amazing items to bring up in class.
(A total of fifteen students made a plea for variety.)

B. Literature and Life
   1. Relate incidents and ideas in literature to our lives.
   2. Do assign literature that appeals to the students' emotional qualities.
   3. Do read things that are timely.
   4. Let the student express his personal ideas and feelings about something he has read before you, the teacher, explain your feelings and beliefs about the same selection.

C. Miscellaneous
   1. Do encourage weak students. Be careful that in doing so you do not offend your strong students. (Very tough.)
   2. Let students lead discussions sometimes. Let students know exactly when assignment is due or when test is scheduled.
   3. Use up-to-date books if possible. Use literature which is more popular with young people.
   4. Make assignments clear, brief, and to the point. Include every student in daily class participation.
   5. Do tie in literature's importance with other subjects.
   6. Do let students read poetry aloud because this helps them understand the ideas of the poem more effectively.
   7. The teacher should express his idea of a literary selection, but he shouldn't force the student to accept his way of thinking.

IV. *What are a few "don'ts" for literature teachers?*

A. Memory Work
   1. No memory work.
   2. Don't require a lot of memorizing for you don't appreciate it and only do it because you have to. Study the biographies of the authors thoroughly and memorize their date of birth and death.
   3. Don't have students memorize authors' names.
   4. Don't ask for a bunch of memorizing.
   (A total of ten students objected to memorizing dates, places, names, etc.)

B. Lectures
   1. Don't lecture.
   2. Don't have a lecture class.
   3. Don't give long lectures and avoid discussion.
   4. Don't just lecture and never let students participate.

C. Discussions
   1. Don't let one person monopolize the discussions.
   2. Don't call on a student who doesn't raise his hand. I think it is very embarrassing because some people, as I, don't get the meaning of the story and they are completely lost.
   3. Don't dominate class discussion.
   4. Don't let a few students dominate class discussion.

D. Assignments
   1. Don't change assignment after making it.
   2. Don't go too fast.
   3. Don't make class responsible for much technical detail about author and selection.
   4. Don't have students write answers to a lot of questions concerning the stories.
   5. Don't give too large assignments for they're only slighted.
   6. Don't assign too much reading material all at once.

E. Miscellaneous
   1. Some teachers have students read what the teacher likes and do not care if the students like it.
   2. Never ridicule an idea presented in class by a student.
   3. Don't ask, "What do you think?" and then expect the answer to be what the teacher thinks.
   4. Don't be a stickler for details.
   5. Don't try to make everyone like literature without showing them what can be learned from it.
   6. Don't criticize modern day literature—this is one of the most disgusting things.
   7. I have only one don't. I don't think a person can tell what another was thinking when he wrote a poem.

ASSUMPTIONS ABOUT THE COMMENTS

Explain why you accept or reject, wholly or in part, the following assumptions related to the preceding comments by college freshmen on literature and teachers of literature.

1. A high school English teacher should not take the college freshmen's comments and suggestions seriously.
2. One can derive from the students' comments and suggestions a series of worthwhile principles on the aims and methods of the high school English teacher.
3. The students' comments and suggestions indicate that some of them had excellent English teachers.
4. The students' answers indicate that they recognize effective teaching.

5. The students' answers to Parts III and IV reveal that they are concerned more with an English teacher's choice of subject matter and methods than his personality.

6. Some of the students seem to rate highly teaching methods that are rejected by most authors of books and magazine articles on teaching English.

7. Some of the students' answers reflect an understanding of what literature can offer a reader.

A Survey of Students' Fears
Before and After
Student Teaching

During the 1965–66 school year the author asked sixty-five Ball State University English majors to answer anonymously in writing the following question before they began part-time (half-day) student teaching: "If you have any fears about student teaching, what are they?" After they completed student teaching, he asked them to respond to, "If you have any fears about your first teaching job, what are they?"

The purpose in asking the questions was to (1) identify students' fears before and after student teachings and (2) compare the number and nature of their fears before and after student teaching. (Before you analyze their answers, see the assumptions on page 306.)

Table I lists the number and nature of students' fears before and after student teaching. Twelve students (18 percent) were "fearless" after student teaching. All the students had one or more fears before student teaching.

TABLE I—FEARS MENTIONED BY SIXTY-FIVE ENGLISH
MAJORS BEFORE AND AFTER STUDENT TEACHING

		BEFORE STUDENT TEACHING	AFTER STUDENT TEACHING
I.	Subject Matter	53	39
II.	Discipline	35	27
III.	Students	34	21
IV.	Critic Teachers	34	0
V.	Administrators	0	9
VI.	Future Colleagues	0	8
VII.	Teaching Load	1	9
VIII.	Miscellaneous	17	25
	Total	174	138

To facilitate comparison in the pages that follow, students' statements about "After Student Teaching" fears appear directly below their "Before Student Teaching" fears:

SUBJECT MATTER

Before Student Teaching

Thirty-three of the fifty-three "Subject-Matter" fears are illustrated by eight "Do-I-know-enough?" statements:
"I fear that students will know more than myself." . . . "My ability to answer or deal with questions of the students." . . . "My unfamiliarity with material I may have to present." . . . "Do I know enough of the subject matter?" . . . "My biggest fear would be running out of things to say or do during a class-room period." . . . "That I don't know any more than the high school students." . . . "I have a fear of being trapped by my students' questions." . . . "I'm afraid students will show me up at times."

Eight of the fifty-three "Subject-Matter" fears are illustrated by four "Do-I-know-how-to-plan-lessons?" statements:
"Being able to write lesson plans quickly and effectively." . . . "I hope I can locate material I need for unit plans or daily lesson plans." . . . "That I will be inadequate in making lesson plans." . . . "I fear that I will make my plans either too long or vice versa."

Five of the fifty-three "Subject-Matter" fears concerned grammar:
"That I don't know my subject matter well enough to teach it, especially grammar and composition." . . . "The only fear I have is that I will get confused when I get into grammar." . . . "That I'll have to teach a grammar class." "My knowledge of grammar is the only thing bothering me at present. I will take English 321 before student teaching; therefore I will be ready." . . . "I fear that my dislike of grammar will show."

Four of the fifty-three "Subject-Matter" fears concerned literature:
"I am afraid my knowledge of literature and especially language will not be adequate for juniors and seniors." . . . "I'm afraid I do not know enough about literature to teach it." . . . "I am afraid I will not be able to bring up questions which will induce real thinking in depth about literature and what the students have read." . . . "Feeling of inadequacy in certain areas of literature, particularly American literature and poetry."

Three of the fifty-three "Subject-Matter" fears concerned evaluation:
"Grading compositions." . . . "That I will be inadequate in knowing how to evaluate a student." . . . "I am not sure about evaluation."

After Student Teaching

Twenty-three of the thirty-nine "Subject-Matter" fears are illustrated by nine "Do-I-know-how-to-organize-material?" statements:

"My main fear is not being able to present subject matter in an effective manner." . . . "I would imagine that organization of the material for a semester would be the most difficult problem I will encounter. For instance, planning activities so that a fairly equal amount of time could be spent on various units such as poetry, short stories, and drama." . . . "I have self-doubt concerning my abilities to adapt to specific grade levels and communicating to these levels effectively. Also I fear that I will be unable to pick out the areas which need to be dealt with." . . . "Programming. How does a new teacher know to set up a schedule for academic, general, and special classes?" . . . "What I have done in student teaching has been predetermined by my critic teacher. I am anxious to know what I can do on my own, in the way of creating new methods of presentation." . . . "Ability to find varied and useful ways to teach English to students who couldn't care less about whether they learned any English or not." . . . "My class next year will consist of students from the complete range of ability. I have only worked with the above-average class; I may find it somewhat difficult to reach *all* the students at their level when I first begin." . . . "Whether or not I can *teach* instead of *follow* the text." . . . "Student teaching has made me realize many inadequacies about myself. I have had problems in putting the material on the students' level."

Five of the thirty-nine "Subject-Matter" fears concern "Do I know enough?"

"I fear being well enough informed about my subject to answer questions that should arise." . . . "My lack of knowledge of subject matter. (My first student teaching assignment was on logic and rhetoric, which was new to me.)" . . . "I don't feel I have an adequate knowledge of the subject matter." . . . "Will I know the subject matter adequately enough?" . . . "Being familiar with the material so that I can make the subject interesting."

Three of the thirty-nine "Subject-Matter" fears concern evaluation:

"I dread making errors in grading." . . . "Not grading correctly, in accordance with the other teachers' standards." . . . "That I will assign unfair grades."

Three of the thirty-nine "Subject-Matter" fears concern teaching outside one's major:

"Teaching in a field not prepared to teach in." . . . "Getting stuck in a small school and having to teach in my minor area which I don't like." . . . "Having to teach in my minor—I feel inadequate in many respects."

Three of the thirty-nine "Subject-Matter" fears concern grammar:

"I don't feel that I am well enough prepared in grammar." . . . "I feel I am lacking especially in grammar and this worries me somewhat." . . . "That my command of grammar is still not adequate."

Two of the thirty-nine "Subject-Matter" fears concern literature:

"I feel my background in grammar is strong; but I think my general literary background is weak, and I may run into trouble there." . . . "I am very concerned about my weakness in knowledge of certain areas of literature. I considered myself well-read until this student-teaching experience, but now I am not sure that I will *ever* have the time to read everything necessary to answer students."

Summary

Before student teaching students were concerned primarily with, "Do I know enough subject matter?" After student teaching, they were concerned primarily with presenting subject matter effectively.

DISCIPLINE

Before Student Teaching

The thirty-five "Discipline" mentions show little variation. These eight examples are representative:

"I fear that I will have discipline problems." . . . "How do I handle discipline problems?" . . . "I am anxious to see whether I can discipline a class." . . . "The problem of discipline bothers me. I am only twenty and will need to establish adult rapport with students." . . . "I may not be able to handle discipline." . . . "I am unfamiliar with the discipline of a particular school. How and how far should I go." . . . "Discipline is always a concern to a beginner, I guess." . . . "Disciplinary problems—I don't know if I'll be able to handle them successfully or not."

After Student Teaching

Thirteen of the twenty-seven "Discipline" fears are illustrated by "Will I be able to handle discipline problems that may come up?" The other fourteen statements relate to student-teaching experiences and are illustrated by:

"My greatest fear about my first teaching position is discipline which will be applicable to myself. I have tried many things, but I have not found that particular method which will work for me. One of my critic teachers forced me to use methods which I do not feel work for me. My other critic teacher told me not to worry, that it will come with time. However, I cannot help but worry whether or not this is one of my problems I will be able to overcome." . . . "I have not experienced any discipline problems in participation or student teaching. Now, I feel that I may have the problem next year. Up until this time I have had above-average students; and the teacher of the class maintained complete discipline, even when I had the class." . . . "Ability to handle discipline better than I have the last few weeks of student teaching." . . . "I have not had discipline problems in student teaching, but I'm still afraid of my first real test." . . . "I have had only academic classes, where the students present no discipline problems. I am afraid that this may cause me to be ill-equipped to handle a heterogeneous group where discipline problems may occur." . . . "Should students who are constantly annoying the class, even after disciplining by you, be sent to the office for disciplining and possible suspension by the principal?" . . . "So far, I have been exceptionally lucky; I have not run into any great discipline problems. I am sure that I will find a few students who will be ready to test the patience of the 'new teacher.' I am quite apprehensive of the situation."

Summary

Before student teaching fear of inability to maintain order in the classroom is quite common. After student teaching students are still apprehensive about discipline problems they expect to meet when they become full-fledged teachers, even though most of them apparently had few serious disciplinary problems as student teachers. They attribute good order in the classroom while student teaching to the presence of the critic teacher.

STUDENTS

Before Student Teaching

Thirteen of the thirty-four "Student" fears are illustrated by five "Can-I-develop-rapport?" questions:

"Maintaining an easy, natural attitude in front of a class and establishing good rapport for better cooperation." . . . "That I will not be able to establish any kind of rapport with my students because I am intensely interested in English and I know they will not be." . . . "That I will be weak in empathizing with students." . . . "Maintaining a healthy teacher-student relationship." . . . "I am afraid I will not be accepted by the students."

Thirteen of the thirty-four "Student" fears are illustrated by five diverse statements:

"I fear that I may not be able to comprehend my students' problems and will be unable to teach to the best of my ability because of this." . . . "If students would laugh at things I do, I wouldn't know what to do." . . . "I am anxious to see whether I can keep my students enthused to some degree over a prolonged period of time." . . . "I am only 20. Some of the students I'll be teaching will be 18-19. Makes for a touchy situation." . . . "Perhaps my demands will be too great for students."

Three of the thirty-four "Student" fears reflected stage fright:

"I fear the initial shock of getting up in front of a new class." . . . "Scared to get up in front of the class for the first time." . . . "Stage fright."

Five of the thirty-four "Student" fears are illustrated by three "Can-I-get-them-to-learn?" statements:

"That I get a bunch of morons to teach." . . . "I am worried about working with slow kids." . . . "That the students won't want to learn."

After Student Teaching

Nine of the twenty-one "Student" fears concern motivation. Examples:

"I wonder about the motivation of students with diverse abilities. Can I keep all students interested?" . . . "What can I do with a student who doesn't care about school, nor do his parents?" . . . "Keeping myself motivated if I teach slow students." . . . "I hope to be able to inspire students as well as instruct them. The feeling one gets when he stares at a group of blank, indifferent faces is not a pleasant one."

Seven of the twenty-one "Student" fears are illustrated by four diverse statements.

"Learning to understand students." . . . "Make-up work for students who have been absent. I have found it hard to keep track of who makes up assignments and what to assign." . . . "Fear that what I may say in class may become twisted when the student relates it to his parents who in turn tell the principal that I am saying the wrong things." . . . "Not being able to devote all the time I should to individual students because there will be so many."

Five of the twenty-one "Student" fears concern "Can I develop rapport?" "Getting the students to respect me as a person as well as a teacher. Sometimes they respect your knowledge, which is desirable, but I want them to respect me as a person—to give them ideas to strive for." . . . "I tend to become very involved in students' individual problems. I have a great deal of empathy for them and their problems. This has not caused a great deal of trouble thus far, but I feel that it could in a regular situation." "Establishing the proper distance between myself and the student." . . . "Sometimes I feel that some of my students consider me a pal rather than a teacher." . . . "The main fear is getting my classes to accept me for what I am and to stop making comparisons with other teachers as quickly as possible."

Summary

"Student" fears numbered thirty-four before student teaching and twenty-one after student teaching. Being understood by high school students and understanding students seem to be serious concerns before and after student teaching.

CRITIC TEACHERS

Before Student Teaching

Fears relating to critic teachers are easily classified. Seventeen of the thirty-four fears concern content and methods. Examples:

"I am rather afraid that I'll get a teacher with whom I disagree, and then I'll have to teach as she sees fit—I won't feel that I'm doing my best because I'll be teaching by her standards, not mine." . . . "That I might be forced into a set teaching pattern by the requirements of workbooks, etc., or that I might fall into a pattern that will be 'easy' for me to maintain." . . . "If I'm in disagreement with the critic teacher, should I concede and do it her way?" . . . "That the critic teacher will demand that I follow his or her methods of teaching, rather than use the ones which I feel I would use more effectively due to my own personality and character." . . . "I fear that I will be student teaching under a teacher who has probably taught for several years and I am supposed to live up to her standards of teaching which she has built up over the years." . . . "Can one use his own methods in teaching such things as poetry?" . . . "Must one fit a rigid plan or is there any elasticity?"

Seventeen of the thirty-four "Critic Teacher" fears concern personal relationships. Examples:

"I am wondering if I will get along with my critic." . . . "That my critic and I will get along together. The critic's recommendation is *so* important." . . . "That I'll have an unsympathetic critic." . . . "Will I get along with my critic?" . . . "What if the teacher I am assigned to resents having a student teacher? Are assignments like this avoided?" . . . "That I'll get a mean and nasty critic."

FUTURE COLLEAGUES AND ADMINISTRATORS

After Student Teaching

Since critic teachers have no administrative authority over beginning teachers, they are not mentioned in the questionnaire completed after student teaching, but administrators received nine mentions and future colleagues eight mentions.

The fears relating to administrators are quoted in full:
"How will department heads, supervisors and principals accept new teaching methods?" . . . "Red tape—I hope I will not be frustrated by red-tape Mickey Mouse, the *Up the Down Staircase* type of thing." . . . "Making the adjustment from being a student to teacher and adjusting to a different type of supervision and evaluation." . . . "I am wondering whether I will approve of administration policies." . . . "I have some administrative fears in regard to school organization or reorganization." . . . "Adapting myself and my principles to those of a stricter, more narrow-minded administration." . . . "I won't allow my personal life to be interfered with (smoking, drinking, dress, etc.) by administrative commands." . . . "Fear of how to talk with my superiors in matters of grave importance." . . . "Will the head of the department dictate what material will be covered during the school year?"

The fears relating to future colleagues are quoted in full:
"Unfortunately, I've found much bickering between teachers. This I don't fear because I won't take the time to degrade a colleague—even if he deserved it!" . . . "More than the children themselves, I fear the observation and snide remarks of fellow teachers." . . . "That I might appear to be unfriendly when I might just be preoccupied or. . . ." . . . "I don't want to appear overly friendly to students or teachers—not to the extent that confidences are exchanged." . . . "Some minor personal things bother me as the social atmosphere and the kind of fashions teachers dress in—but these minor fears will go away once I am established." . . . "Getting a job in a friendly and cooperative school system." . . . "I am afraid of whether I'll be accepted in the group of teachers. I don't want to teach in any school where older teachers are not friendly or do not lend a helping hand." . . . "Learning to like the other teachers and being able to get along with them."

Summary

Before student teaching, the sixty-five students had two fears (each received seventeen mentions) concerning critic teachers: fear of having to follow their methods and fear of not getting along with them. After student teaching students mentioned similar fears concerning (1) administrators (nine mentions) and (2) colleagues (eight mentions).

TEACHING LOAD

Many experienced teachers regard a heavy teaching load as one of their most serious problems. "Load" fears received one mention before student teaching and nine mentions after student teaching.

Before Student Teaching

"I fear that I will have ten hours of homework every night besides my other classes."

After Student Teaching

The following four statements are typical of the nine "Load" fears:
"I fear that I will have to spend too many hours in preparation. I don't want to spend fourteen hours a day teaching." . . . "I fear that I will have so much outside work and preparation that I will be working eighteen hours a day." . . . "I fear that I will have so many different texts and classes that I won't be able to prepare properly." . . . "How do you prepare adequately for five classes daily?"

Summary

Load is not considered a major problem before or after student teaching.

MISCELLANEOUS

Seventeen "Before Student Teaching" fears and twenty-five "After Student Teaching" fears did not seem to fit other classifications, so they were placed under *Miscellaneous*.

Before Student Teaching

Six fears illustrate "Miscellaneous":
"I'm a procrastinator." . . . "Being asked to supervise athletic events as extra-curricular activities. I'm not athletic-minded and am not at all proficient in this field." . . . "How much real responsibility will I have? I am afraid that I will try to do too much or too little." . . . "Is my personality suited to do teaching?" . . . "That I'll never have a class as good as the one I had at Burris."[1] . . . "Where do I learn to mimeograph?"

[1]Burris is a laboratory school where Ball State University students participate prior to student teaching.

IMPROVING ENGLISH INSTRUCTION

After Student Teaching

Eight fears illustrate "Miscellaneous":
"Not enough variety of classes that one might teach." . . . "I fear I, as a teacher, will tend to become a glorified bookkeeper, and I don't want to be. I want to teach—not tally A's, B's, etc." . . . "Following teaching ethics in the particular school in which I teach." . . . "I'm afraid that I'll consider teaching too much of an emotional drain and that I'll want to give up and stay at home." . . . "I'm a little afraid of going out on my own, since I am only twenty. I am contemplating doing graduate work before I teach." . . . "I don't want to teach in a school that is in a low-class district." . . . "Not obtaining a teaching job is my first fear." . . . "I rather fear the idea of teaching in a large city school system somewhat."

COMMENT

Subject-matter fears seem inevitable and are probably desirable. Subject-matter mastery is of necessity a lifelong goal. However, recognition of this dominant fear by university and high school teachers and administrators might lead to policies that will help student teachers and first-year teachers reduce subject-matter fears to a minimum. An accent on careful lesson planning by university methods teachers seems essential. High school teachers and administrators might give student teachers and beginning teachers materials that would acquaint them with the overall goals of the English program and the aims and suggested methods for specific courses.

Fears relating to (1) discipline and (2) establishing effective relationships with students are closely related to those involving subject matter. Most experienced teachers have learned that a curriculum which is relevant to students' concerns reduces discipline problems and helps establish desirable relationships with students. The current emphasis on research may help to give curricula a vitality that will appeal even to potential dropouts.

Students' fears relating to teaching methods of critic teachers seem natural. Newcomers are often impatient with methods used by experienced members of a profession. A dissatisfaction with *what is* is necessary to progress in all fields—agriculture, communication, transportation, medicine, and education. Can this dissatisfaction be directed towards simple research projects that will test the efficacy of students' ideas about teaching? (The author tells students who are disturbed by the methodology of critic teachers that if experimentation is not encouraged during their student-teaching experience, they will still have forty years to test some of their ideas.)

The students' worries about establishing desirable personal relationships with critic teachers also seem natural. Students know that their placement credentials will include evaluations by critic teachers. They know that acceptable grades in student teaching are a must and that critic teachers often decide what the grades will be.

Why students expressed no fears relating to university supervisors seems surprising. Perhaps students learned via the grapevine that the university supervisors usually play a minor role, if any, in determining grades.

One could claim the most easily defended and pertinent assumption implicit in the data gathered in this survey is that student teaching experiences apparently helped twelve of sixty-five students to face their first teaching job with confidence; but a skeptic might contend that one should worry more about those who have "no fears" than those who have some fears about developing (1) subject-matter adequacy, (2) ability to maintain order in the classroom, and (3) satisfactory relationships with students, colleagues, and administrators.

ASSUMPTIONS ABOUT STUDENTS' FEARS
BEFORE AND AFTER STUDENT TEACHING

Explain why you accept or reject, wholly or in part, the following assumptions related to the survey.

1. To know that most students facing student teaching have fears is reassuring.

2. Students' fears about subject-matter inadequacies should be blamed on (1) the university, (2) the student, (3) the high school, (4) no one.

3. Discipline problems can be averted by planning lessons carefully.

4. When high school students are assigned to a new teacher, they are likely to have some fears similar to those expressed by English majors.

5. Critic teachers and college and university supervisors delight in the success of their student teachers.

6. Some of the assumptions under *Comment* are sound; others are questionable.

7. There are more significant questions one could ask student teachers than the two asked in the survey.

A Summary and Evaluation of Twenty-Eight Class Sessions Taught by Fourteen Experienced English Teachers

In 1959–60, the author and fourteen experienced high school English teachers sought the answer to the following question: Will senior high school students in experimental classes who for a period of one school year have frequent teacher-supervised opportunities to write and speak, who receive instruction in grammar and usage based on strengths and weaknesses reflected in their speech and writing, and who learn to relate literature to their own lives, outperform on various tests senior high school students in control classes who are seldom asked to write, who receive instruction in grammar and usage based largely on handbook and workbook exercises, and who see literature primarily as subject matter for objective tests?

During the 1959–60 school year, the author visited the experimental and control classes of the fourteen teachers eight times, and each time (1) summarized what went on in the classes and (2) made suggestions (comments) designed to help the teachers maintain experimental conditions.

Before you begin reading *Observation Report No. 3*, please note that the teachers are labeled A, B, C, D, etc. and summaries are given of what took place in each teacher's control class and experimental class, followed by the authors' comment. Before you begin reading, please turn to page 323 to glance at the assumptions based upon *Observation Report No. 3*.

OBSERVATION REPORT NO. 3[1]

Observations—December 7-15, 1959
In making this series of observations, I discovered that some of you seem to have an improved understanding of what is meant by maintaining experi-

[1] Morsey, *Seminar . . .* , pp. 109–22.

mental conditions. Apparently some of you had not been fully aware of the fact that our project can succeed only if we teach the control classes in approximately the same way we taught them last year, and if we test in our experimental classes some of the theory discussed in our seminars.

A. Control

The teacher asked his students to complete a multiple-choice test consisting of from five to eight questions over each of the following short stories: "The Bishop's Candlesticks," "That's What Happened to Me," "Report on the Barnhouse Effect," and "The Terrible Miss Dove." The students were also asked to answer the following essay questions: "Tell which of the four stories you enjoyed the most and why. Was it due to better handling of plot, characters, or what? Explain completely."

Assignment for the next day: Read Steinbeck's "The Affair at 7, Rue de M—."

A. Experimental

The following essay test had been given the day before over "The Bishop's Candlesticks," "That's What Happened to Me," "Report on the Barnhouse Effect," and "The Terrible Miss Dove":

1. What was the plot of each story?
2. Describe the main character in each story.
3. What would have happened if the story had continued?
4. Which story did you like the best and why?

The teacher explained that each one of the first three questions contains four parts, the last question only one part, and that each one of the total of thirteen parts is worth eight points. The teacher then asked his students to get together in groups of four or five to evaluate the answers to the test. The students' tests were distributed to the various groups by the teacher, who explained that he would also score the tests, return them the next day, and reveal how his grades compared with the grades given by the student groups. The teacher circulated among his students while they evaluated the tests.

When some of the student groups had finished evaluating the tests, the teacher assigned Galsworthy's "Quality." He asked them to consider this question: "Was he (the shoemaker in 'Quality') a foolish person?" Students who had finished the test-evaluation assignment were given a choice of reading "Quality" or writing in their journals.

Towards the end of the period the students were asked whether they had any questions about the short story assigned for today: "The Affair at 7, Rue de M—." The bell rang before the discussion got under way.

Comment

The teacher seems to be making a conscientious effort to teach his control class the way he did last year and to test some new content and methods in his experimental class.

Would it have been well to spend some time in discussing "What are effective answers to the four essay questions?" before having students evaluate the answers? Of course, the teacher could argue that he planned to do just that the next day, or that he was curious to know how well his students would do without any instruction on how to evaluate the answers to the test.

The question "Which story did you like best and why?" calls for judgment on the part of the student; but unless students understand the full significance of the why? in the question, they will probably answer, "I liked 'The Bishop's Candlesticks' best because it was very interesting." A similar question that the teacher asked in the control class would be less likely to be answered with a superficial generalization: "Tell which of the four stories you enjoyed the most and why? Was it due to better handling of plot, characters, or what? Explain completely."

Most students need to be taught to plan and organize their answers to essay questions before they begin writing. Any help you can give students in your experimental classes along this line will help them a great deal when they go to college.

An excellent companion piece for "That's What Happened to Me" is James Thurber's "The Secret Life of Walter Mitty." Using supplementary material that is interesting and worthwhile is an uncommon practice in high school classrooms. When your students study Sandburg or Frost, why not read to the students in your experimental classes a few poems that aren't available in the textbook?

B. Control

The students had been asked to write five sentences illustrating the use of active voice and five sentences illustrating the use of passive voice. Two students wrote active-voice sentences on the blackboard and two other students wrote passive-voice sentences on the board. The sentences were discussed, and the teacher then wrote additional sentences on the board illustrating active and passive voice.

Next, transitive and intransitive verbs were defined and illustrated by students. The same procedure was followed with intransitive linking verbs. The various uses of nouns in sentences were listed on the blackboard. Some time was spent in discussing the use of nouns in apposition.

Assignment: Select twelve words from a list in the textbook and write sentences using the words as nouns and also as some other part of speech. Also, write three sentences illustrating the use of words in apposition.

B. Experimental

The class had been presenting a series of panels on "Prejudice." Today a panel of students discussed "Are People in the United States Prejudiced Against People in Foreign Countries and Their Ideas?" Another panel discussed "The Effects of Prejudice Against Colored People in the South." The following questions were among those raised and discussed by the panel and other members of the class:

1. Do you believe a foreigner should have the same rights in America as an American?

2. Do you believe Americans are prejudiced against "foreign" ideas?

3. What is your attitude toward the Germans, Russians, and Japanese?

4. How long should a foreigner be in this country before he becomes a citizen?

5. How would you feel about a Jewish person moving next to you? a Catholic? a Negro?

Was there an assignment for the next day?

Comment

It seems to me that students should exercise as much care in organizing their contributions to a panel discussion as they do in writing a theme. Most of the brief talks made by panel members lacked organization. Furthermore, most of the statements made by the panel members were unsupported generalizations. It seems to me that unsupported assumptions made by students should be challenged by other students or the teacher. An educated person is one who can present evidence to support the assumptions he makes. The teacher called the attention of the panel members to their failure to explain how prejudices of various kinds originate.

The teacher is making a serious effort to maintain experimental conditions.

C. Control

The spelling lesson consisted of a list of twenty-five words taken from a textbook. The teacher and students then spent the next few minutes in discussing the textbook material on verbs. An assignment involving spotting the simple verb in a twelve-sentence exercise in the textbook was completed. The exercises were exchanged and checked by the students and teacher.

Assignment: Complete two textbook exercises on verbs.

C. Experimental

The teacher opened the class session with, "If you have your themes recopied and ready to hand in, do some writing in your journal." Students had reacted in writing to an article, "Our Home Education for John," in the December, 1959, *Reader's Digest.*

A list of seventy most frequently misspelled words was handed to the students with the admonition that they master it. The teacher explained to me that instead of repeating the formal spelling assignment that he used in his control class, he had asked the students in his experimental class to assume reponsibility for mastering the words in their individual lists (made up of words misspelled in themes and the words in the list of seventy most frequently misspelled words which they are unable to spell).

The students were curious when the teacher confronted them with a box. He told them that they would reach into the box without looking and pick from the box a slip of paper listing a theme topic. He explained that they had been writing themes on their reading, etc., but that they had not had the opportunity to use their imagination. Here are a few of the theme topics that appeared on the slips the students picked from the box: "The Day the Ivory Sank," "How to Build a Better Mousetrap," "What to Do When You Have a Tiger by the Tail," "Why I Admire Harry Truman," "How to Make a Hole-in-One," "How to Raise Twins," and "Life of a Major Leaguer." The teacher spent the remainder of the period in helping individual students plan and write their themes.

Comment

The teacher does an excellent job of maintaining experimental conditions, and he also does an exceptionally fine job during the supervised study part of the period. After the students had picked a theme topic from the box, they began working on it immediately; and there wasn't a single student who avoided the assignment by daydreaming or gossiping with other students. I believe the teacher's success in supervising study can be attributed to the fact that he is skillful in helping students quickly; he gets around to five or six students in just a few minutes.

D. Control

The students gave two-minute talks designed to persuade the audience to take the side of the speaker on a controversial issue.

D. Experimental

Two talks about five minutes in length were given by two boys—one talk on "Oil Paintings," the other on "Weeds." The student audience had been asked to take notes on the two speeches. After the talks were completed and evaluated, the teacher announced that the final speech of the series would be given the next day.

The assignment: Students were asked to organize their notes on the various speeches that had been given over a period of several days and then write a two-page composition related to one of the speeches. They were given the remainder of the period, about twenty minutes, to begin planning the composition.

Comment

The two talks that were given showed evidence of organization, but they lost some of their effectiveness because the speakers relied too heavily on notes they had taken from various sources. One had the feeling that they were merely repeating what they had read in books and magazines. These weaknesses were brought out in the evaluation.

I have noticed that on the four occasions I have observed this teacher's supervised study periods, the students have made very poor use of their time. Some of them study shorthand, some gossip, some work puzzles, and some leave the room. It seems to me that in the experimental class the teacher might try to make his assignments very specific and then circulate about the room to make certain the students are working on them.

E. Control

While the teacher entered the English grades on the students' report cards, the students read quietly at their seats Frost's "Stopping by Woods on a Snowy Evening," "Mending Wall," and "The Road Not Taken." When the report cards had been returned to the students, the students and teacher discussed "Mending Wall." The teacher explained the New England custom of building stone fences and then asked and discussed the following questions with his students: "What was Frost saying? What does the wall stand for? What does the wall do?" The teacher also explained and asked questions about various lines in the poem and showed the relationship between the main idea in the poem and prejudices of all kinds. In introducing "The Road Not Taken," the teacher brought out that life is a series of decisions. He then asked, "Why did he take the less-traveled road? Did he choose the easier of the two paths?"

E. Experimental

While the teacher recorded the English grades on the students' report cards, the students wrote in their journals. When the grades had been entered, the students and teacher discussed Masters' poem "John Horace Burleson," an account of a would-be writer who married a banker's daughter and never got around to writing the great American novel. John Horace Burleson regrets having been sidetracked and concludes that material success is a poor substitute for success as a writer. Prior to discussing "John Horace Burleson," the students had been asked to react in writing to the following questions: "What should one or shouldn't one do in one's own life? What does the poem suggest to you about your own life?" When the poem had been read aloud, the following questions were discussed: "What did Burleson do? Why did he go to

Chicago? Was he a successful man?" After the discussion had been completed the teacher concluded: "Use what you have. Work for what you want. If you have a dream and the ability and ambition to go along with it, try to realize it."

The remainder of the period was spent in discussing "George Gray," a man who feels that he missed the good life because he was afraid to take chances. The teacher asked whether the students believed that Masters approved of George Gray's behavior.

Was there an assignment for the next day?

Comment

It might have been interesting (in the experimental class) to compare "George Gray" with Sandburg's "Mamie." Also, in discussing short poems such as "George Gray" and "John Horace Burleson," one might ask students to state the theme of the poem in one sentence. The teacher did well, it seems to me, in trying to relate the ideas in the poems to the students' lives, an approach that is seldom used by English teachers. The teacher might try to develop in students the ability to ask good questions rather than try to provide all the questions himself.

F. Control

Most of the period was spent in discussing Evelyn Waugh's "The Man Who Liked Dickens." Students began the period by discussing the following questions which had been given to them the preceding day: "Why do people like plays? Why are there so many stagestruck people? Why does the life of an actor seem glamorous? How do radio and television plays differ? How do stage and movie plays differ?" Students volunteered for parts in "The Man Who Liked Dickens" and then read their parts for a while. Questions such as "Why did the hero of the story like Dickens?" and "Was Mr. McMaster a normal person as far as mentality is concerned?" were discussed. During the last twenty minutes the teacher entered grades on the students' grade cards while the students worked on the following assignment: Write out the answers to the first four essay-type questions listed at the end of the play.

F. Experimental

The teacher opened the period with, "Look over the Teen Age Book Club selections for December and January. Let Ray know today or tomorrow what you want to order."

In discussing the drama unit next on the schedule, the teacher made a number of suggestions:

1. Think about some outside project. You might choose to read plays in addition to those in the textbook.

2. There are a number of volumes of plays on my desk that you may use.

Also, *Theatre Arts Magazine* has a complete play each month—"Sunrise at Campobello" in the November issue. The *Indianapolis Star* also carries a list of plays.

3. You may give written or oral reports on the plays you read. Reports should include an evaluation as well as a summary.

4. Plan to report on at least three plays.

5. In your evaluation, what would you look for in addition to enjoyment? Does the subject matter appeal to you? Is the action interesting? Are the characters realistic and natural? Is the theme interesting? In musicals, is the music effective?

6. Instead of reporting on published plays, you might make a list of top dramas on TV. Be sure to defend the selections in your list.

7. Some of you might want to read about Cornell, Hayes, the Barrymores, Lawrence, Evans, Lunt. You might write a sketch of one.

8. You might want to convert a short story into a play.

9. Here is the project of a boy who found advertisements that illustrated the titles of Shakespeare's plays. (The teacher showed his class parts of the boy's project.)

As I understood it, all of the students were to report on three plays; and they were also encouraged to complete one other project that appealed to them.

A student read aloud the material in the textbook introducing Evelyn Waugh's "The Man Who Liked Dickens." The teacher then said to the students, "As you read, determine when you first realize that McMaster had no sympathy toward his fellow men. Also decide which part you would like to read aloud in class. Practice reading the lines aloud."

The teacher began entering grades on report cards while the students worked on "The Man Who Liked Dickens" assignment.

Comment

This teacher uses a lot of imagination in planning his work. His students are always interested in what goes on in the classroom and seem to be enthusiastic about the work that is assigned. Both the control class and experimental class are taught effectively. To vary the procedure in the experimental class, he might have suggested to the students that the next few weeks would be spent on the drama and that he would like to have them get together in groups of four or five to develop a list of interesting and worthwhile projects for such a unit. I should point out that this teacher, unlike most teachers, does as a rule give his students quite a few choices, which is very good.

One of my student teachers once developed a very interesting project in a drama class. He had his students "produce" scenes from six or seven plays that were running on Broadway at the time.

G. Control

During the first half of the period the students and teacher discussed the new regulations concerning school dress that had just been put into effect. During the remainder of the period the material introducing George and Helen Papashvily's "The First Day" was read aloud by the teacher. The students then read the story aloud and discussed it.

G. Experimental

The teacher asked his students to suggest qualities that were responsible for the success of men like Andrew Carnegie. The students suggested the following qualities, which were written on the blackboard by the teacher: desire and drive, faith in self, ability, enthusiasm, extra effort, honesty, sincerity, punctuality, foresight, loyalty, and courtesy. Some of the foregoing qualities were then illustrated by the students and teacher. The teacher then asked, "How did the foregoing fit Andrew Carnegie?" He also asked to what degree the qualities were reflected in the lives of Rockwall in O. Henry's "Mammon and the Archer," John Brown, Abraham Lincoln, and Marian Anderson. The students didn't do very well in answering the questions.

Assignment: Write a paragraph on one of the following topics: "What Does It Take to Achieve a Place in Society?" "What Is Your Idea of a Successful Man?" "Is a Self-Made Man Necessarily a Successful Man?" "Are Modern Businessmen Usually Self-Made Men?"

Comment

It seems to me that it is very difficult for anyone to demonstrate how a list of qualities—ability, honesty, sincerity, loyalty, etc.—are personified in the lives of outstanding Americans. Perhaps the responses would have been better had the teacher asked, "How do you account for Carnegie's success?" and "Would such qualities insure success today? Defend your answer."

I think the topics ("What Is Your Idea of a Successful Man?" "Is a Self-Made Man Necessarily a Successful Man?") on which the students were to write a paragraph are excellent.

One might ask an exceptionally good class to point up the differences, if any, between a successful life and a good life. For example, did Lucinda Matlock (Masters) and Fiddler Jones (Masters) live successful lives even though they were obscure people? Many poets from Laotzu (604–531 B.C.) to W. H. Auden have attempted to define the happy life. It might be interesting and worthwhile to study a series of poems that give counsel on the happy life.

H. Control

The students had been asked to diagram ten sentences that illustrated the use of the gerund. Students placed their diagrams of the ten sentences on the board. These sentences were then checked by the class to see whether they had been diagramed correctly. The following questions were discussed by the teacher and students: "What are the qualities of a gerund? What are its uses? What is the recognizable feature of a gerund that will enable you to recognize it? What are some of its verbal qualities?" The students next identified gerunds and participles in ten textbook sentences.

Assignment: There are twenty words in the textbook ending in *ing*. Select any ten, and use each one in a sentence as a gerund and as a participle. The students had ten minutes left to get started on the assignment. The teacher helped individual students get under way.

H. Experimental

The students had read a *Reader's Digest* article, "Africa's Amazing Treetop Hotel." After a brief discussion of the article, the teacher and students devoted most of the hour in pointing out and discussing the many figures of speech in the article. Students were then asked to write a brief sketch using figurative language. The students spent the last fifteen minutes of the period in organizing and writing the sketch.

Comment

The students showed a great deal of interest in "Africa's Amazing Treetop Hotel" and did a good job of pointing out figures of speech used by the author of the article. It seems to me that in the experimental classes we might help students develop an understanding of the effective use of simile, metaphor, personification, etc., as we have them read poems, short stories, essays, etc. An exercise that might prove useful is to place paragraphs written by students on the board and then analyze them to see how effectively or ineffectively students made use of figures of speech. It seems to me that it is much better to teach figures of speech as a part of the analysis of student and other writing than to devote an occasional period or several periods to an emphasis on figures of speech. In my opinion, this teacher is doing a fine job of maintaining experimental conditions.

I. Control

The teacher and students discussed and illustrated on the blackboard the various uses of the comma. The students were then given a list of twenty-five sentences (taken from their themes) and asked to punctuate them correctly. After the punctuation exercise was completed, students began developing a paragraph growing out of an analysis of one of the following words: *trophy, prevaricate*, etc.

I. Experimental

The students and teacher discussed the various uses of the comma that were illustrated on the blackboard. Students were asked to be aware of the punctuation in a story read aloud by a student. The teacher then dictated a few sentences from the story the student had read and asked his students to punctuate them.

Comment

It seems to me that there wasn't much difference in content and methods between the control and experimental classes. In my opinion, it would be a good idea to base instruction in punctuation in the experimental classes almost entirely on the writings of students. The story-reading technique used in the experimental class seems to be an unusual approach to punctuation. It might work to a degree if students were fully aware of what they were supposed to do. In the approach described above, the student read straight through the story, and that was it. Perhaps the teacher might have stopped the reader occasionally and asked the class to provide punctuation for the last two or three sentences that were read. How many of you have tried this method? What do you think were the results?

J. Control

The first fifteen minutes of the period were spent in analyzing compound sentences that students had written on the board. The remainder of the period was devoted to explaining and getting under way with the following assignment: "Between now and tomorrow write a Christmas story, poem, or editorial. The best one (selected by members of the class) will be published in the next issue of the ——, the school paper. Avoid trite material."

J. Experimental

Students were asked by the teacher to have ready by the next day a story, poem, or editorial for the next issue of the ——, the school paper. He asked those who would like to discuss possible approaches to the assignment with others to get together in groups of four or five; those who would rather work alone were given that opportunity. After ten or fifteen minutes of discussion in groups, each student began working on the topic he had chosen to develop.

Comment

It seems to me that because of the immediate need of material for the ——, not much difference in content and methods could be expected. I wonder, though, why the assignment wasn't made a week or two earlier. It seems to me that most of us would like a little more time if we were asked to complete such an assignment.

K. Control

The students were given a fifteen-word spelling test taken from a textbook. The papers were exchanged, graded, and passed in to the teacher. The students then spent the remainder of the period in completing the following objective test:

_____ 1. makes a statement	a.	stove
_____ 2. happiness	b.	compound personal pronoun
_____ 3. Robert	c.	could have done
_____ 4. indefinite pronoun	d.	this, these
_____ 5. proper adjective	e.	an, the, a
_____ 6. interrogative pronouns	f.	declarative sentence
_____ 7. verb phrase	g.	name of person, place, or thing
_____ 8. common noun	h.	imperative sentence
_____ 9. shows action or state of being	i.	personal pronoun
_____10. not	j.	a preposition
_____11. adverb	k.	abstract noun
_____12. adjective	l.	who, whose, whom, which, what
_____13. pronoun	m.	stands for a noun
_____14. them	n.	verb
_____15. adjectives	o.	Canadian
_____16. asks a question	p.	committee
_____17. concrete noun	q.	exclamatory
_____18. auxiliary verbs	r.	interrogative
_____19. myself	s.	answers the questions "How? When? Where?"
_____20. shows strong or sudden feeling	t.	who, whose, whom, which, that
_____21. of	u.	an adverb
_____22. demonstrative pronouns	v.	answers the questions "Which one? What kind of? How many?"
_____23. relative pronouns	w.	shall, will, should, would
_____24. gives a command	x.	everybody
_____25. noun	y.	proper noun
_____26. collective noun	z.	answer not given

COMPLETION

27. A _____ _____ expresses one main idea.
28. A _____ _____ expresses two or more main ideas.
29. A _____ _____ expresses one main idea (called a _____ clause) and at least one subordinate idea (called a _____ clause).
30. An adjective modifies a _____ and a _____.
31. Any word that may be used alone as a pronoun becomes a _____ _____ when it modifies a noun.
32. An adverb modifies a _____, _____ and _____.
33. A_____ always has an object; if it doesn't it is a _____ instead.
34. A subject and a predicate are the two essential parts of a _____.

A large crowd had been watching the strange cloud.
He gave his old shoes to Goodwill.
American freedom cannot be taken away without a war.
Each of us is carrying a raincoat.
I know that I shall have an enjoyable visit.
Who has been playing with my small car?
Do you know who designed that dress?

Assignment: Students were told there would be no assignment over the week end.

K. Experimental

Students took a spelling test over fifteen words based on words they had misspelled in their compositions, exchanged papers, graded the papers, and passed them to the teacher. The students spent the remainder of the period in taking the same objective test that was given to the students in the control class.

Assignment: Students were told there would be no assignment over the week end.

Comment

While the students were taking the objective test, I talked with the teacher, who told me that he had used the inductive approach in teaching the contents of the test to his experimental students and the traditional approach in his control class.

It seems to me that the teacher might experiment with the following approaches: First, in his experimental class he might have each student keep a list of words the student has misspelled in his compositions; he might also give each student a list of the seventy most commonly misspelled words. Then, instead of spending fifteen or twenty minutes a week giving tests in spelling, he might on Friday (spelling day), or some other day, spend five or ten minutes in checking individual students to see whether they know how to spell certain words on their lists. While he is doing this checking, the students could be working on some other assignment. Students should be allowed to remove from their individual lists the words the teacher feels they have learned how to spell. Second, instead of giving a highly formal objective test over grammatical terminology, he might in the experimental class limit the testing to a performance test consisting of a written composition. He might occasionally use somewhat more formal tests similar to those found in the last chapter of Pooley's Teaching English Grammar.

L. Control

The teacher explained to his students that tomorrow and the next day would be spent in writing a theme growing out of their study of excerpts from Emerson's essays on "Friendship," "Self-Reliance," and "Compensation."

The teacher called the attention of the students to the following lines from Emerson: "Sincerity is the highest compliment you can pay. The world can never be learned by learning its details. Finish each day before you begin the next, and interpose a solid wall of sleep between the two." The teacher then made the comment that one can pick almost any line of Emerson and do a great deal of thinking about it, that Emerson and Thoreau are men that provoke thought; their work has to be studied and not read quickly.

The teacher and his students then discussed the following questions based on excerpts from the three essays:

1. "Friendship": Do you have a friend equal to Emerson's definition? Aren't *ego* and *humility* incompatible? Do you have a friend (Catholic, Jew, Baptist, etc.) with whom you can be completely sincere? Can you talk to your parents about any subject? Can you be perfectly honest at home?

2. "Compensation": Does the theory apply to the invalid? Does it apply to the poor, destitute Chinese?

The students responded very well to the questions that were asked, and they raised some of their own. From time to time the teacher would suggest, "Maybe you would like to write your theme on that topic."

L. Experimental

The students were given the same writing assignment that was given to students in the control class.

Students in the first two rows were asked to spend ten minutes in writing a paragraph in support of Emerson's ideas on friendship. The students in the last two rows were asked to write a brief paragraph opposing Emerson's ideas on friendship. After the students had completed the writing assignment, the students and teacher spent about twenty minutes in discussing the following statements: "I don't want a friend" and "Emerson's idea of *friend* is not possible—no one can live up to it."

A similar ten-minute writing assignment was made on "Compensation." The students in the first two rows were asked to explain why they rejected Emerson's ideas in "Compensation," and the students in the last two rows were asked to support the ideas. After the writing assignment had been completed, the teacher asked, "Why shouldn't I go along with this idea of compensation? Convince me." The discussion was a good one with many students participating. One student did a very good job of explaining why she did not agree with "Every evil has its good."

Comment

This teacher always does an excellent job of teaching in both classes, but I always come out feeling that perhaps his control class is doing even better work than the experimental class. I have observed this teacher's student teachers over many years, and I never saw the excellent content and methods he uses used by his student teachers; their work almost always seemed much more formal.

I think we might pay special attention to the way the teacher related the questions on "Friendship" to the lives of the students. He didn't place the emphasis on what Emerson said, but on how his students applied what Emerson said to their own lives. This is difficult to do, but it is certainly worth trying in your experimental classes.

It seems to me that it would be much better for anthologists to include one complete essay from Emerson than four or five brief excerpts from various essays. I suppose it would be difficult to do; but, whenever possible, we might in our experimental classes make available to students a complete essay from our leading essayists. If no other way is possible, the teacher might occasionally read a complete essay to his students.

Another approach that one might use in the experimental classes is to have students debate the controversial ideas presented by an author such as Emerson. An excellent debate could certainly be developed from the ideas in Emerson's "Compensation," ideas that philosophers have argued about for thousands of years. Of course, some writers on the teaching of English have insisted that debates are not worth the time devoted to them; but it seems quite obvious that public debates are going on all the time in the areas of politics, economics, religion, etc. In using the debate approach, one can get the participation of all of the students if one limits the speeches to a few minutes each and if one has a number of debating teams rather than one.

M. Control

After the students' compositions were returned to them, the teacher spent the next ten minutes explaining to individual students some of the comments he had written on the papers. The students were asked to look up what the textbook had to say about the comments (sentence variation, off the subject, etc.) and report back to the class the next day.

Most of the period was spent in discussing précis writing and in analyzing Knute Rockne's "Qualities That Make or Mar Success," a speech in *Building Better English* that was given many years ago to the salesmen of the Studebaker Corporation. The students dictated the main points in Rockne's speech to the teacher who wrote them on the board. The students were then asked to rewrite a one-paragraph précis they had apparently written the day before. The teacher spent the remainder of the period helping individual students with their assignment.

M. Experimental

Folders containing all of the papers written by the students during the first semester were distributed by a student. Next, TAB News was distributed to students; they spent a few minutes scanning the new offerings.

The remainder of the period was spent in trying to write a précis of one of a list of paragraphs that had been dittoed.

Comment

It seems to me that there weren't any fundamental differences in the content and methods in the two classes. Instead of setting aside a week or so to do précis writing, we might try in our experimental classes to teach this skill as students read, write, and speak.

N. Control

The students and teacher checked an exercise in the workbook on the use of adjectives. The teacher then entered the students' English grades on their report cards.

N. Experimental

The teacher spent fifteen minutes dictating a ninety-five word passage from *Scholastic*. The students were then asked to supply the punctuation and underline the adjectives.

While the students completed the assignment, the teacher entered the students' grades on their report cards. Some of the students finished the assignment in five minutes. Was there another assignment for them to work on?

After the report cards were distributed, students were encouraged to come in after school to talk about their grades.

The teacher suggested to students that they might be thinking of sentences containing prepositional phrases. Some of the sentences would be placed on the board tomorrow.

The teacher stated that two days hence words like *shoes, road, airplane,* etc., would be placed on the blackboard and the students would be asked to write a paragraph on each word; in writing the paragraph students were to use words more specific than the words listed on the board. I did not get a clear understanding of this assignment.

The students next exchanged the passage from *Scholastic* which they had punctuated, and the teacher and students checked it. The teacher told his students that they would talk about the papers in class the next day.

Comment

It seems to me that a number of approaches could have been substituted for the ones used in the experimental class. Fifteen minutes could have been saved by having the passage from Scholastic *duplicated (sans punctuation) and distributed to the students. Better still, the teacher might have based instruction in punctuation on the compositions students are writing and have written. Furthermore, it seems to me that the effective use of adjectives can be taught more successfully if examples of the effective and ineffective use of adjectives in students' themes are placed on the board and analyzed. The same approach could have been used in the next day's assignment: "Write sentences containing prepositional phrases." Do adults ever try to improve their writing by writing a series of sentences containing prepositional phrases? In my opinion, the content and methods exemplified in the experimental class might well be confined to the control class.*

ASSUMPTIONS ABOUT OBSERVATION REPORT NO. 3

Explain why you agree or disagree, wholly or in part, with the following assumptions related to *Observation Report No. 3*:

1. Variations in the teachers' aims are revealed in the kinds of tests they administered.

2. Some of the teachers demonstrated originality and imagination in selecting content and methods.

3. A few of the teachers provided effectively for individual differences among students.

4. The content and methods used in some classes were criticized in this book.

5. Some of the teachers' discussion topics on literature tied in with students' own experiences.

6. The evaluations, stated or implied, under *Comment* are fair.

7. Instruction in the experimental classes was superior to instruction in the control classes.

Two Main Roads Diverge in the Classroom

THE PERFORMANCE ROAD—	THE WORKBOOK-HANDBOOK ROAD—
paved with	*paved with*
performance tests in reading, writing, speaking, and listening to discover where students are academically and	punctuation marks, spelling lists, vocabulary lists, parts of speech, phrases,
guided experiences in reading, writing, speaking, and listening, with grammar and usage instruction related to speech and writing—	clauses, participles, gerunds, simple sentences, compound sentences, complex sentences, and diagraming—
LEADS TO SKILL IN READING, WRITING, SPEAKING, AND LISTENING.	LEADS TO A DEAD END.

APPENDIX 13

To a Skylark

PERCY BYSSHE SHELLEY

Hail to thee, blithe spirit!
Bird thou never wert—
That from heaven or near it
Pourest thy full heart
In profuse strains of unpremeditated art.

Higher still and higher
From the earth thou springest,
Like a cloud of fire;
The blue deep thou wingest,
And singing still dost soar, and soaring ever singest.

In the golden light'ning
Of the sunken sun,
O'er which clouds are bright'ning,
Thou dost float and run,
Like an unbodied joy whose race is just begun.

The pale purple even
Melts around thy flight;
Like a star of heaven,
In the broad daylight
Thou art unseen, but yet I hear thy shrill delight—

Keen as are the arrows
Of that silver sphere
Whose intense lamp narrows
In the white dawn clear,
Until we hardly see, we feel that it is there.

All the earth and air
　　With thy voice is loud,
　　As, when night is bare,
　　From one lonely cloud
The moon rains out her beams, and heaven is overflow'd.

What thou art we know not;
　　What is most like thee?
　　From rainbow clouds there flow not
　　Drops so bright to see,
As from thy presence showers a rain of melody:—

Like a poet hidden
　　In the light of thought,
　　Singing hymns unbidden,
　　Till the world is wrought
To sympathy with hopes and fears it heeded not:

Like a high-born maiden
　　In a palace tower,
　　Soothing her love-laden
　　Soul in secret hour
With music sweet as love, which overflows her bower:

Like a glow-worm golden
　　In a dell of dew,
　　Scattering unbeholden
　　Its aerial hue
Among the flowers and grass which screen it from the view:

Like a rose embower'd
　　In its own green leaves,
　　By warm winds deflower'd,
　　Till the scent it gives
Makes faint with too much sweet these heavy-wingèd thieves.

Sound of vernal showers
　　On the twinkling grass,
　　Rain-awaken'd flowers—
　　All that ever was
Joyous and clear and fresh—thy music doth surpass.

Teach us, sprite or bird,
　　What sweet thoughts are thine:
　　I have never heard
　　Praise of love or wine
That panted forth a flood of rapture so divine.

Chorus hymeneal,
Or triumphal chant,
Match'd with thine would be all
But an empty vaunt—
A thing wherein we feel there is some hidden want.

What objects are the fountains
Of thy happy strain
What fields, or waves, or mountains?
What shapes of sky or plain?
What love of thine own kind? what ignorance of pain?

With thy clear keen joyance
Languor cannot be:
Shadow of annoyance
Never came near thee:
Thou lovest, but ne'er knew love's sad satiety.

Waking or asleep,
Thou of death must deem
Things more true and deep
Than we mortals dream,
Or how could thy notes flow in such a crystal stream?

We look before and after,
And pine for what is not:
Our sincerest laughter
With some pain is fraught;
Our sweetest songs are those that tell of saddest thought.

Yet, if we could scorn
Hate and pride and fear,
If we were things born
Not to shed a tear,
I know not how thy joy we ever should come near.

Better than all measures
Of delightful sound,
Better than all treasures
That in books are found,
Thy skill to poet were, thou scorner of the ground!

Teach me half the gladness
That thy brain must know;
Such harmonious madness
From my lips would flow,
The world should listen then, as I am listening now.

When Lilacs Last in the Dooryard Bloom'd

WALT WHITMAN

1

When lilacs last in the dooryard bloom'd,
And the great star early droop'd in the western sky in the night,
I mourn'd, and yet shall mourn with ever-returning spring.

Ever-returning spring, trinity sure to me you bring,
Lilac blooming perennial and drooping star in the west,
And thought of him I love.

2

O powerful western fallen star!
O shades of night—O moody, tearful night!
O great star disappear'd—O the black murk that hides the star!
O cruel hands that hold me powerless—O helpless soul of me!
O harsh surrounding cloud that will not free my soul.

3

In the dooryard fronting an old farmhouse near the white-wash'd palings,
Stands the lilac-bush tall-growing with heart-shaped leaves of rich green,
With many a pointed blossom rising delicate, with the perfume strong I love,
With every leaf a miracle—and from this bush in the dooryard,
With delicate-color'd blossoms and heart-shaped leaves of rich green,
A sprig with its flower I break.

4

In the swamp in secluded recesses,
A shy and hidden bird is warbling a song.

Solitary the thrush,
The hermit withdrawn to himself, avoiding the settlements,
Sings by himself a song.

Song of the bleeding throat,
Death's outlet song of life, (for well dear brother I know,
If thou wast not granted to sing thou would'st surely die.)

Over the breast of the spring, the land, amid cities,
Amid lanes and through old woods, where lately the violets peep'd from the
    ground, spotting the gray debris,
Amid the grass in the fields each side of the lanes, passing the endless grass,
Passing the yellow-spear'd wheat, every grain from its shroud in the dark-
    brown fields uprisen,
Passing the apple-tree blows of white and pink in the orchards,
Carrying a corpse to where it shall rest in the grave,
Night and day journeys a coffin.

6

Coffin that passes through lanes and streets,
Through day and night with the great cloud darkening the land,
With the pomp of the inloop'd flags with the cities draped in black,
With the show of the States themselves as of crape-veil'd women standing,
With processions long and winding and the flambeaus of the night,
With the countless torches lit, with the silent sea of faces and the unbared
    heads,
With the waiting depot, the arriving coffin, and the somber faces,
With dirges through the night, with the thousand voices rising strong and
    solemn,
With all the mournful voices of the dirges pour'd around the coffin,
The dim-lit churches and the shuddering organs—where amid these you
    journey,
With the tolling tolling bells' perpetual clang,
Here, coffin that slowly passes,
I give you my sprig of lilac.

7

(Nor for you, for one alone,
Blossoms and branches green to coffins all I bring,
For fresh as the morning, thus would I chant a song for you O sane and sacred
    death.

WHEN LILACS LAST IN THE DOORYARD BLOOM'D   329

All over bouquets of roses,
O death, I cover you over with roses and early lilies,
But mostly and now the lilac that blooms the first,
Copious I break, I break the sprigs from the bushes,
With loaded arms I come, pouring for you,
For you and the coffins all of you O death.)

8

O western orb sailing the heaven,
Now I know what you must have meant as a month since I walk'd,
As I walk'd in silence the transparent shadowy night,
As I saw you had something to tell as you bent to me night after night,
As you droop'd from the sky low down as if to my side, (while the other stars
    all look'd on,)
As we wander'd together the solemn night, (for something I know not what
    kept me from sleep,)
As the night advanced, and I saw on the rim of the west how full you were
    of woe,
As I stood on the rising ground in the breeze in the cool transparent night,
As I watch'd where you pass'd and was lost in the netherward black of
    the night,
As my soul in its trouble dissatisfied sank, as where you sad orb,
Concluded, dropt in the night, and was gone.

9

Sing on there in the swamp,
O singer bashful and tender, I hear your notes, I hear your call,
I hear, I come presently, I understand you,
But a moment I linger, for the lustrous star has detain'd me,
The star my departing comrade holds and detains me.

10

O how shall I warble myself for the dead one there I loved?
And how shall I deck my song for the large sweet soul that has gone?
And what shall my perfume be for the grave of him I love?

Sea-winds blown from east and west,
Blown from the Eastern sea and blown from the Western sea, till there on the
    prairies meeting,
These and with these and the breath of my chant,
I'll perfume the grave of him I love.

11

O what shall I hang on the chamber walls?
And what shall the pictures be that I hang on the walls,
To adorn the burial-house of him I love?

Pictures of growing spring and farms and homes,
With the Fourth-month eve at sundown, and the gray smoke lucid and bright,
With floods of the yellow gold of the gorgeous, indolent, sinking sun, burning, expanding the air,
With the fresh sweet herbage under foot, and the pale green leaves of the trees prolific,
In the distance the flowing glaze, the breast of the river, with a wind-dapple here and there,
With ranging hills on the banks, with many a line against the sky, and shadows,
And the city at hand with dwellings so dense, and stacks of chimneys,
And all the scenes of life and the workshops, and the workmen homeward returning.

12

Lo, body and soul—this land,
My own Manhattan with spires, and the sparkling and hurrying tides, and the ships,
The varied and ample land, the South and the North in the light, Ohio's shores and flashing Missouri,
And ever the far-spreading prairies cover'd with grass and corn.

Lo, the most excellent sun so calm and haughty,
The violet and purple morn with just-felt breezes,
The gentle soft-born measureless light,
The miracle spreading bathing all, the fulfill'd noon,
The coming eve delicious, the welcome night and the stars,
Over my cities shining all, enveloping man and land.

13

Sing on, sing on you gray-brown bird,
Sing from the swamps, the recesses, pour your chant from the bushes,
Limitless out of the dusk, out of the cedars and pines.

Sing on dearest brother, warble your reedy song,
Loud human song, with voice of uttermost woe.

O liquid and free and tender!
O wild and loose to my soul—O wondrous singer!
You only I hear—yet the star holds me, (but will soon depart,)
Yet the lilac with mastering odor holds me.

14

Now while I sat in the day and look'd forth,
In the close of the day with its light and the fields of spring, and the farmers preparing their crops,
In the large unconscious scenery of my land with its lakes and forests,
In the heavenly aerial beauty, (after the perturb'd winds and the storms,)

Under the arching heavens of the afternoon swift passing, and the voices of
    children and women,
The many-moving sea-tides, and I saw the ships how they sail'd,
And the summer approaching with richness, and the fields all busy with labor,
And the infinite separate houses, how they all went on, each with its meals and
    minutia of daily usages,
And the streets how their throbbings throbb'd, and the cities pent—lo, then
    and there,
Falling upon them all and among them all, enveloping me with the rest,
Appear'd the cloud, appear'd the long black trail,
And I knew death, its thought, and the sacred knowledge of death.

Then with the knowledge of death as walking one side of me,
And the thought of death close-walking the other side of me,
And I in the middle as with companions, and as holding the hands of com-
    panions,
I fled forth to the hiding receiving night that talks not,
Down to the shores of the water, the path by the swamp in the dimness,
To the solemn shadowy cedars and ghostly pines so still.

And the singer so shy to the rest receiv'd me,
The gray-brown bird I know receiv'd us comrades three,
And he sang the carol of death, and a verse for him I love.

From deep secluded recesses,
From the fragrant cedars and the ghostly pines so still,
Came the carol of the bird.

And the charm of the carol rapt me,
As I held as if by their hands my comrades in the night,
And the voice of my spirit tallied the song of the bird.

Come lovely and soothing death,
Undulate round the world, serenely arriving, arriving,
In the day, in the night, to all, to each,
Sooner or later delicate death.

Prais'd be the fathomless universe,
For life and joy, and for objects and knowledge curious,
And for love, sweet love—but praise! praise! praise!
For the sure-enwinding arms of cool-enfolding death.

Dark mother always gliding near with soft feet,
Have none chanted for thee a chant of fullest welcome?
Then I chant it for thee, I glorify thee above all,
I bring thee a song that when thou must indeed come, come unfalteringly.

Approach strong deliveress,
When it is so, when thou hast taken them I joyously sing the dead,
Lost in the loving floating ocean of thee,
Laved in the flood of thy bliss O death.

From me to thee glad serenades,
Dances for thee I propose saluting thee, adornments and feastings for thee,
And the sights of the open landscape and the high-spread sky are fitting,
And life and the fields, and the huge and thoughtful night.

The night in silence under many a star,
The ocean shore and the husky whispering wave whose voice I know,
And the soul turning to thee O vast and well-veil'd death,
And the body gratefully nestling close to thee.

Over the tree-tops I float thee a song,
Over the rising and sinking waves, over the myriad fields and the prairies wide,
Over the dense-pack'd cities all and the teeming wharves and ways,
I float this carol with joy, with joy to thee O death.

15

To the tally of my soul,
Loud and strong kept up the gray-brown bird,
With pure deliberate notes spreading filling the night.

Loud in the pines and cedars dim,
Clear in the freshness moist and the swamp-perfume,
And I with my comrades there in the night.

While my sight that was bound in my eyes unclosed,
As to long panoramas of visions.

And I saw askant the armies,
I saw as in noiseless dreams hundreds of battle-flags,
Borne through the smoke of the battles and pierc'd with missiles I saw them,
And carried hither and yon through the smoke, and torn and bloody,
And at last but a few shreds left on the staffs, (and all in silence,)
And the staffs all splinter'd and broken.

I saw battle-corpses, myriads of them,
And the white skeletons of young men, I saw them,
I saw the debris and debris of all the slain soldiers of the war,
But I saw they were not as was thought,
They themselves were fully at rest, they suffer'd not,
The living remain'd and suffer'd, the mother suffer'd,
And the wife and the child and the musing comrade suffer'd,
And the armies that remain'd suffer'd.

Passing the visions, passing the night,
Passing, unloosing the hold of my comrades' hands,
Passing the song of the hermit bird and the tallying song of my soul,
Victorious song, death's outlet song, yet varying ever-altering song,
As low and wailing, yet clear the notes, rising and falling, flooding the night,
Sadly sinking and fainting, as warning and warning, and yet again bursting
    with joy,
Covering the earth and filling the spread of the heaven,
As that powerful psalm in the night I heard from recesses,
Passing, I leave thee lilac with heart-shaped leaves,
I leave thee there in the door-yard, blooming, returning with spring.

I cease from my song for thee,
From my gaze on thee in the west, fronting the west, communing with thee,
O comrade lustrous with silver face in the night.

Yet each to keep and all, retrievements out of the night,
The song, the wondrous chant of the gray-brown bird,
And the tallying chant, the echo arous'd in my soul,
With the lustrous and drooping star with the countenance full of woe,
With the holders holding my hand nearing the call of the bird,
Comrades mine and I in the midst, and their memory ever to keep, for the
    dead I loved so well,
For the sweetest, wisest soul of all my days and lands—and this for his
    dear sake,
Lilac and star and bird twined with the chant of my soul,
There in the fragrant pines and the cedars dusk and dim.

The Prodigal Son

KING JAMES VERSION, LUKE 15: 11–32

A certain man had two sons: And the younger of them said to *his* father, Father, give me the portion of goods that falleth *to me*. And he divided unto them *his* living.

And not many days after the younger son gathered all together, and took his journey into a far country, and there wasted his substance with riotous living. And when he had spent all, there arose a mighty famine in that land; and he began to be in want. And he went and joined himself to a citizen of that country; and he sent him into his fields to feed swine. And he would fain have filled his belly with the husks that the swine did eat: and no man gave unto him.

And when he came to himself, he said, How many hired servants of my father's have bread enough and to spare, and I perish with hunger! I will arise and go to my father, and will say unto him, Father, I have sinned against heaven, and before thee, And am no more worthy to be called thy son: make me as one of thy hired servants.

And he arose, and came to his father.

But when he was yet a great way off, his father saw him, and had compassion, and ran, and fell on his neck, and kissed him. And the son said unto him, Father, I have sinned against heaven, and in thy sight, and am no more worthy to be called thy son.

But the father said to his servants, Bring forth the best robe, and put *it* on him; and put a ring on his hand, and shoes on *his* feet: And bring hither the fatted calf, and kill *it*; and let us eat, and be merry: For this my son was dead, and is alive again; he was lost, and is found. And they began to be merry.

Now his elder son was in the field: and as he came and drew nigh to the house, he heard musick and dancing. And he called one of the servants, and asked what these things meant. And he said unto him, Thy brother is come; and thy father hath killed the fatted calf, because he hath received him safe and sound.

And he was angry, and would not go in: therefore came his father out, and intreated him. And he answering said to *his* father, Lo, these many years do I serve thee, neither transgressed I at any time thy commandment: and yet thou never gavest me a kid, that I might make merry with my friends: But as soon as this thy son was come, which hath devoured thy living with harlots, thou hast killed for him the fatted calf.

And he said unto him, Son, thou art ever with me, and all that I have is thine. It was meet that we should make merry, and be glad: for this thy brother was dead, and is alive again; and was lost, and is found.

The Devil and Tom Walker

WASHINGTON IRVING

A few miles from Boston in Massachusetts, there is a deep inlet, winding several miles into the interior of the country from Charles Bay, and terminating in a thickly-wooded swamp or morass. On one side of this inlet is a beautiful dark grove; on the opposite side the land rises abruptly from the water's edge into a high ridge, on which grow a few scattered oaks of great age and immense size. Under one of these gigantic trees, according to old stories, there was a great amount of treasure buried by Kidd the pirate. The inlet allowed a facility to bring the money in a boat secretly and at night to the very foot of the hill; the elevation of the place permitted a good lookout to be kept that no one was at hand; while the remarkable trees formed good landmarks by which the place might easily be found again. The old stories add, moreover, that the devil presided at the hiding of the money, and took it under his guardianship; but this, it is well known, he always does with buried treasure, particularly when it has been ill-gotten. Be that as it may, Kidd never returned to recover his wealth; being shortly after seized at Boston, sent out to England, and there hanged for a pirate.

About the year 1727, just at the time that earthquakes were prevalent in New England, and shook many tall sinners down upon their knees, there lived near this place a meagre, miserly fellow, of the name of Tom Walker. He had a wife as miserly as himself: they were so miserly that they even conspired to cheat each other. Whatever the woman could lay hands on, she hid away; a hen could not cackle but she was on the alert to secure the new-laid egg. Her husband was continually prying about to detect her secret hoards, and many and fierce were the conflicts that took place about what ought to have been common property. They lived in a forlorn-looking house that stood alone, and had an air of starvation. A few straggling savin-trees, emblems of sterility, grew near it; no smoke ever curled from its chimney; no traveller stopped at its door. A miserable horse, whose ribs were as articulate as the bars of a gridiron, stalked about a field, where a thin carpet of moss, scarcely covering the ragged beds of puddingstone, tantalized and balked his hunger; and sometimes he would lean his head over the fence, look piteously at the passer-by, and seem to petition deliverance from this land of famine.

The house and its inmates had altogether a bad name. Tom's wife was a tall termagant, fierce of temper, loud of tongue, and strong of arm. Her voice was often heard in wordy warfare with her husband; and his face sometimes showed signs that their conflicts were not confined to words. No one ventured, however, to interfere between them. The lonely wayfarer shrunk within himself at the horrid clamor and clapper-clawing; eyed the den of discord askance; and hurried on his way, rejoicing, if a bachelor, in his celibacy.

One day that Tom Walker had been to a distant part of the neighborhood, he took what he considered a short cut homeward, through the swamp. Like most short cuts, it was an ill-chosen route. The swamp was thickly grown with great gloomy pines and hemlocks, some of them ninety feet high, which made it dark at noonday, and a retreat for all the owls of the neighborhood. It was full of pits and quagmires, partly covered with weeds and mosses, where the green surface often betrayed the traveller into a gulf of black, smothering mud; there were also dark and stagnant pools, the abodes of the tadpole, the bull-frog, and the watersnake; where the trunks of pines and hemlocks lay half-drowned, half-rotting, looking like alligators sleeping in the mire.

Tom had long been picking his way cautiously through this treacherous forest; stepping from tuft to tuft of rushes and roots, which afforded precarious footholds among deep sloughs; or pacing carefully, like a cat, along the prostrate trunks of trees; startled now and then by the sudden screaming of the bittern, or the quacking of a wild duck rising on the wing from some solitary pool. At length he arrived at a firm piece of ground, which ran out like a peninsula into the deep bosom of the swamp. It had been one of the strongholds of the Indians during their wars with the first colonists. Here they had thrown up a kind of fort, which they had looked upon as almost impregnable, and had used as a place of refuge for their squaws and children. Nothing remained of the old Indian fort but a few embankments, gradually sinking to the level of the surrounding earth, and already overgrown in part by oaks and other forest trees, the foliage of which formed a contrast to the dark pines and hemlocks of the swamp.

It was late in the dusk of evening when Tom Walker reached the old fort, and he paused there awhile to rest himself. Any one but he would have felt unwilling to linger in this lonely, melancholy place, for the common people had a bad opinion of it, from the stories handed down from the time of the Indian wars; when it was asserted that the savages held incantations here, and made sacrifices to the evil spirit.

Tom Walker, however, was not a man to be troubled with any fears of the kind. He reposed himself for some time on the trunk of a fallen hemlock, listening to the boding cry of the tree-toad, and delving with his walking-staff into a mound of black mould at his feet. As he turned up the soil unconsciously, his staff struck against something hard. He raked it out of the vegetable mould, and lo! a cloven skull, with an Indian tomahawk buried deep in it, lay before him. The rust on the weapon showed the time that had elapsed since this death-blow had been given. It was a dreary memento of the fierce struggle that had taken place in this last foothold of the Indian warriors.

"Humph!" said Tom Walker, as he gave it a kick to shake the dirt from it.

"Let that skull alone!" said a gruff voice. Tom lifted up his eyes, and beheld a great black man seated directly opposite him, on the stump of a tree. He was exceedingly surprised, having neither heard nor seen any one approach; and he was still more perplexed on observing, as well as the gathering gloom would permit, that the stranger was neither negro nor Indian. It is true he was dressed in a rude half Indian garb, and had a red belt or sash swathed round his body; but his face was neither black nor copper-color, but swarthy and dingy, and begrimed with soot, as if he had been accustomed to toil among fires and forges. He had a shock of coarse black hair, that stood out from his head in all directions, and bore an axe on his shoulder.

He scowled for a moment at Tom with a pair of great red eyes.

"What are you doing on my grounds?" said the black man, with a hoarse growling voice.

"Your grounds!" said Tom, with a sneer, "no more your grounds than mine; they belong to Deacon Peabody."

"Deacon Peabody be d_____d," said the stranger, "as I flatter myself he will be, if he does not look more to his own sins and less to those of his neighbors. Look yonder, and see how Deacon Peabody is faring."

Tom looked in the direction that the stranger pointed, and beheld one of the great trees, fair and flourishing without, but rotten at the core, and saw that it had been nearly hewn through, so that the first high wind was likely to blow it down. On the bark of the tree was scored the name of Deacon Peabody, an eminent man, who had waxed wealthy by driving shrewd bargains with the Indians. He now looked around, and found most of the tall trees marked with the name of some great man of the colony, and all more or less scored by the axe. The one on which he had been seated, and which had evidently just been hewn down, bore the name of Crowninshield; and he recollected a mighty rich man of that name, who made a vulgar display of wealth, which it was whispered he had acquired by buccaneering.

"He's just ready for burning!" said the black man, with a growl of triumph. "You see I am likely to have a good stock of firewood for winter."

"But what right have you," said Tom, "to cut down Deacon Peabody's timber?"

"The right of a prior claim," said the other. "This woodland belonged to me long before one of your white-faced race put foot upon the soil."

"And pray, who are you, if I may be so bold?" said Tom.

"Oh, I go by various names. I am the wild huntsman in some countries; the black miner in others. In this neighborhood I am known by the name of the black woodsman. I am he to whom the red men consecrated this spot, and in honor of whom they now and then roasted a white man, by way of sweet-smelling sacrifice. Since the red men have been exterminated by you white savages, I amuse myself by presiding at the persecutions of Quakers and Anabaptists; I am the great patron and prompter of slave-dealers, and the grand-master of the Salem witches."

"The upshot of all which is, that, if I mistake not," said Tom, sturdily, "you are he commonly called Old Scratch."

"The same, at your service!" replied the black man, with a half-civil nod.

Such was the opening of this interview, according to the old story; though it has almost too familiar an air to be credited. One would think that to meet with such a singular personage, in this wild, lonely place, would have shaken any man's nerves; but Tom was a hard-minded fellow, not easily daunted, and he had lived so long with a termagant wife, that he did not even fear the devil.

It is said that after this commencement they had a long and earnest conversation together, as Tom returned homeward. The black man told him of great sums of money buried by Kidd the pirate, under the oak-trees on the high ridge, not far from the morass. All these were under his command, and protected by his power, so that none could find them but such as propitiated his favor. These he offered to place within Tom Walker's reach, having conceived an especial kindness for him; but they were to be had only on certain conditions. What these conditions were may be easily surmised, though Tom never disclosed them publicly. They must have been very hard, for he required time to think of them, and he was not a man to stick at trifles when money was in view. When they had reached the edge of the swamp, the stranger paused. "What proof have I that all you have been telling me is true?" said Tom. "There's my signature," said the black man, pressing his finger on Tom's forehead. So saying, he turned off among the thickets of the swamp, and seemed, as Tom said, to go down, down, down, into the earth, until nothing but his head and shoulders could be seen, and so on, until he totally disappeared.

When Tom reached home, he found the black print of a finger burnt, as it were, into his forehead, which nothing could obliterate.

The first news his wife had to tell him was the sudden death of Absalom Crowninshield, the rich buccaneer. It was announced in the papers with the usual flourish, that "A great man had fallen in Israel."

Tom recollected the tree which his black friend had just hewn down, and which was ready for burning. "Let the freebooter roast," said Tom, "who cares!" He now felt convinced that all he had heard and seen was no illusion.

He was not prone to let his wife into his confidence; but as this was an uneasy secret, he willingly shared it with her. All her avarice was awakened at the mention of hidden gold, and she urged her husband to comply with the black man's terms, and secure what would make them wealthy for life. However Tom might have felt disposed to sell himself to the Devil, he was determined not to do so to oblige his wife; so he flatly refused, out of the mere spirit of contradiction. Many and bitter were the quarrels they had on the subject; but the more she talked, the more resolute was Tom not to be damned to please her.

At length she determined to drive the bargain on her own account, and if she succeeded, to keep all the gain to herself. Being of the same fearless temper as her husband, she set off for the old Indian fort towards the close of a summer's day. She was many hours absent. When she came back, she was reserved and sullen in her replies. She spoke something of a black man, whom she had met about twilight hewing at the root of a tall tree. He was sulky, however, and would not come to terms: she was to go again with a propitiatory offering, but what it was she forbore to say.

The next evening she set off again for the swamp, with her apron heavily laden. Tom waited and waited for her, but in vain; midnight came, but she did not make her appearance: morning, noon, night returned, but still she did not come. Tom now grew uneasy for her safety, especially as he found she had carried off in her apron the silver tea-pot and spoons, and every portable article of value. Another night elapsed, another morning came; but no wife. In a word, she was never heard of more.

What was her real fate nobody knows, in consequence of so many pretending to know. It is one of those facts which have become confounded by a variety of historians. Some asserted that she lost her way among the tangled mazes of the swamp, and sank into some pit or slough; others, more uncharitable, hinted that she had eloped with the household booty, and made off to some other province; while others surmised that the tempter had decoyed her into a dismal quagmire, on the top of which her hat was found lying. In confirmation of this, it was said a great black man, with an axe on his shoulder, was seen late that very evening coming out of the swamp, carrying a bundle tied in a check apron, with an air of surly triumph.

The most current and probable story, however, observes, that Tom Walker grew so anxious about the fate of his wife and his property, that he set out at length to seek them both at the Indian fort. During a long summer's afternoon he searched about the gloomy place, but no wife was to be seen. He called her name repeatedly, but she was nowhere to be heard. The bittern alone responded to his voice, as he flew screaming by; or the bull-frog croaked dolefully from a neighboring pool. At length, it is said, just in the brown hour of twilight, when the owls began to hoot, and the bats to flit about, his attention was attracted by the clamor of carrion crows hovering about a cypress-tree. He looked up, and beheld a bundle tied in a check apron, and hanging in the branches of the tree, with a great vulture perched hard by, as if keeping watch upon it. He leaped with joy; for he recognized his wife's apron, and supposed it to contain the household valuables.

"Let us get hold of the property," said he, consolingly to himself, "and we will endeavor to do without the woman."

As he scrambled up the tree, the vulture spread its wide wings, and sailed off, screaming, into the deep shadows of the forest. Tom seized the checked apron, but, woful sight! found nothing but a heart and liver tied up in it!

Such, according to this most authentic old story, was all that was to be found of Tom's wife. She had probably attempted to deal with the black man as she had been accustomed to deal with her husband; but though a female scold is generally considered a match for the devil, yet in this instance she appears to have had the worst of it. She must have died game, however; for it is said Tom noticed many prints of cloven feet deeply stamped about the tree, and found handfuls of hair, that looked as if they had been plucked from the coarse black shock of the woodman. Tom knew his wife's prowess by experience. He shrugged his shoulders, as he looked at the signs of a fierce clapper-clawing. "Egad," said he to himself, "Old Scratch must have had a tough time of it!"

Tom consoled himself for the loss of his property, with the loss of his wife, for he was a man of fortitude. He even felt something like gratitude towards the black woodman, who, he considered, had done him a kindness. He sought, therefore, to cultivate a further acquaintance with him, but for some time without success; the old black-legs played shy, for whatever people may think, he is not always to be had for calling for: he knows how to play his cards when pretty sure of his game.

At length, it is said, when delay had whetted Tom's eagerness to the quick, and prepared him to agree to anything rather than not gain the promised treasure, he met the black man one evening in his usual woodman's dress, with his axe on his shoulder, sauntering along the swamp, and humming a tune. He affected to receive Tom's advances with great indifference, made brief replies, and went on humming his tune.

By degrees, however, Tom brought him to business, and they began to haggle about the terms on which the former was to have the pirate's treasure. There was one condition which need not be mentioned, being generally understood in all cases where the devil grants favors; but there were others about which, though of less importance, he was inflexibly obstinate. He insisted that the money found through his means should be employed in his service. He proposed, therefore, that Tom should employ it in the black traffic; that is to say, that he should fit out a slave-ship. This, however, Tom resolutely refused: he was bad enough in all conscience; but the devil himself could not tempt him to turn slave-trader.

Finding Tom so squeamish on this point, he did not insist upon it, but proposed, instead, that he should turn usurer; the devil being extremely anxious for the increase of usurers, looking upon them as his peculiar people.

To this no objections were made, for it was just to Tom's taste.

"You shall open a broker's shop in Boston next month," said the black man.

"I'll do it to-morrow, if you wish," said Tom Walker.

"You shall lend money at two per cent a month."

"Egad, I'll charge four!" replied Tom Walker.

"You shall extort bonds, foreclose mortgages, drive the merchants to bankruptcy"—

"I'll drive them to the d____l," cried Tom Walker.

"You are the usurer for my money!" said black-legs with delight. "When will you want the rhino?"

"This very night."

"Done!" said the devil.

"Done!" said Tom Walker.—So they shook hands and struck a bargain.

A few days' time saw Tom Walker seated behind his desk in a counting-house in Boston.

His reputation for a ready-moneyed man, who would lend money out for a good consideration, soon spread abroad. Everybody remembers the time of Governor Belcher, when money was particularly scarce. It was a time of paper credit. The country had been deluged with government bills, the famous Land

Bank had been established; there had been a rage for speculating; the people had run mad with schemes for new settlements; for building cities in the wilderness; land-jobbers went about with maps of grants, and townships, and Eldorados, lying nobody knew where, but which everybody was ready to purchase. In a word, the great speculating fever which breaks out every now and then in the country, had raged to an alarming degree, and everybody was dreaming of making sudden fortunes from nothing. As usual the fever had subsided; the dream had gone off, and the imaginary fortunes with it; the patients were left in doleful plight, and the whole country resounded with the consequent cry of "hard times."

At this propitious time of public distress did Tom Walker set up as usurer in Boston. His door was soon thronged by customers. The needy and adventurous; the gambling speculator; the dreaming land-jobber; the thriftless tradesman; the merchant with cracked credit; in short, every one driven to raise money by desperate means and desperate sacrifices, hurried to Tom Walker.

Thus Tom was the universal friend of the needy, and acted like a "friend in need"; that is to say, he always exacted good pay and good security. In proportion to the distress of the applicant was the hardness of his terms. He accumulated bonds and mortgages; gradually squeezed his customers closer and closer: and sent them at length, dry as a sponge, from his door.

In this way he made money hand over hand; became a rich and mighty man, and exalted his cocked hat upon 'Change. He built himself, as usual, a vast house, out of ostentation; but left the greater part of it unfinished and unfurnished, out of parsimony. He even set up a carriage in the fulness of his vainglory, though he nearly starved the horses which drew it; and as the ungreased wheels groaned and screeched on the axletrees, you would have thought you heard the souls of the poor debtors he was squeezing.

As Tom waxed old, however, he grew thoughtful. Having secured the good things of this world, he began to feel anxious about those of the next. He thought with regret on the bargain he had made with his black friend, and set his wits to work to cheat him out of the conditions. He became, therefore, all of a sudden, a violent church-goer. He prayed loudly and strenuously, as if heaven were to be taken by force of lungs. Indeed, one might always tell when he had sinned most during the week, by the clamor of his Sunday devotion. The quiet Christians who had been modestly and steadfastly traveling Zionward, were struck with self-reproach at seeing themselves so suddenly outstripped in their career by this new-made convert. Tom was as rigid in religious as in money matters; he was a stern supervisor and censurer of his neighbors, and seemed to think every sin entered up to their account became a credit on his own side of the page. He even talked of the expediency of reviving the persecution of Quakers and Anabaptists. In a word, Tom's zeal became as notorious as his riches.

Still, in spite of all this strenuous attention to forms, Tom had a lurking dread that the devil, after all, would have his due. That he might not be taken unawares, therefore, it is said he always carried a small Bible in his coat-pocket. He had also a great folio Bible on his counting-house desk, and would frequently be found reading it when people called on business; on such occasions he would lay his green spectacles in the book, to mark the place, while he turned round to drive some usurious bargain.

Some say that Tom grew a little crack-brained in his old days, and that, fancying his end approaching, he had his horse new shod, saddled and bridled, and buried with his feet uppermost; because he supposed that at the last day the world would be turned upside down; in which case he should find his horse standing ready for mounting, and he was determined at the worst to give his old friend a run for it. This, however, is probably a mere old wives' fable. If he really did take such a precaution, it was totally superfluous; at least so says the authentic old legend; which closes his story in the following manner.

One hot summer afternoon in the dog-days, just as a terrible black thunder-gust was coming up, Tom sat in his counting-house, in his white linen cap and India silk morning-gown. He was on the point of foreclosing a mortgage, by which he would complete the ruin of an unlucky land-speculator for whom he had professed the greatest friendship. The poor land-jobber begged him to grant a few months' indulgence. Tom had grown testy and irritated, and refused another day.

"My family will be ruined, and brought upon the parish," said the land-jobber. "Charity begins at home," replied Tom; "I must take care of myself in these hard times."

"You have made so much money out of me," said the speculator.

Tom lost his patience and his piety. "The devil take me," said he, "if I have made a farthing!"

Just then there were three loud knocks at the street-door. He stepped out to see who was there. A black man was holding a black horse, which neighed and stamped with impatience.

"Tom, you're come for," said the black fellow, gruffly. Tom shrank back, but too late. He had left his little Bible at the bottom of his coat-pocket, and his big Bible on the desk buried under the mortgage he was about to foreclose: never was sinner taken more unawares. The black man whisked him like a child into the saddle, gave the horse the lash, and away he galloped, with Tom on his back, in the midst of the thunder-storm. The clerks stuck their pens behind their ears, and stared after him from the windows. Away went Tom Walker, dashing down the streets; his white cap bobbing up and down; his morning-gown fluttering in the wind, and his steed striking fire out of the pavement at every bound. When the clerks turned to look for the black man, he had disappeared.

Tom Walker never returned to foreclose the mortgage. A countryman, who lived on the border of the swamp, reported that in the height of the thunder-gust he had heard a great clattering of hoofs and a howling along the road, and running to the window caught sight of a figure, such as I have described, on a horse that galloped like mad across the fields, over the hills, and down into the black hemlock swamp towards the old Indian fort; and that shortly after a thunder-bolt falling in that direction seeemed to set the whole forest in a blaze.

The good people of Boston shook their heads and shrugged their shoulders, but had been so much accustomed to witches and goblins, and tricks of the devil, in all kinds of shapes, from the first settlement of the colony, that they were not so much horror-struck as might have been expected. Trustees were appointed to take charge of Tom's effects. There was nothing, however, to administer upon. On searching his coffers, all his bonds and mortgages were found reduced to cinders. In place of gold and silver, his iron chest was filled with chips and shavings; two skeletons lay in his stable instead of his half-starved horses, and the very next day his great house took fire and was burnt to the ground.

Such was the end of Tom Walker and his ill-gotten wealth. Let all griping money-brokers lay this story to heart. The truth of it is not to be doubted. The very hole under the oak-trees, whence he dug Kidd's money, is to be seen to this day; and the neighboring swamp and old Indian fort are often haunted in stormy nights by a figure on horseback, in morning-gown and white cap, which is doubtless the troubled spirit of the usurer. In fact, the story has resolved itself into a proverb, and is the origin of that popular saying, so prevalent throughout New England, of "The Devil and Tom Walker."

Gifts

Ralph Waldo Emerson

Gifts of one who loved me—
'Twas high time they came;
When he ceased to love me,
Time they stopped for shame.

It is said that the world is in a state of bankruptcy, that the world owes the world more than the world can pay, and ought to go into chancery, and be sold. I do not think this general insolvency, which involves in some sort all the population, to be the reason of the difficulty experienced at Christmas and New Year, and other times, in bestowing gifts; since it is always so pleasant to be generous, though very vexatious to pay debts. But the impediment lies in the choosing. If, at any time, it comes into my head that a present is due from me to somebody, I am puzzled what to give until the opportunity is gone. Flowers and fruits are always fit presents; flowers, because they are a proud assertion that a ray of beauty outvalues all the utilities of the world. These gay natures contrast with the somewhat stern countenance of ordinary nature: they are like music heard out of a work-house. Nature does not cocker us: we are children, not pets: she is not fond: everything is dealt to us without fear or favor, after severe universal laws. Yet these delicate flowers look like the frolic and interference of love and beauty. Men used to tell us that we love flattery, even though we are not deceived by it, because it shows that we are of importance enough to be courted. Something like that pleasure, the flowers give us: what am I to whom these sweet hints are addressed? Fruits are acceptable gifts, because they are the flower of commodities, and admit of fantastic values being attached to them. If a man should send to me to come a hundred miles to visit him, and should set before me a basket of fine summer-fruit, I should think there was some proportion between the labor and the reward.

For common gifts, necessity makes pertinences and beauty every day, and one is glad when an imperative leaves him no option, since if the man at the door have no shoes, you have not to consider whether you could procure him

346

a paint-box. And as it is always pleasing to see a man eat bread or drink water, in the house or out of doors, so it is always a great satisfaction to supply these first wants. Necessity does everything well. In our condition of universal dependence, it seems heroic to let the petitioner be the judge of his necessity and to give all that is asked, though at great inconvenience. If it be a fantastic desire, it is better to leave to others the office of punishing him. I can think of many parts I should prefer playing to that of the Furies. Next to things of necessity, the rule for a gift, which one of my friends prescribed, is that we might convey to some person that which properly belonged to his character, and was easily associated with him in thought. But our tokens of compliment and love are for the most part barbarous. Rings and other jewels are not gifts, but apologies for gifts. The only gift is a portion of thyself. Thou must bleed for me. Therefore the poet brings his poem; the shepherd, his lamb; the farmer, corn; the miner, a gem; the sailor, coral and sea shells; the painter, his picture; the girl, a handkerchief of her own sewing. This is right and pleasing, for it restores society in so far to its primary basis, when a man's biography is conveyed in his gift, and every man's wealth is an index of his merit. But it is a cold, lifeless business when you go to the shops to buy me something which does not represent your life and talent, but a goldsmith's. This is fit for kings, and rich men who represent kings, and a false state of property, to make presents of gold and silver stuffs, as a kind of symbolical sin-offering, or payment of blackmail.

The law of benefits is a difficult channel, which requires careful sailing, or rude boats. It is not the office of a man to receive gifts. How dare you give them? We wish to be self-sustained. We do not quite forgive a giver. The hand that feeds us is in some danger of being bitten. We can receive anything from love, for that is a way of receiving it from ourselves; but not from any one who assumes to bestow. We sometimes hate the meat which we eat, because there seems something of degrading dependence in living by it.

> "Brother, if Jove to thee a present make,
> Take heed that from his hands thou nothing take."

We ask the whole. Nothing less will content us. We arrange society, if it do not give us besides earth, and fire, and water, opportunity, love, reverence, and objects of veneration.

He is a good man, who can receive a gift well. We are either glad or sorry at a gift, and both emotions are unbecoming. Some violence, I think, is done, some degradation borne, when I rejoice or grieve at a gift. I am sorry when my independence is invaded, or when a gift comes from such as do not know my spirit, and so the act is not supported; and if the gift pleases me overmuch, then I should be ashamed that the donor should read my heart, and see that I love his commodity, and not him. The gift, to be true, must be the flowing of the giver unto me, correspondent to my flowing unto him. When the waters are at level, then my goods pass to him, and his to me. All his are mine, all mine his. I say to him, How can you give me this pot of oil, or this flagon of wine, when all your oil and wine is mine, which belief of mine this gift seems to deny? Hence the fitness of beautiful, not useful things for gifts. This giving is flat usurpation, and therefore when the beneficiary is ungrateful, as all beneficiaries hate all Timons, not at all considering the value of the gift, but looking back to the greater store it was taken from, I rather sympathize with the beneficiary, than with the anger of my lord, Timon. For the expectation of gratitude is mean, and is continually punished by the total insensibility of the obliged person. It is a great happiness to get off without injury and heartburning from one who has had the ill luck to be served by you. It is a very onerous business, this of being served, and the debtor naturally wishes to give you a slap. A golden text for these gentlemen is that which I so admire in the Buddhist, who never thanks, and who says, "Do not flatter your benefactors."

The reason of these discords I conceive to be, that there is no commensurability between a man and any gift. You cannot give anything to a magnanimous person. After you have served him, he at once puts you in debt by his magnanimity. The service a man renders his friend is trivial and selfish compared with the service he knows his friend stood in readiness to yield him, alike before he had begun to serve his friend, and now also. Compared with what good-will I bear my friend, the benefit it is in my power to render him seems small. Besides, our action on each other, good as well as evil, is so incidental and at random that we can seldom hear the acknowledgments of any person who would thank us for a benefit, without some shame and humiliation. We can rarely strike a direct stroke, but must be content with an oblique one; we seldom have the satisfaction of yielding a direct benefit, which is directly received. But rectitude scatters favors on every side without knowing it, and receives with wonder the thanks of all people.

I fear to breathe any treason against the majesty of love, which is the genius and god of gifts, and to whom we must not affect to prescribe. Let him give kingdoms or flower-leaves indifferently. There are persons from whom we always expect fairy tokens; let us not cease to expect them. This is prerogative, and not to be limited by our municipal rules. For the rest, I like to see that we cannot be bought and sold. The best of hospitality and of generosity is also not in the will, but in fate. I find that I am not much to you; you do not need me; you do not feel me; then am I thrust out of doors, though you proffer me house and lands. No services are of any value, but only likeness. When I have attempted to join myself to others by services, it proved an intellectual trick—no more. They eat your service like apples, and leave you out. But love them, and they feel you, and delight in you all the time.

Civil Disobedience

HENRY DAVID THOREAU

I heartily accept the motto,—"That government is best which governs least;" and I should like to see it acted up to more rapidly and systematically. Carried out, it finally amounts to this, which also I believe,—"That government is best which governs not at all;" and when men are prepared for it, that will be the kind of government which they will have. Government is at best but an expedient; but most governments are usually, and all governments are sometimes, inexpedient. The objections which have been brought against a standing army, and they are many and weighty, and deserve to prevail, may also at last be brought against a standing government. The standing army is only an arm of the standing government. The government itself, which is only the mode which the people have chosen to execute their will, is equally liable to be abused and perverted before the people can act through it. Witness the present Mexican war, the work of comparatively a few individuals using the standing government as their tool; for, in the outset, the people would not have consented to this measure.

This American government,—what is it but a tradition, though a recent one, endeavoring to transmit itself unimpaired to posterity, but each instant losing some of its integrity? It has not the vitality and force of a single living man; for a single man can bend it to his will. It is a sort of wooden gun to the people themselves. But it is not the less necessary for this; for the people must have some complicated machinery or other, and hear its din, to satisfy that idea of government which they have. Governments show thus how successfully men can be imposed on, even impose on themselves, for their own advantage. It is excellent, we must all allow. Yet this government never of itself furthered any enterprise, but by the alacrity with which it got out of its way. *It* does not keep the country free. *It* does not settle the West. *It* does not educate. The character inherent in the American people has done all that has been accomplished; and it would have done somewhat more, if the government had not sometimes got in its way. For government is an expedient by which men would fain succeed in letting one another alone; and, as has been said, when it is most expedient, the governed are most let alone by it. Trade and commerce, if they were not made of India-rubber, would never manage to bounce over the obstacles which legislators are continually putting in their way; and, if one were to judge these men wholly by the effects of their actions and not partly by their intentions, they would deserve to be classed and punished with those mischievous persons who put obstructions on the railroads.

But, to speak practically and as a citizen, unlike those who call themselves no-government men, I ask for, not at once no government, but *at once* a better government. Let every man make known what kind of government would command his respect, and that will be one step toward obtaining it.

After all, the practical reason why, when the power is once in the hands of the people, a majority are permitted, and for a long period continue, to rule is not because they are most likely to be in the right, nor because this seems fairest to the minority, but because they are physically the strongest. But a government in which the majority rule in all cases cannot be based on justice, even as far as men understand it. Can there not be a government in which majorities do not virtually decide right and wrong, but conscience?—in which majorities decide only those questions to which the rule of expediency is applicable? Must the citizen ever for a moment, or in the least degree, resign his conscience to the legislator? Why has every man a conscience, then? I think that we should be men first, and subjects afterward. It is not desirable to cultivate a respect for law, so much as for the right. The only obligation which I have a right to assume is to do at any time what I think right. It is truly enough said, that a corporation has no conscience; but a corporation of conscientious men is a corporation *with* a conscience. Law never made men a whit more just; and, by means of their respect for it, even the well-disposed are daily made the agents of injustice. A common and natural result of an undue respect for the law is, that you may see a file of soldiers, colonel, captain, corporal, privates, powder-monkeys, and all, marching in admirable order over hill and dale to the wars, against their wills, ay, against their common sense and consciences, which makes it very steep marching indeed, and produces a palpitation of the heart. They have no doubt that it is a damnable business in which they are concerned; they are all peaceably inclined. Now, what are they? Men at all? or small movable forts and magazines, at the service of some unscrupulous man in power? Visit the Navy-Yard, and behold a marine, such a man as an American government can make, or such as it can make a man with its black arts,—a mere shadow and reminiscence of humanity, a man laid out alive and standing, and already, as one may say, buried under arms with funeral accompaniments, though it may be,—

> "Not a drum was heard, not a funeral note,
> As his corse to the rampart we hurried;
> Not a soldier discharged his farewell shot
> O'er the grave where our hero we buried."

The mass of men serve the state thus, not as men mainly, but as machines, with their bodies. They are the standing army, and the militia, jailers, constables, posse comitatus, etc. In most cases there is no free exercise whatever of the judgment or of the moral sense; but they put themselves on a level with wood and earth and stones; and wooden men can perhaps be manufactured that will serve the purpose as well. Such command no more respect than men of straw or a lump of dirt. They have the same sort of worth only as horses and dogs. Yet such as these even are commonly esteemed good citizens. Others—as most legislators, politicians, lawyers, ministers, and office-holders—serve the state chiefly with their heads; and, as they rarely make any moral distinctions, they are as likely to serve the Devil, without *intending* it, as God. A very few, as heroes, patriots, martyrs, reformers in the great sense, and *men*, serve the state with their consciences also, and so necessarily resist it for the most part; and they are commonly treated as enemies by it. A wise man will only be useful as a man, and will not submit to be "clay," and "stop a hole to keep the wind away," but leave that office to his dust at least:—

> "I am too high-born to be propertied,
> To be a secondary at control,
> Or useful serving-man and instrument
> To any sovereign state throughout the world."

He who gives himself entirely to his fellowmen appears to them useless and selfish; but he who gives himself partially to them is pronounced a benefactor and philanthropist.

How does it become a man to behave toward this American government to-day? I answer, that he cannot without disgrace be associated with it. I cannot for an instant recognize that political organization as *my* government which is the *slave's* government also.

All men recognize the right of revolution; that is, the right to refuse allegiance to, and to resist, the government, when its tyranny or its inefficiency are great and unendurable. But almost all say that such is not the case now. But such was the case, they think, in the Revolution of '75. If one were to tell me that this was a bad government because it taxed certain foreign commodities brought to its ports, it is most probable that I should not make an ado about it, for I can do without them. All machines have their friction; and possibly this does enough good to counterbalance the evil. At any rate, it is a great evil to make a stir about it. But when the friction comes to have its machine, and oppression and robbery are organized, I say, let us not have such a machine any longer. In other words, when a sixth of the population of a nation which has undertaken to be the refuge of liberty are slaves, and a whole country is unjustly overrun and conquered by a foreign army, and subjected to military law, I think that it is not too soon for honest men to rebel and revolutionize. What makes this duty the more urgent is the fact that the country so overrun is not our own, but ours is the invading army.

Paley, a common authority with many on moral questions, in his chapter on the "Duty of Submission to Civil Government," resolves all civil obligation into expediency; and he proceeds to say, "that so long as the interest of the

whole society requires it, that is, so long as the established government cannot be resisted or changed without public inconveniency, it is the will of God
that the established government be obeyed, and no longer. . . . This principle
being admitted, the justice of every particular case of resistance is reduced to
a computation of the quantity of the danger and grievance on the one side,
and of the probability and expense of redressing it on the other." Of this, he
says, every man shall judge for himself. But Paley appears never to have contemplated those cases to which the rule of expediency does not apply, in which
a people, as well as an individual, must do justice, cost what it may. If I have
unjustly wrested a plank from a drowning man, I must restore it to him
though I drown myself. This, according to Paley, would be inconvenient. But
he that would save his life, in such a case, shall lose it. This people must cease
to hold slaves, and to make war on Mexico, though it cost them their existence
as a people.

In their practice, nations agree with Paley; but does any one think that
Massachusetts does exactly what is right at the present crisis?

> "A drab of state, a cloth-o'-silver slut,
> To have her train borne up, and her soul trail in the dirt."

Practically speaking, the opponents to a reform in Massachusetts are not
a hundred thousand politicians at the South, but a hundred thousand merchants
and farmers here, who are more interested in commerce and agriculture than
they are in humanity, and are not prepared to do justice to the slave and to
Mexico, *cost what it may.* I quarrel not with far-off foes, but with those who,
near at home, cooperate with, and do the bidding of, those far away, and
without whom the latter would be harmless. We are accustomed to say, that the
mass of men are unprepared; but improvement is slow, because the few are
not materially wiser or better than the many. It is not so important that many
should be as good as you, as that there be some absolute goodness somewhere;
for that will leaven the whole lump. There are thousands who are *in opinion*
opposed to slavery and to the war, who yet in effect do nothing to put an end
to them; who, esteeming themselves children of Washington and Franklin, sit
down with their hands in their pockets, and say that they know not what to do,
and do nothing; who even postpone the question of freedom to the question of
free-trade, and quietly read the prices-current along with the latest advices
from Mexico, after dinner, and, it may be, fall asleep over them both. What is
the price-current of an honest man and patriot to-day? They hesitate, and they
regret, and sometimes they petition; but they do nothing in earnest and with
effect. They will wait, well disposed, for others to remedy the evil, that they
may no longer have to regret. At most, they give only a cheap vote, and a
feeble countenance and Godspeed, to the right, as it goes by them. There are
nine hundred and ninety-nine patrons of virtue to one virtuous man. But it is
easier to deal with the real possessor of a thing than with the temporary
guardian of it.

All voting is a sort of gaming, like checkers or backgammon, with a slight moral tinge to it, a playing with right and wrong, with moral questions; and betting naturally accompanies it. The character of the voters is not staked. I cast my vote, perchance, as I think right; but I am not vitally concerned that that right should prevail. I am willing to leave it to the majority. Its obligation, therefore, never exceeds that of expediency. Even voting *for the right* is *doing* nothing for it. It is only expressing to men feebly your desire that it should prevail. A wise man will not leave the right to the mercy of chance, nor wish it to prevail through the power of the majority. There is but little virtue in the action of masses of men. When the majority shall at length vote for the abolition of slavery, it will be because they are indifferent to slavery, or because there is but little slavery left to be abolished by their vote. *They* will then be the only slaves. Only *his* vote can hasten the abolition of slavery who asserts his own freedom by his vote.

I hear of a convention to be held at Baltimore, or elsewhere, for the selection of a candidate for the Presidency, made up chiefly of editors, and men who are politicians by profession; but I think, what is it to any independent, intelligent, and respectable man what decision they may come to? Shall we not have the advantage of his wisdom and honesty, nevertheless? Can we not count upon some independent votes? Are there not many individuals in the country who do not attend conventions? But no: I find that the respectable man, so called, has immediately drifted from his position, and despairs of his country, when his country has more reason to despair of him. He forthwith adopts one of the candidates thus selected as the only *available* one, thus proving that he is himself *available* for any purposes of the demagogue. His vote is of no more worth than that of any unprincipled foreigner or hireling native, who may have been bought. O for a man who is a *man*, and, as my neighbor says, has a bone in his back which you cannot pass your hand through! Our statistics are at fault: the population has been returned too large. How many *men* are there to a square thousand miles in this country? Hardly one. Does not America offer any inducement for men to settle here? The American has dwindled into an Odd Fellow,—one who may be known by the development of his organ of gregariousness, and a manifest lack of intellect and cheerful self-reliance; whose first and chief concern, on coming into the world, is to see that the Almshouses are in good repair; and, before yet he has lawfully donned the virile garb, to collect a fund for the support of the widows and orphans that may be; who, in short, ventures to live only by the aid of the Mutual Insurance company, which has promised to bury him decently.

It is not a man's duty, as a matter of course, to devote himself to the eradication of any, even the most enormous wrong; he may still properly have other concerns to engage him; but it is his duty, at least, to wash his hands of it, and, if he gives it no thought longer, not to give it practically his support. If I devote myself to other pursuits and contemplations, I must first see, at least, that I do not pursue them sitting upon another man's shoulders. I must get off him first, that he may pursue his contemplations too. See what gross inconsistency is tolerated. I have heard some of my townsmen say, "I should like to have them order me out to help put down an insurrection of the slaves, or to march to Mexico;—see if I would go;" and yet these very men have each, directly by their allegiance, and so indirectly, at least, by their money, furnished a substitute. The soldier is applauded who refuses to serve in an unjust war by those who do not refuse to sustain the unjust government which makes the war; is applauded by those whose own act and authority he disregards and sets at naught; as if the state were penitent to that degree that it hired one to scourge it while it sinned, but not to that degree that it left off sinning for a moment. Thus, under the name of Order and Civil Government, we are all made at last to pay homage to and support our own meanness. After the first blush of sin comes its indifference; and from immoral it becomes, as it were, *un*moral, and not quite unnecessary to that life which we have made.

The broadest and most prevalent error requires the most disinterested virtue to sustain it. The slight reproach to which the virtue of patriotism is commonly liable, the noble are most likely to incur. Those who, while they disapprove of the character and measures of a government, yield to it their allegiance and support are undoubtedly its most conscientious supporters, and so frequently the most serious obstacles to reform. Some are petitioning the state to dissolve the Union, to disregard the requisitions of the President. Why do they not dissolve it themselves,—the union between themselves and the state,—and refuse to pay their quota into its treasury? Do not they stand in the same relation to the state that the state does to the Union? And have not the same reasons prevented the state from resisting the Union which have prevented them from resisting the state?

How can a man be satisfied to entertain an opinion merely, and enjoy *it*? Is there any enjoyment in it, if his opinion is that he is aggrieved? If you are cheated out of a single dollar by your neighbor, you do not rest satisfied with knowing that you are cheated, or with saying that you are cheated, or even with petitioning him to pay you your due; but you take effectual steps at once to obtain the full amount, and see that you are never cheated again. Action from principle, the perception and the performance of right, changes things and relations; it is essentially revolutionary, and does not consist wholly with anything which was. It not only divides states and churches, it divides families; ay, it divides the *individual*, separating the diabolical in him from the divine.

Unjust laws exist: shall we be content to obey them, or shall we endeavor to amend them, and obey them until we have succeeded, or shall we transgress them at once? Men generally, under such a government as this, think that they ought to wait until they have persuaded the majority to alter them. They think that, if they should resist, the remedy would be worse than the evil. But it is the fault of the government itself that the remedy *is* worse than the evil. *It* makes it worse. Why is it not more apt to anticipate and provide for reform? Why does it not cherish its wise minority? Why does it cry and resist before it is hurt? Why does it not encourage its citizens to be on the alert to point out its faults, and *do* better than it would have them? Why does it always crucify Christ, and excommunicate Copernicus and Luther, and pronounce Washington and Franklin rebels?

One would think, that a deliberate and practical denial of its authority was the only offense never contemplated by government; else, why has it not assigned its definite, its suitable and proportionate penalty? If a man who has no property refuses but once to earn nine shillings for the state, he is put in prison for a period unlimited by any law that I know, and determined only by the discretion of those who placed him there; but if he should steal ninety times nine shillings from the state, he is soon permitted to go at large again.

If the injustice is part of the necessary friction of the machine of government, let it go, let it go: perchance it will wear smooth,—certainly the machine will wear out. If the injustice has a spring, or a pulley, or a rope, or a crank, exclusively for itself, then perhaps you may consider whether the remedy will not be worse than the evil; but if it is of such a nature that it requires you to be the agent of injustice to another, then, I say, break the law. Let your life be a counter friction to stop the machine. What I have to do is to see, at any rate, that I do not lend myself to the wrong which I condemn.

As for adopting the ways which the state has provided for remedying the evil, I know not of such ways. They take too much time, and a man's life will be gone. I have other affairs to attend to. I came into this world, not chiefly to make this a good place to live in, but to live in it, be it good or bad. A man has not everything to do, but something; and because he cannot do *everything*, it is not necessary that he should do *something* wrong. It is not my business to be petitioning the Governor or the Legislature any more than it is theirs to petition me; and if they should not hear my petition, what should I do then? But in this case the state has provided no way: its very Constitution is the evil. This may seem to be harsh and stubborn and unconciliatory; but it is to treat with the utmost kindness and consideration the only spirit that can appreciate or deserves it. So is all change for the better, like birth and death, which convulse the body.

I do not hesitate to say, that those who call themselves Abolitionists should at once effectually withdraw their support, both in person and property, from the government of Massachusetts, and not wait till they constitute a majority of one, before they suffer the right to prevail through them. I think that it is enough if they have God on their side, without waiting for that other one. Moreover, any man more right than his neighbors constitutes a majority of one already.

I meet this American government, or its representative, the state government, directly, and face to face, once a year—no more—in the person of its tax-gatherer; this is the only mode in which a man situated as I am necessarily meets it; and it then says distinctly, Recognize me; and the simplest, the most effectual, and, in the present posture of affairs, the indispensablest mode of treating with it on this head, of expressing your little satisfaction with and love for it, is to deny it then. My civil neighbor, the tax-gatherer, is the very man I have to deal with,—for it is, after all, with men and not with parchment that I quarrel,—and he has voluntarily chosen to be an agent of the government. How shall he ever know well what he is and does as an officer of the government, or as a man, until he is obliged to consider whether he shall treat me, his neighbor, for whom he has respect, as a neighbor and well-disposed man, or as a maniac and disturber of the peace, and see if he can get over this obstruction to his neighborliness without a ruder and more impetuous thought or speech corresponding with his action. I know this well, that if one thousand, if one hundred, if ten men whom I could name,—if then *honest* men only,—ay, if *one* HONEST man, in this State of Massachusetts, *ceasing to hold slaves*, were actually to withdraw from this copartnership, and be locked up in the county jail therefor, it would be the abolition of slavery in America. For it matters not how small the beginning may seem to be: what is once well done is done forever. But we love better to talk about it: that we say is our mission. Reform keeps many scores of newspapers in its service, but not one man. If my esteemed neighbor, the State's ambassador, who will devote his days to the settlement of the question of human rights in the Council Chamber, instead of being threatened with the prisons of Carolina, were to sit down the prisoner of Massachusetts, that State which is so anxious to foist the sin of slavery upon her sister,—though at present she can discover only an act of inhospitality to be the ground of a quarrel with her,—the Legislature would not wholly waive the subject the following winter.

Under a government which imprisons any unjustly, the true place for a just man is also a prison. The proper place to-day, the only place which Massachusetts has provided for her freer and less desponding spirits, is in her prisons, to be put out and locked out of the State by her own act, as they have already put themselves out by their principles. It is there that the fugitive slave, and the Mexican prisoner on parole, and the Indian come to plead the wrongs of his race should find them; on that separate, but more free and honorable ground, where the State places those who are not *with* her, but *against* her,—the only house in a slave State in which a free man can abide with honor. If any think that their influence would be lost there, and their voices no longer afflict the ear of the State, that they would not be as an enemy within its walls, they do not know by how much truth is stronger than error, nor how much more eloquently and effectively he can combat injustice who has experienced a little in his own person. Cast your whole vote, not a strip of paper merely, but your whole influence. A minority is powerless while it conforms to the majority; it is not even a minority then; but it is irresistible when it clogs by its whole weight. If the alternative is to keep all just men in prison, or give up war and slavery, the State will not hesitate which to choose. If a thousand men were not to pay their tax-bills this year, that would not be a violent and bloody measure, as it would be to pay them, and enable the State to commit violence and shed innocent blood. This is, in fact, the definition of a peaceable revolution, if any such is possible. If the tax-gatherer, or any other public officer, asks me, as one has done, "But what shall I do?" my answer is, "If you really wish to do anything, resign your office." When the subject has refused allegiance, and the officer has resigned his office, then the revolution is accomplished. But even suppose blood should flow. Is there not a sort of blood shed when the conscience is wounded? Through this wound a man's real manhood and immortality flow out, and he bleeds to an everlasting death. I see this blood flowing now.

I have contemplated the imprisonment of the offender, rather than the seizure of his goods,—though both will serve the same purpose,—because they who assert the purest right, and consequently are most dangerous to a corrupt State, commonly have not spent much time in accumulating property. To such the State renders comparatively small service, and a slight tax is wont to appear exorbitant, particularly if they are obliged to earn it by special labor with their hands. If there were one who lived wholly without the use of money, the State itself would hesitate to demand it of him. But the rich man—not to make any invidious comparison—is always sold to the institution which makes him rich. Absolutely speaking, the more money, the less virtue; for money comes between a man and his objects, and obtains them for him; and it was certainly no great virtue to obtain it. It puts to rest many questions which he would otherwise be taxed to answer; while the only new question which it puts is the hard but superfluous one, how to spend it. Thus his moral ground is taken from under his feet. The opportunities of living are diminished in proportion as what are called the "means" are increased. The best thing a man can do for his culture when he is rich is to endeavor to carry out those schemes which he entertained when he was poor. Christ answered the Herodians according to their condition. "Show me the tribute-money," said he; —and one took a penny out of his pocket;—if you use money which has the image of Cæsar on it, and which he has made current and valuable, that is, *if you are men of the State*, and gladly enjoy the advantages of Cæsar's government, then pay him back some of his own when he demands it. "Render therefore to Cæsar that which is Cæsar's, and to God those things which are God's," —leaving them no wiser than before as to which was which; for they did not wish to know.

When I converse with the freest of my neighbors, I perceive that, whatever they may say about the magnitude and seriousness of the question, and their regard for the public tranquillity, the long and the short of the matter is, that they cannot spare the protection of the existing government, and they dread the consequences to their property and families of disobedience to it. For my own part, I should not like to think that I ever rely on the protection of the State. But, if I deny the authority of the State when it presents its tax-bill, it will soon take and waste all my property, and so harass me and my children without end. This is hard. This makes it impossible for a man to live honestly, and at the same time comfortably, in outward respects. It will not be worth the while to accumulate property; that would be sure to go again. You must hire or squat somewhere, and raise but a small crop, and eat that soon. You must live within yourself, and depend upon yourself always tucked up and ready for a start, and not have many affairs. A man may grow rich in Turkey even, if he will be in all respects a good subject of the Turkish government. Confucius said: "If a state is governed by the principles of reason, poverty and misery are subjects of shame; if a state is not governed by the principles of reason, riches and honors are the subjects of shame." No: until I want the protection of Massachusetts to be extended to me in some distant Southern port, where my liberty is endangered, or until I am bent solely on building up an estate at home by peaceful enterprise, I can afford to refuse allegiance to Massachusetts, and her right to my property and life. It costs me less in every sense to incur the penalty of disobedience to the State than it would to obey. I should feel as if I were worth less in that case.

Some years ago, the State met me in behalf of the Church, and commanded me to pay a certain sum toward the support of a clergyman whose preaching my father attended, but never I myself. "Pay," it said, "or be locked up in the jail." I declined to pay. But, unfortunately, another man saw fit to pay it. I did not see why the schoolmaster should be taxed to support the priest, and not the priest the schoolmaster; for I was not the State's schoolmaster, but I supported myself by voluntary subscription. I did not see why the lyceum should not present its tax-bill, and have the State to back its demand, as well as the Church. However, at the request of the selectmen, I condescended to make some such statement as this in writing:—"Know all men by these presents, that I, Henry Thoreau, do not wish to be regarded as a member of any incorporated society which I have not joined." This I gave to the town clerk; and he has it. The State, having thus learned that I did not wish to be regarded as a member of that church, has never made a like demand on me since; though it said that it must adhere to its original presumption that time. If I had known how to name them, I should then have signed off in detail from all the societies which I never signed on to; but I did not know where to find a complete list.

I have paid no poll-tax for six years. I was put into a jail once on this account, for one night; and, as I stood considering the walls of solid stone, two or three feet thick, the door of wood and iron, a foot thick, and the iron grating which strained the light, I could not help being struck with the foolishness of that institution which treated me as if I were mere flesh and blood and bones, to be locked up. I wondered that it should have concluded at length that this was the best use it could put me to, and had never thought to avail itself of my services in some way. I saw that, if there was a wall of stone between me and my townsmen, there was a still more difficult one to climb or break through before they could get to be as free as I was. I did not for a moment feel confined, and the walls seemed a great waste of stone and mortar. I felt as if I alone of all my townsmen had paid my tax. They plainly did not know how to treat me, but behaved like persons who are underbred. In every threat and in every compliment there was a blunder; for they thought that my chief desire was to stand the other side of that stone wall. I could not but smile to see how industriously they locked the door on my meditations, which followed them out again without let or hindrance, and *they* were really all that was dangerous. As they could not reach me, they had resolved to punish my body; just as boys, if they cannot come at some person against whom they have a spite, will abuse his dog. I saw that the State was half-witted, that it was timid as a lone woman with her silver spoons, and that it did not know its friends from its foes, and I lost all my remaining respect for it, and pitied it.

Thus the State never intentionally confronts a man's sense, intellectual or moral, but only his body, his senses. It is not armed with superior wit or honesty, but with superior physical strength. I was not born to be forced. I

358

will breathe after my own fashion. Let us see who is the strongest. What force has a multitude? They only can force me who obey a higher law than I. They force me to become like themselves. I do not hear of *men* being *forced* to live this way or that by masses of men. What sort of life were that to live? When I meet a government which says to me, "Your money or your life," why should I be in haste to give it my money? It may be in a great strait, and not know what to do: I cannot help that. It must help itself; do as I do. It is not worth the while to snivel about it. I am not responsible for the successful working of the machinery of society. I am not the son of the engineer. I perceive that, when an acorn and a chestnut fall side by side, the one does not remain inert to make way for the other, but both obey their own laws, and spring and grow and flourish as best they can, till one, perchance, overshadows and destroys the other. If a plant cannot live according to its nature, it dies; and so a man.

The night in prison was novel and interesting enough. The prisoners in their shirt-sleeves were enjoying a chat and the evening air in the doorway, when I entered. But the jailer said, "Come, boys, it is time to lock up;" and so they dispersed, and I heard the sound of their steps returning into the hollow apartments. My room-mate was introduced to me by the jailer as "a first-rate fellow and a clever man." When the door was locked, he showed me where to hang my hat, and how he managed matters there. The rooms were whitewashed once a month; and this one, at least, was the whitest, most simply furnished, and probably the neatest apartment in the town. He naturally wanted to know where I came from, and what brought me there; and, when I had told him, I asked him in my turn how he came there, presuming him to be an honest man, of course; and, as the world goes, I believe he was. "Why," said he, "they accuse me of burning a barn; but I never did it." As near as I could discover, he had probably gone to bed in a barn when drunk, and smoked his pipe there; and so a barn was burnt. He had the reputation of being a clever man, had been there some three months waiting for his trial to come on, and would have to wait as much longer; but he was quite domesticated and contented, since he got his board for nothing, and thought that he was well treated.

He occupied one window, and I the other; and I saw that if one stayed there long, his principal business would be to look out the window. I had soon read all the tracts that were left there, and examined where former prisoners had broken out, and where a grate had been sawed off, and heard the history of the various occupants of that room; for I found that even here there was a history and a gossip which never circulated beyond the walls of the jail. Probably this is the only house in the town where verses are composed, which are afterward printed in a circular form, but not published. I was shown quite a long list of verses which were composed by some young men who had been detected in an attempt to escape, who avenged themselves by singing them.

I pumped my fellow-prisoner as dry as I could, for fear I should never see him again; but at length he showed me which was my bed, and left me to blow out the lamp.

It was like traveling into a far country, such as I had never expected to behold, to lie there for one night. It seemed to me that I never had heard the town-clock strike before, nor the evening sounds of the village; for we slept with the windows open, which were inside the grating. It was to see my native village in the light of the Middle Ages, and our Concord was turned into a Rhine stream, and visions of knights and castles passed before me. They were the voices of old burghers that I heard in the streets. I was an involuntary spectator and auditor of whatever was done and said in the kitchen of the adjacent village-inn,—a wholly new and rare experience to me. It was a closer view of my native town. I was fairly inside of it. I never had seen its institutions before. This is one of its peculiar institutions; for it is a shire town. I began to comprehend what its inhabitants were about.

In the morning, our breakfasts were put through the hole in the door, in small oblong-square tin pans, made to fit, and holding a pint of chocolate, with brown bread, and an iron spoon. When they called for the vessels again, I was green enough to return what bread I had left; but my comrade seized it, and said that I should lay that up for lunch or dinner. Soon after he was let out to work at haying in a neighboring field, whither he went every day, and would not be back till noon; so he bade me good-day, saying that he doubted if he should see me again.

When I came out of prison,—for some one interfered, and paid that tax, —I did not perceive that great changes had taken place on the common, such as he observed who went in a youth and emerged a tottering and gray-headed man; and yet a change had to my eyes come over the scene,—the town, and State, and country,—greater than any that mere time could effect. I saw yet more distinctly the State in which I lived. I saw to what extent the people among whom I lived could be trusted as good neighbors and friends; that their friendship was for summer weather only; that they did not greatly propose to do right; that they were a distinct race from me by their prejudices and superstitions, as the Chinamen and Malays are; that in their sacrifices to humanity they ran no risks, not even to their property; that after all they were not so noble but they treated the thief as he had treated them, and hoped, by a certain outward observance and a few prayers, and by walking in a particular straight though useless path from time to time, to save their souls. This may be to judge my neighbors harshly; for I believe that many of them are not aware that they have such an institution as the jail in their village.

It was formerly the custom in our village, when a poor debtor came out of jail, for his acquaintances to salute him, looking through their fingers, which were crossed to represent the grating of a jail window, "How do ye do?" My neighbors did not thus salute me, but first looked at me, and then at one another, as if I had returned from a long journey. I was put into jail as I was going to the shoemaker's to get a shoe which was mended. When I was let out the next morning, I proceeded to finish my errand, and, having put on my mended shoe, joined a huckleberry party, who were impatient to put themselves under my conduct; and in half an hour,—for the horse was soon tackled, —was in the midst of a huckleberry field, on one of our highest hills, two miles off, and then the State was nowhere to be seen.

This is the whole history of "My Prisons."

I have never declined paying the highway tax, because I am desirous of being a good neighbor as I am of being a bad subject; and as for supporting schools, I am doing my part to educate my fellow-countrymen now. It is for no particular item in the tax-bill that I refuse to pay it. I simply wish to refuse allegiance to the State, to withdraw and stand aloof from it effectually. I do not care to trace the course of my dollar, if I could, till it buys a man or a musket to shoot one with,—the dollar is innocent,—but I am concerned to trace the effects of my allegiance. In fact, I quietly declare war with the State, after my fashion, though I will still make what use and get what advantage of her I can, as is usual in such cases.

If others pay the tax which is demanded of me, from a sympathy with the State, they do but what they have already done in their own case, or rather they abet injustice to a greater extent than the State requires. If they pay the tax from a mistaken interest in the individual taxed, to save his property, or prevent his going to jail, it is because they have not considered wisely how far they let their private feelings interfere with the public good.

This, then, is my position at present. But one cannot be too much on his guard in such a case, lest his action be biased by obstinacy or an undue regard for the opinions of men. Let him see that he does only what belongs to himself and to the hour.

I think sometimes, Why, this people mean well, they are only ignorant; they would do better if they knew how: why give your neighbors this pain to treat you as they are not inclined to? But I think again, This is no reason why I should do as they do, or permit others to suffer much greater pain of a different kind. Again, I sometimes say to myself, When many millions of men, without heat, without ill will, without personal feeling of any kind, demand of you a few shillings only, without the possibility, such is their constitution, of retracting or altering their present demand, and without the possibility, on your side, of appeal to any other millions, why expose yourself to this over-whelming brute force? You do not resist cold and hunger, the winds and the waves, thus obstinately; you quietly submit to a thousand similar necessities. You do not put your head into the fire. But just in proportion as I regard this as not wholly a brute force, but partly a human force, and consider that I have relations to those millions as to so many millions of men, and not of mere brute or inanimate things, I see that appeal is possible, first and instanta-neously, from them to the Maker of them, and, secondly, from them to themselves. But if I put my head deliberately into the fire, there is no appeal to fire or to the Maker of fire, and I have only myself to blame. If I could convince myself that I have any right to be satisfied with men as they are, and to treat them accordingly, and not according, in some respects, to my requisi-tions and expectations of what they and I ought to be, then, like a good Mussulman and fatalist, I should endeavor to be satisfied with things as they are, and say it is the will of God. And, above all, there is this difference be-tween resisting this and a purely brute or natural force, that I can resist this with some effect; but I cannot expect, like Orpheus, to change the nature of the rocks and trees and beasts.

I do not wish to quarrel with any man or nation. I do not wish to split hairs, to make fine distinctions, or set myself up as better than my neighbors. I seek rather, I may say, even an excuse for conforming to the laws of the land. I am but too ready to conform to them. Indeed, I have reason to suspect myself on this head; and each year, as the tax-gatherer comes round, I find myself disposed to review the acts and position of the general and State governments, and the spirit of the people, to discover a pretext for conformity.

> "We must affect our country as our parents,
> And if at any time we alienate
> Our love or industry from doing it honor,
> We must respect effects and teach the soul
> Matter of conscience and religion,
> And not desire of rule or benefit."

I believe that the State will soon be able to take all my work of this sort out of my hands, and then I shall be no better a patriot than my fellow-countrymen. Seen from a lower point of view, the Constitution, with all its faults, is very good; the law and the courts are very respectable; even this State and this American government are, in many respects, very admirable, and rare things, to be thankful for, such as a great many have described them; but seen from a point of view a little higher, they are what I have described them; seen from a higher still, and the highest, who shall say what they are, or that they are worth looking at or thinking of at all?

However, the government does not concern me much, and I shall bestow the fewest possible thoughts on it. It is not many moments that I live under a government, even in this world. If a man is thought-free, fancy-free, imagination-free, that which *is not* never for a long time appearing *to be* to him, unwise rulers or reformers cannot fatally interrupt him.

I know that most men think differently from myself; but those whose lives are by profession devoted to the study of these or kindred subjects content me as little as any. Statesmen and legislators, standing so completely within the institution, never distinctly and nakedly behold it. They speak of moving society, but have no resting-place without it. They may be men of a certain experience and discrimination, and have no doubt invented ingenious and even useful systems, for which we sincerely thank them; but all their wit and usefulness lie within certain not very wide limits. They are wont to forget that the world is not governed by policy and expediency. Webster never goes behind government, and so cannot speak with authority about it. His words are wisdom to those legislators who contemplate no essential reform in the existing government; but for thinkers, and those who legislate for all time, he never once glances at the subject. I know of those whose serene and wise speculations on this theme would soon reveal the limits of his mind's range and hospitality. Yet, compared with the cheap professions of most reformers, and the still cheaper wisdom and eloquence of politicians in general, his are almost the only sensible and valuable words, and we thank Heaven for him. Comparatively, he is always

362

strong, original, and above all, practical. Still, his quality is not wisdom, but prudence. The lawyer's truth is not Truth, but consistency or a consistent expediency. Truth is always in harmony with herself, and is not concerned chiefly to reveal the justice that may consist with wrong-doing. He well deserves to be called, as he has been called, the Defender of the Constitution. There are really no blows to be given by him but defensive ones. He is not a leader, but a follower. His leaders are the men of '87. "I have never made an effort," he says, "and never propose to make an effort; I have never countenanced an effort, and never mean to countenance an effort, to disturb the arrangement as originally made, by which the various States came into the Union." Still thinking of the sanction which the Constitution gives to slavery, he says, "Because it was a part of the original compact,—let it stand." Notwithstanding his special acuteness and ability, he is unable to take a fact out of its merely political relations, and behold it as it lies absolutely to be disposed of by the intellect, —what, for instance, it behooves a man to do here in America to-day with regard to slavery,—but ventures, or is driven, to make some such desperate answer as the following, while professing to speak absolutely, and as a private man,—from which what new and singular code of social duties might be inferred? "The manner," says he, "in which the governments of those States where slavery exists are to regulate it is for their own consideration, under their responsibility to their constituents, to the general laws of propriety, humanity, and justice, and to God. Associations formed elsewhere, springing from a feeling of humanity, or any other cause, have nothing whatever to do with it. They have never received any encouragement from me, and they never will."[1]

They who know of no purer sources of truth, who have traced up its stream no higher, stand, and wisely stand, by the Bible and the Constitution, and drink at it there with reverence and humility; but they who behold where it comes trickling into this lake or that pool, gird up their loins once more, and continue their pilgrimage toward its fountain-head.

No man with a genius for legislation has appeared in America. They are rare in the history of the world. There are orators, politicians, and eloquent men, by the thousand; but the speaker has not yet opened his mouth to speak who is capable of settling the much-vexed questions of the day. We love eloquence for its own sake, and not for any truth which it may utter, or any heroism it may inspire. Our legislators have not yet learned the comparative value of free-trade and of freedom, of union, and of rectitude, to a nation. They have no genius or talent for comparatively humble questions of taxation and finance, commerce and manufactures and agriculture. If we were left solely to the wordy wit of legislators in Congress for our guidance, uncorrected by the seasonable experience and the effectual complaints of the people, America would not long retain her rank among the nations. For eighteen hundred years, though perchance I have no right to say it, the New Testament has been written; yet where is the legislator who has wisdom and practical talent enough to avail himself of the light which it sheds on the science of legislation?

[1] These extracts have been inserted since the lecture was read.

The authority of government, even such as I am willing to submit to,—for I will cheerfully obey those who know and can do better than I, and in many things even those who neither know nor can do so well,—is still an impure one: to be strictly just, it must have the sanction and consent of the governed. It can have no pure right over my person and property but what I concede to it. The progress from an absolute to a limited monarchy, from a limited monarchy to a democracy, is a progress toward a true respect for the individual. Even the Chinese philosopher was wise enough to regard the individual as the basis of the empire. Is a democracy, such as we know it, the last improvement possible in government? Is it not possible to take a step further towards recognizing and organizing the rights of man? There will never be a really free and enlightened State until the State comes to recognize the individual as a higher and independent power, from which all its own power and authority are derived, and treats him accordingly. I please myself with imagining a State at last which can afford to be just to all men, and to treat the individual with respect as a neighbor; which even would not think it inconsistent with its own repose if a few were to live aloof from it, not meddling with it, nor embraced by it, who fulfilled all the duties of neighbors and fellowmen. A State which bore this kind of fruit, and suffered it to drop off as fast as it ripened, would prepare the way for a still more perfect and glorious State, which also I have imagined, but not yet anywhere seen.

The Proposal [1]

ANTON CHEKHOV

DRAMATIS PERSONAE

STEPAN STEPANOVITCH CHUBUKOV, *a landowner.*
NATALYA STEPANOVNA, *his daughter, 25 years old.*
IVAN VASSILEVITCH LOMOV, *a neighbour of* CHUBUKOV, *a large and hearty, but very suspicious landowner.*
The scene is laid at CHUBUKOV'S *country-house.*

A drawing-room in CHUBUKOV'S *house.*

[LOMOV *enters, wearing a dress-jacket and white gloves.* CHUBUKOV *rises to meet him.*]
CHUBUKOV. My dear fellow, Ivan Vassilevitch! I am delighted! [*Squeezes his hand.*] A surprise, my darling. . . . How are you?
LOMOV. Thank you. And how are you?
CHUBUKOV. We just get along somehow, my angel, thanks to your prayers, and so forth. Sit down, please do. . . . Why do you forget your neighbours, my darling? My dear fellow, why are you so formal in your evening dress, gloves, and so forth? Are you going anywhere?
LOMOV. No, I've come only to see you, honoured Stepan Stepanovitch.
CHUBUKOV. Then why are you in evening dress, my good fellow? As if you're paying a New Year's Eve visit!
LOMOV. Well, you see, it's like this. [*Takes his arm.*] I've come to you, honoured Stepan Stepanovitch, to trouble you with a request. Often have I already had the privilege of applying to you for help, and you have always, so to speak . . . I ask your pardon, I am becoming excited. I shall drink some water, honoured Stepan Stepanovitch. [*Drinks.*]
CHUBUKOV [*aside*]. He's come to borrow money! Never! [*Aloud.*] What is it, dear boy?

[1] *The Works of Anton Chekhov* (Roslyn, New York: Walter J. Black, Inc., 1929), pp. 665–674.

LOMOV. You see, Honour Stepanitch . . . I beg pardon, Stepan Honour-itch . . . I mean, I'm awfully excited, as you will notice . . . In short, you alone can help me, though I don't deserve it, of course . . .

CHUBUKOV. Don't beat around the bush, darling! Spit it out! Well?

LOMOV. One moment . . . this very minute. The fact is, I've come to ask the hand of your daughter, Natalya Stepanovna, in marriage.

CHUBUKOV [*joyfully*]. By Jove! Ivan Vassilevitch! Say it again—I didn't hear it all!

LOMOV. I have the honour to ask . . .

CHUBUKOV [*interrupting*]. My dear boy . . . I'm so glad. . . . Yes, indeed. [*Embraces and kisses* LOMOV.] I've been hoping for it for a long time. It's been my long desire. [*Sheds a tear.*] And I've always loved you, my angel, as if you were my own son. May God give you both His help and His love, and I did so much hope . . . What am I behaving in this idiotic way for? I'm giddy with joy, absolutely. Oh, with all my soul . . . I'll go and call Natasha.

LOMOV [*greatly moved*]. Honoured Stepan Stepanovitch, do you think she will consent?

CHUBUKOV. Why, of course, my darling . . . as if she won't consent! She's in love; she's like a lovesick cat. Be right back! [*Exit.*]

LOMOV. It's cold . . . I'm trembling all over, just as if I'd got an exam-ination before me. The great thing is, to decide. If I give myself time to think, to hesitate, to talk, to look for an ideal, or for real love, then I'll never get married. . . . Brr! . . . It's cold! Natalya Stepanovna is an excellent house-keeper, not bad-looking, well-educated. . . . What more do I want? But I'm getting a noise in my ears from excitement. [*Drinks.*] And it's impossible for me not to marry . . . In the first place, I'm already 35—a critical age, so to speak. In the second place, I ought to lead a quiet and regular life . . . I suffer from palpitations, I'm excitable and always getting awfully upset . . . At this very moment my lips are trembling, and there's a twitch in my right eyebrow. . . . But the very worst of all is the way I sleep. I no sooner get into bed and begin to go off when suddenly something in my left side—gives a pull, and I can feel it in my shoulder and head. . . . I jump up like a lunatic, walk about a bit, and lie down again, but as soon as I begin to get off to sleep there's another pull! And this may happen twenty times. . . .

NATALYA STEPANOVNA *comes in.*

NATALYA STEPANOVNA. Well, there! It's you, and papa said, 'Go; there's a merchant come for his goods.' How do you do, Ivan Vassilevitch!

LOMOV. How do you do, honoured Natalya Stepanovna?

NATALYA STEPANOVNA. You must excuse my apron and *négligé* . . . we're shelling peas for drying. Why haven't you been here for such a long time Sit down . . . [*They seat themselves.*] Won't you have some lunch?

LOMOV. No, thank you, I've had some already.

NATALYA STEPANOVNA. Then smoke. . . . Here are the matches. . . . The weather is splendid now, but yesterday it was so wet that the workmen didn't do anything all day. How much hay have you stacked? Just think, I felt greedy and had a whole field cut, and now I'm not at all pleased about it because I'm afraid my hay may rot. I ought to have waited a bit. But what's this? Why, you're in evening dress! Well, I never! Are you going to a ball, or what?— though I must say you look better. . . . Tell me, why are you got up like that?

LOMOV [*excited*]. You see, honoured Natalya Stepanovna . . . the fact is, I've made up my mind to ask you to hear me out. . . . Of course you'll be surprised and perhaps even angry, but a . . . [*Aside.*] It's awfully cold!

NATALYA STEPANOVNA. What's the matter? [*Pause.*] Well?

LOMOV. I shall try to be brief. You must know, honoured Natalya Stepanovna, that I have long, since my childhood, in fact, had the privilege of knowing your family. My late aunt and her husband, from whom, as you know, I inherited my land, always had the greatest respect for your father and your late mother. The Lomovs and the Chubukovs have always had the most friendly, and I might almost say the most affectionate, regard for each other. And, as you know, my land is a near neighbour of yours. You will remember that my Oxen Meadows touch your birchwoods.

NATALYA STEPANOVNA. Excuse my interrupting you. You say, 'my Oxen Meadows. . . .' But are they yours?

LOMOV. Yes, mine.

NATALYA STEPANOVNA. What are you talking about? Oxen Meadows are ours, not yours!

LOMOV. No, mine, honoured Natalya Stepanovna.

NATALYA STEPANOVNA. Well, I never knew that before. How do you make that out?

LOMOV. How? I'm speaking of those Oxen Meadows which are wedged in between your birchwoods and the Burnt Marsh.

NATALYA STEPANOVNA. Yes, yes. . . . They're ours.

LOMOV. No, you're mistaken, honoured Natalya Stepanovna, they're mine.

NATALYA STEPANOVNA. Just think, Ivan Vassilevitch! How long have they been yours?

LOMOV. How long? As long as I can remember.

NATALYA STEPANOVNA. Really, you won't get me to believe that!

LOMOV. But you can see from the documents, honoured Natalya Stepanovna. Oxen Meadows, it's true, were once the subject of dispute, but now everybody knows that they are mine. There's nothing to argue about. You see, my aunt's grandmother gave the free use of these Meadows in perpetuity to the peasants of your father's grandfather, in return for which they were to make bricks for her. The peasants belonging to your father's grandfather had the free use of the Meadows for forty years, and had got into the habit of regarding them as their own, when it happened that . . .

NATALYA STEPANOVNA. No, it isn't at all like that! Both my grandfather and great-grandfather reckoned that their land extended to Burnt Marsh— which means that Oxen Meadows were ours. I don't see what there is to argue about. It's simply silly!

LOMOV. I'll show you the documents, Natalya Stepanovna!

NATALYA STEPANOVNA. No, you're simply joking, or making fun of me. . . . What a surprise! We've had the land for nearly three hundred years, and then we're suddenly told that it isn't ours! Ivan Vassilevitch, I can hardly believe my own ears. . . . These Meadows aren't worth much to me. They only come to five dessiatins, and are worth perhaps 300 roubles, but I can't stand unfairness. Say what you will, but I can't stand unfairness.

Lomov. Hear me out, I implore you! The peasants of your father's grandfather, as I have already had the honour of explaining to you, used to bake bricks for my aunt's grandmother. Now my aunt's grandmother, wishing to make them a pleasant . . .

Natalya Stepanovna. I can't make head or tail of all this about aunts and grandfathers and grandmothers. The Meadows are ours, and that's all.

Lomov. Mine.

Natalya Stepanova. Ours! You can go on proving it for two days on end, you can go and put on fifteen dress-jackets, but I tell you they're ours, ours, ours! I don't want anything of yours and I don't want to give up anything of mine. So there!

Lomov. Natalya Ivanovna, I don't want the Meadows, but I am acting on principle. If you like, I'll make you a present of them.

Natalya Stepanovna. I can make you a present of them myself, because they're mine! Your behaviour, Ivan Vassilevitch, is strange, to say the least! Up to this we have always thought of you as a good neighbour, a friend: last year we lent you our threshing-machine, although on that account we had to put off our own threshing till November, but you behave to us as if we were gipsies. Giving me my own land, indeed! No, really, that's not at all neighbourly! In my opinion, it's even impudent, if you want to know. . . .

Lomov. Then you make out that I'm a land-grabber? Madam, never in my life have I grabbed anybody else's land, and I shan't allow anybody to accuse me of having done so. . . . [*Quickly steps to the carafe and drinks more water.*] Oxen Meadows are mine!

Natalya Stepanovna. It's not true, they're ours!

Lomov. Mine!

Natalya Stepanovna. It's not true! I'll prove it! I'll send my mowers out to the Meadows this very day!

Lomov. What?

Natalya Stepanovna. My mowers will be there this very day!

Lomov. I'll give it to them in the neck!

Natalya Stepanovna. You dare!

Lomov [*clutches at his heart*]. Oxen Meadows are mine! You understand? Mine!

Natalya Stepanovna. Please don't shout! You can shout yourself hoarse in your own house, but here I must ask you to restrain yourself!

Lomov. If it wasn't, madam, for this awful, excruciating palpitation, if my whole inside wasn't upset, I'd talk to you in a different way! [*Yells.*] Oxen Meadows are mine!

Natalya Stepanovna. Ours!

Lomov. Mine!

Natalya Stepanovna. Ours!

Lomov. Mine!

[*Enter* CHUBUKOV.]

CHUBUKOV. What's the matter? What are you shouting at?

NATALYA STEPANOVNA. Papa, please tell to this gentleman who owns Oxen Meadows, we or he?

CHUBUKOV [*to* LOMOV]. Darling, the Meadows are ours!

LOMOV. But, please, Stepan Stepanitch, how can they be yours? Do be a reasonable man! My aunt's grandmother gave the Meadows for the temporary and free use of your grandfather's peasants. The peasants used the land for forty years and got as accustomed to it as if it was their own, when it happened that . . .

CHUBUKOV. Excuse me, my precious. . . . You forget just this, that the peasants didn't pay your grandmother and all that, because the Meadows were in dispute, and so on. And now everybody knows that they're ours. It means that you haven't seen the plan.

LOMOV. I'll prove to you that they're mine!

CHUBUKOV. You won't prove it, my darling.

LOMOV. I shall!

CHUBUKOV. Dear one, why yell like that? You won't prove anything just by yelling. I don't want anything of yours, and don't intend to give up what I have. Why should I? And you know, my beloved, that if you propose to go on arguing about it, I'd much sooner give up the Meadows to the peasants than to you. There!

LOMOV. I don't understand! How have you the right to give away somebody else's property!

CHUBUKOV. You may take it that I know whether I have the right or not. Because, young man, I'm not used to being spoken to in that tone of voice, and so on. I, young man, am twice your age, and ask you to speak to me without agitating yourself, and all that.

LOMOV. No, you just think I'm a fool and want to have me on! You call my land yours, and then you want me to talk to you calmly and politely! Good neighbours don't behave like that, Stepan Stepanitch! You're not a neighbour, you're a grabber!

CHUBUKOV. What's that? What did you say?

NATALYA STEPANOVNA. Papa, send the mowers out to the Meadows at once!

CHUBUKOV. What did you say, sir?

NATALYA STEPANOVNA. Oxen Meadows are ours, and I shan't give them up, shan't give them up, shan't give them up!

LOMOV. We'll see! I'll have the matter taken to court, and then I'll show you!

CHUBUKOV. To court? You can take it to court, and all that! You can! I know you; you're just on the look-out for a chance to go to court, and all that. . . . You pettifogger! All your people were like that! All of them!

LOMOV. Never mind about my people! The Lomovs have all been honourable people, and not one has ever been tried for embezzlement, like your grandfather!

CHUBUKOV. You Lomovs have had lunacy in your family, all of you!

NATALYA STEPANOVNA. All, all, all!

CHUBUKOV. Your grandfather was a drunkard, and your younger aunt, Nastasya Mihailovna, ran away with an architect, and so on. . . .

LOMOV. And your mother was hump-backed. [*Clutches at his heart.*] Something pulling in my side. . . . My head. . . . Help! Water!

CHUBUKOV. Your father was a guzzling gambler!

NATALYA STEPANOVNA. And there haven't been many backbiters to equal your aunt!

LOMOV. My left foot has gone to sleep. . . . You're an intriguer. . . . Oh, my heart! . . . And it's an open secret that before the last elections you bri . . . I can see stars. . . . Where's my hat?

NATALYA STEPANOVNA. It's low! It's dishonest! It's mean!

CHUBUKOV. And you're just a malicious, double-faced intriguer! Yes!

LOMOV. Here's my hat. . . . My heart! . . . Which way? Where's the door? Oh! . . . I think I'm dying. . . . My foot's quite numb. . . . [*Goes to the door.*]

CHUBUKOV [*following him*]. And don't set foot in my house again!

NATALYA STEPANOVNA. Take it to court! We'll see!

LOMOV *staggers out.*

CHUBUKOV. Devil take him! [*Walks about in excitement.*]

NATALYA STEPANOVNA. What a rascal! What trust can one have in one's neighbours after that!

CHUBUKOV. The villain! The scarecrow!

NATALYA STEPANOVNA. The monster! First he takes our land and then he has the impudence to abuse us.

CHUBUKOV. And that blind hen, yes, that turnip-ghost has the confounded cheek to make a proposal, and so on! What? A proposal!

NATALYA STEPANOVNA. What proposal?

CHUBUKOV. Why, he came here so as to propose to you.

NATALYA STEPANOVNA. To propose? To me? Why didn't you tell me so before?

CHUBUKOV. So he dresses up in evening clothes. The stuffed sausage! The wizen-faced frump!

NATALYA STEPANOVNA. To propose to me? Ah! [*Falls into an easy-chair and wails.*] Bring him back! Back! Ah! Bring him here.

CHUBUKOV. Bring whom here?

NATALYA STEPANOVNA. Quick, quick! I'm ill! Fetch him! [*Hysterics.*]

CHUBUKOV. What's that? What's the matter with you? [*Clutches at his head.*] Oh, unhappy man that I am! I'll shoot myself! I'll hang myself! We've done for her!

NATALYA STEPANOVNA. I'm dying! Fetch him!

CHUBUKOV. Tfoo! At once. Don't yell!

Runs out. A pause. NATALYA STEPANOVNA *wails.*

NATALYA STEPANOVNA. What have they done to me! Fetch him back! Fetch him! [*A pause.*]

CHUBUKOV *runs in.*

CHUBUKOV. He's coming, and so on, devil take him! Ouf! Talk to him yourself; I don't want to. . . .

NATALYA STEPANOVNA. [wails]. Fetch him!

CHUBUKOV [yells]. He's coming, I tell you. Oh, what a burden, Lord, to be the father of a grown-up daughter! I'll cut my throat! I will, indeed! We cursed him, abused him, drove him out, and it's all you . . . you!

NATALYA STEPANOVNA. No, it was you!

CHUBUKOV. I tell you it's not my fault. [LOMOV appears at the door.] Now you talk to him yourself. [Exit.]

LOMOV enters, exhausted.

LOMOV. My heart's palpitating awfully. . . . My foot's gone to sleep. . . . There's something keeps pulling in my side. . . .

NATALYA STEPANOVNA. Forgive us, Ivan Vassilevitch, we were all a little heated. . . . I remember now: Oxen Meadows really are yours.

LOMOV. My heart's beating awfully. . . . My Meadows. . . . My eyebrows are both twitching. . . .

NATALYA STEPANOVNA. The Meadows are yours, yes, yours. . . . Do sit down. . . . [They sit.] We were wrong. . . .

LOMOV. I did it on principle. . . . My land is worth little to me, but the principle . . .

NATALYA STEPANOVNA. Yes, the principle, just so. . . . Now let's talk of something else.

LOMOV. The more so as I have evidence. My aunt's grandmother gave the land to your father's grandfather's peasants . . .

NATALYA STEPANOVNA. Yes, yes, let that pass. . . . [Aside.] I wish I knew how to get him started. . . . [Aloud.] Are you going to start shooting soon?

LOMOV. I'm thinking of having a go at the blackcock, honoured Natalya Stepanovna, after the harvest. Oh, have you heard? Just think, what a misfortune I've had! My dog Guess, whom you know, has gone lame.

NATALYA STEPANOVNA. What a pity! Why?

LOMOV. I don't know. . . . Must have got twisted, or bitten by some other dog. . . . [Sighs.] My very best dog, to say nothing of the expense. I gave Mironov 125 roubles for him.

NATALYA STEPANOVNA. It was too much, Ivan Vassilevitch.

LOMOV. I think it was very cheap. He's a first-rate dog.

NATALYA STEPANOVNA. Papa gave 85 roubles for his Squeezer, and Squeezer is heaps better than Guess!

LOMOV. Squeezer better than Guess? What an idea! [Laughs.] Squeezer better than Guess!

NATALYA STEPANOVNA. Of course he's better! Of course, Squeezer is young, he may develop a bit, but on points and pedigree he's better than anything that even Volchantesky has got.

LOMOV. Excuse me, Natalya Stepanovna, but you forget that he is overshot, and an overshot always means the dog is a bad hunter!

NATALYA STEPANOVNA. Overshot, is he? The first time I hear it!

Lomov. I assure you that his lower jaw is shorter than the upper.

Natalya Stepanovna. Have you measured?

Lomov. Yes. He's all right at following, of course, but if you want him to get hold of anything . . .

Natalya Stepanovna. In the first place, our Squeezer is a thoroughbred animal, the son of Harness and Chisels, while there's no getting at the pedigree of your dog at all. . . . He's old and as ugly as a worn-out cab-horse.

Lomov. He is old, but I wouldn't take five Squeezers for him. . . . Why, how can you? . . . Guess is a dog; as for Squeezer, well, it's too funny to argue. . . . Anybody you like has a dog as good as Squeezer . . . you may find them under every bush almost. Twenty-five roubles would be a handsome price to pay for him.

Natalya Stepanovna. There's some demon of contradiction in you to-day, Ivan Vassilevitch. First you pretend that the Meadows are yours; now, that Guess is better than Squeezer. I don't like people who don't say what they mean, because you know perfectly well that Squeezer is a hundred times better than your silly Guess. Why do you want to say it isn't?

Lomov. I see, Natalya Stepanovna, that you consider me either blind or a fool. You must realize that Squeezer is overshot!

Natalya Stepanovna. It's not true.

Lomov. He is!

Natalya Stepanovna. It's not true!

Lomov. Why shout, madam?

Natalya Stepanovna. Why talk rot? It's awful! It's time your Guess was shot, and you compare him with Squeezer!

Lomov. Excuse me; I cannot continue this discussion, my heart is palpitating.

Natalya Stepanovna. I've noticed that those hunters argue most who know least.

Lomov. Madam, please be silent. . . . My heart is going to pieces . . . [Shouts.] Shut up!

Natalya Stepanovna. I shan't shut up until you acknowledge that Squeezer is a hundred times better than your Guess!

Lomov. A hundred times worse! Be hanged to your Squeezer! His head . . . eyes . . . shoulder . . .

Natalya Stepanovna. There's no need to hang your silly Guess; he's half-dead already!

Lomov [weeps]. Shut up! My heart's bursting!

Natalya Stepanovna. I shan't shut up.

Enter Chubukov.

Chubukov. What's the matter now?

Natalya Stepanovna. Papa, tell us truly, which is the better dog, our Squeezer or his Guess.

Lomov. Stepan Stepanovitch, I implore you to tell me just one thing: is your Squeezer overshot or not? Yes or no?

Chubukov. And suppose he is? What does it matter? He's the best dog in the district for all that, and so on.

LOMOV. But isn't my Guess better? Really, now?

CHUBUKOV. Don't excite yourself, my precious one. . . . Allow me. . . . Your Guess certainly has his good points. . . . He's pure-bred, firm on his feet, has well-sprung ribs, and all that. But, my dear man, if you want to know the truth, that dog has two defects: he's old and he's short in the muzzle.

LOMOV. Excuse me, my heart. . . . Let's take the facts. . . . You will remember that on the Marusinsky hunt my Guess ran neck-and-neck with the Count's dog, while your Squeezer was left a whole verst behind.

CHUBUKOV. He got left behind because the Count's whipper-in hit him with his whip.

LOMOV. And with good reason. The dogs are running after a fox, when Squeezer goes and starts worrying a sheep!

CHUBUKOV. It's not true! . . . My dear fellow, I'm very liable to lose my temper, and so, just because of that, let's stop arguing. You started because everybody is always jealous of everybody else's dogs. Yes, we're all like that! You too, sir, aren't blameless! You no sooner notice that some dog is better than your Guess than you begin with this, that . . . and the other . . . and all that. . . . I remember everything!

LOMOV. I remember too!

CHUBUKOV [teasing him]. I remember, too. . . . What do you remember?

LOMOV. My heart . . . my foot's gone to sleep. . . . I can't . . .

NATALYA STEPANOVNA [teasing]. My heart. . . . What sort of a hunter are you? You ought to go and lie on the kitchen oven and catch blackbeetles, not go after foxes! My heart!

CHUBUKOV. Yes really, what sort of a hunter are you, anyway! You ought to sit at home with your palpitations, and not go tracking animals. You could go hunting, but you only go to argue with people and interfere with their dogs and so on. Let's change the subject in case I lose my temper. You're not a hunter at all, anyway!

LOMOV. And are you a hunter? You only go hunting to get in with the Count and to intrigue. . . . Oh, my heart! . . . You're an intriguer!

CHUBUKOV. What? I an intriguer? [Shouts.] Shut up!

LOMOV. Intriguer!

CHUBUKOV. Boy! Pup!

LOMOV. Old rat! Jesuit!

CHUBUKOV. Shut up or I'll shoot you like a partridge! You fool!

LOMOV. Everybody knows that—oh my heart!—your late wife used to beat you. . . . My feet . . . temples . . . sparks. . . . I fall, I fall!

CHUBUKOV. And you're under the slipper of your housekeeper!

LOMOV. There, there, there . . . my heart's burst! My shoulder's come off. . . . Where is my shoulder? . . . I die. [Falls into an armchair.] A doctor! [Faints.]

CHUBUKOV. Boy! Milksop! Fool! I'm sick! [Drinks water.] Sick!

NATALYA STEPANOVNA. What sort of a hunter are you? You can't even sit on a horse. [To her father.] Papa, what's the matter with him? Papa! Look, papa! [Screams.] Ivan Vassilevitch! He's dead!

CHUBUKOV. I'm sick! . . . I can't breathe! . . . Air!

Natalya Stepanovna.   He's dead. [*Pulls* Lomov's *sleeve*.] Ivan Vassile-vitch! Ivan Vassilevitch! What have you done to me? He's dead. [*Falls into an armchair.*] A doctor, a doctor! [*Hysterics.*]

Chubukov.   Oh! . . . What is it? What's the matter?

Natalya Stepanovna [*wails*]. He's dead . . . dead!

Chubukov.   Who's dead? [*Looks at* Lomov.] So he is! My word! Water! A doctor! [*Lifts a tumbler to* Lomov's *mouth*.] Drink this! . . . No, he doesn't drink. . . . It means he's dead, and all that. . . . I'm the most unhappy of men! Why don't I put a bullet into my brain? Why haven't I cut my throat yet? What am I waiting for? Give me a knife! Give me a pistol! [Lomov *moves*.] He seems to be coming round. . . . Drink some water! That's right. . . .

Lomov.   I see stars . . . mist. . . . Where am I?

Chubukov.   Hurry up and get married and—well, to the devil with you! She's willing! [*He puts* Lomov's *hand into his daughter's*.] She's willing and all that. I give you my blessing and so on. Only leave me in peace!

Lomov [*getting up*]. Eh? What? To whom?

Chubukov.   She's willing. Well? Kiss and be damned to you!

Natalya Stepanovna [*wails*]. He's alive. . . . Yes, yes, I'm willing. . . .

Chubukov.   Kiss each other!

Lomov.   Eh? Kiss whom? [*They kiss*.] Very nice, too. Excuse me, what's it all about? Oh, now I understand . . . my heart . . . stars . . . I'm happy. Natalya Stepanovna. . . . [*Kisses her hand*.] My foot's gone to sleep. . . .

Natalya Stepanovna.   I . . . I'm happy too. . . .

Chubukov.   What a weight off my shoulders. . . . Ouf!

Natalya Stepanovna.   But . . . still you will admit now that Guess is worse than Squeezer.

Lomov.   Better!

Natalya Stepanovna.   Worse!

Chubukov.   Well, that's a way to start your family bliss! Have some champagne!

Lomov.   He's better!

Natalya Stepanovna.   Worse! worse! worse!

Chubukov [*trying to shout her down*].   Champagne! Champagne!

CURTAIN

Bibliography

DEVELOPING GOALS

Alberty, Harold, *Reorganizing the High School Curriculum*. New York: The Macmillan Company, 1953.

Anderson, Robert H., *Teaching in a World of Change*. New York: Harcourt, Brace and World, Inc., 1966.

Brubacher, John S., *A History of the Problems of Education*. Second Edition. New York: McGraw-Hill Book Company, Inc., 1966.

Brubacher, John S., *Modern Philosophies of Education*. New York: McGraw-Hill Book Company, Inc., 1962.

Bruner, Jerome, *The Process of Education*. Cambridge: Harvard University Press, 1960.

Butts, R. Freeman and Lawrence A. Cremin, *A History of Education in American Culture*. New York: Henry Holt and Company, 1953.

Chauncey, Henry, ed., *Talks on American Education*. New York: Bureau of Publications, Columbia University, 1962.

Conant, James B., *The American High School Today*. New York: McGraw-Hill Book Company, Inc., 1959.

Conant, James B., *The Education of American Teachers*. New York: McGraw-Hill Book Company, Inc., 1963.

Cremin, Lawrence A., *The Transformation of the School: Progressivism in American Education, 1876–1957*. New York: Alfred A. Knopf, Inc., 1961.

Full, Harold, ed., *Controversy in American Education, An Anthology of Crucial Issues*. New York: The Macmillan Company, 1967.

Good, H. G., *A History of American Education*. New York: The Macmillan Company, 1962.

Good, H. G., *A History of Western Education*. New York: The Macmillan Company, 1960.

King, Edmund J., *Other Schools and Ours*. New York: Holt, Rinehart and Winston, Inc., 1963.

Morris, Van Cleve, *Philosophy and the American School*. Boston: Houghton Mifflin Company, 1961.

Phenix, Philip H., *Philosophy of Education*. New York: Holt, Rinehart and Winston, Inc., 1958.

Scheffler, Israel, ed., *Philosophy of Education*. Boston: Allyn and Bacon, Inc., 1958.

Thut, I. N. and Don Adams, *Educational Patterns in Contemporary Societies*. New York: McGraw-Hill Book Company, 1964.

Wilds, Elmer Harrison and K. V. Lottich, *The Foundations of Modern Education*. Third Edition. New York: Holt, Rinehart and Winston, Inc., 1961.

Wiles, Kimball, *The Changing Curriculum of the American High School*. Englewood Cliffs, N. J.: Prentice-Hall, Inc., 1963.

EVALUATION

Black, Hillel, *They Shall Not Pass*. New York: William Morrow and Company, Inc., 1963.

Buros, Oscar Krisen, *Fifth Mental Measurements Yearbook*. Highland Park, N.J.: Gryphon Press, 1959.

Downie, N. M., *Fundamentals of Measurement: Techniques and Practices*. New York: Oxford University Press, Inc., 1958.

Educational Testing Service, *Making the Classroom Test*. Princeton, N. J., 1961.

Gross, Martin L., *The Brain Watchers*. New York: Random House, Inc., 1962.

Hoffman, Banesh, *The Tyranny of Testing*. New York: Crowell-Collier Press, 1962.

Remmers, H. H. and D. H. Radler, *The American Teen Ager*. Indianapolis: Bobbs-Merrill Company, Inc., 1957.

Wood, Dorothy Adkins, *Test Construction: Development and Interpretation of Achievement Tests*. Columbus, Ohio: Charles E. Merrill Books, Inc., 1960.

GENERAL BOOKS ON TEACHING

Ashton-Warner, Sylvia, *Teacher*. New York: Simon and Schuster, 1963.

Barzun, Jacques, *Teacher in America*. Garden City, N. Y.: Doubleday Anchor Books, Doubleday and Company, Inc., 1954.

Braithwaite, Edward R., *To Sir, with Love*. Englewood Cliffs, New Jersey: Prentice-Hall, Inc., 1959.

Church, Virginia, *Teachers Are People*. Santa Barbara, Calif.: W. Hebberd, 1945.

Eggleston, Edward, *The Hoosier Schoolmaster*. New York: Grosset and Dunlap, Inc., 1892.

Highet, Gilbert, *The Art of Teaching*. New York: Vintage Books, 1956.

Kaufman, Bel, *Up the Down Staircase*. New York: Avon Books, 1966.

Neill, A. S., *Summerhill*. New York: Hart Publishing Co., 1960.

Stuart, Jesse, *The Thread That Runs So True*. New York: Charles Scribner's Sons, 1949.

NATURE OF LANGUAGE

Alexander, Henry, *The Story of Our Language*. Garden City, N. Y.: Doubleday and Company, Inc., 1962.

Allen, Harold, ed., *Applied English Linguistics*. New York: Appleton-Century-Crofts, Inc., 1964.

Allen, Harold B. and Verna L. Newsome, Thomas H. Wetmore, Helen J. Throckmorton, Enola Borghe, *New Dimensions in English*. Wichita: McCormick-Mathers Publishing Company, Inc., 1966.

Bailey, Dudley, ed., *Introductory Language Essays*. New York: W. W. Norton and Company, Inc., 1965.

Baugh, Albert C., *A History of the English Language*. New York: Appleton-Century-Crofts, Inc., 1957.

Booth, Wayne C., *The Rhetoric of Fiction*. Chicago: The University of Chicago Press, 1961.

Bryant, Margaret M., *Current American Usage*. New York: Funk and Wagnalls, 1962.

Carroll, John B., *The Study of Language*. Cambridge, Mass.: Harvard University Press, 1959.

Chase, Stuart, *The Tyranny of Words* (1938) and *The Power of Words* (1954). New York: Harcourt, Brace and Company.

Christensen, Francis, *Notes Toward a New Rhetoric*. New York: Harper and Row Publishers, 1967.

Dean, Leonard F. and Kenneth G. Wilson, eds., *Essays on Language and Usage*. New York: Oxford University Press, Inc., 1959.

Gleason, Henry A., *Linguistics and English Grammar*. New York: Holt, Rinehart and Winston, Inc., 1965.

Goldberg, Isaac, *The Wonder of Words*. New York: Frederick Ungar Publishing Company, 1957.

Hall, Robert A., *Leave Your Language Alone.* Ithaca, N. Y.: Linguistica, 1950.

Hayakawa, S. I., *Language in Thought and Action.* New York: Harcourt, Brace and Company, 1964.

Hogben, Lancelot, ed., Frederick Bodmer, *The Loom of Language.* New York: W. W. Norton and Company, Inc., 1944.

Johnson, Wendell, *People in Quandaries.* New York: Harper and Brothers, 1946.

Korzybski, Alfred, *Science and Sanity.* Lancaster, Pa.: The Science Press Company, Distributors, 1941.

Laird, Charlton and Robert M. Gorrell, eds., *English as Language: Backgrounds, Development, Usage.* New York: Harcourt, Brace, and World Inc., 1961.

Laird, Charlton, *The Miracle of Language.* Greenwich, Conn.: Fawcett Publications, Inc., 1962.

Lee, Irving, *Language Habits in Human Affairs.* New York: Harper and Brothers, Publishers, 1941.

Lee, Irving, ed., A. B. Johnson, *The Meaning of Words Analyzed into Words and Unverbal Things, and Unverbal Things Classified into Intellections, Sensations and Emotions.* Milwaukee: J. W. Chamberlain, 1948.

Marckwardt, Albert H., *American English.* New York: Oxford University Press, Inc., 1958.

Marckwardt, Albert H. and Fred G. Walcott, *Facts about Current English Usage.* New York: Appleton-Century-Crofts, Inc., 1938.

Mencken, Henry L., *The American Language.* New York: Alfred A. Knopf, Inc., 1936. *Supplement One, The American Language,* 1945, and *Supplement Two, The American Language,* 1945.

Mencken, Henry L., *The American Language,* 1963, revised by David McCord. New York: Random House, Inc., 1963.

Ogden, C. K. and I. A. Richards, *The Meaning of Meaning.* New York: Harcourt, Brace and Company, 1943.

Pei, Mario, *The Story of English.* Greenwich, Conn.: Fawcett Publications, Inc., 1962.

Schlauch, Margaret, *The Gift of Language.* New York: Dover Publications, Inc., 1955.

Walpole, Hugh R., *Semantics: The Nature of Words and Their Meanings.* New York: W. W. Norton and Company, Inc., 1939.

RESEARCH

American Educational Research Association (a department of the N.E.A.), *Review of Educational Research: Language Arts and Fine Arts*, Vol. 37, No. 2, April, 1967.

Barnes, John B., *Educational Research for the Classroom Teacher.* New York: G. P. Putnam's Sons, 1960.

Corey, Stephen M., *Action Research to Improve School Practices.* New York: Bureau of Publications, Columbia University, 1953.

Gage, N. L., ed., *Handbook of Research on Teaching.* Chicago: Rand McNally and Company, 1963.

Harris, Chester W., ed., *Encyclopedia of Educational Research.* New York: The Macmillan Company, 1960.

Loban, Walter, *The Language of Elementary School Children.* Champaign, Illinois: National Council of Teachers of English, 1963.

Mouly, George J., *The Science of Educational Research.* New York: American Book Company, 1963.

N. C. T. E., *Research in the Teaching of English* (semiannual periodical).

Needed Research in the Teaching of English, U.S. Department of Health, Education and Welfare, Office of Education, Monograph No. 11, Washington, D.C., 1963.

Shane, Harold G. and June Grant Mulry, *Improving Language Arts Instruction Through Research.* Washington, D.C.: Association for Supervision and Curriculum Development, NEA, 1963.

TEACHING ENGLISH

Altick, Richard D., *Preface to Critical Reading.* New York: Holt, Rinehart and Winston, Inc., 1962.

Bernstein, Abraham, *Teaching English in the High School.* New York: Random House, Inc., 1961.

Burton, Dwight L., *Literature Study in the High Schools.* New York: Holt, Rinehart and Winston, Inc., 1964.

Chall, Jeanne S., *Learning to Read: The Great Debate.* New York: McGraw-Hill Book Company, 1968.

The Commission on the English Curriculum, National Council of Teachers of English, *The English Language Arts in the Secondary School.* New York: Appleton-Century-Crofts, Inc., 1956.

Cross, E. A. and Elizabeth Carney, *Teaching English in the High School*. New York: The Macmillan Company, 1950.

DeBoer, John and others, *Teaching Secondary English*. New York: McGraw-Hill Book Company, Inc., 1951.

Dunning, Stephen, *Teaching Literature to Adolescents*. New York: Scott, Foresman and Co., 1966.

Evans, William H. and Jerry L. Walker, *New Trends in the Teaching of English in Secondary Schools*. Chicago: Rand McNally and Co., 1966.

Fowler, Mary Elizabeth, *Teaching Language, Composition and Literature*. New York: McGraw-Hill Book Co., 1965.

Fries, Charles Carpenter, *American English Grammar*. New York: D. Appleton-Century Company, Inc., 1940.

Fries, Charles Carpenter, *Linguistics and Reading*. New York: Holt, Rinehart, and Winston, Inc., 1963.

Gordon, Edward J. and Edward S. Noyes, *Essays on the Teaching of English*. New York: Appleton-Century-Crofts, Inc., 1960.

Guth, Hans P., *English Today and Tomorrow: A Guide for Teachers of English*. Englewood Cliffs, N.J.: Prentice-Hall, Inc., 1964.

Hook, J. N., *The Teaching of High School English*. Third Edition. New York: The Ronald Press Company, 1965.

Jenkinson, Edward B., *What Is Language?* Bloomington: Indiana University Press, 1967.

Jenkinson, Edward B. and Philip B. Daghlian, eds., *Books for Teachers of English: An Annotated Bibliography*. Bloomington: Indiana University Press, 1968.

Jenkinson, Edward B. and Jane Stouder Hawley, eds., *On Teaching Literature—Essays for Secondary School Teachers*. Bloomington: Indiana University Press, 1967.

Jewett, Arno and Joseph Mersand, Doris V. Gunderson, eds., *Improving English Skills of Culturally Different Youth*, Washington, D. C.: U. S. Department of Health, Education and Welfare. Office of Education, 1964.

Kennedy, Arthur G., *English Usage: A Study of Policy and Procedure*. New York: D. Appleton-Century Company, Inc., 1942.

LaBrant, Lou, *We Teach English*. New York: Harcourt, Brace and Company, 1951.

Lazarus, Arnold and Rozanne Knudson, *Selected Objectives for the English Language Arts: Grades 7–12*. New York: Houghton Mifflin Co., 1967.

Lewis, John S. and Jean C. Sisk, *Teaching English: 7–12*. New York: American Book Company, 1963.

Loban, Walter, Margaret Ryan, and James R. Squire, *Teaching Language and Literature: Grades 7–12*. New York: Harcourt, Brace and World, Inc., 1961.

Marckwardt, Albert H., *Linguistics and the Teaching of English*. Bloomington: Indiana University Press, 1966.

Marksheffel, Ned, *Better Reading in the Secondary School*. New York: Ronald Press, 1966.

Mersand, Joseph, *Index to Plays: With Suggestions for Teaching*. New York: The Scarecrow Press, Inc., 1966.

Mirrielees, Lucia B., *Teaching Composition and Literature in Junior and Senior High Schools*. New York: Harcourt, Brace and Company, 1937.

Moffett, James, *A Student-Centered Language Arts Curriculum, Grades K–13: A Handbook for Teachers*. Boston: Houghton Mifflin Company, 1968.

Newsome, Berna L., *Structural Grammar in the Classroom*. Oshkosh, Wisc.: Wisconsin Council of Teachers of English, Wisconsin State College, 1961.

Otto, Wayne and Richard A. McMenemy, *Corrective and Remedial Teaching*. Boston: Houghton Mifflin Co., 1966.

Poley, Irvin C., *Speaking of Teaching*. Philadelphia: Germantown Friends School, 1957.

Pooley, Robert C., *Teaching English Grammar*. New York: Appleton-Century-Crofts, Inc., 1957.

Pooley, Robert C., *Teaching English Usage*. New York: Appleton-Century-Crofts, Inc., 1946.

Roberts, Paul, *English Sentences*. New York: Harcourt, Brace and World, Inc., 1962.

Roberts, Paul, *Patterns of English*. New York: Harcourt, Brace and World, Inc., 1956.

Roberts, Paul, *Understanding Grammar*. New York: Harper and Brothers, Publishers, 1954.

Rodgers, Mary Columbro, *New Design in the Teaching of English*. Scranton, Pennsylvania: International Textbook Company, 1968.

Rosenblatt, Louise M., *Literature as Exploration*. New York: D. Appleton-Century Company, Inc., 1938.

Sauer, Edwin H., *English in the Secondary School*. New York: Holt, Rinehart and Winston, Inc., 1961.

Seely, Howard Francis, *Enjoying Poetry in School.* New York: Johnson Publishing Company, 1931.

Seely, Howard Francis, *On Teaching English.* New York: American Book Company, 1933.

Sheridan, Marion C., Harold H. Owen, Jr., Ken Macrorie, Fred Marcus, *The Motion Picture and the Teaching of English.* New York: Appleton-Century-Crofts, 1965.

Smith, James A., *Creative Teaching of the Language Arts in the Elementary School.* Boston: Allyn and Bacon, Inc., 1967.

Stone, George Winchester, ed., *Issues, Problems, and Approaches in the Teaching of English.* New York; Holt, Rinehart and Winston, Inc., 1961.

The Teachers Guide to Media and Methods (formerly *School Paperback Journal*). 124 East 40 Street, New York, New York 10016: Media and Methods Institute, Inc.

Weiss, M. Jerry, ed., *An English Teacher's Reader.* New York: Odyssey Press, Inc., 1962.

Wolfe, Don, *Creative Ways to Teach English: Grades 7–12.* Second Edition. New York: Odyssey Press, Inc., 1966.

INDEX

383

reading motivation, 29
school subscriptions to, 35-36
worthwhile, 74
Mankind, problems of, 32
Mass media, 33-36
collecting information on, 35
language problem, 34
learning problem, 33
Mass media experiences, including, 36
Memorization of rules, boring, 26, 28
Metaphor, 166
Method:
clarity and vitality in, 24
developing, 214, 216
divergence in, 324
goal attainment and, 5
in new grammar, 145
in oral composition, 122-123
student participation in selecting, 13
Motivation, 217
disadvantaged students, 29
goals and, 25
group, 190
knowledge of, 214
through lesson planning, 62
problem-solving approach, 31
reading and, 29
slow learners, 44
of students, 217
in teaching literature, 99
Movies:
learning problem, 33, 35
literary presentations by, 34

Narrative poems, 89
National Council of Teachers of English, 207-208
Nationalism, through vernacular literature, 71
New grammar, 143-147
approach to, 146-147
editing drafts, 147
New situations, transfer of learning to, 27
Newspapers:
disadvantaged students and, 44
learning problem, 34, 35
quality, 36
reading motivation, 29
school subscriptions to, 35-36
worthwhile, 74
Nonreaders, 66, 69-70
Note-taking, 135-136
Novel, teaching the, 90-92

Objective tests, 187-188
placement tests and, 112

Office of Education, U. S., 208-209
Oral composition:
bashful students, 126
criticizing, 123
effective, 120-130
evaluating, 125
interest in, 122
rating form, 123-124
research projects, 212
standards in, 122
student's preparation for, 124, 125
traditional units, 122
Oral expression, testing, 86
Orientation, two-valued, 169
Originality, concept of, 107

Paperbacks:
in classroom library, 92
literature and, 203-204
research on, 203-204
use of, 92
Parts of speech, in new grammar, 145
Past learning, applying, 26-27
Patriotism, and democracy, 11
Performance tests, 25
in experimental and control classes, 29
goals and, 27
Philosophy:
defining, 1-2
of education, 3-6
interdisciplinary, 40-44
of life, 3-4
of teaching English, 13-15
Perfection, defined, 28
Performance, effective speech and, 120-121
Performance method, 324
Performance tests, 27
disadvantaged students and, 45
Personal pronouns, objective/subjective case forms, 156
Placement tests, and objective tests, 112
Plays:
Laughton-Boyer approach to, 95
one-act, in junior high, 93
senior high, 93-94
Poetry:
appreciation of, 52
boredom with, overcoming, 59
lesson plan, 59
teaching of, 80-84
understanding, 52, 81
unit plan, 62
Practice, in skills, 28-29
Problem curriculum, 43
Problem solving, 31-33
Problem-solving approach, 31